A SHORT HISTORY OF TRANSPORT IN JAPAN

A Short History of Transport in Japan from Ancient Times to the Present

John Andrew Black

https://www.openbookpublishers.com

© 2022 John Andrew Black

This work is licensed under an Attribution-NonCommercial 4.0 International (CC BY-NC 4.0). This license allows you to share, copy, distribute and transmit the text; to adapt the text for non-commercial purposes of the text providing attribution is made to the authors (but not in any way that suggests that they endorse you or your use of the work). Attribution should include the following information:

John Andrew Black, *A Short History of Transport in Japan from Ancient Times to the Present*. Cambridge, UK: Open Book Publishers, 2022, https://doi.org/10.11647/OBP.0281

Copyright and permissions for the reuse of many of the images included in this publication differ from the above. This information is provided in the captions.

Every effort has been made to identify and contact copyright holders and any omission or error will be corrected if notification is made to the publisher.

In order to access detailed and updated information on the license, please visit https://doi.org/10.11647/OBP.0281#copyright. Further details about CC licenses are available at https://creativecommons.org/licenses/by-nc/4.0/

All external links were active at the time of publication unless otherwise stated and have been archived via the Internet Archive Wayback Machine at https://archive.org/web

Digital material and resources associated with this volume are available at https://doi.org/10.11647/OBP.0281#resources

ISBN Paperback: 9781800643567
ISBN Hardback: 9781800643574
ISBN Digital (PDF): 9781800643581
ISBN Digital ebook (EPUB): 9781800643598
ISBN Digital ebook (AZW3): 9781800643604
ISBN XML: 9781800643611
ISBN Digital ebook (HTML): 9781800646674
DOI: 10.11647/OBP.0281

Cover image: "Transformation—from Steam Engines to Super-Conducting Maglev Railway Technology". The reproduction of this painting is allowed by permission from its owner, Yoshitsugu Hayashi, Senior Research Professor, Chūbu University, Nagoya, Japan, and was photographed by Mr Kiyoaki Suzuki. The cover was designed by Anna Gatti.

Table of Contents

Foreword	vii
Preface	xi
Acknowledgements	xv
1. Introduction	1
2. Japanese Institutions and Organisations	15
3. Ports and Shipping	69
4. Canals, Rivers and Lakes	99
5. Roads	121
6. Railways	155
7. Civil Aviation and Airports	183
8. Urban Planning Institutions and the Integration of Land Use and Transport	223
9. Conclusions	255
List of Figures	285
List of Tables	287
Index	291
About the Cover	301

Foreword

Professor John A. Black (below I refer to him as John) and I first met in August 1986. I presented a city simulation model that was under development at the time at the session he chaired at a land-use and transportation symposium at Monash University, Melbourne. I knew his name from *The Land-Use Transport System*, co-authored with Professor Blunden, but I remember being quite surprised because I never thought he would be such a young Professor. On the way back from the symposium, I stopped by in Sydney and visited his UNSW's laboratory. It has been 35 years since then, and our relationship between public and private has continued. In the meantime, I have taken care of him in Japan, but for most of the time he has continued to help me.

John's co-authorship of *The Land-Use Transport System* represented the first masterpiece on the interaction between transportation and land use and is the starting point for researchers in relevant fields. Since then, John has been active as an internationally prestigious researcher in a wide range of transportation-related fields, from transportation engineering to finance. One of these contributions was in the World Conference on Transport Research Society (WCTRS), at the 5th conference in Yokohama in 1989, when I was the secretary-general of the executive committee. At that time, he cooperated with the management organizers as a member of the thesis award selection committee. From then on, he actively participated in the management of the WCTRS academic society, and, in 1995, invited the 7th Congress to Sydney that became a great success with him as the Chair of the Organizing Committee. Since then, he has made a great contribution to the development of WCTRS as a member of the International Steering Committee. There are many other things to mention, such as him leading the launch of the timely *Journal Transportation Research D: Transport and the Environment*.

In 1999, I was able to secure an invitation Professor position at Tohoku University, where I was a Professor at the time, so I recommended John as a candidate to the personnel committee without hesitation. In addition to international recognition, his ability to deliver academically and his engaging personality were the reasons for his recommendation. After coming to Sendai, I instructed doctoral students from Mexico, Thailand, and Japan who were enrolled in my laboratory. They received more enthusiastic guidance than I gave them, and were greatly inspired by a world-renowned professor, who deepened their research approach. They grew spiritually and are now active themselves as researchers of internauional standing. John has been conducting joint research with many Japanese researchers other than myself through encounters at international conferences, and so on, not only in Japan but around the world. He has co-authored dozens of papers with Japanese researchers. In addition, he has contributed widely to the provision of international information to Japanese researchers, including reviews of publications in English by Japanese people.

In addition, when looking at things other than academic, John has a deep general knowledge of Japan. He studied under a famous Japanese painter, drew ink paintings, and wrote haiku with various friends. I am impressed by his continued interest in Japan. From time to time, is not uncommon for me to rush to find out the answer to questions in emails about Japanese matters.

This book can be said to be the results of one of John's insatiable inquisitive spirits from the transport academic field to the general liberal arts field. The publication of this book may be an end break for John, but I believe that it will be an opportunity for readers to deepen the connection with Japan, foster new encounters, and develop new themes.

6 June 2021
Kazuaki Miyamoto
Professor Emeritus of Tohoku University
Professor Emeritus of Tokyo City University

序文

Professor John A Black（以下Johnと呼ばせてもらおう。）とはじめて会ったのは1986年の8月であった。メルボルンのMonash大学で開かれた土地利用と交通に関するシンポジウムにおいて彼が座長をしたセッションで、私がその時開発中であった都市シミュレーションモデルの発表をした時である。それまでも彼の名前はBlunden教授との共著「The Land-Use Transport System」で知ってはいたが、まさか、こんなに若い青年教授とは思ってもいなかったので随分驚いたことを覚えている。その帰路シドニーに立ち寄り、UNSWの研究室を訪問した。それから早35年、公私にわたる付き合いが続いている。その間、少しは私が彼の世話をしたこともあるが、ほとんどの場合は継続して彼に助けられてきている。

Johnの共著「The Land-Use Transport System」は交通と土地利用の相互作用について最初に書かれた名著で、関係する分野の研究者がその研究の基点としている。それを皮切りに、Johnは交通関連の広い分野で交通工学からファイナンスにわたり国際的に権威ある研究者として活躍してきている。その一つの場として世界交通学会（WCTRS: World Conference on Transport Research Society）が挙げられるが、その最初は私が実行委員会の幹事長をした1989年の横浜での第5回学会である。その時は、論文賞選考委員会のメンバーとして大会運営に協力してくれた。それを契機に、WCTRSの学会運営に積極的に参加し、1995年には第7回大会をシドニーに招致し、実行委員長（Chair of Organizing Committee）として大成功を収めた。その後もSteering CommitteeメンバーとしてWCTRSの発展に多大な貢献を果たしてきている。他にも枚挙のいとまがないが、時宜を得た雑誌であるTransportation Research D: Transport and the Environment Journalの立ち上げをリードしたこと等があげられる。

1999年になるが、私が当時教授をしていた東北大学で招聘教授のポストを確保することが出来たので、迷わずJohnを候補者として人事委員会に推薦した。国際的な知名度に加えその行動力と人柄が何よりの推薦理由

であった。来仙後、私の研究室に在籍していたメキシコ、タイ、そして日本人の博士課程学生の指導をしてもらった。私以上に熱心な指導を、しかも世界的に著名な教授から受けた彼らは大いに刺激を受け、研究の深度を深めると共に精神的にも成長し、現在は国際的な研究者として活躍している。Johnは日本国内だけではなく、世界各地での国際学会等における出会いを通して、私以外にも多くの日本人研究者と共同研究をして来ており、日本人との共著論文が数十に及んでいる。さらに日本人による英語での出版等のreviewをはじめ、日本人研究者への国際的な情報提供でも広く貢献してきている。

一方、学術面以外に目を転じると、Johnは日本に対する全般的な造詣が深いことが挙げられる。有名な日本人画家に師事して水墨画を描き、また、多彩な交友関係の友人と俳句を詠むなど、日本のことに関しては悉く興味を持ち続けていることに感心させられる。時々着信する日本の事柄に関する質問メールの中には、私が知らなくて慌てて調べることも少なくない。そのJohnの学術分野から一般教養分野にわたる継続して飽くなき探究心の一つの集大成が本書と言うことが出来よう。

本書の出版はJohnにとっては一つの区切りであろうが、これまでの日本とのつながりをより深めるとともに新たな出会いを育み、新たなテーマに発展する契機となることを信じている。

2021年6月

東北大学（Tohoku University）名誉教授
東京都市大学（Tokyo City University）名誉教授
宮本和明（Kazuaki Miyamoto）

Preface

Nearly 50 years ago, my passion for Japan was fired when I stayed in a farmhouse near Ōami (now Ōamishirasato City) in Chiba Prefecture and jogged through sloping hills, and what were, in those days, majestic scenes of rice ripening in paddy fields. Over subsequent years, as the farmlands disappeared under Tōkyō's urban sprawl, my research, teaching and consultancy took me frequently to Japan where I received appointments at three universities. In my spare time, I either travelled extensively across Japan (in addition to my research) or read books on Japanese history, literature and poetry, including visiting historical sites following in the footsteps of the famous haiku poet, Matsuo Bashō (1644–1694). To more fully understand these walking pilgrimages that Bashō undertook I studied Tokugawa history and the main characters behind military, political and economic change during the Edō period (1603–1867).

The genesis of the idea to convert this accumulated Japanese experience into a book on the history of transport and the changes to institutions and organisations was prompted when Emeritus Professor Malcolm Tull, Murdoch University, Australia, drew my attention to the theory of the new institutional economics (NIE) applied to port administration and governance. Malcolm organised an international conference on maritime history held in Perth, Australia, in 2016, so I applied concepts of institutions and organisations to trace the history of port development in the Ōsaka region from ancient times to the beginning of the Meiji restoration (Black and Lee, 2016), extending the narrative to the present (Black, 2021). Using a similar research methodology, chapters on other transport modes and integrated land-use and transport developments were added.

In compiling this manuscript, no one source of funding has been received: instead, grants and support over the years have come from diverse sources. In terms of acknowledging these sources, that, in addition to the specifics of the research projects that I cite in this Preface, I thank the following: The Japan Society for the Promotion of Science (two Long-term Fellowships); The Center for North East Asian Studies at Tōhoku

University, Sendai (two Visiting Professorships); The Graduate School of Environmental Studies, Nagoya University (Visiting Professor); Faculty of Engineering, Saitama University (Visiting Professor); the United Nations Development Program on Managing Rapidly Growing Asian Cities; the East Asia Society for Transportation Studies International Collaborative Activity (EASTS-ICA); the Economic Intelligence Unit of *The Economist* on an institutional analysis of public-private partnerships (PPP) and economic infrastructure in Japan; the UNSW Sydney special studies program for research into international airports and the environment; and Urban Research and Planning (URaP) International, North Strathfield, NSW, Australia, for funding research into: land-use developments at major railway stations in Japan; on tsunami evacuation modelling in Miyagi, Iwate and Kagawa Prefectures; and with social capital funding in Takamatsu, Shikōku. An appointment at Southern Cross University in 2017–2018 as an Adjunct Professor to advise Professor Scott Smith, Dean of Engineering, Science and the Environment on academic links with Japan has given me support to complete aspects of my research through funding from the Australian Government's New Colombo Plan to mentor Australian engineering students in Japan.

In addition, some of the research findings are the result of collaborative efforts with colleagues in Japan and elsewhere over many years. My Japanese friends have translated material from Japanese into English: Dr Masaki Arioka; Ms Michiko Arioka; Dr Ji Myong Lee; and Dr Kaori Shimasaki. Competitive funding (with Professor Danang Parakesit, Universitas Gadjah Mada, Indonesia) under the Australian-Indonesian Governance Reform Program (AIGRP), administered through the Crawford School at the Australian National University, allowed me to visit Tōkyō and discuss financing for metro systems and transit-oriented developments. The Planning Research Centre at Sydney University (Professor Ed Blakely, Professor John Renne, Dr Santos Bista), in association with Jackson Teece Architects (Mr David Chesterman, Mr Carlos Frias and Ms Nadira Yapa), undertook a transport-oriented development study for the New South Wales Roads and Traffic Authority (now Transport for NSW), where, in Japan, the following people provided valuable information: Dr Masafumi Ota, Manager, Project Coordinating Secretariat, Planning and Administration Division, Railway Headquarters, Tōkyū Corporation, Tōkyō; Mr Dongkun Oh, Assistant

Manager, Residential Realty Division, Residential (Development) Headquarters, Tōkyū Corporation, Tōkyō.

The propositions of institutions and organisations as a conceptual framework for the history of transport in Japan were tested at the Oxford School of the Environment, Transport Studies Unit during a research seminar held in February 2017 (Black, 2017). I am indebted to Professor Tim Schwanen, Director, for hosting me in 2017, and also to his academic colleagues, Emeritus Professor David Banister and Dr Geoff Dudley, for providing advice on possible conceptual frameworks, and to Dr Heuishil Chang for her research into aspects of contemporary Japanese society. Reginald Fisk, former policy advisor to the NSW Minister for Roads, Duncan Gay, has provided invaluable advice on the general workings of institutions—parliament, government and the bureaucracy. The research on canals was greatly assisted by Tsuyoshi Shimasaki (Minato Museum, Tōyama).

There are so many people to thank, but five Japanese research colleagues must be acknowledged at the outset. First, my oldest academic colleague is Emeritus Professor Kazuaki Miyamoto, now advising Pacific Consultants International, Tōkyō, who kindly wrote the Preface to this book. Secondly, my oldest Japanese research collaborator is Dr Chiaki Kuranami, Padeco, Tōkyō, a doctoral student of mine from the late 1970s, who invited me to stay in his parents' farmhouse in Chiba Prefecture in 1983. It was in that year when I first met Professor Hideo Nakamura (Tōkyō University)—the leading transport academic at the time—with whom I shared an appointment on the World Conference on Transport Research Society International Steering Committee. Fourthly, Professor Yoshisugu Hayashi (formerly Nagoya University) and now a Senior Research Professor at Chūbu University, and his graduate students at Nagoya University, all have provided a source of intellectual stimulation on urban development and transport issues in Japan. Of more importance in the final checking of this manuscript is the gift that Professor Hayashi gave me: *Japan—An Illustrated Encyclopedia* (Kodansha, 1993). He said that I knew more about the history of Japan than he did and added that everything I needed to know was in that encyclopedia. His modest admission about the first point was incorrect, but he was certainly right about the latter statement. Fifthly, Dr Masaki Arioka, whom I met when he was the Kumagai Gumi Director of the Sydney Harbor Tunnel construction project and I was undertaking an independent review of the tunnel traffic forecasts for the New South Wales Department of Planning and Environment. He is a founder member of the Tōkyō-based NPO Strategic Lifecycle Infrastructure Management (SLIM)—an NPO that I joined to assist with the debris management study following the March 2011 Northeast Japan earthquake and tsunami. Many of Dr Arioka's senior engineering colleagues, such as Emeritus Professor Katsuhiko Kuroda at Kōbe University (on ports), have accompanied me on fieldtrips and given me insights into many of the construction projects on which they were involved.

Finally, none of this research would have been possible without the continued support of my wife, Professor Deborah Black. She not only pursued a full-time career as a senior academic at UNSW Sydney, and then as Deputy Dean Student Life in the Medical Faculty at the University of Sydney, but she also brought up our children during the periods of my absence in Japan.

On 31 December 2020, my mother, Betty Black, would have been 100 years old, so, in her memory, I dedicate this book to her with affection. She greatly supported me, and encouraged my school and university education, all at the expense of her educational opportunity in the mid-1950s by declining an offer from her then employer to enroll in optometry at London University. When she worked as an executive assistant at Odhams Press, London, prior to the Second World War, she dealt with communications with Japanese publishers so it could be said there has been a family Japanese connection for over 80 years.

References

Black, J. (2017) "Hakanai (儚い): The Transformation of Transport Organisations in Japan from Archaic Times—Searching for Conceptual Frameworks", Seminar, Transport Studies Unit, Oxford School of the Environment, Oxford University, 14 February 2017, http://www.tsu.ox.ac.uk/events/170214.html

Black, J., and Jimyoung Lee (2016) "Osaka Ports from Ancient Times to the Meiji Restoration: Institutions and Organisations", in *Old Worlds, New Worlds? Emerging Themes in Maritime History*, 7th IMEHA International Congress 27 June to 1 July 2016. Murdoch University, Perth, Western Australia, 57.

Black, J. A. (2021) "Ports and Intermodal Transport—Institutions and Organisations: The Setō Inland Sea, Japan, from Archaic Times to the Present", *World Review of Intermodal Transportation Research*, *World Review of Intermodal Transportation Research*, 10 (3), 269–303.

Acknowledgements

Many people contributed to the production of this book. I thank Dr Alessandra Tosi, the Managing Director of Open Book Publishers, for her advice on the publication process. I also thank Lucy Barnes for the production of the book, Sam Noble for his careful editing, Luca Baffa and Melissa Purkiss for their advice on the illustrations, and Anna Gatti for designing the book cover. The book cover is courtesy of Professor Yoshitsugu Hayashi and his oil painting that was photographed by Mr Kiyoaki Suzuki, clerical staff at Chūbu University Japan.

Professor Travis Waller, Head of the School of Civil and Environmental Engineering, UNSW Sydney, provided a generous grant that allowed this research to be completed for publication.

On copyright matters, Kazuaki Miyamoto, Emeritus Professor of Tohoku University (who also provided Figure 8) helped in obtaining permission for material from Japanese government websites through his professional network: Mr. Ryohei Miura, Vice Mayor, The City of Toyama and seconded from the Ministry of Infrastructure, Land, Transport and Tourism; Mr. Koichi Nemoto, Geospatial Information Authority of Japan; Mr. Keiji Kozawa, Director, Haneda Airport Construction Office, Ministry of Land, Infrastructure, Transport and Tourism; Mr. Takao Ueki, Director, Nagasaki Airport Administrative Office, Ministry of Land, Infrastructure, Transport and Tourism; Mr. Hajime Tanaka, Road Bureau, Ministry of Land, Infrastructure, Transport and Tourism.

In addition, Mr. Takayuki Noami, Director of Renewal Project, Renewal and Construction Bureau, Metropolitan Expressway Company Limited organised Copyright © Shutoko Associate Company Limited all rights reserved for Figure 2. Mr Kensuke Tamura, General Manager, International Department, East Japan Railway Culture Foundation, Tokyo, provided the original for Figure 4. Ms Kate Kavanagh. Assistant Manager, Central Japan Railway Company, Sydney Office, organised permission to reproduce Figures 5 and 6.

1. Introduction

The cover to this book alludes to technological change in transport where a magnetic levitation rail car is seen projecting from the firebox of a mid-19th century British railway steam engine. The stories behind these inventions, and numerous others, that have progressed all forms of transport over land, sea and air, are the *people* in the institutions and organisations whose policies, rules and regulations have brought ideas to fruition. Here, 'institution' means the mechanisms of governance of a geographical territory. A distinguishing feature of a primitive society is "social organisation" (Nash, 1967: 5) but this evolves with different historical epochs each having distinctive and complex institutions.

The term 'institution' for a nation extends from its constitution to other governing organisations that have a less secure constitutional basis, such as provincial and local government, the bureaucracy, political parties, trade unions and lobby groups. As Hague and Harrop remark "As we move away from the heartland of constitutionally mandated structures, the term 'organisation' tends to supplant the word 'institution'" (2001: 63).[1]

Throughout history, it is largely the power sanctioned by central governing institutions that progress personal mobility and the ability to move goods. This book is a short history embracing all modes of transport in Japan. The themes identify the governing authorities of institutions and describe what factors have influenced their major transformations over time, and demonstrate, at the same time, how transport has evolved. When interpreting the history of transport, one way to understand the distinction between the institutions and

---

1 For an extensive exposition of these, sometimes subtle, distinctions, the reader is referred to Duina (2011), who provides a detailed introductory discussion of the characteristics of institutions and organisations, or to Alston (*et al.*, 2018).

organisations of the economy—respectively, the public (government) and the private sectors, or the civic and civil sectors[2]—is to think of the political institutions of government extending back over time and to consider their long-term evolutions, in which are embedded much shorter-term changes in transport innovation and administration.

In the descriptive narrative and interpretations of institutions and organisations covered in subsequent chapters, the following transport-related questions are posed.

1. Throughout the history of transport innovations and policies that relate to the movement of people and freight—from archaic times to the present—both civic and civil society have been intimately entwined in one way or another to deliver progress, change and technological and managerial innovation. Who were the relevant institutions and organisations in society? What were their respective roles in relation to the movement of traffic on all transport modes, especially issues of authority and power relations?

2. By placing people at the centre of this enquiry, an obvious parallel question would be: who were the key players behind the changes in these institutions and organisations and what tangible things did they achieve in the transport sector?

3. The transfer of knowledge and its adoption that, in turn, influences change is facilitated by the technology of transport and communications available at any point in history (Grayling, 2016), so to what extent is any country influenced by overseas ideas in the transformation of its institutions, organisations and transport?

4. What might the future look like in terms of institutions, society and transport?

Such questions are answered in this book with a case study of transport in Japan from archaic times to the present. This book represents a vastly

---

2   For a more concrete, micro example of such interactions involving civic and civil society see a case study of urban transport policy in Sydney, Australia (Black *et al.*, 1982).

more ambitious extension of the author's description of institutional changes and the changes in the provision of transport infrastructure services in Australia 'bookended' between the 1956 Melbourne Summer Olympic Games and the 2000 Sydney Summer Olympic and Paralympic Games (Black, 1999). These questions can be addressed more readily in relation to contemporary societies where data are freely available. Every advanced economy, including that of Japan, would have detailed descriptions, accessible in the public domain, on its institutional and organisational arrangements for transport, including its regulatory framework: who plans, approves, funds and finances, builds and maintains transport infrastructure. However, to reveal the past entails interpreting material from a wide range of sources.

To tease out the evolution of institutions, organisations and transport requires a broad search of historical accounts written both in English and in Japanese. Published in English, there is scholarship rich in details of ancient and modern aspects of Japan, its politics and economy. Computer search engines and the website Academia allow access to data bases that contain relevant articles. Extensive use of Google translator was made to convert text in kanji and katakana into English. As with some historical writings, there are variants in dates in the original source material, so I have resolved these differences by resort to *Japan: An Illustrated Encyclopedia* (Kodansha, 1993), written by leading Japanologists. Material extracted from published secondary sources has been carefully checked from this encyclopedia.

The methodology on which the manuscript is based also includes: extensive site inspections of all form of transport infrastructure; visits to museums and art galleries—especially the woodblock prints of Hiroshige and Hokusai that depict famous scenes on medieval roads; publications and reports in English and in Japanese; reference to old maps and artworks; and historical novels, such as *The Tale of the Heike*[3] Interpretations of data collected have been aided by my numerous Japanese academic colleagues, and by the engineering members of the Not for Profit Organisation (NPO), Strategic Life-cycle Infrastructure Management (SLIM), Tōkyō, whose members arranged fieldwork

---

3   Heike means the "House of Taira"—where "Taira" was the original *uji* (or clan) name of the house.

excursions for me to the many transport projects that they helped build, or they studied when they were students in the 1950s and 1960s.

In surveying the contemporary transport scene, when attempting to answer some of the questions posed earlier, government officials and consultants have been interviewed. Today, in Japan, there are three tiers of government—national, prefectural (and city) and local. The civic sector comprises an elected Parliament, government bureaucracies of which the Ministry of Land, Infrastructure, Transport and Tourism is the most relevant to the transport sector. The sector is a mixed one, with government-owned ports, canals and airports, prefectural highway departments, private railway companies, public and private bus services, private-sector logistics companies, and, of course, a population wedded to personal mobility with motor cars and bicycles. Examples of such fieldwork and interviews by the author include published studies on railways and transit-oriented development (Black *et al.*, 2016), Ōsaka seaports and canals (Black, 2021) and emissions from the Hanshin Ports (Styhre *et al.*, 2017), and unpublished investigations into roads and airports.

Study Area and Time Periods

For convenience of exposition, and for its historical association with the formation of the early Japanese state (Kawanabe *et al.*, 2012), most of the selected case study area comprises of the Kantō region in central Honshū (containing the prefectures of Tōkyō, Chiba, Saitama, Kanagawa, Gumma, Ibaraki and Tōchigi) and of the Kansai region (a historical and cultural term loosely applied to Ōsaka, Kyōto and Kōbe). Today, Kansai (https://en.wikipedia.org/wiki/Kansai_region#/media/File:Kinki-en.png) and Kantō are distinct regions in the minds of Japanese people. Used in documents some time before the 10th century, Kansai ("west of the barrier") is in contradistinction to Kantō ("east of the barrier"). Added to this study area is the Hokuriku region to the north of the Japanese Alps because of its historical trade links with the core study area between Ōsaka and Tōkyō. The study area includes a well-defined geographical region on Honshū Island that the Japanese refer to as the *Tōkaidō Megaroporisu* or the "Super Mega Region" (https://transportgeography.org/contents/applications/transportation-mega-urban-region/tokyo-osaka-corridor-tokaido/).

The *Tōkaidō Megaroporisu* is a general term for the approximately 500 km stretch of land that accounts for only 17 per cent of the nation's area along the Pacific coast of the island of Honshū extending westwards from Tōkyō to Ōsaka and Kōbe. This region is the political, cultural and economic heartland of Japan. As of January 2020, its population was 66.48 million (just over half of the national population) and its annual GDP (in 2016) was 311 trillion yen—very similar to the GDP of the United Kingdom (Central Japan Railway Company, 2020: 22).

Nevertheless, certain transport developments require discussion that extend beyond this land-based study area—air travel and ocean and coastal shipping being obvious cases in point. Historical sea routes of Japan connecting China, Korea and other Southeast Asian countries via the Setō Inland Sea are considered as an integral part of the core study area. Another example is the early fortified trading seaport of Dazaifu on the Sea of Japan (near present day Hakata). Similarly, when discussing developments in aviation in the first half of the 20th century, it should be noted that Japan had overseas territories in China, Taiwan and Korea.

The time frame starts with the "dawn of civilisation" in Japan (Deal, 2005: 12) and ends up today, with speculations on possible reforms to the Japanese transport sector in 2022 and beyond. A periodisation scheme is adopted that divides the continuous flow of social events and institutions into a number of discrete time periods. As such, any classification scheme is a historical concept devised by historians. An obvious starting point for a non-historian is to consult *The Cambridge History of Japan* (Hall *et al.*, 1990, 1993, 1999) where the defined periods are labelled: ancient; Heian; early medieval; Edō; and modern, or to look at the chronology in Wikipedia (2021).

However, I have preferred to use a classification from a Japanese scholar partly because his classification of time periods has been devised in the context of legal history whereby "...law is that which regulates social activities and organizations..." (Ishii, 1980: ix). Table 1 shows these convenient time periods used for later analysis of social institutions with the addition of an amended contemporary period to bring events up to date. Ishii's detailed chronological table (Ishii, 1980: 133–153), that ends in 1951, uses both the Western calendar year and the Japanese year based on the reign of each Emperor (from 562 A.D.) so these approximate dates have been added to Table 1 to make the classification easier for non-Japanese readers to understand.

Table 1. Time Periods—Analysis of Institutions and Organisations.
Source: based on Ishii, 1980: viii.

Time Period	Western Calendar	Description of Period
Archaic	250 B.C.–603 A.D.	Tribal (Religious) State
Ancient	603–967	*Ritsuryō* State
Medieval	967–1467	Early Feudal
Early Modern	1467–1858	Centralised Feudal
Modern	1858–1945	Modern Monarchy
Contemporary	1945–2022	Modern Democratic

Significance

A multi-disciplinary, social science perspective is taken with the book being of interest to a variety of disciplines. They include historians, geographers, political scientists, sociologists and any students in Japanese courses dealing with technology and society. In addition to transport researchers and students, the book may also be of interest to the general reader. For researchers of the new institutional economics (Williamson, 2000), the case study approach will be of interest because North (1991: 97) mentions institutions as "humanly devised" twice in the first five lines of his article. Furthermore, Japanese transport researchers, who are less familiar with this line of inquiry, can take inspiration from the approach in formulating their own area-based, research case studies with the benefit of being able to access primary data sources in their own language.

This book aims to complement the understanding of institutional arrangements of the governance, planning and evaluation in the transport sector, and to the ways these activities interact to shape the spatial economy of any nation. An understanding of the political framework in any era is essential in understanding the context, how transport functioned at the time and the impacts transport had on society. Finer (1997: 1) notes that the history of polities involves understanding "the structures of government under which groups of men live, and its relationship towards them."

Apart from the socio-technical transition literature (Geels, 2012), little has been written about institutional and organisational transformations when applied to transport. No Western scholar has attempted to interpret the long-term development of the Japanese transport sector by paying attention to all modes of transport within the context of political economy. The closest studies of this kind are the book *Rikisha to Rapid Transit: Urban Public Transport Systems and Policy in Southeast Asia* (Rimmer, 1986) and books by Hauser (1974), who studied the Tokugawa era and economic institutional change in the cotton industry, by Vaporis (1994) on Tokugawa road administration and by Traganou (2004) on barriers to travel in the Tokugawa period.

With a greater understanding of the historical factors underpinning the dynamics of (transport) institutional and organisational change in the past it is possible to look more critically at current institutional arrangements and to assess the reforms that might be needed such that transport services support society in a more economic, environmentally sustainable and equitable way. As noted by van Vliet (2002: 35), the widespread global application of newly emerging transport and communication technologies is reshaping the physical, economic fabric of cities: these require new institutional arrangements.

Understanding of the role of modern governments is essential when considering the financial aspect of infrastructure development. Various projections of infrastructure requirements in urban and rural areas of Japan, and the capacity of governments to fund infrastructure from traditional sources of revenue, such as income tax, show a shortfall such that private-sector finance will be needed to plug the gap. This situation has led in the 1990s to private finance initiatives (PFI) in the UK and in Japan, and public-private partnerships (PPP) in Australia, and in other Asia-Pacific countries (Economic Intelligence Unit, 2012).

Studying the contents of this book raises the contemporary question as to what is the appropriate role of governments in economic development policy? One view is that transport infrastructure and services are social overhead capital and therefore should be provided, and maintained, by the government as monopoly enterprises. Another view is that such markets should be contestable and that the role of government should be policy, regulation and strategic planning with outcomes being transport project development and the procurement of construction, operation and maintenance services based on which party can offer the highest value for money to society. How this plays out in Japan in the future will be shaped partially by past and present experiences by people, their political motivations and the policies they introduced.

Organisation of the Chapters

The next chapter elaborates on the concept of institutions and provides the political context for the case study material on all modes of transport in Japan by outlining the important institutions and other organisations and how they have evolved and changed from archaic times to the modern period. These include: the hunter-gather society of the Jōmon, where there were clans but no institutions; the rise of clan chiefs and defined territories in the Yayoi period; the unification of parts of western Japan in the 2nd century and the institution of Emperor (Griffis, 1915); the over-reaching control of the Emperor's Court; the rise of the warlords and the imposition of three military governments until 1868; a rapid modernisation of the economy with the Meiji Restoration and westernised model of government in a monarchical democracy; and, finally, the current democratic form of government and its bureaucratic departments in Japan.

Apart from the obvious importance of walking to any society, the most appropriate transport mode to start with is water because sea transport provided the means for the early inhabitants of Japan to communicate with nearby states, especially on mainland China and Korea. Therefore, Chapter 3 analyses the organisation of ports and domestic and coastal shipping. This includes the ancient and medieval ports at the Eastern end of the Setō Inland Sea, such as Naniwa, Sakai, Ishiyama Honganji, Watanabe and Hyōgo. Coastal trade became an important feature of the Japanese economy from the early 17th century. As Western powers forced the opening of selected ports in the mid-19th century, and as the economy modernised in the 20th century, port improvements took place to accommodate international shipping. The post-Second World War economic boom of the 1960s onwards required further port expansion, and the introduction of container shipping in the late 1960s necessitated large facilities and extensive land reclamation. Increased global maritime competition has forced government intervention into the way Japanese ports are owned and financed of which the Hanshin port of Kōbe and Ōsaka is a good example.

Canal transport and lakes are forms of water transport (rivers have played a limited transport role in Japan because of the mountainous topography and fluvial infrastructure improvements have served to regulate surges in water flow and avoid excess flooding) that deserve a separate chapter (Chapter 4). The ancient period essentially set the pattern of canal and river management for millennia with landowners reliant on local knowledge for construction, operation and maintenance. In fact, the canals that were constructed in the commercial ports of Ōsaka and Edō from the 17th century were not financed by governments but were built entirely by the resources and capital of the merchant class. The ancient cultural and political locus of Japan was around Lake Biwa and Kyōto, so various ambitious plans were proposed by warlords that involved large-scale canals linking the Sea of Japan and the Pacific Ocean. All were aborted because of topography. It was not until the late 19th century that a canal was constructed between Lake Biwa and Kyōto for the purposes of moving freight, providing irrigation and generating electricity.

Ways of moving over the landscape on foot or by horse stretch back to when the Japanese archipelago was settled, but any sense of building and maintaining a network of roads dates from state formation in 6th century (Chapter 5). Later, in the medieval period, as the country descended into civil war, the *daimyō* (the great war lords owning large domains) used corvée labour for road building purposes. The third military government (Tokugawa) used roads and barriers[4] to maintain tight security and control over the country that followed the barrier policies and post stations introduced by the Taira edicts in the 7th century. During the early modernisation of Japan, there was little road investment because railways were a construction priority. Highway and expressway construction is predominantly a post-Second World War phenomenon that went hand in hand with the Japanese Government's

---

4 In Japan, these "barrier stations" were small fortified structures on main roads. Used in the Middle Ages, the British word "turnpike" was a spiked barrier across a road for defence, especially against horsemen (Jackman, 1916: 218–227).

promotion of a domestic automobile industry and policies to raise the standard of living that included private car ownership.

As the feudal past in Japan was swept aside (partly through external pressures), railways (Chapter 6) were constructed at the beginning of the Meiji Restoration under the influence of overseas money and expertise. Competition to expand the network ensued between the government and private sectors, until, as in many countries, the government nationalised the railways. Post-Second World War Japanese railways is a story of the financial difficulties of government railways and the establishment of regional business enterprises. In addition, Chapter 6 is the story of the history of the successful bullet train (*Shinkansen*) that has captured international attention. The unique reasons behind its development and success are explored in this chapter, along with its technological advancement in the 500 km/hr maglev train that is under construction between Tōkyō and Nagoya.

Air passenger transport is an obvious competitor to high-speed rail in the long-distance passenger markets of Japan. Chapter 7 traces the history of Japanese aviation in the early part of the 20th century, initially limited to military aircraft, but soon expanding into domestic services. Both the national government and private enterprise were involved in offering air services until the government nationalised the airline companies. The main theme is the organisation of airports and civil aviation in the post-Second World War period, including the rise of domestic and international air carriers. From military aerodromes to the most modern of airports, such as Haneda and Narita in or near to Tōkyō, and Kansai and Kōbe serving the Ōsaka region, the national government has been the prime mover with policies, regulations and airport financing in the aviation sector.

Anyone who reads scholarly articles about transport would have heard of the plea to "integrate land use and transport".[5] How the Japanese have tackled this feature of urban development is described in Chapter 8 with a case study of the Tōkyō metropolis, where the land readjustment program, transit-oriented development and land-value capture feature prominently. Planning for integrated land-use and

---

5   This has been a reoccurring transport conference theme worldwide since the concept of "integration" was introduced in a report for the Ministry of Transport, British Government, by Baroness Sharp (1970).

transport in Tōkyō regional new towns is also described. Examples of transit-oriented development are drawn from railway stations where the author and colleagues conducted field studies and interviews. Globally, there is an ongoing 'smart city' movement and examples from the study area are described. Looking to the future, the Japanese Government is promoting Society 5.0 and the vision and components are outlined in this chapter. Chapters 2–8 each contain their concluding sections and are supported by separate lists of references.

In the Conclusions (Chapter 9) the early questions posed are re-packaged and answered when addressing transport institutions and organisations. What are the respective roles of civil and civic society in providing transport at specific points in history? What activities did they actually perform in their respective social institutions in delivering transport infrastructure and services? Who were the key players in these transport institutions and organisations and what tangible things did they achieve? Were the progression of evolutionary paths of institutions and organisations slow and conservative, or were the paths abruptly disrupted, and for what internal or external reasons? Who were the dominant players behind these changes? And the transfer of knowledge and its adoption in most societies influences transitions, so to what extent has Japan been dependent on overseas ideas in the transformation of its institutions and organisations? Finally, Chapter 9 also considers the future of key aspects of Japanese society and speculates on some of the institutional and organisational challenges that might be facing Japan into the middle of the 21st century.

References

Alston, E., L. J. Alston, B. Mueller and T. Nonnenmacher (2018) *Institutional and Organizational Analysis: Concepts and Applications.* Cambridge University Press, Cambridge.

Black, J. A. (1999) "The Provision of Transport Infrastructure and Transport Services", in P. N. Troy (ed.) *Serving the City: The Challenge for Australian Institutions.* Pluto Press, Sydney, 80–105.

Black, J. A. (2021) "Ports and Intermodal Transport—Institutions and Organisations: The Setō Inland Sea, Japan, from Archaic Times to the Present", *World Review of Intermodal Transportation Research*, 10 (3), 269–303.

Black, J., C. Kuranami and P. J. Rimmer (1982) "Transport—Land Use Issues, Problems and Policy Implications: Sydney Since the Thirties", *8th Australian Transport Research Forum: Forum Papers, Volume 1*, 92–118.

Black, J., K. Tara and P. Pakzad (2016) "Planning and Design Elements for Transit Oriented Developments/ Smart Cities: Examples of Cultural Borrowings", *Procedia Engineering*, Proceeding of Sustainable Development of Civil, Urban and Transportation Engineering, Ho Chi Min City, Vietnam, April 2016, 142, 2–9.

Central Japan Railway Company (2020) *Central Japan Railway Company Annual Report*. Central Japan Railway Company, Nagoya.

Deal, W. E. (2005) *Handbook to Life in Medieval and Early Modern Japan*. Oxford University Press, Oxford.

Duina, F. (2011) *Institutions and the Economy*. Polity Press, Cambridge.

Economist Intelligence Unit (2012) *Evaluating the Environment for Public-Private Partnerships in Asia Pacific: The 2011 Infrascope—Findings and Methodology*. The Economist Intelligence Unit Ltd., and Asian Development Bank, Manila.

Finer, S. E. (1997) *The History of Government from the Earliest Times: Volume I Ancient Monarchies and Empires*. Oxford University Press, Oxford.

Geels, F. W. (2012) "A Socio-Technical Analysis of Low Carbon Transitions: Introducing the Multi-Level Perspective into Transport Studies", *Journal of Transport Geography*, 24, 471–482.

Grayling, A. C. (2016) *The Age of Genius—The Seventeenth Century & The Birth of The Modern Mind*. Bloomsbury, London.

Griffis, W. E. (1915) *The Mikado: Institution and Person*. Princeton University Press, Princeton, New Jersey.

Hague, R., and M. Harrop (2001) *Comparative Government and Politics: An Introduction, 5th Edition*. Palgrave, Basingstoke, Hants.

Hall, J. W., M. B. Jansen, Madoka Kanai and D. Twitchett (eds) (1990) *The Cambridge History of Japan, Volume III Medieval Japan Edited by Kozo Yamamura*. Cambridge University Press, Cambridge.

Hall, J. W., M. B. Jansen, Madoka Kanai and D. Twitchett (eds) (1993) *The Cambridge History of Japan, Volume I Ancient Japan Edited by Delmer M. Brown*. Cambridge University Press, Cambridge.

Hall, J. W., M. B. Jansen, Madoka Kanai and D. Twitchett (eds) (1999) *The Cambridge History of Japan, Volume II Heian Japan Edited by D. H. Shively and W. H. McCullough*. Cambridge University Press, Cambridge.

Hauser, W. B. (1974) *Economic Institutional Change in Tokugawa Japan: Osaka and the Kinai Cotton Trade*. Cambridge University Press, Cambridge.

Ishii, Ryosuke (1980) *A History of Political Institutions in Japan*. The Japan Foundation, Tokyo.

Jackman, W. T. (1916) *The Development of Modern Transportation in England, 2 Volumes*. Cambridge University Press, Cambridge.

Kawanabe, Hiroya, Machiko Nishino and Masayoshi Maehata (eds) (2012) *Lake Biwa: Interactions between Nature and People*. Springer, Dordtrecht.

Kodansha (1993) *Japan: An Illustrated Encyclopedia*. Kodansha, Bunkyo-ku, Tokyo.

Lake Biwa Comprehensive Preservation Liaison Coordination Council Office/ Metropolitan Areas Development Division, City and Regional Development Bureau, Ministry of Land, Infrastructure and Transport (2003) *Lake Biwa Comprehensive Preservation Initiatives—Seeking Harmonious Coexistence with the Lake's Ecosystem*. Ministry of Land, Infrastructure and Transport, Chiyoda-ku, Tokyo.

MacMillan, M. (2020) *War: How Conflict Shapes Us*. Profile Books, London.

Nash, M. (1967) "The Organization of Economic Life", in G. Dalton (ed.) *Tribal and Peasant Economies: Readings in Economic Anthropology*. The Natural History Press, Garden City, New York, 3–28.

North, D. C. (1991) "Institutions", *Journal of Economic Perspectives*, 5 (1), 97–112.

Rimmer, P. J. (1986) *Rikisha to Rapid Transit: Urban Public Transport Systems and Policy in Southeast Asia*. Pergamon, Sydney.

Sharp, E. A., Lady (1970) *Transport Planning: The Men for the Job—A Report to the Minister of Transport*. Her Majesty's Stationery Office, London.

Styhre, L., H. Winnes, J. Black, Jimyoung Lee and H. Le-Griffin (2017) "Greenhouse Gas Emissions from Ships in Ports—Case Studies in Four Continents", *Transportation Research D: Transport and Environment*, 54, 212–224.

Traganou, J. (2004) *The Tokaido Road: Traveling and Representation in Edo and Meiji Japan*. Routledge Curzon, New York.

Tyler, R. (2012) *The Tale of the Heike*, translated by Royall Tyler. Viking Penguin, London.

Van Vliet, W. (2002) "Cities in a Globalizing World: From Engines of Growth to Agents of Change", *Environment & Urbanization*, 14 (1), 31–40.

Vaporis, C. N. (1994) *Breaking Barriers: Travel and the State in Early Modern Japan*. Harvard University Press, Cambridge, Mass.

Wikipedia (2021) "Timeline of Japanese History", https://en.wikipedia.org/wiki/Timeline_of_Japanese_history

Williamson, O. E. (2000) "The New Institutional Economics: Taking Stock, Looking Ahead", *Journal of Economic Literature*, 38, 595–613.

2. Japanese Institutions and Organisations

…institutionalization is an articulation or integration of the actions of a plurality of actors in a specific type of action in which the various actors accept jointly a set of harmonious rules regarding goals and procedures (Mayhew, 1983: 116–117).

Introduction

The aim of this chapter is to give an overview of the major developments in state formation, Japanese political institutions and commercial organisations in the archaic, ancient, medieval, early modern, modern and contemporary times. The lengthy conclusions to this chapter summarise the main points about institutional and organisational transitions or reforms.

The archaic period saw the importation of Yayoi culture from China and Korea via Kyūshū to co-exist with, and later supplant, the first wave of immigration from continental Asia—the Jōmon hunter gathers. Families formed larger units of clans ruled by chiefs until consolidations of territories though kinship ties and territorial conquest eventually forged the Yamato State that covered much of western Japan.

The ancient period saw the expansion of territory away from the Yamato heartland, primarily in the direction of the north-east of the island of Honshū. By the 7th century, codification of laws and the construction of large administrative capitals indicate the consolidation of a "state institution" with the Emperor at the pinnacle of power. But this early phenomenon of strong, politically active Emperors was short-lived: from the 9th through to the mid-19th centuries Emperors had little political influence. Other figures came to rule in the name of the

Emperor: first, aristocratic families linked to the Imperial Court in Kyōto and, then, military families with diverse social and political bases.

The medieval period in Japan was a feudal age that was not static but underwent successive dislocations of its institutions through civil warfare. As with the Marxian history (Jameson, 1974) that all hitherto existing societies are histories of class struggles (freeman and slave; patrician and plebian; lord and serf), feudal Japan can be summarily described as a long conflict involving the institution of Emperor and its nobles being usurped by warlords (*daimyō*) who gained territories through military conquest. Some warlords were politically and militarily adroit enough to establish two successive military governments (Kamakura and Muromachi). In a predominantly politically fragmented and decentralised country, where borders frequently shifted through civil wars, the *daimyō* were, in essence, the local government institutions of the day wielding power as landlords over their peasants in their domains.

Dislocations occurred because of the actions of individuals. In the early modern period, three warlords are associated with the unification of Japan in the late 16th century—Oda Nobunaga, Toyotomi Hideyoshi and Tokugawa Ieyasu (who created the third military government that lasted from 1603 until 1868). They also helped create a more prosperous economy by recognising monopoly organisations and delegating trade and transport to the merchant class that increasingly became more financially secure as time went by.

After the restoration of the Emperor in 1868, the modern era is characterised by attempts to catch up with major Western powers by borrowing ideas on law, political institutions and technology. Social institutions that are more familiar to us today were formed: an elected parliament, national, prefectural and local governments (and their executive agencies) and organisations, such as powerful industry conglomerates and lobby groups.

Another round of major reform followed in Japan with the occupation by the U.S.A. and its allies after the Pacific War. A new constitution was written by Americans based on the British model. By and large, in the contemporary period, the institutions and organisations established in the immediate post-war era continue to this day. The military and powerful pre-war industrial companies had been disbanded, allowing skilled personnel to be transferred into government and industry research. The post-war economy boomed to the extent that by the 1980s Japan was one of the three largest economies in the world.

Archaic Tribal (Religious) State

Migrations and the Earliest Inhabitants

The societies that have evolved across the Japanese archipelago owe their origins entirely to *external* influences. Lineages of all humans can be traced to East Africa some 70 thousand years ago (Harari, 2011: 16, and Map 1, p. 16) before reaching East Asia (Harari, 2011: 23). During the last Ice Age, ending 15,000 years ago, Japan was connected to continental Asia through several land bridges. The relevant routes for the migration into Japan were as follows: the Ryūkyū Islands to Taiwan and Kyūshū; the link from Kyūshū to the Korean peninsula; and the connection of Hokkaidō to Sakhalin and the Siberian mainland. (The Philippines and Indonesia were also connected to the Asian mainland.) These links allowed migrations from China and Austronesia towards Japan about 35 thousand years ago. The Ainu (or *Emishi*) came from Siberia and settled in Hokkaidō and Honshū some 15,000 years ago, just before the water levels started rising again.

Autosomal DNA analyses and population expansion models (Ding *et al.*, 2011) indicate at least two waves of migration. The first wave— the Upper Paleolithic people of the Jōmon hunter-gatherer culture, represented by the Minatogawa Man in Okinawa—began around 50,000 B.C. and reached a peak at about 10,000 B.C. (Ding *et al.*, 2011: 19; Moiseyev, 2009). This culture was distributed widely on the Japanese archipelago from the southernmost Okinawa to the northernmost Hokkaidō (Hay, 2016).

The second wave of migration travelled to the Japanese Archipelago around 2,300 years B.C. These Mongoloid populations, called the Yayoi, differed from the Jōmon people in origin, and began to immigrate into Japan, specifically to Kyūshū and also along the coastline of the Sea of Japan (Yanshina, 2019: 9). Hudson suggests (2006: 421) that the Yayoi period saw the largest relative influx of immigrants from the

Chinese mainland and the Korean peninsula that heralded in innovative agricultural practices.

The first evidence of woven cloth in Japan is thought to have appeared in the early part of the Yayoi period (900 B.C.—A.D. 300) when spinning and weaving technologies were brought from Korea along with an agricultural package including the cultivation of rice and millet (Nelson et al., 2020: 11, and Fig.3, p. 13). Archeological sites in Japan reveal Yayoi-period spindle whorls were made from clay, stone, wood or bone and antler.

Jōmon and Yayoi Institutions

The Jōmon period (about 10,000–300 B.C.) is divided into stages (Initial, Early, Middle, Late and Final) based on archeological evidence as the technology of the culture, unsurprisingly, developed at different rates across the Japanese archipelago (Kodansha, 1993: 691–694). This hunter-gather culture began with the emergence of pottery and ended with the introduction of rice paddy agriculture and long-distance trade (Yoshida and Ertl, 2016). '"Primitive tribes" cement their social order by believing in spirits' (Harari, 2011: 31): "The tribe did not serve as a permanent political framework...there were no institutions." (ibid.: 52).

The Jōmon lived in relatively small tribes, estimated about 24 individuals per human settlement. Shamanistic practices, possibly influenced by Daoist practices from China, have been identified that suggest some hierarchical structuring of society. In the Middle and Late Jōmon periods, archeological excavations point to fisherman inventing an array of tools and techniques for deep-sea fishing (Kodansha, 1993: 693) that implied the construction of small boats and, by implication, some hierarchical control in the organisation of hunter-gather labour for lake, river, coastal and sea-faring fishing.

The population sizes of each human settlement of the Yayoi communities were larger, at 57 individuals (Ding et al., 2011:20). Crawford (1992) suggests the transition from hunter-gathers to agriculture in Japan was not a singular process but that there were at least four distinctive transitions.[1] The political system and style

---

[1] The Jōmon-Yayoi transition is the most important problem for the study of ethnicity in Japanese archaeology (Hudson, 2006: 418).

of human settlements changed significantly. Community leaders increasingly associated the rice granary and control over storage to gain "centralized power" (Hosowa, 2014: 67). Yayoi communities, and their contemporaries on the Korean peninsula, were in constant contact.

> A system of social ranking of elite and commoners existed, but among the elite, a formal hierarchy did not emerge until the end of the Yayoi Period when some segments of lineages became very powerful and were linked in a network. (Pearson, 2016: 21).

Based on cultural landscapes, fossil records and human remains (Uchiyama *et al.*, 2014), the Yayoi soon dominated the Japanese archipelago and completed their expansion around 300 A.D. but never fully replaced the Ainu tribes to the northeast.

Yayoi society was structured around agriculture with clan chiefs in command. The development of rice cultivation regions in Japan has been closely related to progress in the development of irrigation systems (Tabayashi, 1987). River irrigation systems for paddy fields extended across wide areas, especially in eastern Japan. The combination of these natural and man-made water courses formed the basis of rural infrastructure that also facilitated the movement of agricultural produce from the Yayoi period into the 20th century. The enduring feature of managing this Yayoi landscape was grass-roots organisations and cooperation and a decentralised administration.

Yamatai and Yamato States

From the Yayoi period (c. 300 B.C.) to the formation of Yamato State around 250 A.D., archaeological evidence suggests that the rise of social groupings, political control and small kingdoms were gradually incorporated into kingdom federations (Brown, 1993a: 4). The influx of Korean Bronze Age culture led to two distinctive religious and cultural spheres: one centred in northern Kyūshū; the other around Lake Biwa in the Kinai Region—the five "home" provinces of Yamato, Yamashiro, Kawachi, Izumi and Settsu. According to a Chinese Han (202 B.C.-220 A.D.) history, "Japan" (*Wa*) then had "over one hundred" separate countries (Ishii, 1980: 133). In the early days of state formation, "status and alliances were not based on place, for loyalties would shift with a family, not necessarily with territory" (Nelson, 2014: 89).

During the later Kōfun period (300–538 A.D.), Pearson (2016: 25), whilst acknowledging the debate around archaic political institutions, suggests that there was a complex political system in which social classes were controlled by elites who monopolised production and used military force to control or expand territory. Social prestige was derived from lineage, from tutelary deities and from ancestors linked to *uji* chiefs. Gradually, the clan of Yamato became paramount and interactions between far-flung tribes increased. Each *uji* earned extra prestige from the marriage of women in their clan with members of the Imperial *uji* (Culeddu, 2013: 62) underpinning the formation of Yamatai. (The confusion over the name of this embryonic country derives from different readings of ancient Chinese ideograms.)

These rulers based their beliefs on mystical Shintōism: they justified that they were a divine race whose ancestors came from Heaven, whilst those subdued were born on earth and therefore "ordained to subjection" (Griffis, 1915: 26). The chief god of Shintōism is *Amaterasu*, the Sun God—the direct ancestor of later Japanese Emperors and Empresses.[2] Barnes (2014) suggests that the mystical beliefs were derived from Chinese Daoism and the myth of *Xi Wang Mu* (The Queen of the West).

Towards the end of the 2nd century twenty-eight independent states pledged loyalty to Queen Himiko (c. 170–248) of the Yamatai state that was probably located in the Kinai Region—although that location is disputed by scholars (Harding, 2020: 10). Queen Himiko helped establish a single line of priestly and hereditary rulers in the Yamato region that gained control later over most of the Japanese islands, through inter-marriage and kinship ties (Barnes, 2014: 10), and parts of the Korean peninsula (Brown, 1993a: 1–2, 22). After becoming ruler of *Wa*, Queen Himiko confined herself to the inner recesses of the Court and the "mundane" affairs of state were left to others, possibly under the authority of her brother. The state was "tightly governed, and marked by a social hierarchy so vivid and entrenched..." (Harding, 2020: 17).

This established the precedent that the Emperor of Japan—whose authority was based on divinely-informed rule—does not personally run the government (Ishii, 1980:7), and this continues as Imperial

---

2   This belief is certainly a much later historical invention because Griffis (1915: 28) suggests Buddhist priests retrospectively invented many titles for the Yamato tribe, probably in the 6th century A.D.

policy. The state expanded through territorial conquest. King Yuryaku (reigned 418–479) sent a memorial to the Sung Court (420–479) that gave a brief description of how political unification was achieved in Japan after successive rulers had forcefully defeated other contenders for hegemony (Wang, 1994: 27).

These territories of land under the direct rule of the King/Queen (Emperor) required administration and this gave rise to the Court-appointed governors (*kuni no miyatsuko*), who sometimes were the local chieftains. Provinces (*kuni*) and districts (*agata*) served as the local government arms of centralised control by the Court. This hierarchical control of land and sea resources by clans and tribes (institutions of governance) reinforced the centralisation of political power. During their rise to power the Yamato lineage established no permanent capital until 313 A.D. when Emperor Nintōku (uncertain dates for his reign are 313 to 399) built Takatsu no Miya at Naniwa, situated at the inner recesses of the large Ōsaka Bay on a marshy delta of major rivers that made it of strategic importance for seaborne and inland waterway traffic. The importance of ideas imported from continental Asia were facilitated by maritime transport.

A "remarkable transformation" (Harding, 2020: 23) of the Yamato State, involving long and frequently bloody internal wars, took place in central Honshū in the 6th and 7th centuries that fashioned the archipelago's first recognisable state (Toshiya, 1993). Mixing fact with fiction, the "Great Sovereigns" morphed into the "Heavenly Sovereigns" (or Emperors as rendered in English), as elaborated upon by Harding (2020: 24–28) with particular reference to the legendary Prince Shōtoku (573–621).

The influence of continental Chinese culture grew including the codification of state law and the construction of large administrative capitals (Heijo-kyō in 710; Heian-kyō in 794), with their substantial administrative components. The Yamato State issued eight official directives between 715 and 840 that encouraged the cultivation of crops other than rice (Hudson, 2019: Table 1, p. 32) to diversify the state revenue base. From the 890s onwards, the Chinese *Zhenguan Zhengyao* (The Essentials of Government in the Zhenguan era) was known to have been circulating in Japan and was a source of reference for the

Kamakura, Muromachi and Tokugawa military governments (Kornicki, 2016: 169–171).

The Institution of Emperor

The most enduring institution is that of the Emperor of Japan and its earlier manifestations—some of which are surrounded in myth (Ishii, 1980: 3; Kidder, 1993). Japan claims to have the world's oldest unbroken line of rulers. Issued in 1889, the preamble to the constitution reads:

> Having by virtue of the glories of Our Ancestors ascended the Throne of a lineal succession unbroken for ages eternal...The rights of sovereignty of the State We have inherited from our Ancestors, and We shall bequeath them to Our descendants (Griffis, 1915: 22).

In this preamble, there are seventeen articles that define the place of the Emperor as the "fountain of order, power and privilege". In fact, as emphasised by Gordon (2003: 2–3), the early phenomenon of strong, politically active Emperors was short-lived: Emperors from the 9th through to the 19th centuries had little political influence and they predominantly played a ceremonial role as priests in the indigenous Shintō tradition. Other figures came to rule in the name of the Emperor: first aristocratic families linked to the Imperial Court and then military families with diverse social and political bases.

Ancient Period, 603–967

The ancient period was heralded in with a shift from court appointments based on hereditary titles (the *kabane* system) to one based on merit, despite the opposition of the *uji* chieftains. In 603, a new twelve-tier system of Court ranks was established with those ranks bestowed on recipients by the Emperor according to merit and ability. Reformers first moved to strengthen the government's control (Mitsusada, 1993: 194), then Nakatomi no Kamakari (Fujiwara no Kamatari) and Prince Naka no Oe (later Emperor Tenji) finally broke the power of the *uji* chieftains (Kodansha, 1993: 1496–1497).

Emperor Kōtoku (597–654) called a meeting in 645 of new ministers and made them swear an oath of allegiance affirming the principle that it was the Emperor—and not the chieftains—who should rule the state.

The Taika Reform edict was proclaimed on the first day of first month of 646. It was a Four-Article Edict that abolished Imperial and local magnate service communities and lands (setting up a system of government stipends), set up a new Imperial Capital and established a system of local and village government (Kiley, 1999). This administration was directly concerned with managing the fundamental resource—land.

The edict ordered the compilation of registers for population, taxation and the state allocation of land, and it substituted a product tax (levied on households and paddy land) for a labour tax (so, yō and chō). In 649, eight ministries were responsible for various areas of the new government and 100 official posts were decreed (Ishii, 1980: 20). Also, as suggested by Mitsusada (1993: 197–199), and of lasting relevance to the history of military institutions, was that the Taika Reforms established the "position of *seii taishōgun* (征夷大将軍)", or "generalissimo who conquers the barbarians"—the supreme military chief. The mandate was to quell frontier rebellions within Japan, especially in the northeast of Honshū where the indigenous tribes of the *Emishi* (Ainu) fought defiantly against intrusions into their traditional territories.

Institutional reforms in the ancient period were substantially influenced by external factors to Japan—although they took about half a century to resolve. First, in 663, a Chinese T'ang force defeated a naval expedition at the Battle of Hakusukinoe (off the southwest coast of the Korean peninsula): administrative reforms based on the Chinese model occurred. Secondly, the Sinophile Emperor Saga (786–842; reigned 809–823) strengthened the Japanese legal-bureaucratic state after the 810 "Kusuko Incident" when the former Emperor Heizei, who abdicated, staged a coup d'état.[3]

Thirdly, a social code of behaviour, with strong Confucian influences from China, became formalised. The Chinese-inspired *ritsuryō* codes were more than mere ideograms (words) on a page: they reflected a "legal cosmology" that rested on metaphysical assumptions about the nature of the universe and the place of people within it. The maintenance of social order was premised on vertical relations of hierarchy and subordination where every person had a specific role and specific duties

---

3   The abdicated Emperor Heizei (774–824; reigned 806–809) attempted to come out of retirement by staging a coup d'état against Emperor Saga with the help of his chief consort Fujiwara no Kusu.

(Celudda, 2010: 356): relations between ruler and subject; husband and wife; father and son; elder and young brother; and between friends.

This strengthening of the central government led to an expansion of its territories on the island of Honshū. It took almost half a century for the enactment of Taihō Code (702 A.D.) that was based on the adoption of the Chinese-style (T'ang Dynasty) law (Ishii, 1980: 30). A commission of aristocrats and Court officials, which included Prince Osakabe (died 705) and Fujiwara no Fuhito (659–720), compiled the code. It consisted of six volumes of penal law and 11 volumes of administrative law (revised in 718 as the *Yōrōryō* Code, as explained by Migliore and Manieri (2020)).

The Code finally broke down the clan-title system by making appointments to secular and priestly functions. As the entire country (which now included the provinces of Mutsu and Dewa, but not the island of Hokkaidō) was now placed under the direct control of the Emperor's government, a new system of land administration was introduced. The country was divided into three types of administrative units—*kuni, kori* and *sato* (fifty-household groups).

There were three T'ang-style taxes sanctioned by the government (Ishii, 1980: 27–28). *So* was a 3 per cent tax on the rice harvest but most of the rice was transported within the *kuni* for local government expenses. *Chō* was a tax imposed on local products other than rice and this included the expense and physical effort (transaction costs) of delivering the payment to the central government. *Yō* was a tax on labour at 10 days per year but could be substituted in lieu with local products. The latter two taxes were the responsibility of each household who were also obliged to transport the products to the capital—whether by water or by land.

The land law of 711 allowed aristocrats and local gentry to obtain permission from provincial governors to cultivate a piece of virgin land at their own expense—essentially, the formation of the manor system (*shōen*). Towards the close of the ancient period the reclamation of new lands through irrigation—largely by private individuals (influential families, temples and shrines)—was decreed to be private property, immune from confiscation by the state in perpetuity. This resulted in large-scale private agglomerations of land that were exempt from taxation and this had implications later with the rise of regional warlords.

Early Medieval Period, 967–1467

The early part of this period in Japanese history is characterised by a Chief Imperial Advisor (*kanpaku*) who was selected to take control over the administrative apparatus of government. Appointees to the role of Chief Imperial Advisor controlled politics only until 1185 when their influence was superseded by the political primacy of retired Emperors (*insei* system): "personal or individual relationships proved the main determinants of civil affairs" (Ishii, 1980: 34). The *insei* system (with the retirement of Emperor Go-shirakawa) gave way to joint political hegemony by the Court nobility (*kuge*) and by the leaders of the warrior houses (*buke*).

Kamakura Bakufu,[4] 1192–1333

At the beginning of this era, the Heike family monopolised Court positions, and other posts, by virtue of their military power and financial wealth. When the warlord Minamoto no Yoritomo crushed the forces of the Heike the warrior families throughout the country pledged loyalty to him as their leader. After confiscating Heike estates in central and western Japan, he had the Imperial Court appoint stewards for the estates and constables for the provinces. The Imperial Court officially recognised Minamoto no Yoritomo's position of the "chief of the warrior houses" (*buke no tōryō*). This paved the way for the warrior class to dominate the country under the Kamakura *bakufu* system (1192–1333) that was based on kinship ties and property inheritance (Gouge, 2017).

The leadership of the Kamakura government was drawn from descendants of former governors, holders of military commissions and managers of *shōen* estates. Headed by the *Shōgun*, and based in Kamakura, the new 'central' government was supported by the regional warlords (*buke*) and the *bushi*[5] who were appointed to administer policies in each

---

4 Literally 'tent government'.
5 *Bushi* (military gentry) were the warrior elite that emerged in the provinces of pre-modern Japan from the early 10th century (Kodansha, 1993: 1306). By the late 12th century they became the ruling class of the country (until 1868) and were more widely known as samurai ("One who Serves").

provincial government institution (*shugo*) and in the *shōen* estates where local warriors (*jitō*[6] or *gesu*) had seized administrative control.

The structure of the central institutions of government were well defined under the supreme governing body, the Council of State (Kodansha, 1993: 724). At the head of this hierarchy was the *Shōgun*, followed by the *Shōgunal* Regent (*shikken*). The Council of State was made up of the heads of the Documents Office, or Administrative Board from 1191 (financial affairs), the Board of Inquiry (legal matters), the Board of Retainers (dealing with general affairs) and the High Court.

The local institutions that were also represented on the Council of State were; the Kyōto Military Governor (*Kyōto shugo*); the Kyūshū Commissioner (*chinzei bugyō*); the General Commissioner of Oshu (*Oshu sobugyō*); the Military Governors (*shugo*); and the Land Stewards (*jitō*). *Bugyō* is a term from the Heian period (794–1185) meaning to carry out orders received from a superior. This reflected the hierarchical nature of Confucianism.

Confucianism and Neo-Confucianism (introduced to Japan in the 12th century) helped to legitimise the *bushi*'s authority and superiority over the other social classes. The warrior society was strictly ranked into three classes. At the top, with comparatively small numbers, were the *Shōgun*'s vassals on whom were bestowed letters of confirmation that recognised their proprietorship of land and the right to govern in that domain. The second tier in the hierarchy was composed of samurai. The third tier was made up of lightly armed foot soldiers.

Go seibai shiki mo ku (the Formulatory of Adjudications) is the law code established by the Kamakura *Shōgunate* (1192–1333) to codify warrior house law. This specifies both the relationship of vassal to *Shōgun* and the administration of warrior domains that remained in place (together with the periodic promulgation of supplementary articles, *suika*) until the mid-19th century—all predicated on the Confucian ideology of loyalty.

Shugo were local officials appointed to each province as part of national public administration. From the 1190s the *bakufu* assigned *shugo* to identify, and to register, suitable warriors who deserved recognition as *go kenin*. Their formal duties were initially to organise palace guard

---

6   *Jitō*—Their historical importance is their role in the warrior class's struggle against absentee *shōen* proprietors (Kodansha, 1993: 687).

duties, but they soon expanded to having the jurisdiction to punish rebellions (formalised in 1232 under the "Three Regulations for Great Crimes" legislation).

The demise of the Kamakura *bakufu* was caused by a number of factors. The attempted Mongol invasion of Japan had been a drain on the economy, and new taxes had to be levied to maintain defensive preparations for the future. There was disaffection among those warriors who expected rewards for their participation in the conflicts. Additionally, inheritances had divided family properties, and landowners increasingly had to turn to moneylenders for support. Roving bands of *rōnin* (samurai without a lord or master) further threatened the stability of the *bakufu*.

To further weaken the Imperial Court, the *bakufu* decided to allow two contending Imperial lines (the Southern Court and the Northern Court) to alternate on the throne. In 1331, the *bakufu* attempted to exile Emperor Go-Daigo, but loyalist forces reacted, aided by Ashikaga Takauji (1305–1358), a constable who turned against Kamakura when dispatched to put down Go-Daigo's rebellion. This period of reform, known as the Kemmu Restoration (1333–1336), aimed, unsuccessfully, at strengthening the position of the Emperor and reasserting the primacy of the Court nobles over the *bushi*. The long war between the Courts lasted from 1336 to 1392. Early in the conflict, the Northern Court contender was installed by Ashikaga Takuji, who became the new *Shōgun* in 1338.

Muromachi Shōgunate, 1338–1573

Japan's second military regime was characterised by expanded authority over all military and political affairs that included responsibility for foreign diplomacy and trade. Two men are credited with giving shape to the machinery of government (Kodansha, 1993: 1020). The *Shōgun*'s younger brother, Ashikaga Tadayoshi, established the administrative organs of government by following the Kamakura model. The *Shōgun* was directly responsible for local administration. Through the *Shōgun*'s deputies in the Kantō region were the institutions of the Muromachi *Shōgunate*. In addition, reporting to the *Shōgun* were the deputies from Kyūshū, Ōshū (the ancient provinces of northeast Honshū) and Ushū (today, the prefectures of Akita and Yamagata). The remaining part of local administration comprised of the military governers (*shugo*) and the military land stewards (*jitō*).

Miyagawa with Kiley (1990) explain the rise of the institution of *shugo* as "military governors" of provinces during the Muromachi period:

> It is essential to bear in mind the importance of the institution of kokujin [provincial men] lordship within the total political system of the Muromachi period [...] kokujin lordship was the fundamental institution upon which that order rested. (Miyakawa with Kiley, 1990: 99).

Gradually, the *shugo* were given more extensive powers by the *bakufu*, including: the power to execute judgment in cases regarding land; to arrest and punish those accused of unlawful harvesting; and to administer *hanzei*—a system whereby half of the income from certain estates was expropriated for military purposes. Another power was the authority to collect *tansen*, which originally was an extraordinary levy measured in cash and imposed uniformly throughout each province on each *tan* (about one-third of an acre) of "public land".

By the middle of the 15th century, in compensation for the burden of collecting these taxes, the *shugo* had asserted the right to levy *shugo tansen* and *shugo* corvée. This *bakufu-shugo* institutional arrangement structure was "the guarantor of kokujin lordship at the local level" (Miyagawa with Kiley, 1990) but the system of independent *kokujin* lordships on *shōen* estates began to decline in the latter half of the 15th century.

During the two and one-half centuries, stretching from the wars between the Northern and Southern Courts to the Sengoku period, the institutional arrangements shifted substantially. The *shōen* system of the "Imperial state" structure and its proprietors—court nobles and temples as proprietors—finally collapsed, and actual power in the provinces was exercised first by the *kokujin* and then by a new class of warrior lords, the *sengoku-daimyō*. For example, the Hosokawa family[7]—a branch of the Ashikaga family originally from Hosokawa village in Mikawa Province (now Aichi Prefecture)—illustrates this shift of power towards the warrior houses and its enduring nature over the following centuries.

---

7   The Hosokawa clan supported Tokugawa Ieyasu at the Battle of Sekigahara in 1600 and were rewarded with the position of *tōzama daimyō* (literally "outside vassals") in the Tokugawa *bakufu* throughout the Edō period up to the Meiji Restoration of 1868 (Kodansha, 1993: 1618).

The head of the clan, Hosokawa Akiuji (d. 1352), assisted Ashikaga Takauji in his rise to form a government. In return, the family was made military governor (*shugo*) of seven provinces in central Honshū and Shikōkū, and traditionally held the post of *Shōgunal* deputy (Kodansha, 1993: 567). For example, Hosokawa Katsumoto (1430–1473) succeeded his father as *shugo* of Settsu that included the administration of the important port of Sakai with its trade links with China.

In the Muromachi era, the *sengoku-daimyō* had to deal with villagers (Nagahara with Yamamura, 1990: 108) and the status of merchants and tradesmen. These relationships led to an explosion of land and sea transport networks (Yamamura, 1993: 381–383) and the rise of "transport and trade" *organisations*. In particular, Ashikaga Yoshimitsu (1358–1408), the highest-ranking member of the Imperial Court, forged (after he had retired from public office) a tributary trade relationship with Ming China that lasted for about a century. This heralded both the assertion of a positive foreign policy on the part of the *bakufu* and the *bakufu*'s usurpation from the Imperial Court of the right to deal with foreign heads of state. By this act, the Muromachi *bakufu* set the precedent for the particular balance of authority between Emperor and *Shōgun* for the next four hundred and fifty years.

Early Modern Period, 1467–1858

By the 16th century the provinces were firmly in the hands of the *sengoku-daimyō*. This undermined the power of the Muromachi *Shōgunate*. The military and political changes, and the development of warfare in *sengoku* Japan, were driven by deep structural changes in rulership, administration, social structures and conflicts (Morillo, 1995: 100). The collapse of national political systems of legitimacy unleashed competition at a lower level amongst the *daimyō*. The *daimyō* discovered that such competition was most effectively carried out through the conquest and effective governance of compact territorial bases.

They developed administrative, financial and human resources, and built more effective local states. One example was the powerful warlord, Oda Nobunaga (1534–1582), who ousted Ashikaga Yoshiaki (resigned as *Shōgun* in 1588) from Kyōto in 1573. Oda Nobunaga's way of consolidating territories included a war against the Pure Land

Buddhist sectarians based in Honganji (Ōsaka) who had land and lucrative trading networks.

The Rise of Guild Organisations and Trade in the Muromachi Era

Under the *shōen* system of self-sufficiency all non-agricultural activities—the manufacture of luxury and special products, the construction and service trades, the exchange of goods—were controlled by the *shōen* proprietor. Village blacksmiths, roof thatchers and carpenters met the needs of the farming community, and artisans produced the luxury goods necessary for the aristocratic class. Such goods were not freely produced for a general market, nor were they freely traded for commercial profit. A dual peasant system emerged where the small, weak peasants subordinated themselves to more powerful peasants (*myōshu* class[8]).

It became common in villages to manufacture products, such as noodles, rice vinegar, lamp oil and blinds crafted from bamboo, for sale in the towns that were beginning to emerge around castles. The peasants who made such products formed themselves under the protection of a powerful noble family, a warlord or a religious patron into *za*—the counterpart to the European medieval guild—that emerged in the late 11th century, and flourished especially in Kyōto from the Muromachi period onwards (Nagahara, 1990: 330–331). Only in the Muromachi period did the *za* monopolise the production, transport and sale of commodities—an embyonic *organisation* in Japan's history.

The almost ceaseless civil warfare during the Ōnin no Ran (1467–1477) might give the impression of a dark picture of destruction across the region around Kyōto, but those warlords holding land increased yields and, in fact, promoted industry through the *za* system. Their merchandise (especially salt, sake, malt, vegetable oils and paper) was exempt from tolls, from duties imposed in transit and from market taxes. Recognition of these privileges took the form of paying 'fees' to their

---

8   *Myōshu* were commoners given privileges by *shōen* owners as local landholders from the 10th—16th centuries (Kodansha, 1993: 1026–1027). They were responsible for collecting taxes and labour services from their families and sub-ordinate families. As the *shōen* system declined some were given samurai equivalent status and became armed vassals of provincial barons (*kokujin*) who, in turn, had allegiances to the military governor (*shugo*).

patrons, who were predominantly the noble families, the local warlords, Shintō shrines and Buddhist temples.

Guilds were officially abolished nationally around 1590 by the actions of Oda Nobunaga and Toyotomi Hideyoshi. Old feudal barriers were broken down by Oda Nobunaga, whose policy of the incorporation of large conquered territories eliminated many barriers to trade. Oda Nobunaga fashioned political institutions that his successors used to good effect in establishing and sustaining the Tokugawa peace from 1603 to 1868 (Gordon, 2003: 10). Merchants rose in importance to facilitate the extensive trade networks of the religious and secular organisations.

Oda Nobunaga allowed relatively autonomous village organisations to thrive as long as they paid him taxes. He developed a bureaucratic program of tax collection, where specialised tax collectors dealt directly with villages and returned the revenue to Oda Nobunaga and his vassals. In this, Oda Nobunaga took 'proprietorship' from these petty landowners, and, in exchange, he guaranteed them an income reflecting the size and output of their land. He also established the right to reassign a subordinate lord to another domain.

Oda Nobunaga, and, later, Toyotomi Hideyoshi, eliminated the *za* with their policy of free markets and guilds (*rakuichi-rakuza*) but in doing so created new guilds under their protection. Merchants opposed guilds as being monopolistic and restrictive of trade and found ways to circumvent policies: some merchants located in small seaports dealt with the administrators of the *buke* estates and arranged for the movement of their agricultural surpluses by sea.

Piracy as an Organisation

'Piracy' represents a good example of the blurring between *institutions* and *organisations*. Piracy in medieval Japan might be best thought of as an economic partnership between *de facto* local government (warlords) and private enterprise. Japan's land-based warlords accepted the autonomy of "pirates" and, in fact, competed to sponsor these multi-functional "sea-lord brigands" who could administer coastal estates, fight sea battles, protect shipping and carry out trade as well as seizing cargoes from foreign ships (Petrucci, 2010).

According to Shapinsky (2010, 2014), the "pirates" thought of themselves as sea lords. Over the course of time, "pirates" became maritime magnates who wielded increasing amounts of political and economic power by developing autonomous maritime domains that operated outside the auspices of state authority. With opportunities to make great profits it was natural that unlicensed trade grew in volume, especially through the hands of an *organisation* of "pirates" (Sanson, 1961: 265–270).

The chaotic world of *sengoku* Japan has been characterised by Clulow (2009: 25) as a "failed state" with endemic conflict fuelled by a proliferation of weapons and competing warrior groups. Since the collapse of the Ashikaga shogunate in 1467 and the onset of Japan's warring states (*sengoku*) period (1467–1568), no central authority had been able to exert real power over the archipelago's maritime fringes. Piracy underpinned these local coastal economies of Japan (Tamaki, 2014: 257), providing a reliable source of income to local warlords and creating employment for coastal communities.

In addition, during the 16th century, *daimyō* on the outlying western islands began to appropriate the title of *nihonkokuō shi* (Japan's official overseas diplomatic emissaries). Lacking the military power to prevent fraudulent use of that title, the Muromachi *bakufu* was helpless to prevent regional rulers from pursuing foreign trade and diplomatic relations (Murdoch with Yamagata, 1903). Far from taking steps to prevent their domains from becoming bases for illegal trade or piracy, the lords of Japan's westernmost provinces (including the Sō of Tsushima, the Ōuchi near the western tip Honshū, and the Ōtomo, Matsuura, and Shimazu of Kyūshū) were eager to pocket a share of the profits from such trade (Murai, n.d.).

The Eradication of Piracy and State Incorporation

Following in the path of Oda Nobunaga, Toyotomi Hideyoshi built up powerful coalition of domains with an objective of unifying all Japanese provinces. Under the tutelage of Oda Nobunaga his wealth expanded rapidly in an environment of rampant extra-legal, extra-national economic activity of maritime smuggling. He began to trade by way of *shuin sen* (ships used for foreign trade) with the formal permission of the Muromachi *bakufu* (Tamaki, 2014: 259). As his military power expanded, Toyotomi Hideyoshi incorporated some of the pirate clans into his war machine to gain more territory.

As for those remaining pirates, Toyotomi Hideyoshi initiated a campaign consisting of three steps: identification; disarmament; and enforcement. The key moment was on 29 August 1588, when he issued two decrees that, combined, aimed to eradicate pirate organisations: the "sword-hunt" edict; and an anti-piracy regulation. The anti-piracy edict specifically targeted coastal communities by ordering that "the sea captains and the fishermen of the provinces and the seashores, all those who go in ships to the sea, shall immediately be investigated" (de Bray et al., 2002: 459). Once they were identified, these sea peoples were compelled to sign oaths declaring that they would no longer engage in piracy.

The edict extended central government control over the maritime fringes of the Japanese archipelago for the first time, effectively moving the "marginal men", who were so central to piracy, out of the margins and into the legal structures (Clulow, 2009) of *institutions*. Japanese sea power became a centralising political force during the late 16th century, as demonstrated by the two maritime invasions of the Korean peninsula during the Imjin Wars of 1592–1598 (Hawley, 2005; Turnbull, 2002).

Isolated pirate attacks continued to be recorded well into the 17th century, but Toyotomi Hideyoshi's efforts transformed piracy from an *organisation* that could be conducted with virtual impunity into a far more sporadic and marginal business that entailed great risks where smaller pirate *organisations* remained outside the pale of a centralised government. Details on how the smuggling of valuable goods from overseas countries into Japan continued during the later Edō period by organised networks is described by Knoest (2016).

Edō Period—Bakuhan System of Government

The Edō period (Deal, 2005: 12) heralded the unification of the country under the Tokugawa military government. The Battle of Sekigahara (1600) confirmed the hegemony of Tokugawa Ieyasu, who was appointed by the Emperor as *Shōgun* in 1603. He set about building a castle and reconstructing the city that became Edō (Naito, 2003; Kodansha, 1993: 314). The Edō period saw the immediate transfer of political and economic power away from the Kansai region to the Kantō region.

Roughly three-quarters of Japan was governed by *daimyō* (*han* provincial government), about 15 per cent by the Tokugawa *bakufu*, and an additional 10 per cent by vassals loyal to the Tokugawa. Approximately 2 per cent of the land was in the hands of the Imperial Family, temples and shrines. The Tokugawa *Shōgunate* is best described as a fiscal-military state (Tamaki, 2011) where the overriding policy was to ensure the successful succession of the House of Tokugawa.[9]

The *bakufu* had absolute central political power over the fate of the *daimyō* and could even remove them from a domain. The iron fist of a national government reached its zenith once the country of powerful independent fiefdoms of some 250 domains had been finally unified in the very early 17th century. *Han* allocation reached its maturity under the third Tokugawa *Shōgun*. Tokugawa Iemitsu (1604–1651), established the right to confiscate *daimyō* lands and give them to other *daimyō* he considered more reliable to ensure the hegemony of the Tokugawa clan and its allies in other domains.[10] He also exercised power by ordering some *daimyō* to trade domains, which weakened them considerably. He confiscated portions of many domains and gave them to lieutenants under his direct command.

Tokugawa Iemitsu effectively controlled over about five million *koku*, or about one-fifth of Japan's cultivated land (Gordon, 2003: 13). He was especially tough on the *daimyō* who had opposed his grandfather in the Battle of Sekigahara. He took the land of former opponents of the regime and granted them to his most loyal *daimyō* allies—the *fudai daimyō*. He protected his power base by building a concentric pattern of Tokugawa

---

9   This is best illustrated by consulting the Tokugawa family genealogy (Kodansha, 1993: 1577) with its fifteen Tokugawa *Shōguns* who were supported by the *gosanke* (Three Successor Houses)—*daimyō* families from the domains of Mito, Ōwari and Kii—who were expected to supply the *Shōgun* with military forces against any *daimyō* challengers and to enable successors in the event a *Shōgun* who died without a male issue.

10 Tokugawa *Shōgunate* power in first fifty years was to control the provinces with the active allocation and withdrawal of domains. 172 new *daimyōs* were created and 206 were given fief increases for notable service; there were 281 occasions that *daimyōs* were transferred from one domain to another with the quality of the new fief in proportion to service rendered; and 213 *daimyōs* lost all or part of their estates in punishment (Kodansha, 1993: 1580). The principal officials of the Tokugawa *Shōgunate* were held by the *fudai* (hereditary vassal) *daimyōs* with other lesser offices held by the *hatamoto* and *gokenin* (liege vassals) such that governance was in the hands of the most powerful warlords. This *bakuhan* system of governance is the name given by modern Japanese scholars to the political structure established by the Tokugawa house in the early part of the 17th century.

house lands close to Edō, surrounded by lands of allied *fudai daimyō* and Tokugawa relatives called *shinpan*. He placed the former opponents—the *tozama daimyō*—in lands at the farthest reaches of the three main islands of Honshū, Kyūshū and Shikōkū.

Governance under the Tokugawa functioned in a complex way through a system of layered hierarchical spheres of authority, each of which retained autonomy. Each *daimyō*—the *Shōgunate*'s direct vassal—ruled his own domain (*han*). Buddhist temples, Shintō shrines and other organisations, such as merchant guilds and certain other associations, were similarly self-governing. All of these *interlocking institutional and organisational spheres* enjoyed a large degree of autonomy so long as they fulfilled their obligations to the relevant authorities directly above them in the hierarchy.

The Office of *Shōgun* nominally headed the *bakufu* and this office was invested in 15 successive heads of the Tokugawa family in an unbroken line that eventually came to an end in 1867 with the resignation of Tokugawa Yoshinobu. Directly supporting the Office of *Shōgun* were the junior councillors: Chiefs of the Pages and Attendants; Inspectors; Captains of the Bodyguards and Inner Guards; and Magistrates, Accountants, Tax Collectors and Policemen (Kodansha, 1993: 1580). This structure would allow the House of Tokugawa to retain supreme power throughout the land, especially with police powers to spy on operations in the *han* domains.

To reinforce absolute *Shōgun* power were seven senior officials reporting directly to the *Shōgun*. These positions were held by loyal, hereditary vassals (*fudai*): the Great Elder (*tairo*)—a position rarely occupied; Senior Councillors (*roju*); Master of *Shōgunal* Ceremonies (*soshaban*); Commissioner of Temples and Shrines (*jisha bugyō*); Kyōto Deputy (*Kyōto shoshidai*); Keeper of Ōsaka Castle (*Ōsaka jodai*); and the Grand Chamberlain (*sobayonin*). Civil and judicial administration was rationalised during the Tokugawa *Shōgunate* when the *bugyōs* became of much lesser importance as administrators were confined to holding middle ranks with well-defined duties.

Military and security governance were of paramount importance dealing with the Emperor's Court in Kyōto and maintaining Tokugawa hegemony. Responsible to the Senior Councillors were 10 official positions: Edō City Commissioners; Commissioners of Finance (*kanjo bugyō*); Comptrollers (*kanjo gimiyaku*); Inspectors General (*ometsuke*); Commissioners of Distant Provinces (*ongaku bugyō*); Captains of the

Great Guard (*obangashira*); Keepers of Edō Castle (*rusui*); Envoys to the Court (*kinrizuki*); Masters of Court Ceremony (*koke*); and Chamberlains (*sobashu*).

Finer (1997a: 15–16) has identified the link in all countries between the emergence of the civil bureaucracy and the raising and maintenance of military forces. He explains the structure of the Tokugawa *bakufu* in light of an organisation chart (Finer, 1997b: Figure 4.1.1, p. 1103). The pertinent thing he noted was Japan's huge and intricate civil bureaucracy: it was a highly effective police state that was "despotic, harsh, unequal and bureaucratic" (Finer, 1997b: 1103).

Provincial governments (*han*) were responsible for the implementation of national edicts. An important concept for instilling correct behaviour in provincial local officials was that of *bokumin* texts imported from China that influenced the administrative ethos and practice within the *bakuhan* system of government (Brown, 2009: 291–292). The Confucian scholar Yamaga Sokō (1622–1685) revised the *bokumin* ideal to suit the ruling warrior class. Over time and combined with "Records of Wise Rulers" (*meikunroku*), a Confucian-style "people as the base" ideology was created, whereby local magistrates would function as "benevolent" officials looking out for the welfare of the people and promoting the stability of the *bakufu* and the *han*.

The Tokugawa *bakufu* actively utilised foreign policy and trade as a means of consolidating its legitimacy in ruling Japan. Instead of dealing directly with foreign trade, the *bakufu* transferred the authority to conduct trade to the *daimyō* of Satsuma and Tsushima. Satsuma conducted trade with China via Ryūkyū, and Tsushima traded with Korea. This avoided the sovereign-vassal relationship with China (Colaccino, 2014: 33). Instead of kowtowing to China as a vassal or tribute state, Tokugawa Ieyasu initiated his own vermillion seal (*shuin*, 朱印), thereby declaring Japan as a country independent of China.

Paradoxically, this stance not only restricted, but greatly encouraged and enforced mutual exchange with China (Schottenhammer, 2008: 333–334). For example, the 1631 Tokugawa regulations specified that trading activities with Chinese ships outside of Nagasaki were prohibited, that a non-negotiable price for silk imports was set, and that mobility of any Chinese living in Nagasaki became restricted. In 1688, the *bakufu* issued a regulation, drafted by Arai Hakuseki (1657–1725), restricting the annual number of ships being allowed to enter Nagasaki harbour (Schottenhammer, 2008: 337, footnote 37). Both sides (for a Chinese perspective see Schottenhammer, 2013) were dissatisfied with the regulations and so smuggling continued to be prevalent.

As time went by, the successive *Shōguns'* attempts to gain better control over foreign trade involved policy changes and the formation of a large administrative bureaucracy. For example, the *Shōgunate* administrator (*bugyō*) of Kyūshū in 1681 employed 1,041 officials—a figure that almost doubled by 1724 (Schottenhammer, 2008: 335). By adapting Western ideas (from the Dutch and Portuguese), especially in the maritime field, Tokugawa Ieyasu and his successors developed a sufficiently powerful modern naval fleet. By the 1630s, the *bakufu* could back-up the *sakoku* edicts ("seclusion") with Japanese sea power that could control movements into and out of its coastal waters.

However, maritime borders were not impregnable to the circulation of Chinese administrative and strategic military ideas: through news and reports delivered by ships, the *bakufu* kept abreast of overseas conflicts such as the transition from the Ming to the Qing dynasty (1618–1683) and the port concessions yielded by China from 1842 to 1844 to the British, American and French Governments. China's government and its administration was of general interest to the Japanese rulers (Schottenhammer, 2008: 355). For example, *Shōgun* Tokugawa Yoshimune ordered Fukami Kudayū (a third-generation Japanese of Chinese origin) to translate into Japanese the *Collected Statutes of the Great Qing Dynasty* (*Da Qing Huidian*).

Local Government by Merchants

For over 250 years Itami was governed by the *sengoku-daimyō*, as was typical of most of Japan. The relevant governance of Japan in this era was provided by the local *daimyō*. After a series of unusual events in the late 17th century, the merchants of Itami County (about 16 km north-northwest of the present-day Ōsaka Railway Station) were assigned the task of local administration. The temporal dynamics of this unusual example of governamce by merchants are summarised in Table 2 that gives the timeline, the key events and the unusual sequence of institutional/ organisational structures governing Itami County in Settsu.

The Itami clan constructed a castle in the early Muromachi period and its domain covered Itami County. During the Warring period in

1574, forces of Oda Nobunaga captured the castle and his General in Settsu, Araki Murashige, was put in charge, and vastly expanded the castle. A few years later, Araki was accused of siding with enemies of Oda Nobunaga. Forces of Toyotomi Hideyoshi loyal to Oda Nobunaga captured the castle in 1579 and subsequently dismantled it. Following Oda Nobunaga's death in 1582, Itami was placed under the direct control of the Imperial Court and, in essence, became a de-militarised protectorate (Brecher, 2010: 22–25).

Table 2. Institutional Shifts in the Administration of Itami, Settsu Province, from the Mid-14th century to the Mid-19th century.
Source: Based on Kodansha, 1993, and Brecher, 2010.

Time Period	Major Event	Dominant Institution
Mid-14th century	Itami clan constructs a castle	*Sengoku-daimyō*
1574	Itami castle attacked by forces of Oda Nobunaga then castle was substantially enlarged by Araki Murashige—a general in Settsu for Oda Nobunaga	*Sengoku-daimyō*
1579	Successful siege and dismantling of castle by Toyotomi Hideyoshi following accusation that Araki conspired with the Mori Clan—enemies of Oda Nobunaga	*Sengoku-daimyō*
1582	After Nobunaga's death Itami placed under direct control of Imperial Court and declared *musoku-chō* (land outside warrior jurisdiction)	Imperial Court
June 1615	Re-appropriated by the Tokugawa *bakufu* during Ieyasu successful siege of Ōsaka Castle against Toyotomi Hideyoshi clan	Tokugawa *Bakufu*
1661	*Bakufu* swap land at Uji (for the establishment of temple for Ōbaku sect of Zen Buddhism) owned by the Konoe clan for land in Itami County	Konoe—Senior of Five Houses (Go-sekke) of Fujiwara Clan and high court officials eligible for post of Regent

Time Period	Major Event	Dominant Institution
1697	The Konoe clan formalised previous arrangements by placing administrative and judicial affairs in the hands of an appointed merchant council	Merchant Council of 24 Members from Sake Brewing Houses (*sōshukurō*)
1871	Konoe clan return land to Meiji government	National and Prefectural Government

The Tokugawa *bakufu* regained control of Itami after Tokugawa Ieyasu's successful siege of Ōsaka Castle in 1615, when the Toyotomi clan was finally crushed. In 1661, the *bakufu* reassigned land in Itami County to the Konoe clan—one of the Five Great Houses from the Fujiwara Clan—who swapped their land holding at Gokanoshō in Uji (southern outskirts of Kyōto) because the *bakufu* had been searching for a suitable site on which to construct Manpukuji—a head temple for the Ōbaku sect of Zen Buddhism that had recently arrived from China.

During the Edō period, Itami's independence from *bakufu* and *daimyō* control resulted in the Konoe clan's responsibilities being similar to those born by the *bakufu* and *daimyō* but this form of governance proved advantageous from a taxation point of view. The annual tax burden divided amongst the estimated number of households would have constituted "no more than a trifle" compared with tax rates imposed by the *daimyōs*, which varied widely, but, generally, amounted to 30–40 per cent of a village's assessed land productivity (Brechard, 2010: 25).

Furthermore, a Konoe representative did not staff Itami's town office: it was allowed to function as a semi-independent civil government. In 1697, the Konoe formally placed administration and judicial affairs in the hands of an appointed council of twenty-four elders (*sōshukurō*). Council members were formalised with a "pseudo-aristocratic status" that entitled them more prestige and authority than village headmen. The council dispatched to Kyōto monthly reports of the town's political, administrative and judicial affairs and was responsible for collecting and remitting taxes to Kyōto. This institution of local governance continued to operate until the Meiji Restoration when the Konoe family returned its land to the national government.

Merchant Organisations in the Edō Period

Merchants were denied the means of achieving any degree of political power (unlike European merchants in medieval times). They were the lowest class in Neo-Confucian Japan because they were tainted for handling money and called "odious toads". A close correlation can be found between the increase in production and the rapid development of commerce (Sheldon, 1958: 3). Initially, the main commodity traded by merchants was tax rice (*kuramai*) but there were other important traded commodities such as sugar, paper and indigo. Trading activities were conducted in the *daimyō* residence.

Later, office locations shifted, and domain officials supervised the activities of the merchants who were forced into new types of *organisations* (monopolies) that prevented competition and gave protection (Sheldon, 1958: 39–40). Government policy opposed monopolistic guilds[11] because of potential collusion with domain officials that would raise prices. Against official hostility, trade associations or guilds (*nakama*), and their divisions (*kumi*), developed as monopolistic organisations. The wholesaling functions were organised as family enterprises in a similar way to *nakama* and called *ton'ya*. As storage and shipping agents in rural areas began to compete against those located in the more major cities, merchant shippers turned away from the urban *ton'ya* to rely more heavily on those wholesalers in smaller towns who charged lower fees.

Merchants ingratiated themselves with central and local government authorities with gifts and bribes in order to receive protection and special privileges in the early Tokugawa era. These protected merchants managed the huge construction projects across the country: construction of castles; *daimyō* residences and samurai quarters; temples; and warehouses. In the middle- to late-Tokugawa period, large family enterprises, with a main house and branch families, were created through a family constitution. Morck and Nakamura (2005: 371–373)

---

11 Guilds, abolished under Oda Nobunaga, were reinstated over the course of the Edō period, with merchants paying a small fee for membership in organisations that enjoyed monopoly privileges at the marketplaces. The *bakufu* did permit certain monopolistic organisations: for policing and control; foreign trade at Nagasaki; pawnshops (Edō and Ōsaka); second-hand dealers (Edō and Ōsaka); public bathhouses (in Edō); and peddlers and hairdressers (Edō). Entrance fees to government and a small annual membership fee were levied.

sketch out the early history of two of these family enterprises (Mitsui and Sumitomo).

The financial influence of merchants in trade was on the ascendency. By the late 18th century, merchant houses worth more than 200,000 *ryō* numbered more than two hundred. With one *ryō* being ostensibly equal in value to one *koku* of rice, this made the wealth of these merchant houses equivalent to that of some of the wealthiest of *daimyō*. The financial status of the latter was on the decline with the imposition of the costs associated with the alternate year residency in the capital imposed by the *Shōgun*.

The *bakufu* was not very capable of (nor interested in) imposing any consistent economic policies because the semi-official orthodoxy of political economy was *shushigaku* or Neo-Confucianism[12] (Najita, 1998). Each *han* could decide its tax rates, and other economic regulations, or encourage certain industries (so long as it was not explicitly prohibited by the *bakufu*). Rice tax was levied by the *daimyō* on villages (not individual farmers), and village representatives allocated the rice tax burden amongst all villagers. Tax rice was stored in granaries on *daimyō* or *Shōgunal* lands and was dispensed to their retainers as stipends. Tax rice was also sent to the various domain offices (*kurayashiki*) in the major towns, such as Ōsaka, where it was sold on the commercial market.

The business responses to government policies by the Ōsaka merchants were to build the town's infrastructure and its port, and to ensure that Ōsaka enjoyed a central function in the national economy through the rice trade at Dōjima (see Chapter 3). The Ōsaka merchants developed an increasingly monopolistic grasp on the rice trade, determining prices not only within Ōsaka, but also in the entire Kinai (Home Provinces) area, that, indirectly, had a considerable impact on prices in Edō. Trade at the Ōsaka market was made through rice bills (*kome kitte*). The claim over rice in kind represented by the rice bill was protected by the *bakufu* and enforced by law. It was a means to reduce the transaction costs of trading large volumes of rice.

According to McClain and Wakita (1999), rice merchants propelled Japan into a more modern era of economic development. Since

---

12 The 397-volume *dai nihon shi* condemns the old aristocratic institutions as decadent whilst extolling the moral virtues of military governance (Kodansha, 1993: 544). See Najita (1998) and Culeddu (2009: 198–200) for more details on the Neo-Confucian philosophy.

samurai, including the *daimyō* were paid in rice, the rice brokers and moneychangers (両替商, *ryōgaeshō*) played a crucial role in the emerging early modern economy of Japan. Over the course of the Edō period, the entire economy would not only shift from rice to coin, but would also see the introduction, and spread, of paper money initiated and facilitated by the Dōjima *organisations*. In 1720, the *bakufu* authorised the concept of trading in futures (延べ米 or *nobemai*) as described by Moss and Kintgen (2009).

Institutions and *organisations* dealing in rice were both complex and their relative positions changed over time. The Dōjima Rice Exchange (堂島米市場, *Dōjima kome ichiba*, 堂島米会所) developed independently and privately as a wholesale market west of Ōsaka Castle on a slender island between the Shijima and Dōjima rivers. The Rice Exchange was established in 1697 when the Yodoya merchant house received a license from the *bakufu* and became the most dominant enterprise. Enabling this sophisticated trading mechanism was a national distribution network and a judicial system established by the *Shōgunate*. The Tokugawa *Shōgunate* chartered the Rice Exchange in 1730.[13] After being dissolved because of claims that merchants were hording rice during times of shortages it later became officially sanctioned, sponsored and organised again by the *bakufu* in 1773. The Rice Exchange was reorganised in 1868 under the Meiji Restoration, before being dissolved entirely in 1939 when it was absorbed into the National Government Rice Agency (日本米穀株式会).

The Tokugawa government recognised it was unable to abolish the *nakama* and reversed its policy to create the regulatory framework under which commerce was to develop until 1843 (Sheldon, 1958: 110–130). As the *bakufu*'s financial position deteriorated in the late 18th century, and amidst widespread famines and rioting, forced loans were levied on

---

13   In the first years of the 1730s, as the result of poor harvests and trade issues, the price of rice plummeted. Speculators and various conspiracies within the brokers' community played games with the system, keeping vast stores of rice in the warehouses, which ensured low prices. The samurai, whose stipends were paid in rice, panicked over the exchange rate into coin. The *bakufu* set a price floor in 1735. Over the fifteen years or so, until roughly 1750, the government stepped in on a number of occasions to attempt to stabilise or to control the economy. Eventually, the Rice Exchange was reintroduced in 1773, under *bakufu* sponsorship, regulation, and organisation because the government finally understood the economic power of the Rice Exchange in supporting the national economy, determining exchange rates, and even creating paper money.

wealthy merchants. This emergency measure was used 16 times by the central government (Sheldon, 1958: 119). Eventually, the Tempō Reform (1841–1843) of Mizuno Tadakuni (1794–1851) gave orders to dissolve the *ton'ya* and *nakama*, thereby effectively destroying this specific organisation of commerce. With the interference of transport trading networks, Tadakuni resigned in 1843 and the monopolistic bodies were reinstated in 1851.

The failure of this reform "showed that the Tokugawa Bakufu had lost its right to exist. The history of the Meiji Restoration had already begun" (Sheldon, 1958:129). The failure of reforms merely demonstrated an incapable and out-of-date government: it simply attempted to control the people with varying methods of austerity (Robinson-Yamaguchi, 2015: 55–56). Corruption in government and society was becoming relatively commonplace and the scholarly social critic, Rai Sanyō (1780–1832) wrote *Nihon Gaishi (Unofficial History of Japan)* and presented it in 1827 to Matsudaira Sadanobu (1759–1829), a senior councillor in the Tokugawa *bakufu*, that made the case for governmental reform.

Saito and Settsu (2006) explain in detail how capital was mobilised for rural-centred growth in production and commerce, and how the quasi-capital markets worked in both the Ōsaka economy and in the countryside. One thing that separated the Tokugawa financial systems from the those of the early-Meiji is that the late-Tokugawa local economies were never integrated into one national market. Links between the local domain economies were weak, and the Ōsaka-centred system of credit chain was virtually cut off from those of the growing rural economies (Saito and Settsu, 2006: 13).

Pressure for political reform came also from organisations such as the Mito School of Thought, derived from Shintōism and Confucianism, and founded by Tokugawa Mitsukuni, *daimyō* of Mito province (now part of Ibaraki Prefecture). The School was established to compile the 1720 edition of *Dai Nihon Shi (History of Great Japan)* but from 1841 under Tokugawa Nariaki (1800–1860) the School fostered Western learning and *"Sonnō Jōi"* ("Revere the Emperor, Expel the Barbarians"). This movement believed "the Emperor was the son of Heaven and thus the rightful ruler of Japan" and that "the foreign 'barbarians' had no right being in Japan, which to them was a 'Divine Realm'" (Robinson-Yamaguchi, 2015: 50).

Kurofune and International Influences on Reform

"*Kurofune*" is the Japanese term used to refer to all Western ships that legally visited Japan from the 16th century to the late 19th century through the designated port of entry at Nagasaki (the island of Dejima). These ships were painted black as their hulls were caulked with pitch and their wooden superstructures were tarred—unlike the colour of ships from China and Southeast Asia. In 1615, Tokugawa Ieyasu had issued a regulation that effectively stripped the Court of all but its ritual functions (Finer, 1997b: 1101) so the *bakufu* had never sought Imperial sanction for any of its political decisions—that is until Commodore Perry of the United States appeared in Japanese waters with his black ships and a letter to the Emperor politely requesting that Japan enter into international trade relations and open up selective ports to American ships for refuelling and taking on provisions.

In June 1853, the U.S. East India Fleet, commanded by Commodore Matthew C. Perry (1794–1858), entered Uraga Harbour near Yokohama, where his four, well built, black ships left a deep impression on the Japanese people. He presented to the *Shōgun* his credentials and a letter from the President of the United States of America that proposed open maritime trade. All political forces in Japan had unanimously reinforced an isolationist policy but the uneasy presence of American gunboats left the *bakufu* with no alternative but to sign a treaty of friendship with the United States of America.

In March 1854, acceding to Commodore Perry's demands that were backed by threats of armed force, the government of Japan signed a "Treaty of Peace and Amity between the Emperor of Japan and the United States of America." In 1858, the *bakufu* was obliged to sign another treaty of amity and commerce with Townsend Harris, the Consul-General of the United States of America. The *bakufu* were apprehensive about the views of the Imperial Court on the signing of these treaties and sought Imperial sanction for the treaty of amity and commerce (Ishii, 1980: 94). The Court denied permission through an Imperial edict and this dealt a humiliating blow to enlist cooperation and advice from other *daimyō* who ultimately challenged the *bakufu*'s legitimacy to monopolise political power.

The "Treaty of Amity and Commerce" was followed by similar treaties signed with Holland, Russia, the United Kingdom and France (McOmie, 2006; Natalizia, 2014). They were unequal treaties in the sense that Japan had no jurisdiction over foreigners in their country, there was no Tokugawa government control over trade and no control over the money exchange rate. This resulted in a large outflow of Japanese gold (Sano, 2013: 8). The opening-up of a few Japanese ports to foreign trade (Sadler, 1937: 239–245) caused dissent amongst some of the *daimyō* of the western provinces that eventually led to a coup (Sadler, 1937: 246–257).

Antecedents to the Meiji Restoration

After 1858 some *daimyō* from the western provinces established direct contact with the Court and the Court itself began to re-engage in political activities. One of the most powerful of the *tozama* domains, Chōshū, led those who called for an overthrow of the *bakufu*, whilst another *tozama* domain, Satsuma, wanted a power-sharing relationship with the *bakufu*, the Court and other prominent *tozama* domains. Japanese historians point to 1858 as the starting point of "the modern period".

At this point, it is worth interjecting a note on the role played by a Scottish-born entrepreneur, Thomas Glover (1838–1911), who moved from Shanghai to Nagasaki in 1859 to manage the newly established Nagasaki office of Jardine, Matheson & Company, initially exporting green tea. The *daimyō* of Satsuma commissioned Glover to build six saw factories and three sugar factories that provided the industrial might to finance the Imperialist military stockpile. In addition, he smuggled out of Japan, through the port of Yokohama, Itō Hirobumi and Inoue Kaoru, two of the "Chōshū Five", to attend lectures in the Chemistry Department at University College London. They returned full of enthusiasm for Western technology and British products.

In the autumn of 1865, Glover had facilitated an illegal arms trade through Satsuma to Chōshū. In February of the following year, he sold Satsuma sixteen steamers—all aimed to destroy the *bakufu*. This trade allowed Chōshū to arm 11,000 frontline forces with Minié rifles that had an effective range of 550 metres against the 46 metres of the *bakufu*'s antiquated muskets. This gave Chōshū the technological edge necessary to defeat the *bakufu* in a military campaign in July 1866. Other

British citizens also meddled in Japanese affairs on the back of various incidents.[14]

Kawashima (2020: 89) explains that the "intricate subtleties of the Meiji Restoration" cannot be reduced to a simple polarity of conservatives versus reformists as it took place against the backdrop of "the cross-pollination" of varying ideologies. The details of a complex series of events may be found in Beasley (1972) and in Kodansha (1993: 948–953). In essence, internal dissention in Japan over foreign relations and the refusal of Emperor Kōmei (reigned 1846–1867) to sign the foreign treaties were important factors in the overthrow of the Tokugawa *Shōgunate* in 1868. In addition to the opening of more ports to international trade (Hakodate, Nagasaki, Yokohama, Hyōgo, Ōsaka and Niigata), a more punitive measure in 1866 was the reduction of duties to a uniform rate of 5 per cent *ad valorem*.

This political situation forced Emperor Kōmei to assume a more active role in state affairs than any of his predecessors. As the U.S.A. and European powers were demanding that Japan be opened to trade, the Emperor insisted that Japan should remain "closed" and the "Western Barbarians" be expelled. The Emperor wanted a closer unity of the Court and the Tokugawa *Shōgunate* to repel external pressures on Japan's sovereignty (Todd, 1991: 203), although this alliance never eventuated.

Within Japan, it had become increasingly obvious that the old social order of *shinōkōshō* (hierarchy of samurai at the top, followed by farmers and artisans, with merchants being at the bottom) no longer reflected the reality of life. Intellectuals, such as Motōri Norinaga (1730–1801) and Aizawa Seishisai (1781–1863), influenced the *sonnō jōi* (尊皇攘夷) movement and this ultimately contributed to the weakening of the Tokugawa regime (Pickl-Kolaczia, 2017: 202–203).

---

14   British businessmen, in trying to promote trade, helped drain the *bakufu*'s finances. On 22 October 1864 a convention was signed in compensation for Chōshū's blockade of shipping in the Shimonoseki Straits. The British Government demanded that the *bakufu* either pay an indemnity of U.S. $300,000 (U.S. $4.95 million in 2020 prices), or, as the British Government preferred that Japan open another "treaty port". After the Imperial ratification by the Emperor, Sir Ernest Satow (1843–1929), a British Diplomat (Brailey, 1992), recounts that rather than risk the unpopularity of opening another port, the *bakufu* agreed to pay, but only in instalments. This proposal illustrates the tremendous burden that these indemnities placed on *bakufu* finances estimated to be about the equivalent of one-third of annual revenue.

Emperor Kōmei was to be the symbol of a new era for Japan with the protagonists behind the Meiji Restoration aiming to create a strong and positive image of the Emperor amongst the population, including his elevated position in this world and his divine status as a direct descendant of Amaterasu. At the core of this restoration of the institution of Emperor stood a system of ancestral worship that befitted the Imperial Family. While such a system had existed between the 7th and 9th century, it was all but forgotten during the Edō era.

The renewal of this systematic ancestral worship during the Bunkyū era (1861–1864) included the restoration of decayed Imperial tombs (Pickl-Kolaczia, 2017: 203). The main protagonist behind the Bunkyū Restoration was Toda Tadayuki (1809–1883) from Utsunomiya who successfully petitioned the *bakufu* to allocate a budget that allowed 58 tombs and places of cremation to be restored or completely recreated between 1862 and 1865 (Pickl-Kolaczia, 2017: 212).

Following clashes in 1864 and 1866 between the Tokugawa government and Chōshū forces, both *tozama* domains, with support from several influential Court nobles, agreed to work jointly to restore Imperial rule. On 9 November 1867, Chōshū and Satsuma obtained Imperial permission to attack *bakufu* forces: the *Shōgun*, Tokugawa Keiki, the 15th and last *Shōgun*, was declared an Enemy of the Court and all *bakufu* domains were confiscated.

Modern Monarchy

Meiji Era

The years from 1868 to 1912, when Emperor Mutsuhito died, are referred to as the Meiji era. Emperor Mutsuhito succeeded to the position of "chief of the warriors" with the rights of the *daimyō* remaining intact. The Meiji Restoration represented not only internal reform (Allinson and Anievas, 2010)—an example of institutional persistence (Ogata, 2015)—but a signal to the international community that "Japan had embarked upon the path of 'modernization'" (Kawashima, 2020: 89). On 6 April 1868, Emperor Meiji issued the Charter Oath, which promised that assemblies would be established to deal with all matters through public discussion and that "evil feudalistic customs of the past" would be abolished. The *han* lands and their subjects were returned to the Emperor in 1869, but it was not until 1871 when the *han* system was finally abolished (Ishii, 1980: 96). The former feudal lords were required to return their lands to the Emperor in 1870.

The Meiji government from 1868 to 1881 was greatly influenced by European legal theory, especially the French liberal doctrine of popular rights (Sims, 1998). In the government's restoration of the ancient system of Imperial rule, it also resurrected the *ritsuryō* antecedents and the Sinified legal system. Renewal was generated through "the 'revival of antiquity'" (Kawashima, 2020: 89). Ramaioli (2021) explains how *kokutai* (国体)—the spiritual notion of the essence of the Japanese polity—interacts with the constitutional model Japan has adopted since the Meiji Restoration.

On 6 April 1868, the Emperor issued a five-article Charter Oath outlining the principles to be followed by his government (Ishii, 1980: 98). On 3 January 1868, a formal declaration was issued of the restoration of the Emperor along with a new administrative structure that conformed to the ancient style of direct Imperial control over political affairs. Three new posts were established directly under the Emperor: prime minister; senior councillors; and junior councillors.

In June, the new government adopted a new fundamental law (*seitaishō*) that contained a mixture of ancient Japanese and American concepts of public administration: the tripartite division of governmental powers—legislative assembly (*giseikan*) with its upper and lower chambers; judiciary (*keihōkan*); and executive administration (*gyōseikan*).

These sweeping reforms transformed Japan from a feudal society to a modern industrial state, and that led to the administrative restructuring of the country into prefectures that exist today. The men responsible for this implementation of centralised and prefectural systems were Kidō Koin and Okubo Toshimichi—samurai from Chōshū and Satsuma respectively (Taylor, 2007: 3). Samurai reinvented themselves as bureaucrats in central and local administration (Paşca, 2016: 125), and became "the brains" in Japan's push to modernise, "but the merchants were the muscle, as they carried the whole financial burden of such an enterprise" (Paşca, 2016: 122).

An Imperial edict of 1881 stated that a parliament would open in 1890 with preparatory work studying the constitutions of other countries. A parliament that opened in November 1890—the First Imperial *Diet*—was convened and Japan became a constitutional monarchy along with the implementation of a new constitution (Ishii, 1980: 114–116). The new regime placed heavy emphasis on the importance of the Emperor in ruling Japan. The *Diet* (Parliament) was established, with the Emperor placed as the sovereign of state hierarchically at the head of the army, navy, executive and legislative powers.

Following more than a millennium of precedent, the ruling elder statesmen (*genrō*) held the actual power to run the state. The Meiji Constitution was finally promulgated in 1889, investing the Emperor with full sovereignty and declaring him "sacred and inviolable" (Kodansha, 1998: 950). The system of national government (the Imperial Household Agency; *Diet* as the Lower House), provincial government and local government were created, and all institutions were modernised along Western lines.

The basis for Japan's current style of government was founded in this period by emulating the, then, "superior" Western powers. Japan sent various delegations to major Western societies in order to study and emulate their parliaments and bureaucracies. From this international scanning, specific institutions were seen as leading examples of dominant models. Some traditional modes of thought continued: the ideal of *bokumin* was reproduced as part of the administrative ideology of the new Home Ministry, going on to inform the elitist ethos of that institution until its dissolution in 1947 (Brown, 2006: 293).

As the government's program of regional integration gained pace a new structure of central administration was required. Seven ministries were created: civil affairs; finance; foreign affairs; Imperial Household; industrial affairs; justice; and military affairs. As the *han* system was abolished—to be replaced by prefecture governments—further adjustments were made to the central administration (Ishii, 1980: 102–112). Communications was added to the above ministries as authority was transferred to a cabinet in 1885 based again along European lines. Ports, harbours, railways, roads and other types of economic infrastructure were established at this time. The Meiji-era creation of a professional bureaucracy, and the efforts of non-party political elites in the late Taishō and early Shōwa periods, were to counter the expansion of party power.

The Meiji era commenced with no private entrepreneurs who had the capital or confidence to modernise the economy. In the first fifteen years of the Meiji period, the government transformed the economy from an agrarian one to an industrialised state by investing in public works such as railways, shipping, communication, ports, and lighthouses. The Meiji government enacted the 1894 Anglo-Japanese Treaty of Commerce and Navigation, a long-awaited event that put an end to half a century of national humiliation by eliminating foreign rights of extraterritoriality and largely restoring tariff autonomy (Phipps, 2015: 1). The Meiji government also invested a high percentage of national revenue in importing Western technology and expertise.

The Japanese searched the world for the best institutions of capitalism and changed their institutions more radically and more often than in any other major industrial economy (Morck and Nakamura, 2005: 367). In the late 19th century, the government capitalised and subsidised numerous state-owned enterprises, but failures triggered a fiscal crisis. To restore public finances, Japan implemented a policy of mass privatisation (Morck and Nakamura, 2007: 4). Wealthy family merchant houses of the Edō period (Mitsui, Sumitomo), and other entrepreneurs, assembled former state-owned enterprises into *zaibatsu*.

At the apex of a *zaibatsu* pyramid was a family partnership (later a family corporation), which controlled several public corporations, each of which controlled other public corporations, each of which controlled yet other public companies, and so on. The families organised a new firm to float equity for each new venture and organised them into pyramidal groups. Corporate governance in Japan was characterised by the *zaibatsu* until they were dismantled by American occupying forces in 1945.

Decline of Constitutional Monarchy, 1931–1945

The decline of a constitutional monarchy in Japan from 1931 to 1945 can be attributed to the rise of military influences—not entirely unrelated to the expansion of Japan's overseas territories. Taiwan (Formosa) and the Pescadores were ceded by China as a result of the Sino-Japanese War (1894–1895), the southern half of Sakhalin Island (southward from latitude 50 degrees) became Japanese territory following the Russo-Japanese War (1904–1905), Korea was annexed in 1910 and, after the

First World War (when Japan was a Western ally), those South Sea islands north of the equator that were former German colonial territories were placed under Japanese mandate.

A neo-colonial expansionist philosophy emerged along with the administration of new territories. Ignoring government policy of the non-proliferation of warfare, military forces took over Manchuria in March 1932 and installed Puyi as Head of State and, in 1934, as the puppet Chinese Emperor of Manchukuō. In May 1932, a group of naval officers and non-commissioned officers assassinated the Japanese Prime Minister and the Japanese President that brought an end to political party government with the introduction of "National Unity" cabinets (Ishii, 1980: 122). The National General Mobilization Act of 1938 deprived the *Diet* of the right to deliberate on state affairs. The military government policy was promulgated by invoking the Emperor's authority.

During the Pacific War, government institutions replaced corporate organisations. Japan nationalised many major corporations, subordinating them to central planning. The Temporary Funds Adjustments Law of 1937 created the *Kikakuin* (Planning Agency) to direct economic planning and administration following Soviet models of the 1930s (Morck and Nakamura, 2005: 368–369). Corporate boards had to obtain government approval to make any important decisions, such as changing their articles of incorporation or issuing equity and debt. In 1939, further government decrees abolished boards' rights to set dividends. In 1943, another decree abolished boards' rights to appoint managers and reassigned this power to the *Kikakuin*.

Modern Democratic State, 1945–2022

What happened to institutions and organisations in the contemporary period is only sketched in outline because there is an abundance of available documentation for the reader to pursue this topic in more detail (for example, Burks, 1966). What is essential to note here is there was a new definition of the Emperor as "a non-divine symbol of the Japanese nation (as he was declared to be in an Imperial rescript on January 1, 1946)" (Ishii, 1980: 130). Within two weeks of Japan's surrender in the Pacific War, Allied occupying forces began landing on Honshū. The main administrative body for the Occupation was technically the Far Eastern Commission, headquartered in Washington and made up of representatives of the thirteen nations who had fought Japan. In Tōkyō, the Allied Council (representing the U.S.A., U.S.S.R., Britain and China) was to oversee policy implementation.

However, real power rested with the U.S.A., especially the Supreme Allied Commander of the Pacific, General Douglas MacArthur, who was given the responsibility of supervising the dismantling of the Japanese war machine and its socioeconomic underpinnings (Andressen, 2002: 118). On 2 October 1945, in Tōkyō, the General Headquarters of the Allied Powers was formally established under the direction of General MacArthur, Supreme Commander for the Allied Powers (SCAP). A draft of a new constitution originated in the General Headquarters of the Allied Powers and underwent very minor modifications by the Japanese Government before receiving Imperial sanction. Six months later on 3 November 1946 the new constitution came into effect. It stated that sovereignty is vested in the people while the Emperor is regarded simply as a symbol of state (Ishii, 1980: 130).

The constitution, written by U.S. occupation staff and imposed upon a reluctant Japanese government after Japanese authorities failed to make satisfactory progress in the view of occupation leaders, still serves as the foundation of Japanese democracy (Andressen, 2002: 113). The new American-designed constitution, written in under a week, was based on the British model, which was closer to Japan's pre-war system than America's (Andressen, 2002: 120).

In dismantling Japan's war industries, the big four *zaibatsu* (Mitsui, Mitsubishi, Yasuda and Sumitomo) were special targets: 83 of their holding companies were broken up. Approximately 3,000 senior businessmen were removed from their jobs. The smaller subsidiary companies were separated from the core businesses, and their ability to work together was limited by tax reform and laws against collusion (such as the *Anti-Monopoly Law* of 1947). In 1948, with a relaxation of the policy of purging the *zaibatsu*, a modified form of the *zaibatsu*, called the *keiretsu kigyō* ('aligned companies') emerged. They were similar in structure to their predecessors though more loosely linked and no longer family owned. They did, however, retain their original appellations, so, once again, the names Mitsui, Mitsubishi, Yasuda and Sumitomo became commonplace in Japan (Andressen, 2002: 124).

Under the 1946 Constitution a bicameral *Diet* was established as the highest organ of authority, with the House of Representatives and a House of Councillors (both popularly elected) as a Lower House. Executive power is vested in the Cabinet—responsible to the *Diet*. The Japanese Constitution importantly gave encouragement to local self-government and to administrative decentralisation. Until 1994, the House of Representatives consisted of 512 members elected from 130 districts, with each electoral district having anywhere from two to six *Diet* seats. In 1994, the lower-house system was significantly modified to 300 single-member districts throughout Japan, where local voters choose lower house members and 200 seats in eleven national blocks that are awarded based on proportional representation (Ellington, 2002: 116).

In the post-war period, the Japanese economy recovered: Japan was given foreign aid to build up its infrastructure and industrial base (the 1947 American aid budget for the country was approximately U.S. $400 million (Andressen, 2002: 124). The historical development of policies and institutions related to the manufacturing industry post-1949 are summarised by the World Bank (2020, Table 2.1, pp. 29–31). With the end of the Allied Occupation in 1952 the machinery of government was formally returned to Japanese control. Following the end of the U.S. occupation, Japanese firms began pre-empting takeovers by acquiring *white squire* positions in each other (Morck and Nakamura, 2005: 369). A *white squire* is a friendly firm that buys a block of stock in a target firm to protect it from a raider. If the friendly firm takes the target over entirely, it is called a *white knight*. Major banks were often engaged in arranging these inter-corporate equity placements. These holdings, the *keiretsu* system of the 1950s, expanded in the 1960s, and are characteristic of Japanese big business today.

The conservative Liberal and Democratic parties dominated. The first Prime Minister of note was Yoshida Shigeru (1878–1967), a pre-war diplomat who was appointed Prime Minister in 1946 with the goal to restore the fundamental characteristics of Japanese society, "while maintaining the values of the Meiji restoration—a strong government and a regulated society" (Andressen, 2002: 122). The event that dramatically changed the structure of Japan's economy was the outbreak of the Korean War in June 1950.

The American military, which became part of a larger U.N. force, had to secure a massive supply of war items very quickly to stop the sudden invasion of South Korea by the North. The result was U.S. $4 billion (U.S.

$43 billion in 2020 prices) in orders for Japanese companies for "special procurements" (*tokuju*), consisting primarily of motor vehicles, textiles and communications equipment—the subsequent development of these industries propelled Japan as a global manufacturing giant (Andressen, 2002: 125).

The Japanese often refer to the 1960s as the 'Golden Years'. It was a time when Japanese society came together to rebuild the country and the result was astounding economic success. Ikeda Hayato (1899–1965; Prime Minister from 1960–1964) announced in 1960 that Japanese per capita incomes would double by 1970 (they did so by 1967), to U.S. $2,800 (in 2020 prices). Economic growth gave citizens a clear, common goal ("GNP nationalism") around which they could organise their social institutions (Andressen, 2002: 137). In 1964, Japan joined the group of industrialised nations—the Organisation of Economic Cooperation and Development (OECD)—and became the third largest economy in the world (behind the U.S.A. and West Germany) by the end of the decade. GNP had increased approximately six-fold between 1970 and 1990 (Andressen, 2002: 176).

However, the end of the 'bubble economy' caused widespread damage and loss of confidence—both in the economy and in the government during the 1990s with stagnation that was exacerbated by an ageing population. From 1992 onwards various stimulus packages were produced, including massive injections of money (U.S. $84 billion in 1992, U.S. $119 billion in 1993, U.S. $150 billion in 1994, U.S. $75 billion in 1995, U.S. $123 billion in 1998 and U.S. $137 billion in 1999) as well as tax cuts, and financial aid to banks and smaller businesses.

Bank bailouts were a particular focus with the establishment of a 'bridge bank' in 1998 to take over some U.S. $540 billion in bank debt, thereby isolating the problem and eliminating widespread bankruptcies in this sector. Bank mergers were also organised (Sumitomo and Sakura Banks, and Asahi and Tokai Banks) to strengthen the banking sector, but this also led to substantial job losses. These measures failed to revive the economy, partly because much of the money was spent on infrastructure projects (U.S. $183 billion since 1998 alone). All that infrastructure spending achieved was to reinforce the 'cozy relationship' between the Japanese government (especially the Ministry of Construction) and construction companies.

Fundamental political reform did not seem to be forthcoming (Andressen, 2002: 185). This demonstrates the considerable inertia in a conservative government system. National government bureaucrats were the academic elite who were recruited from the top of the classes of the very best Japanese universities (Ellington, 2002: 119). Bureaucratic style was reinforced by informal personal connections—usually begun at university. Andressen (2002: 9) suggests that politicians have little time to gain expertise within a portfolio and therefore tend to formulate new laws based on the lobbying from business and their electorates.

The implication is that "over time the bureaucracy has come to be a centre of power, often seemingly independent of politicians". However, competition between bureaucrats and their departments "tends to ...inhibit change" (Andressen, 2002: 9). The conservative nature of Japanese politics reflects the ongoing tension between different sources of power in Japan. The question 'Who runs Japan?' was considered in the mid 1990s by the journalist, Karl van Wolferen, who published *The Enigma of Japanese Power* (van Wolferen, 1989). This was followed by Chalmers Johnson's *Japan: Who Governs?* Conventional wisdom has it that there exists an "iron triangle" of power in the Japan: big business; bureaucrats; and politicians (Andressen 2002: 148–149). From a survey of 1,600 civic society organisations, they think they have no influence on government policy making (Tsujinaka and Pekkanen, 2007).

Along with these economic problems came political ones. Some argue that with the passing of Emperor Hirohito in early 1989 there was some concern (especially amongst the older Japanese) over cultural continuity because the institution of Emperor has long been the cultural core of Japanese society. There were concerns that a younger, more outward-looking Emperor might undermine the 63 years of stability that saw the country through the worst period in its history. However, the pomp and circumstance of the November 1990 accession ceremonies of the new Emperor (Akihito) reinforced, rather than undermined, the country's cultural traditions.

Conclusions

Table 3 summarises who were the dominant institutions at the national government level in Japanese society from ancient times to Japan in 2022. The stability (or collapse) of a political community must be distinguished from the collapse of a regime—synonymous with the form of rule or the form of polity (Finer, 1997a: 14). Regimes may change but perhaps not so rapidly as political communities do. Similarly, the people at the top of the hierarchy of these legitimate regimes are simply those who hold the authority roles at any one point in time. As decision-making authorities their turnover may be very rapid without in any way altering the essential characteristics of the regime itself.

Table 3. Dominant Japanese Institutions from Ancient Times to 2022.
Source: Author.

Time Period	Western Calendar	Dominant Institution
Archaic	250 B.C.–603 A.D.	Independent clan chiefs; Unification of territories—Yamato State; Emperor
Ancient	603–967	Emperor and Court Nobility
Medieval	967–1467	Marginalisation of Emperor; Rise of Warrior Houses; Kamakura & Muromachi *Shōgunates*
Early Modern	1467–1858	Civil War; Unification; Tokugawa *Shōgunate*; *bakuhan* government
Modern	1858–1945	Restoration of Divine Emperor; System of democratic government: Military dominating government
Contemporary	1945–2022	Defeat in War; Non-divine Emperor; New Constitution

What were the main factors, and the key events, that help explain the institutional change in governance summarised in the above table? In summary, Table 4 identifies the key historical events in the six broad time periods that brought about the transitions of national institutions of governance in Japan. The transitions cover the archaic, ancient, medieval, early modern, modern and contemporary periods.

Table 4. Major Factors Explaining Institutional Change in Japan.
Source: Author.

Time Period	Major Events
Archaic	Jōmon hunter-gathers replaced by Yayoi migration from continental Asia and establishment of clans (*uji* chiefs); Kingdom federations—territory expansion through war, marriage and kinship ties; consolidation of Yamato State; Royalty evoked a divine race whose ancestors came from Heaven (based on Esoteric Daoism or mystical Shintōism) creation of institution of Emperor; Court-appointed governors administer the country; Territorial expansion at expense of indigenous *Emishi* (Ainu)
Ancient	Imperial House controls Japan; Consolidation of power Emperor's administration supplants that of the independent chieftains; Taika Reform (646) creates military position of *seii taishōgun*; Taihō Code (702) adopts Chinese-style law and Chinese-inspired *ritsuryō* codes and Confucian social order
Medieval	Estate administration by court nobles delegated to land stewards leading the rise of the military class; Warrior Houses; Marginalisation of Emperor; Government by military Kamakura and Muromachi *Shōgunates*
Early Modern	Civil War; Unification of Japan; Military government by Tokugawa *shogunate* with 250 years of peace; *Bakuhan* system of government; Increasing influence of foreign nations; Weakening of Tokugawa *bakufu* and victory to Chōshū and Satsuma *daimyōs*
Modern	Restoration of Divine Emperor; System of Western democratic government; Modernisation of bureaucracy; Rise of military
Contemporary	Defeat in Second World War; Non-divine Emperor; Modern democratic nation; Hosting Summer Olympics in 1964 & 2021

Who were the individuals behind some of these changes in the evolutionary paths of national institutions? As Griffis (1915: 54–55) points out that the origins of two modern Japanese parties can be traced to the era 1575 to 1604. The idea of the "Federalist" is traced to Toyotomi Hideyoshi whereas the Imperialists are traced back to the *daimyōs* of

Satsuma and Chōshū in their influential role leading to the restoration of the Emperor to power. The elder statesmen of the Meiji period (1868–1912) were Ōkubo Toshimichi (1830–1878) and Itō Hirobumi (1841–1909). Table 5 puts a name against the institutional changes identified in Tables 3 and 4 despite the inherent problem of over-simplification and selectivity.

Table 5. Selected Key Players in National Institutional Change in Japan from Archaic Times to the Present Day.
Source: Author.

Transformative Event and Date	Instigator
Yamatai State created from coalition of chiefdoms (c. 200)	Queen Himiko
Imperial House gains control of Western Japan (645)	Fujiwara no Kamatari; Prince Naka no Oe
Oath of allegiance: principle that Emperor should rule the state not the chieftains (645); Taika Reform edict (646)	Emperor Kotoku
Taihō Code—Compilation and adoption of the Chinese-style law penal administrative law (702)	Prince Osakabe; Fujiwara no Fuhito
Imperial Court officially recognise Kamakura *Shōgunate* when warrior families throughout Japan pledge loyalty the "chief of the warrior houses" (*buke no tōryō*) (1193)	Minamoto no Yoritomo
Formation of Muromachi *Shōgunate* (1338)	Ashikaga Takauji
Muromachi *Shōgunate* ousted from Kyōto (1573); Ashikaga Yoshiaki resigned as *Shōgun* (1588)	Oda Nobunaga
Eradication and state incorporation of "piracy" organisations—issue of two decrees (the 'sword-hunt' edict; and an anti-piracy regulation (1588)	Toyotomi Hideyoshi
Battle of Sekigahara confirmed the hegemony of Tokugawa Ieyasu (1600); Tokugawa *Shōgunate* (1603) that governed for two-and-a-half centuries	Tokugawa Ieyasu
Foreign demands—the U.S. East India Fleet enters Uraga Harbour; international treaties and a selective open port policy (1853)	Commodore Matthew Perry
Chōshū and Satsuma obtain Imperial permission to attack *bakufu* forces (1867) and the Meiji Restoration	*Daimyōs* of Chōshū and Satsuma

Transformative Event and Date	Instigator
Japan modernises and a colonial power; Defeated in Second World War; Occupation forces write new constitution and a bicameral *Diet* (1946)	General Douglas MacArthur
Modern, democratic state welcomed by the international community by hosting Tōkyō Olympics in 1964 and 2021	Government of Japan

The limited and restrictive policies of the Tokugawa military regime during the Edō period largely ignored economic development in a predominantly agrarian society. When an appraisal of those government services is made (Finer, 1997b: 1114–1123) there is clearly no direct involvement that relates to transport—except in the area of taxation policy with its implications on the physical movement of rice. The expansion of commerce was in the hands of the merchant class.

The new institutional economics suggests that dependency paths do get reversed. The case of the Dōjima Rice Exchange demonstrates that over its three-century history it variously served private interests before becoming an arm of the Japanese national government. The merchants originally set the detailed rules for trade in the rice market, including the tradition of tipping a bucket of water to indicate the suspension of daily trading that determined the price of rice. Following the collapse of the Tokugawa government, a new rice marketing system, the *Ōsaka Dōjima Komesho Kaisho*, was established then renamed in 1893 as the *Ōsaka Dōjima Beikoku Torihikisho* (Ōsaka Dōjima Rice Market Place). The government-sponsored *Nihon Beikoku Kabushiki Kaisha* (Japan Rice Company Limited) absorbed this in 1939 to control rice distribution and its price during a period of scarcity. From 1968 onwards the government has been taking measures to cope with a rice surplus (Hayami and Godo, 1997; Kodansha, 1998: 1263).

Another example of reversing path dependency is that the Tokugawa government recognised it was unable to abolish merchant guilds and reversed its policy to create the regulatory framework under which commerce was to develop until 1843. As the *bakufu*'s financial position deteriorated in the late 18th century, and amidst widespread famines and rioting, forced loans were levied on wealthy merchants—and this emergency measure was used 16 times by the central government. Eventually, the Tempō Reform (1841–1843) dissolved the *ton'ya* and *nakama*, thereby effectively destroying this specific organisation of commerce. However, with the disruption to trading networks monopolistic bodies were reinstated in 1851.

From around 1,100 guilds (*za*) sprang up under the protection of regional warlords but it was not until the Muromachi period that they monopolised the production, transport and sale of commodities. Peasants who made such products also formed themselves under the protection of a powerful noble family or a religious patron into guilds. During the *Ōnin no Ran*, warlords holding land increased yields, and, in fact, promoted and recognised commerce through the *za* system. Merchants opposed guilds as being monopolistic and restrictive of trade. Guilds were officially abolished nationally around 1590 by the feudal lords Oda Nobunaga and Toyotomi Hideyoshi to encourage free markets but then encouraged new guilds under their protection.

At first, the merchant trading activities were conducted in the *daimyō* residence, but, later, office locations shifted elsewhere where domain officials supervised the activities. Merchants were forced into new types of *organisations* that were protective in nature: organisations that prevented competition (monopolies); merchant-class solidarity; and protection. Government policy opposed monopolistic guilds because of potential collusion with officials that would raise prices. Samurai and peasant classes alike supported this policy. Against official hostility, trade associates or guilds developed.

Institutions and *organisations* dealing in rice were both complex and their relative positions changed over time. The Dōjima Rice Exchange developed in Ōsaka in 1697 independently and privately as a wholesale market through a license from the Tokugawa *Shōgunate*. Enabling this sophisticated trading mechanism was a national distribution network and a judicial system established by the *Shōgunate*. The Rice Exchange was chartered in 1730 but was then dissolved because of claims that merchants were hoarding rice during times of shortages. In 1773, it became officially sanctioned, sponsored and organised again by the *bakufu*. The Rice Exchange was reorganised in 1868 under the Meiji Restoration, before being dissolved entirely in 1939 when it was absorbed into the National Government Rice Agency.

During the Tokugawa *Shōgunate*, the jurisdictional governance of land in Japan was predominantly the *bakuhan* system although counter-intuitive examples of local government by the merchant class can be found. For example, in the late 17th century, a merchant council of 24 members from sake brewing houses in Itami County were assigned the task of local administration (see Table 3). The merchant administration lasted until 1871 when the *daimyō* land was returned to the Meiji government.

The Meiji government introduced the institution of capitalism (Allinson and Anievas, 2010). During its crash modernisation, Japan adopted a legal system largely based on German civil law. Thus, Japanese law was subjected to a variety of old and new (external) influences (Ishii, 1980: 91–92). Public bond trading began in the 1870s, and in 1878 the Tōkyō and Ōsaka Stock Exchanges were formed and subjected to regulation under the Stock Exchange Ordinance. Leading merchant families issued stock to finance industrialisation, and the great pyramidal *zaibatsu* groups were formed and came to dominate the Japanese economy. They were dismantled during the Allied Occupation of Japan when a new form of corporate governance emerged in the 1950s—the *keiretsu* formed as a defence mechanism against corporate takeovers (Morck and Nakamura, 2005: 434).

In the contemporary politics of the Western World, and of Japan, it is the transport bureaucracies, in one form or another, that have been permanent features of governments for over a century or more. Modern transport bureaucracies are relatively permanent and unchanging in the short- to medium-term and can be thought of as a fixture of the regime. The story as to how transport was organised and administered from archaic times to the present unfolds in the subsequent chapters.

References

Allinson, J. C., and A. Anievas (2010) "The Uneven and Combined Development of the Meiji Restoration: A Passive Revolutionary Road to Capitalist Modernity", *Capital & Class*, 34 (3), 469–490.

Andressen, C. (2002) *A Short History of Japan: From Samurai to Sony*. Allen & Unwin, Crows Nest, New South Wales.

Barnes, G. L. (2014) "A Hypothesis for Early Kofun Rulership", *Japan Review*, 27, 3–29.

Beasley, W. G. (1972) *The Meiji Restoration*. Stanford University Press, Stanford, California.

Brailey, N. (1992) "Sir Ernest Satow, Japan and Asia: The Trials of a Diplomat in the Age of High Imperialism", *The Historical Journal*, 35 (1), 115–150.

Brecher, W. P. (2010) "Brewing Spirits, Brewing Songs: Saké, Haikai, and the Aestheticization of Suburban Space in Edo Period Itami", *Japan Studies Review*, 14, 17–44.

Brown, D. M. (1993a) "Introduction", in J. W. Hall, M. B. Jansen, Madoka Kanai and D. Twitchett (eds) (1993) *The Cambridge History of Japan, Volume I Ancient Japan Edited by Delmer M. Brown*. Cambridge University Press, Cambridge, 1–47.

Brown, D. M. (1993b) "The Yamato Kingdom", in *The Cambridge History of Japan, Volume I Ancient Japan*, 108–162.

Brown, R. H. (2009) "Shepherds of the People: Yasuoka Masahiro and the New Bureaucrats in Early Showa Japan", *Journal of Japanese Studies*, 35 (2), 285–319.

Burks, A. W. (1966) *The Government of Japan*. Methuen & Co. Ltd., London.

Clulow, A. (2009) "The Pirate Returns: Historical Models, East Asia and the War against Somali Piracy", *The Asia-Pacific Journal*, 7 (25.3), 1–11.

Colaccino, N. (2014) "Creation of Monopoly: The Influence of the Dutch East India Company in Tokugawa Foreign Policy", unpublished PhD thesis, Department of History, University of Michigan, Ann Arbor, Michigan.

Crawford, G. W. (1992) "The Transitions to Agriculture in Japan", in A. B. Gebauer and T. D. Price (eds) (1992) *Transitions to Agriculture in Prehistory—Monographs in World Archaeology No.4*. Prehistory Press, Madison, Wisconsin, 117–132.

Crawford, G. W. (2011) "Advances in Understanding Early Agriculture in Japan", *Current Anthropology*, 52, Supplement 4, S331–S345.

Culeddu, M. P. (2009) "Daimyō Principles in the Tokugawa Era. An Essay on Itakura Shigenori and Some of His Contemporaries", *Rivista Studi Orientali*, Impaginato 03/11/09, 187–204.

Culeddu, M. P. (2010) "Shimazu Yukihisa and the Four Junshi in Sadowara. A Loyalty Case in Tokugawa Japan", *Ming Qing Studies 2010*, 351–361.

Culeddu, M. P. (2013) "The Samurai Bond of Loyalty: Transition from Blood Ties through Self-Interested Allegiance to Absolute Devotion", *Journal of Cultural Interaction in East Asia*, 4, 61–72.

Deal, W. E. (2005) *Handbook to Life in Medieval and Early Modern Japan*. Oxford University Press, Oxford.

de Bary, T., D. Keene, G. Tanabe and P. Varley (eds) (2002) *Sources of Japanese Tradition, Volume One: From Earliest Times to 1600*. Columbia University Press, New York.

Ding, Qi-Liang, Chuan-Chao Wang, S. E. Farina and Hui Li (2011) "Mapping Human Genetic Diversity on the Japanese Archipelago", *Advances in Anthropology*, 1 (2), 19–25.

Ellington, L. (2002) *Japan: A Global Studies Handbook*. ABC-CLIO, Santa Barbara, California.

Finer, S. E. (1997a) *The History of Government from the Earliest Times: Volume I Ancient Monarchies and Empires*. Oxford University Press, Oxford.

Finer, S. E. (1997b) "I—Tokugawa Japan, 1600–1745, Asia", in Finer (1997) *The History of Government from the Earliest Times: Volume III Empires, Monarchies, and the Modern State*. Oxford University Press, Oxford, 1077–1128.

Gordon, A. (2003) *A Modern History of Japan: From Tokugawa Times to the Present*. Oxford University Press, Oxford.

Gouge, K. L. (2017) "The Ties that Bind: Kinship, Inheritance, and the Environment in Medieval Japan", unpublished PhD Thesis, University of Michigan, Horace H. Rackman School of Graduate Studies, Ann Arbor, Michigan.

Griffis, W. E. (1915) *The Mikado: Institution and Person—A Study of the Internal Political Forces of Japan*. Princeton University Press, Princeton, New Jersey.

Harari, Y. N. (2015) *Sapiens: A Brief History of Humankind*. Vintage, London.

Harding, C. (2020) *The Japanese: A History in Twenty Lives*. Allen Lane, London.

Hawley, S. (2005) *The Imjin Wars: Japan's Sixteenth-Century Invasion of Korea and Attempt to Conquer China*. Royal Asiatic Society, Korea Branch, Seoul, and the Institute of East Asian Studies, University of California Berkeley, Berkeley, California.

Hay, M. (2016) "The Origins of the Japanese People", http://wa-pedia.com

Hayami, Yujiro, and Yoshihisa Godo (1997) "Economics and Politics of Rice Policy in Japan: A Perspective on the Uruguay Round", in Takatoshi Ito and A. O. Krueger (eds) (1997) *Regionalism versus Multilateral Trade Arrangements, NBER-EASE Volume 6*. University of Chicago Press, Chicago, 371–404, http://www.nber.org/chapters/c8606

Hosowa, Leo Aoi (2014) "The 'Routine-scape' and Social Structuralization in the Formation of Japanese Agricultural Societies", *Geografiska Annaler: Series B Human Geography*, 96 (1), 67–82.

Hudson, M. J. (2019) "Towards a Prehistory of the Great Divergence: The Bronze Age Roots of Japan's Premodern Economy", *Documenta Praehistorica*, XLVI, 30–43.

Ishii, Ryosuke (1980) *A History of Political Institutions in Japan*. The Japan Foundation, Tokyo.

Jameson, F. (1974) *Marxism and Form: 20th-Century Dialectical Theories of Literature*. Princeton University Press, Princeton, New Jersey.

Kawashima, Shin (2020) "Japan: The Meiji Restoration, 1868", in P. Furtado (ed.) (2020) *Revolutions: How They Changed History and What They Mean Today*. Thames and Hudson, London, 85–95.

Kidder, J. E. (1993) "The Earliest Societies in Japan", in *The Cambridge History of Japan, Volume I Ancient Japan*, 48–107.

Kiley, C. J. (1999) "Provincial Administration and Land Tenure in Early Heian", in J. W. Hall, M. B. Jansen, Madoka Kanai and D. Twitchett (eds) (1999) *The Cambridge History of Japan, Volume II Heian Japan Edited by D. H. Shively and W. H. McCullough*. Cambridge University Press, Cambridge, 236–340.

Knoest, J. (2016) "'The Japanese Connection': Self-Organized Smuggling Networks in Nagasaki Circa 1666–1742", in C. Antunes and A. Polónia (eds) (2016) *Beyond Empires—Global, Self-Organizing, Cross-Imperial Networks, 1500–1800*. Koninklijke Brill NV, Leiden, 88–137.

Kodansha (1993) *Japan: An Illustrated Encyclopedia*. Kodansha, Bunkyo-ku, Tokyo.

Kornicki, P. F. (2016) "A Tang-Dynasty Manual of Governance and the East Asian Vernaculars", *Sunkyun Journal of East Asian Studies*, 16 (2), 163–177.

Mayhew, L. H. (1983) *Talcott Parsons on Institutions and Social Evolution: Selected Readings*. Chicago University Press, Chicago.

McClain, J. L., and Osamu Wakita (eds) (1999) *Osaka: The Merchants' Capital of Early Modern Japan*. Cornell University Press, Ithaca, New York.

McOmie, W. (2006) *The Opening of Japan, 1853–1855: A Comparative Study of the American, British, Dutch and Russian Naval Expeditions to Compel the Tokugawa Shogunate to Conclude Treaties and Open Ports to their Ships*. Global Oriental, Folkestone, Kent.

Migliore, M. C., and A. Manieri (2020) "Book 7 of the Yōrōryō: A Research and Translation Project", *Academic Letters*, December, Article 36, 1–4.

Mitsusada, Inoue (1993) "The Century of Reform", in *The Cambridge History of Japan, Volume I Ancient Japan*, 163–220.

Miyagawa, Mitsuru, with C. J. Kiley (1990) "From Shoen to Chigyo: Proprietary Lordship and the Structure of Local Power", in J. W. Hall, M. B. Jansen, Madoka Kanai and D. Twitchett (eds) *The Cambridge History of Japan, Volume III Medieval Japan Edited by Kozo Yamamura*. Cambridge University Press, Cambridge, 89–106.

Moiseyev, V. G. (2009) "On the Origin of the Ryukyu Islanders: The Integration of Craniometric and Cranial Nonmetric Data", *Archaeology Ethnology & Anthropology of Eurasia*, 37 (4), 146–152.

Morck, R. K., and Masao Nakamura (2005) "A Frog in a Well Knows Nothing of the Ocean: A History of Corporate Ownership in Japan", in R. K. Morck (ed.) *A History of Corporate Governance around the World: Family Business Groups to Professional Managers*. University of Chicago Press, Chicago.

Morck, R., and Masao Nakamura (2007) "Business Groups and the Big Push: Meiji Japan's Mass Privatization and Subsequent Growth", *NBER Working Paper*, No. 13171, June. National Bureau of Economic Research, Cambridge, Mass.

Morillo, S. (1995) "Guns and Government: A Comparative Study of Europe and Japan", *Journal of World History*, 6 (1), 75–106.

Moss, D. A., and E. Kintgen (2009) "The Dojima Rice Market and the Origins of Futures Trading", *Harvard Business School Case 709-044, January 2009*.

Murai, Shōsuke (n.d.) "Japan in East Asian History: From the Medieval Through the Premodern Periods—Extranational Pirate-Traders of East Asia", http://www.nippon.com/en/features/c00101/

Murdoch, J., in collaboration with Isoh Yamagata (1903) "A History of Japan during the Century of Early Foreign Intercourse (1542–1651)", http://www.maproom.org/00/05/index.php

Nagahara, Keiji (1990) "The Medieval Peasant", in *The Cambridge History of Japan, Volume III Medieval Japan*, 301–343.

Nagahara, Keiji, with Kozo Yamamura (1990) "Village Communities and Daimyo Power", in *The Cambridge History of Japan, Volume III Medieval Japan*, 107–125.

Naito, Akira, illustrated by Kazuo Hozumi (2003) *Edo, The City That Became Tokyo: An Illustrated History*. Kodansha International, Tokyo.

Najita, Tetsuo (1998) *Tokugawa Political Economy*. Cambridge University Press, Cambridge.

Natalizia, G. (2014) "External Shocks, International Status and the Change of Regime in the Japan of the Meiji Restoration", in A. F. Biagini and G. Motta (eds) (2014) *Empires and Nations from the Eighteenth to the Twentieth Century: Volume 1*. Cambridge Scholars Publishing, Newcastle-upon-Tyne, pp. 345–353.

Nelson, S. M. (2014) "Relationships between Silla 新羅 and Yamato 大和", *Crossroads—Studies on the History of Exchange Relations in the East Asian World*, 9, 83–96.

Nelson, S., I. Zhushchikhovskaya, T. Li, M. Hudson and M. Robbeets (2020) "Tracing Population Movements in Ancient East Asia Through the Linguistics and Archaeology of Textile Production", *Evolutionary Human Sciences*, 2 (e5), 1–20.

Ogata, K. (2015) "The Emperor is Dead! Long live the Emperor!: A Study of Institutional Persistence", *Management & Organizational History*, 10 (1), 21–38.

Paşca, R. (2016) "Modernity as Continuity: The Samurai and the Merchants in 'Post-historical' Tokugawa Japan", *The Bulletin of the Research Institute for Japanese Studies*, 8, March, 119–130.

Pearson, R. (2016) *Ōsaka Archaeology*. Archaeopress Publishing Ltd., Oxford.

Petrucci, M. G. (2010) "Pillaging, Gunpowder, and Christianity in Late Sixteenth-Century Japan", in R. J. Anthony (ed.) (2010) *Elusive Pirates, Pervasive Smugglers: Violence and Clandestine Trade in the Greater China Seas*. University of Hong Kong Press, Hong Kong, 59–71.

Pickl-Kolaczia, B. (2017) "The Bunkyū Restoration: The Restoration of Imperial Tombs and Re-Design of Imperial Ancestor Worship", *Vienna Journal of East Asian Studies*, 9, 201–234.

Phipps, C. L. (2015) *Empires on the Waterfront: Japan's Ports and Power, 1858–1899*. Harvard East Asian Monographs, Vol. 373, Harvard University Asia Center, Boston, Mass.

Ramaioli, F. L. (2021) "From the Gods of Heavens: Kokutai, Myth and Law in Japanese History, 1825–1947", *Academia Letters*, Article 2349, https://doi.org/10.20935/AL2349

Robinson-Yamaguchi, E. (2015) "Expelling the Barbarian and the Last Stand: Examining the Newly Established Meiji Government's Reaction to Foreign Pressure and National Strife in 1868". 愛知県立大学外国語学部紀要第 47 号(地域研究・国際学編) [*The Journal of the Faculty of Foreign Studies, Aichi Prefectural University, No. 47 Area Studies and International Relations*], 47–81.

Sadler, A. L. (1937) *The Maker of Modern Japan: The Life of Tokugawa Ieyasu*. George Allen & Unwin, London.

Saito, Osamu and Tokihiko Settsu (2006) "Money, Credit and Smithian Growth in Tokugawa Japan", *Institute of Economic Research, Hitotsubashi University, Discussion Paper Series*, No. 139. Kunitachi, Tokyo.

Sansom, G. (1961) *A History of Japan, 1334–1615*. Cressett Press, London.

Schottenhammer, A. (2008) "Japan—The Tiny Dwarf? Sino-Japanese Relations from *Kangxi* to the Early Qianlong Resigns", in A. Schottenhammer (ed.) (2008) *The East Asian Mediterranean—Maritime Crossroads of Culture, Commerce, and Human Migration*. Otto Harrassowitz, Wiesbaden, Germany, 331–388.

Schottenhammer, A. (2013) "Empire and Periphery? The Qing Empire's Relations with Japan and the Ryūkyūs (1644–c. 1800), A Comparison", *The Medieval History Journal*, 16 (1), 139–196.

Shapinsky, P. D. (2010) "From Sea Bandits to Sea Lords: Nonstate Violence and Pirate Identities in Fifteenth- and Sixteenth-Century Japan", in R. J. Antony (ed.) (2010) *Elusive Pirates, Pervasive Smugglers: Violence and Clandestine Trade in the Greater China Seas*. Hong Kong University Press, Hong Kong, 27–42.

Shapinsky, P. D. (2014) *Lords of the Sea: Pirates, Violence, and Commerce in Late Medieval Japan, Monograph No. 76*, Center for Japanese Studies, University of Michigan, Ann Arbor, Michigan.

Sheldon, C. D. (1973) *The Rise of the Merchant Class in Tokugawa Japan 1600–1868: An Introductory Survey*. Russell & Russell, New York, reissued from 1958 publication by The Association for Asian Studies.

Sims, R. (1998) *French Policy Towards the Bakufu and Meiji Japan 1854–95*. Japan Library, Imprint of Curzon Press, Richmond, Surrey.

Tabayashi, Akira (1987) "Irrigation Systems in Japan", *Geographical Review of Japan*, 60, Ser. B (1), 41–65.

Tamaki, Toshiaki (2014) "Japanese Economic Growth during the Edo Period", 京都産業大学経済学レビュー, No.1 (2014, 平成26年3月), 255–266.

Tamaki, Toshiaki (2011) "A Fiscal-Military State without Wars: The Relations between the Military Regime and Economic Development in TOKUGAWA Japan", in S. Conway and R. Torres Sanchez (eds) (2011) *The Spending of States: Military Expenditure during the Long Eighteenth Century—Patterns, Organisation, and Consequences, 1650–1815*. Vdm Verlag Dr. Müller, Berlin, 155–179.

Taylor, D. (2017) "Bullet Train to Modernization: How Emulation of Western Ideals and Forward Thinking Leadership Contributed to the Success of Meiji Restoration's Push Towards a Modern Japan", unpublished semester paper California State University Fullerton for Dr William Haddad.

Todd, H. (1991) "A Glimpse above the Clouds: The Japanese Court in 1859", *The British Library Journal*, 198–220, https://www.academia.edu/29827630/A_glimpse_above_the_clouds_the_Japanese_Court_in_1859

Toshiya, Torao (1993) "Nara Economic and Social Institutions", in *The Cambridge History of Japan, Volume I Ancient Japan*, 414–452.

Tsujinaka, Yutaka and R. Pekkanen (2007) "Civil Society and Interest Groups in Contemporary Japan", *Pacific Affairs*, 80 (3), 419–437.

Turnbull, S. (2002) *The Samurai Invasion of Korea 1592–98*. Cassell & Co., London.

Uchiyama, Junzo, J. C. Gillam, Leo Aoi Hosoya, K. Lindstrom and P. Jordan (2014) "Investigating Neolithization of Cultural Landscapes in East Asia: The NEOMAP Project", *Journal of World History*, https://doi.org/10.1007/s10963-014-9079-8

Van Wolferen, K. (1989) *The Enigma of Japanese Power*. MacMillan, London.

Wang, Zhen Ping (1994) "Speaking with a Forked Tongue: Diplomatic Correspondence between China and Japan, 238–608 A.D.", *Journal of the American Oriental Society*, 114 (1), 23–32.

World Bank (2020) *Resilient Industries in Japan: Lessons Learned in Japan on Enhancing Competitive Industries in the Face of Disasters Caused by Natural Hazards*. World Bank, Washington, D. C.

Yamamura, Kozo (1990a) "Introduction", in *The Cambridge History of Japan, Volume III Medieval Japan*, 1–10.

Yamamura, Kozo (1990b) "The Growth of Commerce in Medieval Japan", in *The Cambridge History of Japan, Volume III Medieval Japan*, 344–395.

Yanshina, O. (2019) "Understanding the Specific Nature of the East Asia Neolithic Transition", *Documenta Praehistorica*, XLVI, 6–29.

Yoshida, Yasuyuki, and J. Ertl (2016) "Archaeological Practice and Social Movements: Ethnography of Jomon Archaeology and the Public", *Journal of the International Center for Cultural Resource Studies 2, Kanazawa University*, https://www.academia.edu/35219785/Archaeological_Practice_and_Social_Movements_Ethnography_of_Jomon_Archaeology_and_the_Public?auto=download

3. Ports and Shipping

The cherry trees are in full bloom
Now, while at the palace by the sea
Of wave-bright Naniwa...

13th Day of the Second Month, 755 A. D.[1]

Introduction

As a maritime nation, both domestic trade on coastal ships and international shipping trade through Japanese seaports have been the engines of the country's economic prosperity. In this chapter, the prime focus is on ports in the Ōsaka Bay at the eastern end of the Setō Inland Sea. The historical time period is from archaic times to the present day. The themes of port-related institutions and organisations in the Ōsaka Bay region are broadly representative of ports in other parts of Japan.

The justification for this choice of Ōsaka Bay is that it has a rich maritime history that has been documented continuously from the time when the Emperor moved his capital and established the Port of Naniwa (from the *Kojiki*, 712 A. D. and the *Nihon Shoki*, 720 A. D.). Furthermore, institutional changes to port ownership and administration described for Ōsaka Bay for over a millennium can be translated to the evolution of ports in other parts of Japan, especially during the period since the Second World War.

This chapter does not attempt to describe the configuration of ancient and medieval ports or to recount the physical changes in scale and function to seaports. An ancient mariner returning to the shoreline of Ōsaka Bay (formerly called Naniwa Bay) clearly would not recognise the vast extent of land reclamation at the eastern end of the Setō Inland

---

1 Quoted by McClain and Osamu, 1999: 3.

Sea, the man-made islands and docks that make up the modern Hanshin port and the extensive metropolis of Ōsaka and Kōbe (see, for example, Kawanabe *et al.*, 2012). Neither does the chapter trace the history of Japanese naval ships and their bases (currently, the main ports of the Japan Maritime Self-Defence Force are at Yokosuka—32 km south of Yokohama, and at Kure—24 km south-south west of Hiroshima).

There are studies published in English on Ōsaka ports that contain information not covered in this chapter. The evolution of the ports of Naniwa, Watanabe, Ishiyama Honganji, Sakai and Ōsaka, in relation to their political and their functional role from the 5th century, is admirably summarised in English by Wakita (1999) and Sakaehara (2009). Pearson (2016) documents, in detail, the archeological evidence on the ancient port at Naniwa. Asao (*et al.*, 1999) give a detailed history of Sakai, and Yamasaki (*et al.*, 2010) describe the history of nearby Kōbe (Ōwara no tsu/Hyōgo). However, the focus here is more on port governance and the organisation of domestic shipping.

The chapter is organised in the following way, first with some general background information on the essential geographical features of Ōsaka Bay, noting the very early geomorphological processes that have altered river estuaries. The second section outlines ports and shipping from archaic times. The third section describes Ōsaka ports in the ancient period. This is followed by an explanation of the administration of ports in the Edō period when the merchant class organised ports and shipping. Sections follow on the beginning of the Meiji era—when Western models of port administration—were introduced through to the present day with the recent Japanese National Government policy of creating the Hanshin super-container port (Ōsaka and Kōbe Ports). The final section considers the policy of land reclamation because this has facilitated port infrastructure development as well as post-war industrialisation.

The Geography of Ōsaka Bay

During the time of human occupation in Japan geomorphological processes have transformed the delta area of the Yamato and Yodo Rivers from a marine bay (Ōsaka Bay) to a fresh-water lagoon and finally to dry land (Pearson, 2016: 8–9 and Figure 2.2). Similar processes would have modified river estuaries in other parts of Japan. The greatest transformations to the natural coastline have been made by man with the land reclamation programs dating from Edō times but intensifying with port developments in the latter part of the 20th century and early 21st century.

The waterway systems southwards of Lake Biwa (Kawanabe et al., 2012) provided natural arteries for ancient domestic trade, with links to international trade routes through Ōsaka Bay (formerly Naniwa Bay). The Setō Inland Sea allows ships to pass on their journeys to and from China and Korea through relatively sheltered waters compared with the more exposed ocean route via the Kii Strait south of Shikōkū Island.

The Use of the Sea in Archaic Times

Water transport has been of great importance from ancient times with the discovery of primitive dugout canoes and other fishing artifacts at various archeological sites confirming a strong association with the sea from late Palaeothic and Jōmon times (10,000 B.C. to 300 B.C.) onwards. This technology allowed coastal settlements to forage further afield rather than the restricted hinterland of travel on foot (Hudson, 2017: 108). In this same period, evidence from ceramic fragments points to long-distance maritime trade between Kyūshū and both the Ryūkūs and the Korean peninsula (Hudson, 2017: 110).

In the Palaeothic period there is evidence of obsidian found on Honshū having been transported by sea from the off-shore volcanic island of Kōzushima (Hudson, 2017:106)—about 56 km south of the Honshū mainland at Shimoda. A dugout canoe made from the muku tree (*aphanante aspera*) discovered in Chiba prefecture, was measured at 7.45 metres in length and was dated around 3,000 B.C. (Naumann, 2000: 50–51). Archeological findings of dugout canoes from the late and final Jōmon periods indicate coastal travel, deep-sea fishing and trade, as obsidian was found only on islands off the coast of Honshū (and in Korea).

However, as Hudson (2017:111) notes there is "no direct information regarding social measures aimed at the governance of the sea." It is certain that the chiefdoms and early states of western Japan in the Yayoi and Kōfun periods used bronze mirrors and glass beads from the south of the Korean peninsula (the Gaya Confederacy before it was invaded by Silla in 562) and mainland China as symbols of political power.

There are three Shintō shrine complexes in northern Kyūshū dedicated to female sea-deities. Hetsumiya, located at the coastal town of Genkai, Fukuoka, is dedicated to the deity Ichiki-shima-hime. The other two temples are in the Genkai Sea: Nakatsumiya on the island of Ōshima dedicated to the deity Taki-tsu-hime; and Ōki-tsu-miya on the island of Ōkinoshima and dedicated to Tagori-hime. Between the 4th and the 9th centuries these shrines were located at the points of embarkation and disembarkation for the official diplomatic missions between Japan and Silla (Korea) and China (Kodansha, 1993: 1013; Nelson, 2014).

The Yamato Kingdom gained access to these important sea routes by defeating the Iwai Rebellion in present day Fukuoka Prefecture (Hudson, 2017: 112). From the Kōfun period onwards, Dazaifu was an important military centre for the Yamato period from whence armies were dispatched to defend its Korean territory (the Kingdom of Mimana). A branch of the Yamato Court was established in Dazaifu from 663 (Heritage of Japan, 2020).

In 665, Japan lost 400 battle ships to a joint T'ang and Silla force at the mouth of the Kum (Geum) River that empties into the Yellow Sea. Later, Chinese Song dynasty (960–1279) ships came to Dazaifu and traded with representatives of various temples and shrines and their attached estates. Little trade was carried out by the central government of Japan. From the end of the 10th century to the beginning of the 12th century the most important centre for trade was Dazaifu that had an organisation especially established for foreign trade.

Administration of Ancient Ōsaka Ports

In ancient times, powerful clans ruling as an *institution* would have controlled maritime ports. It is uncertain when Japanese ships first explored beyond their shores, nor are there descriptions of the seaports from where they embarked, but the first written evidence of a 'Japanese' envoy visiting China (Schottenhammer, 2013) is recorded in the *Hou Hanshu* (57 A.D.) which stated that the *Wa* (倭) brought tribute to the Chinese Court (textiles, sapan wood, bows and arrows, slaves and white pearls). In return, the Chinese Court sent silk fabrics, gold objects, bronze mirrors, pearls, lead and cinnabar. From the 1st century A.D., Chinese records (*wei zhi*) mention the land of *Wa* composed of a number of states that joined a league in around 180 A.D. under the headship of Himiko, Queen of Yamatai, and who sent an envoy to the State of Wei (魏, 220–265) in 239 A.D.

Brown (1993) describes the *institutional* arrangements under the Yamato King control system (during the 5th century) as one where chiefs of clan (*uji*) dominated the politics of ancient Japan. The system would have evolved from previous eras (see McClain and Wakita, 1999: 1–4). The clan system, with family allegiances, would have exercised hierarchical control of the workforce of farmers and fishermen. It can be speculated, with a high degree of plausibility, that, from the earliest times, port operations would have been handled, under supervision, by those who specialised in navigating the river and coastal waters, who knew where to land boats and who acted as the wharfinger keeping account of the comings and goings of produce and other goods. Domestic and international exchange would have been facilitated through a peasant and slave labour force under the institutional control of the clan chief.

Twice the Wei rulers, Mingdi (reigned 227–239) and Shaodi (reigned 240–253), sent embassies to Japan (238 and 247) and four Japanese embassies were dispatched to Wei. An international port at Suminoe (Suminoe no tsu, 住吉津), was located just to the south of the modern Sumiyoshi Grand Shrine (containing the Gods of Seafarers) on the Yamato River. Sumiyoshi port is as old as Naniwa, being important from the 5th century onwards. The port had important state-related functions. This is where the Japanese envoys and military flotilla assembled before departure. From Sumiyoshi port the direct overland route to Asuka was shorter than from other ports.

A more centralised institution of the Emperor's Court emerged over time (Asuka Enlightenment) and made extensive use of Chinese techniques for expanding state power (Mitsusada with Brown, 1993). Japan adopted not only art and culture from China but, more or less, its complete administrative system. The T'ang Dynasty government set up the *Shi Bo Si* (市舶)—its Oceangoing and Marketing Department—in many coastal ports for the administration of foreign economy-related affairs by sea, including the export of silk products to Japan (Chaffee, 2010). Therefore, it is most certain that equivalent port-related functions were duplicated in Japan. Ruling elites (acting 'on behalf' of the authority of the Emperor) introduced and reinforced the basic regulations on coastal and international shipping. Sets of maritime regulations (*kaisen shikimoku* or *kaisen taihō*) reveal information about seafaring practices in the medieval period.

The dates of maritime regulations that include articles on coastal trade ships, riverboats and port regulations are disputed because of their frequent recopying from documents dated 1223 (Damian, 2014: 2). Though few trade-related documents from the medieval period have survived the centuries, one set of port records provides much information about coastal shipping. The Records of Incoming Ships at the Hyōgo Northern Checkpoint (*hyōgo kitaseki irifune nōchō*) record data for over 1900 vessels that passed through the checkpoint at Hyōgo (today part of Kōbe City), in 1445 and the first two months of 1446 (Hayashiya, 1981). Each dated entry notes the port of registry of the ship, the type and volume of cargoes carried, such as salt and ceramics (Damian, 2014), the taxes levied on the items and dates collected, the name of the ship's captain and the name of the warehouse manager that handled the incoming items. The records show the flow of goods from the provinces to Hyōgo—gateway to the central court region of Kyōto.

The Role of Temples and Shipping Agents

As early as the 7th century, Zen Buddhism was introduced into Japan from China. Although it was being taught by the 8th and 9th centuries, as a foreign religion, it failed to prosper until the early Kamakura period (1185–1333), when the Japanese nobility adopted it. The temples as *organisations* were a consumer of vast amounts of building materials, agricultural produce and soon developed expansive trading networks.

In addition, shipping *organisations* that had appeared earlier, and continued to develop during the Kamakura period, were the agents who took rice and other products of the *shōen* estates on consignment for distribution to markets (*toimaru*) and the co-operative guilds (*za*) that provided favourable reciprocal trade advantages and reduced competition (Pearson, 2016: 97).

Ōsaka Ports During the Medieval Period

The key towns, shrines and early ports of Ōsaka Bay were Naniwa no Tsu, Sakai, Ōwada no Tomari (Hyōgo), Watanabe and Ishiyama Honganji. The characteristics of their governance is described ranging from Naniwa no Tsu as an Imperial port until its decline, Sakai as a port administered by town merchants and Ishiyama Honganji run by a Buddhist sect with extensive regional trading networks.

Naniwa no Tsu

By the time that a port (Naniwa no tsu or Naniwazu, 難波津) was established at Naniwa, a complex administrative system was in place. Sakaehara (2009: 4–7) traces the origins of a port at Naniwa (some time in the late 5th century in the reign of Emperor Nintoku) to the building of Naniwa no Horie—a canal cut through the Uemachi Tablelands that acted both as a flood control barrier and a shortened route to the ocean from inland settlements via the Yodo and Yamato Rivers. Sakaehara (2009) notes the construction—near to the probable location of the port—of large storehouses with a floor area of some 82–98 square metres—probably to keep war supplies because the *Wa*'s traditional ally on the Korean peninsula, Paekche, was being invaded by the northern state of Koguryo. With the fall of Paekche, new immigrants, including the Paekche royal clan, played an important role in the technological advancement of Japan.

Naniwa became an important seat of government and international trading centre carrying Japanese envoys to China during the T'ang Dynasty and where military flotillas were assembled. Ocean-going ships with crews of about 50 people could be pulled up on the beaches that were protected by rock berms. Seagoing ships carrying cargoes weighing up to 20 to 30 *koku*[2] (roughly 3,600 to 5,400 kg) docked in the area of the Naniwa where the cargoes were transferred to riverboats of 9 metres in length (Pearson, 2016: 55). A line of temples and manors of

---

2 *Koku* (from the Edō era) is an important standard volumetric measurement of milled rice equal to 180.4 litres (enough to feed one adult for a year). Tax assessments, stipends to samurai and the wealth of *daimyō* were calculated in *koku* (Kodansha, 1993: 816).

temples controlled the transfer point between ships on the Inland Sea and riverboats. Both private and state trade was shipped through the Horie Canal.

Diplomatic missions to China from the 5th to the 8th century departed from Naniwa. These ships typically carried 150 people and they travelled in convoys of two to four ships, occasionally more (Pearson, 2016: 55). McClain and Wakita (1999: 3) attribute the ability for the Yamato lineage to extend its boundaries of dominance in central Japan to the convenient transport of soldiers and goods through Naniwa. In 645, Emperor Kōtoku built his palace, Naniwa-no-nagara-no-toyosaki-no-miya (難波長柄豊碕宮), in Ōsaka, making this area the capital (Naniwa-kyō).

By the time of Emperor Tenmu (reigned 672–686) the city measured about 3 km by 4 km in extent, with a walled government compound, some two hundred blocks for the aristocrat residents, and shops and homes for merchants, artisans and service workers (McClain and Wakita, 1999: 5). Government facilities for diplomatic functions, and residences for visiting diplomats, were constructed (Sakaehara, 2009: 7–8). The capital was short-lived, before moving inland to Heijo-kyō. Naniwa continued as a port of political, military, economic and transport importance serving the new inland capitals of various Emperors with palaces located in Nara and Kyōto.

The domestic port function of Naniwa is further clarified when the system of administrative laws (*ritsuryō*), issued from the capital Heijo-kyō, is explained. With the consolidation of the taxation system in the 8th century, taxes from all parts of western Japan were shipped by sea to Naniwa before being transshipped along the river systems to the capital. These taxes were special products from different regions (*chō*), different products paid in lieu of labour tax (*yō*) and the fixed amount of rice supplied as a ration to different offices each year. Many of the nobles, officials and clergy who were based in the capital also owned estates in parts of western Japan, and around Naniwa, and tributes from these estates were also assembled in Naniwa.

Naniwa lost its political and diplomatic importance as a port when Heijo-kyō and its subordinate town of Naniwa-kyō were integrated into a new capital at Nagaoka-kyō in 784. Despite its decline, a port close to the site continued to function but other nearby communities emerged as important centres of commerce, trade and religion during the Heian

(794–1185) and the Kamakura (1185–1333) periods (McClain and Wakita, 1999: 6).

In 785, a new canal connecting the Mikuni River (present-day Kanzaki River) and the Yodo River allowed ships from the Setō Inland Sea to by-pass Naniwa Port and dock either at Nagaoka-kyō, Yamazaki no tsu or Yodo tsu. Although considerably downgraded in its significance, trade continued at Naniwa because it is known, for example, that a merchant, Bunya no Miyatamaro (died 843 but date uncertain), amassed a fortune trading with Silla (Korea) during the mid-9th century (Sakaehara, 2009: 9). As pointed out by Wakita (1999: 25), the shift in the centre of economic gravity did not leave the Uemachi Plateau a "desolate wilderness" because people remained in the locality and continued to make a living from river transport or shipping.

Sakai

One of the best examples of a port administered by the merchant class is that of Sakai, located on the head of the Setō Inland Sea, a few kilometres south of Suminoe no tsu, and close to the boundaries of the provinces of Izumi, Kawachi and Settsu (Asao *et al.*, 1999). In the 14th century, the area was an Imperial manor estate (*shōen*) producing salt for sale, but then became the base for fishing vessels supplying the Kasuga Shrine near Nara (Sansom, 1961: 189). The convenience of its location formed the base for the movement of army supplies during the civil conflict of 1337 to 1392 between the Southern and the Northern Courts.

During the next civil conflict, the *Ōnin no Ran* (1467–1477), shipping movements in the Setō Inland Sea became increasingly dangerous and trade shifted to the port of Sakai. The town of Sakai was surrounded by a moat and prospered through its administration by merchants (*naya-shu* or *kaigo-shu*). Merchants thrived on the trade with the Ming dynasty (1368–1644) established in 1401 by the third Muromachi *Shōgun*, Ashikaga Yoshimitsu, largely because ships utilised the Kii Channel then sailed to southern Kyūshū thereby avoiding piracy in the Setō Inland Sea (Osaka Toshi Kogaku Center, 1999: 18). However, ships were subject to more exposed weather and more dangerous sailing conditions.

After the civil wars, the town of Sakai was rebuilt in the early 15th century and granted special privileges by the Muromachi *bakufu* for domestic and international trade. Japanese maritime trade grew rapidly in the 14th and early 15th centuries, and the enterprise of merchants, through licensed trade with China, brought great profit to the merchants and their *daimyō* protectors, and, sometimes, their sponsors. For example, the reported gross profit of sales in China was a factor of three based on a 1493 voyage out of Sakai (Sansom, 1961: 271). In 1548, both sides terminated trade missions (Sansom, 1961: 266) being replaced by unlicensed trade, especially by Japanese pirates (although the ships contained crews that were predominantly Chinese nationals).

After about 1500, Sakai replaced Hyōgo (under the direct control of the Muromachi *bakufu*) as the usual port of departure, for political and security reasons documented by Sansom (1961: 270–272). Sakai merchants organised and financed most of the voyages originating in the Home Counties. Sakai merchants also traded in the Setō Inland Sea by paying protection money to the Murakami "pirates" and facilitating trade for the Honganji Temple.

Ōwada no Tomari (Hyōgo)

During the Nara period (710–784), the port of Kōbe, known then as Ōwada no Tomari, was already a major port of trade with China and other foreign countries. For a short time, the capital of Japan was moved from Kyōto to Kōbe's Fukuhara district. At the same time, Hyōgo became a centre of military activity. Battles between the Heike and Genji clans occurred there, including the decisive Battle of Ichi no Tani in 1184.[3] In later years, Hyōgo's port played an important role as a maritime centre for both the Setō Inland Sea and the Sea of Japan. It was also a rest station along the Saigoku Highway—a major highway that went from Kyōto to western Japan (Kobe Trade Information Office, http://cityofkobe.org/about-kobe/history/).

---

3   A decisive battle during the Gempei War fought at the Taira defensive position to the west of Kōbe. The Taira clan (a strength of about 5,000 troops) were defeated by Minamoto no Yoshisune and Minamoto no Nororiyori (a strength of about 3,000 troops).

Watanabe no Tsu

At the beginning of the 10th century an Imperial estate called Ōe no Mikuriya was established in the provinces of Settsu and Kawachi. Watanabe no tsu, located on the south bank of the Yodo River, was a relay point to transport foods to the Emperor in Heijo-kyō. Court nobility sailed to Watanabe-no-tsu then travelled on foot southwards to make pilgrimages to Shitennōji Temple, to the 117 temples on Koyasan (now Wakayama Prefecture), or further, across the mountainous Kii Peninsula to the Kumano shrines (now Mie Prefecture).

The port also functioned as an auxiliary port for coastal shipping in the Setō Inland Sea in the 11th century. Its administration was atypical because the *jitō* managers of the Imperial estate (*shōen*), the Watanabe clan, with a powerful navy, were appointed chief of police (*kebiishi*) and exercised marine police authority in the port and river estuaries. The port underwent a major transformation in late Heian and Kamakura periods evolving from a warehousing and transshipment centre to lumberyards and storehouses belonging to religious organisations and rich families.

Commencing in 1196, it was Tōdaiji's Abbot, Shunjō Chōgen, who developed a better port, protected by stone levees and piers, to accommodate oceangoing vessels (Wakita, 1999: 29). Its main function was for the transport of building materials for the temples and hence it was a private port. However, it did charge a small fee for any ship docking there—especially grain ships. Wakita (1999: 33) notes the paucity of historical documentation but speculates that local residents took over the self-governing organisation of Watanabe port—as occurred at Sakai and Tennōji.

Ishiyama Honganji

From 1533 to 1580, the temple and town located at the estuary of the rivers Yodo and Yamato was the origins of the modern city of Ōsaka. It was the headquarters of a religious and secular organisation of the Honganji—a major branch of the Buddhist True Pure Land Sect (*Jodō shinshu*). The temple was founded in 1496 but grew into a large town within the temple complex all surrounded by moats and fortified walls

(Kodansha, 1993: 633). Ishiyama Honganji thus became a centre of religion and commerce that stretched across the province as a vast power structure described in the *Japan: An Illustrated Encyclopedia* (Kodansha, 1993: 633) as a "religious monarchy".

The temple's 10-year war with Oda Nobunaga was lost: when the temple surrendered in 1580 it was burnt on the orders of the *rennyō* (abbot). Recognising its strategic location, Toyotomi Hideyoshi built Ōsaka Castle (that stands today as a renovated monument) on the same site and he moved into this fortress in 1584. He restored Ōsaka's central place in Japanese trading affairs, as well as building up his maritime power and fortune, initially in association with pirate trade before eradicating piracy, as explained earlier in Chapter 2, and by the Japan Heritage Portal Hub (2019).

Arnason (2010) describes in detail the rise of this region of Japan that became a "secondary state" (*institution*). After Toyotomi Hideyoshi gained hegemony and built his base in Ōsaka in 1583, the Ōsaka port (still a river port) became a renewed centre of international and domestic trade. Many of the canals based on the river system were excavated during his reign and that of his son. On Toyotomi Hideyoshi's death, his son, Toyotomi Hideyori, became *daimyō* of a large and prosperous domain centred on Ōsaka Castle. However, in 1614, Tokugawa Ieyasu found a pretext to denounce Toyotomi Hideyori (1593–1615) for subversive actions, defeating him in field battles. The castle finally surrendered in June 1615 when the domain was transferred into Tokugawa control. This is an important point when port developments during the Edō period, especially those at Ōsaka, are discussed below.

Port Administration in the Edō Era

Ōsaka became a region under the direct control of the Tokugawa *Shōgunate* in 1619. The extraordinary role of Ōsaka as a nerve centre of much trade and of financial support to the *Shōgunate* explains the importance of the *bugyōsho* (奉行所) of Ōsaka, and also why the *bugyō* was either consulted, or, on occasions, directed by the Edō *machi bugyō* (町奉行) acting for the *Shōgunate*. Edō's officials seem to have been passive in documenting the inflow of goods to Edō and were often content to rely on detail from Nagasaki (Dejima for foreign trade) or Ōsaka, where the *bugyōsho* acted as a powerful agent of the *Shōgunate*.

3. Ports and Shipping

Cullen (2010) explains that the key institution of coastal trade in Japan during the Edō era reflected three circumstances: the central trading importance of Ōsaka; the rising consumer market of Edō; and the scale of trade in sensitive commodities between these two dominant ports. The *bugyō* of Ōsaka was a central figure, acting on instructions from the Tokugawa *bakufu*. Administration of a port was divided between the national institution of the *rōjū* (老中)—in effect a cabinet of the *bakufu*—and the *kanjōsho* (勘定所), or Finance Office, and the local *machi bugyō* (magistrate of towns). Coastal trade was primarily a concern of the *machi bugyōsho*: there is little evidence that *kanjōsho*, *rōjū* or the *Shōgun*, intervened directly in port affairs (Cullen, 2009: 187). Under the *machi bugyō*, the workhorses were the *machi doshiyori* (町年寄) who were the wholesalers (*ton'ya*, 問屋) or guilds that represented them.

The plans for the excavations of canals in Ōsaka and the inspection of commodities, were administrated by the *machi bugyō*. However, most of the infrastructure of Ōsaka built between the late 16th and the 17th centuries—flood control on the major rivers, land reclamation, urban canals, main roads as urban thoroughfares and port development—were constructed by wealthy citizens of Ōsaka and not by the government. Under the permission of the *bakufu*, townspeople constructed canals in the marshes including Dōtombori that was completed in 1615 by the merchant Doton Nariyasu (Yamamukai, 2004: 12).

For example, Suminokura Ryōi (1554–1614) excavated several canals in Ōsaka including the Hozugawa and the Takasegawa to facilitate economy activities. Sand and soil excavated from these constructions were used in town creation (Nagai, 2004: 5)—a town area that was approximately 5km by 5km. They also built numerous bridges to the extent the town was called *Naniwa Happyakuya-bashi* (Naniwa's 808 bridges).[4] Of the estimated 200 bridges in this area only 6 per cent were built by the *bakufu* (Matsumura, 2004: 16). Wealthy merchants and citizens living along the streets of individual bridges built and maintained the vast majority of these bridges.

The *bakufu* asked Kawamura Zuiken (1617–1699) to plan the secure transport of commodities to Edō and developed coastal shipping routes in 1671 and 1672. By the 17th century ships plying the coastal trades (*hokkokubune*) had a capacity of 1,000 *koku* (98 gross tons). The Ōsaka

---

4   In Japanese, "808" is a metaphor for a very large number.

port was one of main ports of call on these routes. The construction of Edō as the new capital required large quantities of timber and stone from the provinces that stimulated coastal shipping.

Itami (see Chapter 2) was one of twelve towns that formed Settsu's sake brewing belt. From breweries outside the castle at Itami, an array of brands and labels in casks were exported to suppliers active in Edō (*kudari-zake*). Casks were transported first by horse to a point on the Kanzaki River about 8 km away, transshipped by boat to the port of Denbō, and finally loaded onto barrel barges (*taru kaisen*) bound for Edō. In the 1730s, Itami's sake exports bound for Edō exceeded 180,000 casks valued at about 64,800 *koku*, and demand pushed this amount progressively higher (Brecher, 2010: 27). The shipping route improved in 1784 when the Itami brewers finally received permission from the *bakufu* to use boats on the Ina River, allowing door-to-door water transport that delivered sake into Edō within a week, or sometimes less.

Together with improved coastal shipping, developments of transport infrastructure attracted commodity markets, such as the Zakoba fish market, the Tenma fresh food market and the Dōjima rice market, along the rivers and canals that brought prosperity to the Ōsaka region. Organised in 1694, the Ōsaka 24-wholesale group (*nijuushi kumi ton'ya*) and the 10-wholesale group (*to kumi ton'ya*) operated a virtual monopoly transport system of cargo ships (*higaki kaisen*) between Ōsaka and Edō. The economic rise of the merchants, at the expense of the *daimyōs* and their samurai retainers, was further reinforced because these organisations also operated as moneylenders and financiers.

Many coastal areas of Japan also grew over the course of the 18th and into the 19th centuries. They became more prosperous and more interconnected, and their locally active ports transformed into more prominent regional ports. For example, the port of Shimoda on the Izu peninsula on the island of Honshū (nowadays Shizuoka Prefecture) developed as it acted as a security point for the *bakufu*, where all ships bound for Edō were required to dock there for inspection up to 1721. The layout of these coastal ports in the Edō is typified by the port of Takamatsu on the northern part of Shikōkū Island (Figure 1). The castle is protected by a moat. Other canals provide safe haven for ships.

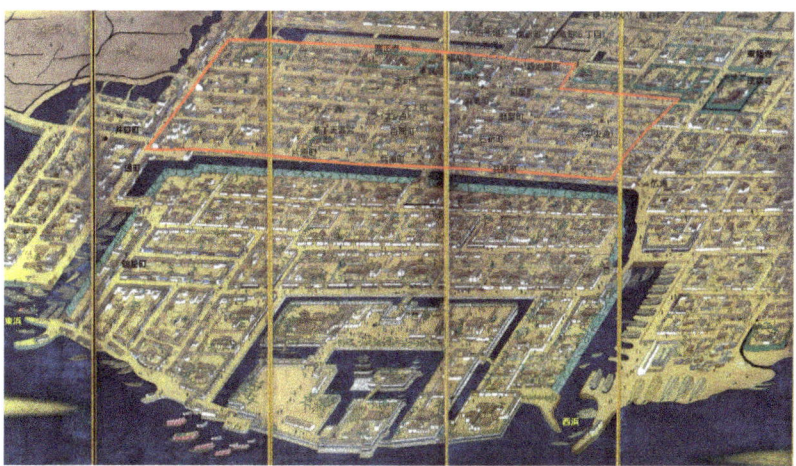

Figure 1. Screen Painting of Takamatsu Castle and its Port During the Edō Period.
Source: Photograph by author in Kagawa Museum, Takamatsu, Shikōkū, Japan.

Port Administration in the Modern Monarchy Era

From the mid-19th century, Japan realised the need for trade in vital raw materials, such as oil, iron ore, and industrial products, and for a strong navy for defence. Phipps (2015) has written a book on the economic history of the commercial expansion of ports from 1858 until the early Meiji era by tracing maritime networks of exchange, transport, and information. Construction, or purchase, of ocean-going ships was given fresh emphasis in Japan. At the end of the 19th century, government subsidies to shipbuilders encouraged the industry, but it was only the pressures of the First World War that gave Japanese shipping companies the lion's share of Japanese foreign trade.

The Meiji government's policy of modernisation under a centralised government was designed to help Japan catch up with advanced Western nations. Japan's ports and harbours matured under the Meiji government's policy of industrial promotion, national wealth and military strength. Ports, harbours, railways, roads and other types of economic infrastructure were established at this time. The modernisation of the Japanese economy can be aptly illustrated with the case of Kōbe Port. In the U.S.-Japan Treaty of Trade and Amity (1858) Hyōgo was declared a designated open port under the treaty.

Under a Meiji government policy enacted in 1873, ports were deemed "government-owned structures", which brought them under national government jurisdiction (Japan, Ministry of Land Infrastructure and Transport, n.d.). These facilities were ranked (Class One, Two and Three), and the government was directly responsible for the improvement of the five major Class One ports (including Ōsaka and Kōbe) which were central to the country's international trade. The port of Ōsaka opened to foreign trade on 15 July 1868 but soon found it necessary to construct a new port because large vessels could not navigate along the rivers due to accumulation of silt.

Construction started at Tempozan, Ōsaka, in 1897 under a plan of a Dutch engineer, De Rijke,[5] with a budget as equivalent of 20 times the city's annual budget. Tempozan wharf opened in 1922 and work on the port was finally finished in 1929. Further reconstruction and renovation work started in 1935 with the Central Pier being completed in 1944. Allied bombing severely damaged the port facilities in 1945 and they were further damaged as a result of the 1946 Shōwa Nankai earthquake of the 21 December 1945.

Class two and three ports were either under the sole jurisdiction of local governments or they were managed by prefecture and municipal governments. At that time, however, the Japanese constitution did not provide for autonomous local government, and the responsibility for these ports was in the hands of the prefecture governor, who was appointed by the national government. Local government merely served as the management body, bearing the expenses involved in managing the ports and harbours, while the administration of these facilities was actually directed by the national government.

At the end of the 19th century, a new *institution*—the Port Customhouse—was placed under the direct jurisdiction of the Japan Ministry of Finance. Around 1897, all laws and regulations concerning customs administration, particularly the *Customs Law* and the *Customs Tariff Law*, were enacted to reflect the provisions of the new treaties imposed on the country by foreign powers. At the same time, a new Customs organisational chart was set up, consisting of a secretariat, one division and six sections. The staff numbered a total of 1,240.

---

5   Kamibayashi (2009) documents the civil engineering works in Japan, including the flood control of the Yodogawa, by Johannis de Rijke (1842–1913) and others.

This virtually laid the foundation of the present Japan Customs Administration (Japan, Department of Customs, 2021).

In 1924, the Cabinet of Prime Minister Katō Takaaki (1860–1926) implemented administrative reorganisation by integrating the whole responsibility of port and harbour administration into the Customs Department. Under an Imperial ordinance, the local harbour departments, which had previously been under the jurisdiction of the Ministry of Home Affairs, were all transferred to Customs. Japan's external trade declined with the intensification of military activities. Shipping was brought under state control to reinforce military transport capacity and customhouses were closed. The Marine Transportation Bureau assumed authority for their personnel and facilities.

Naval ship building grew rapidly at the same time, and, by 1940, Japan had one of the largest and most powerful navies ever built in the world, totalling 15 battleships and battlecruisers, 7 aircraft carriers, 66 cruisers, 164 destroyers and 66 submarines. Following Japan's surrender in the Second World War, and in accordance with the "Memorandum on the Japan Customs System" issued in 1946 by the General Headquarters of the Allied Forces, the Ministry of Finance again took the responsibility for all Customs matters.

Port Administration in the Modern Democratic Era

After the Second World War, the *Port and Harbor Act* (1950) dramatically shifted port administration from the central government to local governments. American General Headquarters, which essentially controlled Japan at that time, ordered the Japanese Government to draw up a Port Act that would force local governments to assume port management by adopting the then current U.S.A. port authority system.

Hayashi and Seta (2012) describe the conflict between the central government (who wanted to remain in a position of power and influence) and the big five port cities including Kōbe and Yokohama who kept asking for priority treatment. Shibata (2008) notes that the major ports were already being developed by local government funds. In fact, the *Port and Harbor Act* defines a "port management body" as the Port Authority or a local public entity. Major port cities, including the city of Ōsaka (on 1 July 1952) have entitled themselves to a port management body under the Ōsaka Municipal Government. (Almost all other ports are managed by prefecture governments; unions manage only a few ports.)

For example, there are four port areas on Ōsaka Bay, and they are administrated by each local government: Ōsaka Port by the City; Sakai Senboku Port by Ōsaka Prefecture; Kōbe Port by the Kōbe City; and Amagasaki-Nishinomiya-Ashiya Port by Hyōgo Prefecture. This regional decentralisation of port administration has resulted in competitive bidding by governments to develop ports in every coastal region of the country some of which are scarcely viable economically. Terada (2012) explains this proliferation of ports in considerable detail.

With the increasing container shipping in global maritime markets since the 1960s, the Ministry of Transport planned to institute a public corporation that would develop and manage international container terminals in Kōbe Port, Yokohama port and Nagoya port. The first two named cities, and the Nagoya Port Association—as port management bodies—however, repelled the plan, as the central government intended the corporations to take over port administration. Furthermore, the Ministry of Finance objected to the plan on financial grounds. After the Ministry of Transport lobbied the ruling party, the plan finally ended up as the *International Container Terminal Corporation Act* in August 1967— effectively establishing two Port Development Authorities, 外貿埠頭公団 (PDA hereinafter) as public corporations: the Keihin PDA financed by Tōkyō Metropolis and Yokohama City; and the Hanshin Foreign Trade Terminal Public Corporation (PDA) by Ōsaka City and Kōbe City.

The national government and private companies also invested into these PDAs. Since the PDAs took responsibilities not only in developing, but also managing, international container terminals, it led to a dualised administration in Ōsaka port. For the construction of many liner berths and container terminals, the "Hanshin and Keihin Port Authority" was founded by the investment of the central government in 1967. But, in 1982, the Authority was dissolved, and assets were transferred to public corporations established by local governments. Hanshin PDA was replaced by Kōbe PMC and Ōsaka PMC as affiliated organisations of the ports.

The trade in the container shipping industry declined after the Oil Shocks of 1973 and the over-development and surplus capacity of container wharves became a significant issue in Japan. Two PDAs were nominated for abolishment in the Administration Reform Commission.

The Cabinet made a decision in December 1977 to abolish the PDAs. On this issue of abolishing PDAs, conflicts inevitably arose amongst institutions of government and organisations: the Ministry of Transport appealed the decision with its objections; container-shipping companies, who had invested into PDAs, claimed a right to take over the container terminals; and the city governments, including Ōsaka City, welcomed the opportunity to take over the functions of PDAs.

Those conflicts lasted until another political decision was made in 1980: to replace the PDAs with a new institution of a Port Management Corporation, 埠頭公社 (PMC) in each port without any changes in the financial status for private companies. The cities took over the container terminals and the PMCs were under the supervision of the central government (the Ministry of Transport). After 1985, the national government formulated several plans with a basic aim of implementing a "Multipolar Pattern Japan" that encouraged local governments to have a claim for an international container port.

The intent of the final plan was to develop 39 new international container ports over 15 years (from 1986 to 2000). The number of international container ports in Japan increased eleven times from 6 ports in the 1960s to 66 ports in 2007. This National Ports Policy (Japan, Ministry of Land, Infrastructure, Transport and Tourism, 2009) eventually forced port management bodies into domestic competition for attracting shipping liners. At the same time, other Asian ports, such as Singapore, Hong Kong and Pusan, introduced their own container services. Falling behind those countries, the Japanese government reversed its policy so as to centralise port investment and the container freight: it first designated the Hanshin port (Ōsaka Port and Kōbe Port) as one of three "super hub ports" in 2004 and later designated them as one of two "strategic international container ports" in 2010.

The Hanshin Ports are allowed to apply for preferential funds from the national government. In accordance with those centralisation policies, the national government has promoted the privatisation of PMCs in order "to make them more economically efficient operations and to respond to customers' need". The Japan Ministry of Land, Infrastructure, Transport and Tourism (2019), concluded that existing port administrations had difficulties in responding to both shipping liners' and shippers' requests because they were public-sector institutions. The Ministry suggested that a private company, such as a limited company, is a superior model for administrating a container port. Under the consideration of nominating a strategic international container port, the national government determined the feasibility of efficient management from the private sector as one of the criteria.

Ōsaka Port subsequently privatised its PMC to the Ōsaka Port Corporation with 100 per cent capital from the City of Ōsaka in 2010 (Kawasaki *et al.*, 2020). As a result, Ōsaka Port has three elements in its container port administration: the national government; the local government of Ōsaka City; and the Ōsaka Port Corporation. In addition to its old container terminal developed and managed by the Ōsaka City or PDA/PMC, a "strategic international container port" with a container pier has been developed: the wharf-land is owned by local government and other equipment, such as cranes, by Ōsaka Port Corporation. In addition, for the Hanshin Port, the Kōbe—Ōsaka International Port Corporation was launched by the national government (34% of capital), the City of Kōbe (31% of capital), the City of Ōsaka (31% of capital) and city banks (4% of capital).

As in most countries, Japanese port functions, such as administration, piloting, dredging and infrastructure development, are a combination of responsibilities shared by both public and private sectors. Public service ports are predominantly managed by the government except that certain functions, such as dredging, may be shared with private companies. The landlord model is common to many ports throughout the world where a government corporation administers the port and 'owns' the surrounding water such as the approach and departure channels; other functions are shared or are the responsibility of the private sector. As implied by the name of a privatised port, most functions are managed by the private sector except for pilotage or the environmental approval for marine dredging.

Land Reclamation

One of the most extraordinary physical and economic developments in Japan, especially in the era after the Pacific War, has been the degree of land reclamation that has been undertaken in its oceans and bays (see https://japanpropertycentral.com/real-estate-faq/reclaimed-land-in-japan/). Whilst some of this has been driven by the need for container terminals, the planning of such reclamation has included the integration of other land uses such as commercial, residential, roads and recreational. The City of Kōbe provides one example of the extent of land reclamation in Ōsaka Bay (https://sustainableworldports.org/project/port-of-kobe-environmental-measures-in-reclamation-projects/). The mining of material from Mount Rokkō, and the transportation of spoil by slurry pipeline into the bay, is an engineering feat in its own right. In addition to port and airport functions, land on the reclaimed new islands in the sea were sold to developers as residential, commercial and other urban land use. Locally called the "Kōbe Business Model", land reclamation has generated income from both land and sea.

However, one problem of constructing facilities on landfill is the liquefactions that occur during major earthquakes. In January 1995 an earthquake of a magnitude 7.2 on the Richter scale, with an epicentre on the nearby island of Awaji, devasted the Kōbe area causing loss of life and major damage to structures (Chung, 1996, Figure 4.5.4, p. 294).

Conclusions

Migration to the islands of Japan followed land bridges where the hunter-gather culture exploited shallow coastal waters for fishing from dug-out canoes. As society advanced with the influx of Yayoi people from continental Asia local clans formed, along with clan chiefs who exercised control over maritime resources. With the birth of the Yamatai Kingdom, centralised command over these resources occurred. Suminoe and Naniwa ports were *institutional* artifacts of a succession of the clan leaders, Kings of *Wa* and Emperors using primarily their diplomacy with China and Korea for trade in precious and symbolic items of power and their domestic movement of taxation rice and other products to the capital.

Just as Naniwa had supplanted Suminoe as an international point of embarkation and disembarkation Naniwa declined with the construction of a canal on the Yodo River and the rise of Watanabe—a port up-river on Imperial estates (*shōen*) and closer to the capital. Acting on the authority of the Emperor, samurai administered this port and formed a marine police force. The interpretation of the shifting patterns of control of international trade through Japanese ports from 600 to 1868 is summarised in Table 6, showing the dominant players over time who controlled international trade through Japanese ports.

From 600 until the tribute trade with the Sui and T'ang was abolished in Middle Heian times, the Emperor (*institution*) and his administration exercised tight control. Chinese merchants (*organisations*) entered this national policy vacuum with private international trade. Diplomatic trade resumed in the 10th to 13th centuries but it was now strongly controlled by the decentralised *institutions* of the warlords (in essence local government). With the rise of regional warlords and military governments from the Kamakura period onwards, in coastal fiefdoms, especially to the west of Japan, maritime piracy as an *organisation* was rife and the evidence of strong alliances between pirates as "lords of the sea" and the regional warlords (*institutions*) support one proposition of the new institutional economics: the existence of nested institutions.

Table 6. Dominant Players Controlling International Trade, Japan, from 600–1868.
Source: Author with assistance from Dr Naoya Akita.

Period	Description	Trade Type	Dominant Players Managing Trade
Asuka 600–618	Envoys to Sui	Tribute	Emperor—powerful
Nara 618–894	Envoys to T'ang	Tribute	Emperor—powerful
Middle Heian	Tribute trade abolished	Private	Chinese merchants—weak control
End of Heian (10th—13th C)	Free trade	Diplomatic	*Buke*—Decentralised but strong control
Early Kamakura	Chaotic—rise of early *wako* pirates	Private	Regional warlords—weak control
Middle Muromachi	Ming Trade	Tribute	*Shōgun*—powerful
Late Muromachi	Ming Trade—late *wako* pirates	Tribute	*Shōgun, daimyō*, merchants—weak control
Azuchi—Momoyama	Nanbanboeki	Private	*Kanpaku*—powerful
Edō 1603–1868	Regulated Isolation	National	*Shōgun*—powerful

3. *Ports and Shipping*   91

One of the first unifiers of Japan, Toyotomi Hideyoshi, grew rich by participating in this illegal, international trade, destroyed the trading religious monarchy and port at Ishiyama Honganji (*organisation*) to secure a strategic site for the future Ōsaka Castle. With the unification of the country in the Edō period the Tokugawa government regained powerful control of international trade that included a policy of not paying tribute to Chinese Emperors.

Table 7 summarises the arguments presented in the earlier, substantive part of the chapter by considering the six ancient ports in the Ōsaka region in terms of whether the port administration was predominantly through an institution or an organisation, who were the dominant parties in port affairs, what were main landmark events that led to the functioning of each port and who were the main agents of change from one historical period to another.

Table 7. Early Ōsaka Ports in History—Institutional and
Organisational Analysis.
Source: Author.

Port (date)	Suminoe (< 5th C)	Naniwa (5–11th C)	Watanabe (11–16th C)	Ishiyama Honganji (16th C)	Sakai (16th C)
Administration	*Institution*	*Institution*	*Institution*	*Organisation*	*Organisation*
Dominant Party	*Wa* clans; Emperor	Emperor	Emperor; *Daimyō*	Buddhist Temple	Merchants
Landmark Events	Diplomacy with China Korea	Diplomacy; Taxation	Canal built on Yodo; Marine police	Land allocation to powerful elites	Trade with Ming; Piracy in Setō Inland Sea
Agents of Change	Decline of tribute trade with China	Canal building enhancing strategic location; capital at Naniwa	Canal building by-passing Naniwa to inland capital	Destroyed by warlord Toyotomi Hideyoshi	Toyotomi Hideyoshi control; Transfer of merchants to Ōsaka

The table illustrates the considerable variation in governance and who was responsible for major events. Suminoe, Naniwa and Watanabe were the creation of the ruling elites of *uji* clan chiefs and the Imperial Court whereas the ports of Ishiyama Honganji and Sakai were administered respectively by a religious order and by a merchant association.

Administration of the port of Sakai can be interpreted as an 'outlier' in the medieval period in as much that it was run by merchant associations not by a regional warlord. Pirates often identified themselves not only with looting/pillaging associates but also with groups of wealthy merchants, often tied to the *egoshu*—the rich merchant associations of Sakai. During the *Ōnin no Ran* (1467–1477) shipping movements, the Setō Inland Sea became increasingly dangerous and trade shifted to the port of Sakai where it prospered in a town administered by merchants (called *nayashu* and later *kaigoshu*). They thrived on the trade with Ming dynasty China established by the third Muromachi *Shōgun*, Ashikaga Yoshimitsu. Port administration changed dramatically when Toyotomi Hideyoshi captured the town and transferred merchants to Ōsaka to grow the commercial activities of that embryonic town.

By 1619, Ōsaka Castle had been taken by the House of Tokugawa and its seaport theoretically was administered with broad oversight by the *machi bugyō* appointed by the *Shōgunate* (national institution) in the case of legal disputes arising. Port governance under the Tokugawa functioned in a complex way through a system of layered hierarchical spheres of authority, each of which retained some degree of autonomy. Despite the Ōsaka Port being located on a Tokugawa domain its infrastructure development of river works, canal construction, land reclamation, bridge building and warehouses was the result of private merchants' initiatives (*organisations*). Much of this development was paid from merchant profits made from the transport and handling of rice (then the national currency) to the new capital of Edō.

During the Edō period, there were conflicts over international trade providing examples of policy reversals. For example, from the Chinese trading perspective, merchants and officials were critical of the low copper imports from Japan as a result of problems in the procurement of export copper from Japanese mines (Schottenhammer, 2008: 339). In 1701, the Japanese institutional response was to open a copper office (*dōza*, 銅座), which managed the transport of copper to China until 1712–1713 when it was closed down.

Foreign intervention and the military force of Western powers were factors shattering the institutional stability of the Tokugawa *bakufu*, which had lasted for two and a half centuries. The threat of the U.S.

black ships backing up demands for free international trade and the opening of ports Japan forced the *Shōgun* to consult with all *daimyōs* as a political precedent and with it came a perceived weakness of command that eventually resulted in the downfall of the regime and the reinstatement of the institution of Emperor. The Meiji Restoration brought in Western-styled democratic institutions with the ownership of ports being radically re-organised under the control of the national government. After the Second World War, the *Port and Harbor Act* (1950), strongly influenced by U.S. advisors during the Allied occupation of Japan, shifted port administration from the central government to local governments.

In the post-war era the development of ports and their administration followed much along Western lines. From approximately 1950–1970, the supply of berths for liners increased; from 1970–2000, container terminals were constructed, and many urban waterfronts were developed, much of them on reclaimed land; and from the 21st century onwards there was a move towards port re-organisation and the privatisation of container terminals. For example, the Hanshin Ports are allowed to apply for preferential funds from the national government. Ōsaka Port subsequently privatised its management to the Ōsaka Port Corporation with 100 per cent capital from the City of Ōsaka in 2010. 'Consequently, container port administration in Ōsaka Port comprises three elements: the national government; the local government of Ōsaka City; and the Ōsaka Port Corporation. In addition, in October 2014, the Hanshin Port, Kōbe-Ōsaka International Port Corporation was launched by the national government (34% of capital), the City of Kōbe (31% of capital), the City of Ōsaka (31% of capital) and city banks (4% of capital).

Successful development policy entails an understanding of the dynamics of economic change if the policies pursued are to have the desired consequences. The directions of major port developments require a broad understanding of the relative roles of national, provincial and local governments in port and shipping policy. In Japan, this narrative of the history of port administration would suggest a temporal sequence highlighting the relative importance of: *uji* clan chiefs and the Emperor; 'provincial government'—the military power of the regional *daimyō*— then private interests (merchants) taking over port construction and trade development (taxation rice) during the Edō era, albeit under the careful scrutiny of a national military government; followed by Meiji government policies of modernisation—much along western lines for port administration; and finally national government intervention to make Japanese container ports more internationally competitive with the Hanshin "super port" model of administration.

References

Arnason, J. P. (2010) *Social Theory and Japanese Experience: The Dual Civilization*. Routledge, Oxford.

Asao, Naohiro, Towao Sakaehara, Hiroshi Niki and Yasunao Kojita (1999) 堺の歴史 [*History of Sakai: The Origin of a Self-Governing City*]. Kadokawa Shoten, Tokyo.

Brecher, W. P. (2010) "Brewing Spirits, Brewing Songs: Saké, Haikai, and the Aestheticization of Suburban Space in Edo Period Itami", *Japan Studies Review*, 14, 17–44.

Brown, D. M. (1993) "The Yamato Kingdom", in J. W. Hall, M. B. Jansen, Madoka Kanai and D. Twitchett (eds) (1993) *The Cambridge History of Japan, Volume I Ancient Japan*. Cambridge University Press, Cambridge, 108–162.

Chaffee, J. (2010) "Song China and the Multi-state and Commercial World of East Asia", *Crossroads—Studies on the History of Exchange Relations in the East Asian World*, 1, 33–54.

Chung, R. (ed.) (1996) "The January 17, 1995 Hyogoku-Nanbu (Kobe) Earthquake: Performance of Structures, Lifelines and Fire Protection Equipment". *National Institute of Standards and Technology, Special Publication 901*. U.S. Government Printing Office, Washington, D. C.

City of Osaka (2014) *Watashitachi no Kurashito Osaka Kou* (わたしたちのくらしと大阪港), No. 39, n.p.

Cullen, L. M. (2009) "Statistics of Tokugawa Coastal Trade and Bakumatsu and Early Meiji Foreign Trade", *Japan Review*, 21, 183–223.

Damian, M. (2014) "A Geographic Analysis of Traders and Trade Goods in Japan's Late Medieval Seto Inland Sea", Second Asia-Pacific Regional Conference on Underwater Cultural Heritage, Honolulu, Hawaii, May 2014.

Hayashi, Masahiro and Fumihiko Seta (2012) *Kouwan Seibi Jigyouniokeru Gyousei Taiseito Senryaku Houkouseini Tsuiteno Kenkyu* (港湾整備事業における行政体制の実態と戦略的方向性についての研究), 17–18, http://www.mlit.go.jp/common/000140768.pdf

Hayami, Yujiro and Yoshihisa Godo (1997) "Economics and Politics of Rice Policy in Japan: A Perspective on the Uruguay Round", in Takatoshi Ito and

A. O. Krueger, eds, *Regionalism versus Multilateral Trade Arrangements, NBER-EASE Volume 6*. University of Chicago Press, Chicago, 371–404.

Hayashiya, T. (ed.) (1981) *Hyōgo Kitaseki Irifune Nōchō*. Chuo Koron Bijutsu Shuppan, Tokyo.

Heritage of Japan (2020) "Defense Projects of Dazaifu: The 'Water Fortress'", https://heritageofjapan.wordpress.com/inception-of-the-imperial-system-asuka-era/the-ruins-of-asuka-yamato/the-architecture-of-asuka/engineering-marvels-dazaifus-water-fortress/

Hudson, M. J. (2017) "The Sea and Early Societies in the Japanese Islands", in P. de Souza, P. Arnaud and C. Buchet (eds) (2017) *The Sea in History—The Ancient World*, Boydell & Brewer, Martlesham, Suffolk, 102–113.

Japan, Department of Customs (2021) "History of Japan Customs", https://www.customs.go.jp/english/zeikan/history_e.htm

Japan, Ministry of Land, Infrastructure, Transport and Tourism (2009) "Ports and Harbours in Japan", http://www.mlit.go.jp/kowan/english/appendix/1.html

Japan, Ministry of Land, Infrastructure, Transport and Tourism (2019) *White Paper on Land, Infrastructure, Transport and Tourism in Japan, 2017*. Tokyo, Ministry of Land, Infrastructure, Transport and Tourism,://www.mlit.go.jp/en/statistics/white-paper-mlit-2019.html

Japan Heritage Portal Site (2019) "Murakami Kaizoku: Japan's Largest 'Pirate Group and their Territory in the Geiyo Archipeligo—Story 36", https://japan-heritage.bunka.go.jp/en/stories/story036/

Kamibayashi, Yoshiyuki (2009) "Two Dutch Engineers and Improvements of Public Works in Japan", *Proceedings of the Third International Congress on Construction History*, May 2009, Cottbus, Germany, https://structurae.net/en/literature/conference-paper/two-dutch-engineers-and-improvements-of-public-works-in-japan

Kawanabe, Hiroya, Nishino, Machiko and Maehata, Masayoshi (eds) (2012) *Lake Biwa: Interactions Between Nature and People*. Springer, Dordtrecht.

Kawasaki, Tomoya, Hoshi Tagawa, Toshihiro Watanabe and Shinya Hanaoka (2020) "The Effects of Consolidation and Privatization of Ports in Proximity: A Case study of the Kobe and Osaka Ports," *The Asian Journal of Shipping and Logistics*, 35 (1), 1–12.

Kodansha (1993) *Japan: An Illustrated Encyclopedia*. Kodansha, Bunkyo-ku, Tokyo.

MLIT (2019) "Main Points of the 9th Five-Year Port Consolidation Plan", Ministry of Land, Infrastructure, Transport and Tourism, Tokyo, http://www.mlit.go.jp/english/ports/kowan4.html

McClain, J. L., and Osamu Wakita (1999) "Osaka Across the Ages", in J. L. McClain and Osamu Wakita (eds) (1999) *Osaka: The Merchants' Capital of Early Modern Japan*. Cornell University Press, Ithaca, New York, 1–21.

McClain, J. L., and Osamu Wakita (eds) (1999) *Osaka: The Merchants' Capital of Early Modern Japan*. Cornell University Press, Ithaca, New York.

Matsumura, Hiroshi (2004) "Bridges: Highlights of Osaka's Urbanscape', *Osaka, Osaka City Foundation for Urban Technology, OSAKA and its Technology*, No. 45, 16–21.

Mitsusada, Inoue, with D. M. Brown (1993) "The Century of Reform", in *The Cambridge History of Japan, Volume I Ancient Japan*, 163–220.

Nagai, Fumihiro (2004) "Initiatives for Restoring 'Water Metropolis Osaka'", *Osaka, Osaka City Foundation for Urban Technology, OSAKA and its Technology*, No. 45, 5–10.

Naumann, N. (2000) *Japanese Prehistory: The Material and Spiritual Culture of the Jōmon Period*, Asien- und Afrika-Studien 6 der Humbolt-Unversitat zu Berlin. Harrissowtz-Verlag, Wiesbaden.

Nelson, S. M. (2014) "Relationships between Silla 新羅 and Yamato 大和", *Crossroads—Studies on the History of Exchange Relations in the East Asian World*, 9, 83–96.

Osaka Toshi Kogaku Center (1999) *OSAKA—MILLENNIUM CITY Sen Nen Toshi Machi Zukuri Monogatari*. Zaidan Hozin, Osaka Toshi Kogaku Center, Osaka.

Pearson, R. (2016) "Japanese Medieval Trading Towns: Sakai and Tosaminato", *Japanese Journal of Archaeology*, 3, 89–116.

Phipps, C. L. (2015) *Empires on the Waterfront: Japan's Ports and Power, 1858–1899*. Harvard University Asia Center, Cambridge, Mass.

Sakaehara, Towao (2009) "The Port of Osaka: From Ancient Times to Today", in A. Graf and Chua Beng Huat (eds) (2009) *Port Cities in Asia and Europe*. Routledge, London, 3–18.

Sansom, G. (1961) *A History of Japan 1334–1615*. The Cresset Press, London.

Schottenhammer, A. (2012) "The 'China Seas' in World History: A General Outline of the Role of Chinese and East Asian Maritime Space from its Origins to c. 1800," *Journal of Marine and Island Cultures*, 1 (2), 263–286.

Shibata, Etsuko (2008) "戦後経済の流れと港湾政策の検討(前編・1982年まで" (Sengo Keizaino Nagareto Kouwan Seisakuno Kentou. Zenpen, 1982 Nenmade)", 海事交通研究 第57集.

Terada, Hideko (2002) "Port Construction Subsidies in Japan and the Way They Discourage Private Sector Investment in Port Development", *IAME Panama 2002 International Steering Committee Conference Proceedings*, held in Panama on 13–15 November 2002, 1–24.

Wakita, Haruko (1999) "Ports, Markets, and Medieval Urbanism in the Osaka Region", in J. L. McClain and Osamu Wakita (eds) (1999) *Osaka: The Merchants' Capital of Early Modern Japan*. Cornell University Press, Ithaca, New York, 22–43.

Yamamukai, Kaoru (2004) "Dotombori Riverfront Development Project—Towards Regenerating the Water Metropolis", *Osaka, Osaka City Foundation for Urban Technology, OSAKA and its Technology*, No. 45, 11–15.

Yamasaki, Takeshi, Tanigawa Kanae and G. D. Ness (2010) "Kobe and Niigata: Situation and Site in the Development of Two Japanese Port Cities", in F. Broeze (ed.) (2010) *Gateways of Asia—Port Cities of Asia in the 13th-20th Centuries*. Routledge, London, 233–264.

4. Canals, Rivers and Lakes

An official is on his mettle
When riding in a *choki*[1]

Introduction

The transport of produce by natural water courses of rivers and lakes is one of mankind's oldest means of communication that allowed food to be carried over more extended distances from farms to settlements. Modifications to the landscape, in the form of ditches, dikes and narrow canals, were initially to improve agricultural productivity but had only a minor effect of improving transport efficiency. In the case of Japan, over the millennia, it has been the constant drive at a local level to improve irrigation systems that have had the co-benefits to water transport rather than the construction of a national network of canals as occurred in many other countries. The essential pattern of Japanese agriculture had, at its heart, river irrigation systems (Tabayashi,1987; Kuroishi, 2019).

A sizable proportion of this chapter deals with canals in rural, agricultural regions of the study area. In the overall scheme of things, river transport is of minor importance because engineering works were directed to flood control and urban water supply. The narrative follows the chronology adopted in Chapter 1, where in the archaic period dugout canoes were key artefacts of the hunter-gatherer society. The ancient period essentially set the pattern of canal and river management for millennia with landowners reliant on local knowledge for construction, operation and maintenance. In the early medieval to the early modern periods, the ancient cultural and political locus of Japan was around

---

1   A *choki* was a small boat used in Edō times to ferry samurai to and from the red-light district of Yoshiwara in Edō. The poetic style is *senryū*—in this case, where the *chōnin* (townsfolk) are mocking their social superiors (Kato, 1997: 205).

Lake Biwa and Kyōto, so various ambitious plans by warlords involved large-scale canals linking the Sea of Japan and the Pacific Ocean, but they were aborted because of the mountainous terrain.

The canal infrastructure that was constructed in the commercial ports of Ōsaka and Edō during the early modern period was entirely the resources and capital of the merchant class (Chapter 3). This chapter then focuses on an early Meiji period engineering marvel: Lake Biwa Canal between Ōtsu and Kyōto, based on material in Lake Biwa Comprehensive Preservation Liaison Coordination Council Office/ Metropolitan Areas Development Division, City and Regional Development Bureau, Ministry of Land, Infrastructure and Transport (2003), van Gasteren (2001), and Sakuro (1894). Finally, the administration of rivers and canals from the Meiji period onwards, especially the contemporary role of the Ministry of Infrastructure, Land, Transport and Tourism, is explained from a regulatory perspective with the *River Act* (1896; amended 1964). The next section explains why the topography on Honshū island was unsuitable for a network of canals for transport purposes.

The Importance of Topography

Topography is a significant factor as to whether rivers are navigable and whether there is economic value in canal construction. It is worth comparing the island of Honshū with a country of similar area. Japan and Great Britain offer relevant comparisons: Honshū is an island with an area of 227,963 sq. km (roughly 1,300 km long and from 50 to 250 km wide); England, Scotland and Wales, combined, have a similar area of 229,462 sq. km (the distance from Land's End in England to John O'Groats in Scotland is 970 km). In these two countries, as of 1600— when Japan's population was approximately 5 million and that of Great Britain 4.8 million—rivers, inland waterways and coastal shipping provided the main means of transporting bulk materials and the occasional passenger.

There are clear topographical differences between Japan and Great Britain. The navigable parts of English river systems are more extensive than those in Japan because of the lower mean terrain, whereas most of Japan, apart from coastal fringes, is predominantly mountainous or hilly. The longest rivers in Great Britain are the Severn (354 km), the

Thames (346 km), the Trent (297 km), the Great Ouse (230 km) and the Wye (215 km). Japanese rivers rise in the mountainous spines and plateaux that run along most of central Honshū and are short and fast flowing, especially after alpine snow melt. The latter rivers are less suitable for transport purposes.

The largest drainage basin in Japan is the Tonegawa (Tone River)—322 km long with its source at Mount Ōminakami in the Echigo Mountains and it flows into the Pacific Ocean at Chōshi in Chiba Prefecture. Emptying into Ise Bay, the Kisogawa (Kiso River) is 227 km long, with headwaters between the Hida and Kiso Mountains. (Details on the Shinano, Tone and Yoda Rivers can be found on the homepage of the Australian Bureau of Meteorology (2019)). The Arakawa is 169 km long with its source in the Kantō Mountains then passing through Saitama and Tōkyō prefectures with its lower reaches referred to as the Sumidagawa (Sumida River) where it enters into Tōkyō Bay. Despite the dangers of the fast-flowing rivers, currents and shoals, river navigation was negotiated by Japanese boatmen whose skills have been honed from Jōmon times.

Based on the above conditions, there was no obvious incentive in Japan to think about investment in canals to extend the river systems as a national waterway network. This investment happened in Britain from 1741 onwards.[2] These transport developments in Britain were driven by local projects: with private landowners as entrepreneurs (many initially exploiting coal); finance raised locally—primarily from those likely to benefit from the canal; consortia of business interests forming joint-stock companies; and, importantly, the rise of skilled surveyors and engineers (Barker and Savage, 1974: 36–44). As described by Osborne (2013: 266–282), it was private capital that invested in British canals from the day that the Duke of Bridgewater's proposal was approved by the UK Parliament in March 1759 to build a canal that linked coalmines at Worsley to Manchester. In comparison, the Tokugawa *bakufu* had little economic interest in business and therefore canal construction.

---

2   In the UK, there is a wealth of published material on inland water transport, such as Willan (1936); Hadfield (1968) and Barker and Savage (1974).

Archaic Period

In Jōmon times, the coastlines and rivers were obvious sources of fish. The shoreline of Lake Biwa was an especially important location for Jōmon peoples and their hunter-gather lifestyles because of its abundance of food from land and water. Approximately 460 rivers of various sizes flow into Lake Biwa with a unique arrangement of attached lakes (most now filled for paddy fields) but only one outflow (the Seta River) that eventually empties into Ōsaka Bay as the Yodo River as a communications corridor (Uemura, 2012). Dated from the early Jōmon period, more than 30 dugout canoes (*maruki-bune*) have been discovered—the largest number ever found in Japan.

Ancient Period

In the early Yayoi period, water management was exercised by farmers where irrigation dikes drained paddy fields on the natural wetlands. As agriculture extended to upland areas in the 2nd century B.C. intake dams stretched across streams up to 10 metres wide and diversion canals were created. Inter-community organisations created canals 20 to 30 metres wide on alluvial uplands. Excavations at Toro (Shizuoka Prefecture) uncovered third century paddy fields totalling 7.5 hectares and irrigated by a canal more than 370 metres long (Tabayashi, 1987: 57).

According to Tabayashi (1987: 58), only a strong government could carry out the ambitious program of constructing and maintaining the well-ordered pattern of rural fields, paths and ditches, known as the *jōri* system. These waterways would have also served to transport rice. The *jōri* system of land division was introduced after the Taika Reform of 645 where tracts of land were divided into squares with sides measuring six *chō* (654 metres). This system made it possible for government to allocate land to cultivators, but the system was discontinued during the Heian period (794–1183).

As covered in Chapter 3, canals were indispensable elements of port expansions from ancient times through to the Edō period (Sakura, 2014). Dating the Horie Canal is difficult but there is no doubt of its importance by the 6th and 7th centuries A.D. The total length of the artificial canal was 3 km and was cut through three parallel sand bars, each separated by narrow lagoons, immediately to the north of the Uemachi Terrace in the Ōsaka region (Pearson, 2016, Figure 5.18, p. 50).

Medieval Period

Variously, both institutions and organisations—local elites, the regional *daimyō*, merchants, influential politicians or local government—have been instrumental in formulating ambitious plans for canals throughout Japanese history to connect Lake Biwa with the ocean. Given the ancient cultural and political locus of Japan was around Lake Biwa and Kyōto, these plans involved large-scale canals linking the Sea of Japan and the Pacific Ocean (Yoda, 2012:294). Towards the end of the Heian period, Taira no Kiyomori (1118–1181)—head of a powerful warrior clan— ordered his son, Shigemori, the local governor (*shugo*) of Echizen Province to build a 25-km long canal starting from Shiotsu in the north of Lake Biwa towards Tsuruga facing the Sea of Japan. The obstruction of Mount Fukasake caused work to stop 12 km from the port of Shiotsu, where a statue of *jizo bosatsu* (patron saint of dead children) was erected.

The legitimacy of the national government decreased so that it no longer carried out major water utilisation, river flood control or canal projects and improvements were organised by local authorities such as by the *shōen* estates and by the *daimyō*. Clearly, the skills to build canals in Japan existed from the 12th century when there was a tradition of building elaborate systems of moats around castles. The *Jinkouki*—a book on mathematics for the education of ordinary people published first in 1627—sets out examples of the calculation of volumes of soil to excavate (Wasan Institute, 2000: 135–137).

Early Modern

River Management

During the Warring States period, warlords developed the vast alluvial flood plains on major rivers that set up a cycle of flood damage and flood control measures. As noted by Aoyama (1999: 2) this led to the expansion of "local government" river administrative districts and the "integration of river administration measures". A specific example is the 128-km long Fujigawa that rises from Nokogiriyama (2,685 metres) in northwest Yamanashi as the Kamanashigawa then changes its name to the Fujigawa before emptying into Suruga Bay (Shizuoka Prefecture). During the *sengoku* period, many *daimyō* used advanced castle engineering to control the upper and middle reaches of wild rivers (Tabayashi, 1987: 58). For example, the local warlord Takeda Shingen built extensive dikes (*Shingen—zusumi*) along the Kamanashigawa to control the latitudinal inundation of floodwaters.

Continuing the time-honoured approach to irrigation practices, the Tokugawa government formed water management association of villages in each region to ensure the collective operation and maintenance of water facilities as well as to regulate both water rights and distribution systems in each village. In general, land development efforts during the Edō period brought a rapid expansion of paddy fields and of rice yields. Paddy areas doubled and rice production tripled. New laws and policies shaped the relationship between water rights, ownership of land, the village community system and taxation.

Both land and water were managed and owned by all village residents and agricultural works and environmental management became an everyday matter (Kuroishi, 2019: 155). The "Kantō method" attempted to control flood waters by widening riverbeds, by lengthening rivers through the creation of meanders, by sending excess water into holding basins and by altering the paths of rivers (Tabayashi, 1987:58). By the mid-Edō period, the provincial "integration of river administration measures" become the national government's river administrative system.

From a national transport perspective, the Tokugawa government was primarily interested in rivers as a strategic means of imposing control of the country along the major highways radiating from Edō. Boats were essential in the crossing of rivers and bays on the national highway system of the Tōkaidō. From the militaristic perspective, the Tokugawa government regarded the shallow ford of the Seta River near Ōsaka as a strategic point for transporting an army across the river. Therefore, it was naturally reluctant to dredge the riverbed despite it hindering economic progress. In fact, during the Edō period, the government allowed dredging only five times over 200 years.

Occasionally, infrastructure projects were undertaken by the national government. For example, between 1624 and 1674, the Tokugawa *bakufu* constructed an extensive dike system to protect populated areas along the lower reaches of the Fuji River near the castle town of Sunpu. Water transport from Suruga Bay up-stream prospered in the Edō and early Meiji periods. Commercial river services were withdrawn in 1923.

Canals in the Edō Period

Kanazawa, located on the coast of the Sea of Japan, 260 km north northwest of Kyōto, was one of the largest of cities by population during the Edō era. In 1631, the castle was destroyed by fire. Maeda Toshitsugu (1617–1674), the *daimyō* of Kaga (today, Ishikawa Prefecture), ordered the construction of the Tatsumi Canal (11 km long of which 4 km are in tunnel), primarily for the purpose of fire protection and also to provide water for the gardens and moats of the rebuilt castle. The canal was completed in 1632. However, there is no evidence that it was used for transport purposes.

Kyōto was also an important city with respect to canal development in the Edō era. Toyotomi Hideyoshi granted a formal trade licence (*shuinjō*) to Suminokura Ryōi (1554–1614), to manage overseas trading operations by importing goods from a tributary state of the Ming Dynasty, Yue Nan (now Vietnam). When Toyotomi Hideyoshi died in 1598, Suminokura Ryōi became a trusted advisor and supplier of merchandise to Tokugawa Ieyasu and he was granted a *shuinjō* licence by his new patron to continue his overseas trading business.

The first canal constructed in Kyōto demonstrates the dynamics of the three-way interactions amongst merchant organisations and the *daimyō* and *bakufu*. Between 1605 and 1611, Suminokura Ryōi formed an enterprise with the other two leading merchant families (Chaya Shirōjirō and Gotō Shōzaburō) to construct canals and to make the four rivers of Kyōto (Tenryu, Takase, Fuji and Hozu Rivers) more navigable for shipping goods. The Takase River in central Kyōto is, in effect, a 9.7-km long canal that rises from Nijō-Kiyamachi, meeting the Uji River at Fushimi Port, and crosses the Kamo River on its way. It was constructed in 1611 and contributed substantially to the economic prosperity of the city.

Similarly, the short sections of canals built around the port areas of Edō and Ōsaka were primarily the initiatives of merchant organisations. The growing economic importance of merchants in the early Edō period has been documented in the previous chapter with respect to land reclamation and canals that enhanced the rapid development of both ports. Colour wood-block prints of the time depict the canal frontages in the commercial district of Nihonbashi in Edō and the commercial canals of Ōsaka (Hashizume, 2019; Reith-Banks, 2019).

The earliest modifications to the undulating terrain surrounding modern-day Tōkyō were undertaken in the mid-15th century. In 1467, Ōta Dōkan (1432–1486), a warrior and military strategist, was the architect and builder of a fortress at Edō for Uesugi Sadamasa (who, in 1439, had been appointed Governor-General of the Kantō region). The first civil work undertaken in Edō changed the route of the Hira River for defence moats around the castle and to link the castle with the port (Sakura, 2014, Fig, 1, p. 296)—the transhipment point for the goods that were transported from Kamakura (Sakura, 2014: 925).

To secure the fortification of Edō Castle from attack an elaborate system of moats and canals were dug, including access to Tokugawa land at Hama-Rikyū (now a public park) on marshes in Hibiya Bay that provided rich duck shooting and hawking opportunities. Quarrying of Kanda Hill provided the material for land reclamation that became the merchant town of Edō, as extensively documented by Sadler (1937), Naito (1993) and Kato (2000). The early construction initiatives ordered by Tokugawa Ieyasu included a defensive moat to the east of the castle and short parallel canals from Edō Bay for ships and boats to access the castle.

In the layout of the castle and surrounds, Tokugawa Ieyasu continued the Japanese tradition of cultural borrowings from the Chinese. He was clearly aware of the layout of Chinese Imperial cities and of the study of geomancy. There is much political symbolism in the layout of early Edō with the castle on the highest ground surrounded by the *daimyō* mansions, with the line of sight to Mount Fuji providing a spiritual axis for the castle. In the northeast corner—the traditional location for major temples that would act as a defence from evil forces—sat Sansō-ji, the oldest Buddhist temple in Tōkyō founded in 628.

Thirty-six square enclosure gates (*masugata*) controlled access to the city. As further defence in the northeast were the *Shōgunal* vassals' mansions. Lower-ranking samurai lived in different areas. Parts of the southwestern section of the city were merchant and artisan districts. The commercial centre was located around Nihonbashi (Bridge of Japan)—between the castle to its west, and the river to its east—this centre was connected to the Sumida River, and a canal extended to the port providing access to incoming and outgoing shipping trade. To construct the city, building materials were commanded from the *daimyō* estates and shipped to Edō.

On Tokugawa Ieyasu's authority, Ōkubo Tōgoro (date of birth unknown, died 1617) dug a waterway from Koishikawa (in present-day Bunkyō Ward) to satisfy the needs of the burgeoning new town growing up around Nihonbashi. By 1629, this rudimentary supply line had been expanded into the Kanda Canal, which channelled supplies from Inokashira Pond in present-day Mitaka into the Kanda River, then into a canal cut through the surrounding hillsides. After filling the ponds and streams in the Kōrakuen Garden (constructed by Tokugawa Yorifusa, the 11th son of Tokugawa Ieyasu) over an area of some 70,000 square metres, the canal waters then entered the heart of the city along a wooden aqueduct across the Kanda River.

Altogether, this water system served the eastern sections of Edō, supplying about 25 per cent of the total demand. The extent of the natural river systems and the canals can be interpreted from a map of Edō in 1849 (Reith-Banks, 2019). Transport by a small wood craft (*choki-bune*) propelled by a pole pushing off the canal's bottom became the common means of getting from point to point, with wooden bridges across canals for road transport. Today, visitors to Tōkyō would be largely unaware of the original canal system because they have been filled in to make way for road and rail constructions (Seidensticker, 2019).

The original courses of rivers have changed substantially, especially the Tone River (Sakura, 2014, Figures 2 and 3, pp, 927–928). The Ginza district of Tōkyō provides a good example of how canals have been replaced by more modern transport infrastructure (Tokyo Reporter, 2008). On the first floor of the Shiodome Media Tower, an exhibition of aerial photographs of the area taken from a balloon one century ago were on display. The images show how the roads, bridges and canals in existence from the Edō era have intermingled to produce the contemporary streetscape of Tōkyō (Figure 2).

Figure 2. Major Buildings in Modern Tōkyō Superimposed on the Original Canal System of Ginza, c. 1900 (Scale: from Higashi Ginza Station in the south to Shin-Sukibashi in the north = approximately 1 km).
Source: Tokyo Reporter, 2008.

Lake Biwa Transport and Canals

In the Azuchi-Momoyama period (1568–1600), Toyotomi Hideyoshi, during his land grab to unify Japan, revived an ancient plan to connect Lake Biwa with the Sea of Japan. He ordered the owner of Tsuruga lands, Ōtani Yoshitsugu (1558–1600), to build a canal from Oura on Lake Biwa to Tsuruga located on the Sea of Japan. These works were aborted because of the difficult mountainous terrain. The 12-km long canal is named *taiko no ketsu wari bori* [the taiko's morning sickness canal]. On numerous occasions throughout the Edō period, merchants resurrected the idea of linking Lake Biwa to the Sea of Japan, but all were thwarted by opposition either from the Tokugawa *bakufu*, or from local villages along any proposed route.

Lake Biwa itself was, of course, navigable. The navigation and management of later *maruko* ships, and their design, corresponding to the depths of Lake Biwa, can be determined from ancient documents written and bequeathed to Katayama Minato, Tsukide Minato and Oura Minato who in the Edō period were resident in the former Ika-gun (Lake Biwa). Furthermore "*The Katayama Minato Katayama*" document and the "*Tsukide Minato Takebes*" document describe Lake Biwa water transport during the Edō era. The numbers of the *maruko* ships (*maruko bune*) and the circle ships (*maru bune*) exceeded 1,300 in the golden age of transport on Lake Biwa in the 18th century (Kawanabe et al., 2019).

Lake Biwa water transport in the Edō era was the economic lifeline of the country carrying cargo and passengers from as far away as in the north of Japan to Kyōto and Ōsaka and offering an alternative means of travel on a part of the road journey from Kyōto to Edō. The principal freight was rice that came from regions north of Kyōto along the Sea of Japan coast, overland to the north end of Lake Biwa, then overland again at the south end of the lake to the Yodo River and on to Ōsaka. In a similar fashion, travellers taking the more expensive boat option used Lake Biwa and the Yodo River to avoid parts of the Nakasendō and Tōkaidō highways.

The objective of connecting Lake Biwa with the Sea of Japan at Tsuruga was revived again in the 19th century. At the end of Edō period, Maeda Yoshiyasu, *daimyō* of the Kaga domain (Ishikawa Prefecture), asked the mathematician Ishiguro Nobuyoshi (1760–1836) to survey the area in order to build a more efficient transport system between Kyōto and the Kaga domain. He started from the Tsuruga area and created a highly precise route survey from Tsuruga to Lake Biwa (recent research for the Shinminato Historical Museum by Shimasaki[3] has verified the accuracy of this survey). Ishiguro also measured onwards from Lake Biwa to Ōtsu and made a very rough preliminary plan in 10 days. However, the Tokugawa government was unravelling fast, and the *daimyō* no longer had power of influence on the national government, so Ishiguro Nobuyoshi was not able to continue his survey in that area.

Modern Period

Lake Biwa Canal

In the early Meiji era, Kyōto was having water shortage problems. The city government lobbied the national government to construct a canal (*biwako sosui*) from Lake Biwa to the city (City of Kyoto, n.d.). In 1868, with the transfer of the national capital from Kyōto to Tōkyō, the city witnessed an economic decline. The Prefecture Mayor, Kunimichi Kitagaki (1836–1916), was appointed in 1881 and aspired to inject new life back into the community by commissioning the construction

---

3   Material collected during an interview with Mr Yoshitsu Shimasaki at the Shinminato Museum, Imizu City, Tōyama Prefecture, Japan.

of Lake Biwa Canal for the purposes of town water supply, irrigating surrounding paddy fields, water to fight fires and electrical power generation for cotton spinning.

It is pertinent to note that in a state recently liberated from feudalism and emerging as a modern democratic state the proposed Lake Biwa Canal project was not without its opponents. Many local farmers along the proposed route of the canal were opposed to its construction but the negotiated outcome of the conflict was a promise that the canal would provide irrigated water to the rice paddies in seasons when the rainfall was insufficient for a good rice harvest (Kitagaki, 2010).

The historical significance of this integrated development project is that it was the first project in the Meiji era that did not involve foreign engineers. Minami Ichirobe and Shimada Michio conducted the survey and made the plan based on Western mathematics—although their work was possibly based on Ishiguro's earlier survey because the route is almost the same and the locations of the outlets are exactly as Ishiguro Nobuyoshi had planned. Preparatory work was also undertaken for a transport canal, with Minami Ichirobe (who had been the chief engineer working with the Dutch advisor van Doorn on the construction of the Asaka Canal in Fukushima Prefecture) conducting a preliminary route survey. Shimada Michio made the necessary measurement of the route between Ōtsu on Lake Biwa and Kyōto—a 20-km long canal. The volume of rock estimated in the tunnelling through the mountain at Mount Nagana had been previously calculated in a thesis at Imperial College London—illustrating again the influence of foreign technology in the early Meiji period.

Tanabe Sakuro, a graduate of the School of Engineering, Imperial University of Tōkyō, was engaged by the Kyōto Prefecture as Chief Civil Engineer and started work on the project in May 1883. Permission to begin construction was sought from the national government in May 1884 who gave authorisation in January 1885 but with approval for a more ambitious building plan. Today, this is known in the construction industry as "scope creep" that effectively doubled the initial budget allocation by the local government of 600,000 yen.

The Prefecture Assembly resolved to proceed and financed the revised project by imposing heavier taxes on Kyōto residents. The construction cost estimate was 1,250,000 silver dollars (twice the annual budget of the Prefecture) with one-quarter paid for by a national government grant, one-third paid by the Meiji Emperor and the remainder raised through local taxation (van Gasteren, 2001). The canal was completed by navvy labour (altogether involving 4 million workers) within five years with three tunnels, including the 2,436-metre long tunnel through Mount Nagana that required bricks and timber especially for the purpose, and generated a brickwork factory nearby. An impression of the canal at Ōtsu on Lake Biwa as it looks today is obtained from the photograph in Figure 3.

Figure 3. Photograph of the Lake Biwa Canal at Ōtsu on Lake Biwa, 2018.
Source: Photographs by Author and Dr Masaki Arioka.

The difference in height between Lake Biwa and Kyōto is approximately 73 metres with a mean grade of 1: 0.00037. Its width is from 6 to 10 metres—advantageous to the water transport of goods (primarily rice and cotton) coming from the Lake Biwa hinterland to Kyōto and beyond. The canal stimulated agricultural production around Lake Biwa and the goods transport canal opened up the markets in Kyōto and Ōsaka as the road alternative means of transport was costly on the unsealed Sanjō road that was especially difficult for laden packhorses and porters in the hilly terrain—slippery after rain and impassable after snow. However, the return journey from Kyōto is against the gravity flow of water so the barges had to be poled by boatmen and pulled by assistants using ropes. Traffic is only one-way in the narrow tunnels so that boat ponds were constructed at the tunnel portals to allow boats to pass each other.

When the Kyōto City Council was created in April 1889 it took ownership of the canal on completion exactly one year later in 1890. In June of that year work commenced on the Kamo River canal that would allow goods to be transshipped from the Lake Biwa Canal via the Kamo and Yoda rivers to Ōsaka. In 1891, the first phase of the Keage Power Station was completed with power delivery commencing six months later. At the eastern end of Lake Biwa Canal is an ingenious device that solved the steep gradient problem. A scale working-model of this is on display in the Lake Biwa Canal Museum of Kyōto (http://www.city.kyoto.lg.jp/suido). At either end of the double track incline railway is a metal open carriage that is designed to take the wooden boat. Gravity takes the carriage on wheels downwards pulling the other carriage upwards. The rails extend a short way underwater so effectively the boats float on and off of the carriages.

The economic impact of the multi-functional canal is especially interesting. In fact, by far the greatest income from the canal came from selling electricity to the emerging industrialisation processes in Kyōto: fabrics and silk; tobacco factories; engineering machinery; and electrical goods. The farmers received water for irrigation when they needed it, and the reservoir of water was a source for fire protection given that the buildings in Kyōto were then constructed of timber.

Lake Biwa Canal was a transport artery that brought goods and new wealth to the city and for the waterpower it provided in the stimulation of new industries, such as cotton spinning. The canal facilitated the construction of Japan's first industrial hydro-electric power generation plant using a Pelton waterwheel (a water impulse turbine patented in 1880) and a Stanley generator. The energy generated by the water wheels allowed the spinning of cotton. The Kyōto City Water Department commemorated the 100th Anniversary of the completion of Canal

Number 1 with a three-volume collection in the Lake Biwa Museum that is a rich source of data for further analysis.

In 1923, there was another grand plan to link Ōsaka to Tsuruga via Lake Biwa. As the military influence on the national government of Japan increased, Yoshida Kozaburo, an army captain, proposed the "Great Hanton Canal" linking Ōsaka with Tsuruga (Yoda, 2012: 294). The plan included lowering the level of Lake Biwa by a staggering 43 metres to reduce the number of locks required along the route. This would have reduced the surface area of the lake by about one-half and would have resulted in reclaimed land for cultivation. However, its main policy objective was to allow the movement of 4,000-ton warships and 3,000-ton steamships. Twelve years later, the Chief Engineer of the Lake Biwa Canal expanded on this plan, re-branding it as the Great Lake Biwa Canal that would allow 10,000-ton ships to pass through this proposed waterway complex.

This plan of linking the Setō Inland Sea with the Sea of Japan was aborted with the onset of the Pacific War. In the mid-20th century this planned transport infrastructure was clearly obsolete. It therefore appears somewhat anachronistic that, in 1961, a partnership between a political entrepreneur, Baron Ono Tomochika, and the Mayor of Yokkaichi (a small town in Mie prefecture at the head of Ise Bay on its west bank) came up with a new plan to cut a canal joining Ise Bay with the Sea of Japan. The overall distance was about 130 km with a substantial portion of the route using the current level of Lake Biwa.

Meiji Administration of Rivers and Canals

The Imperial Constitution of 1889 stimulated work on new laws and regulations including the 1896 *River Law* that contained many pre-Meiji practices (Aoyama, 1999: Word of Recommendation). The 1896 *River Act* was one of the earliest comprehensive modern river codes in the world (Infrastructure Development Institute, 1999). Its purpose was water control and thus the law contained only one Article (Number 28) on river transport: that covered prohibitions, restrictions and permission for the navigation of boats/ships and rafts. The national government was the regulatory authority for major rivers and prefectural government the authority for smaller rivers. In essence, the relevant river administrator specifies the maximum dimensions of boats and ships and their draught that are permitted to pass through the various locks on the river system. Various revisions were made during the modern era.

In the same year that the first *River Act* was promulgated, the great flood of 1896 caused serious damage in the Kyōto region, including 111 casualties and 7,885 collapsed houses. Local government initiated a large-scale disaster prevention program, targeting the entire Lake Biwa and the Yodo River Basin. The program comprised of the widening and dredging of the shallow fords of the Seta River, construction of the Nango Araizeki Weir, and improvement works on the lower reaches of the Uji and the Yodo Rivers.

As a result, the Seta River flow capacity increased fourfold. Weir gates were installed to maintain the water level of Lake Biwa and the flow of the Seta River control. The gates, however, were manually operated, requiring one full day to open and two days to close. It is clear that Japanese canals in the modern era were primarily constructed and modified for the purposes of flood mitigation.

Modern Democratic Period

After the end of the Pacific War, Japan underwent substantial social and economic change to the extent that the *River Law* required reform. Japan had constructed some 3,000 dams since this first law. A new *River Act* in 1964 dealt primarily with water control, water rights and allocation, and, in essence, divided rivers into class A (national government management—today, its administration is by the Ministry of Land, Infrastructure, Transport and Tourism) and Class B (prefectural government management). Management of the former involves a wide range of players from government institutions and private organisations, as detailed in the Tone River case study published by the OECD (2015).

Two of the most important flood control activities are the central government's administration of levees and sluice gates (Atsumi, 2009), including the planning and administration of super levees (Hashiguti et al., 2009; Nakamura et al., 2013). When the *River Act* was amended in 1997—where rapid post-war industrialisation had polluted and degraded rivers—it included more emphasis on "environmental conservation".

Recently, the Japan Ministry of Land, Infrastructure, Transport and Tourism (2019: 87) revised the *River Act* to promote a greater involvement of more organisations in civil society to contribute towards river conservation: "river administrators may designate private organizations such as NPOs that conduct activities related to active river maintenance and conservation of the river environment..." The River Cooperative Organization System provides assistance for river management projects. For example, the Ecology Research Club Hiroshima is a river cooperative organisation that conducts activities such as participating in activities to beautify the Ota River, providing hands-on learning for children, training instructors and observing tidal flats at discharge channels (Japan Ministry of Land, Infrastructure, Transport and Tourism, 2019: 88, Figure 3–2–8).

Another example of the involvement of non-government organisations is the promotion of recreational boat cruising for domestic and international tourists. In March 2018, after 67 years, a tourist boat cruise connecting Kyōto with Lake Biwa was revived. Lake Biwa Canal Cruise is available by advance reservation only. A 12-person boat travels down the canal. In 2018, the Canal Cruise operated from 29 March to 28 May and from 6 October to 28 November to capture scenery in the distinctly Japanese 'four seasons' (https://japan-magazine.jnto.go.jp/en/special_keihan04.html).

Conclusions

For reasons of mountainous terrain on Honshū, rivers have played little part in the history of transport in Japan other than where coastal roads required a boat crossing from one bank of the river to the other. Water transport has been related to the constant drive at a local level to improve irrigation systems that have had the co-benefits to water transport rather than the construction of a national network of canals as occurred in many other countries. Over the centuries these rivers in Japan have been modified not for navigation and transport but more for irrigation, flood control and water supply. For example, the course of the Tone River has been artificially changed to prevent flooding of the Edō and Tone canals that were built in more recent years in Saitama, Musashi and Asaka to supply water to Tōkyō. An estuary barrage was constructed to control the salinity of up-stream water (www.water.go.jp).

Japan had no 'canal age' and the story of canals can best be summarised by the author as "the age of aborted canals". The little there was of canal construction in Japan dates from at least the 6th century although there have been numerous plans to cut across the island of Honshū to link the Sea of Japan with the Pacific Ocean via Lake Biwa. Table 8 lists these plans with the proposed routes (that amounts to 24 km of construction), the instigators and the approximate dates of each plan. A sketch map of the routes proposed for the various canal plans that have been summarised in Table 8 can be found in Yoda (2012, Figure 1, p. 294). It should be noted that the sketch map is a little deceptive because it does not show the mountainous terrain that blunted construction between the northern end of Lake from Oura and Shiotsu to Tsuranga. Topography explains why the maximum length of canal construction was only 12 km.

Table 8. Canal Plans to Link the Sea of Japan with the Pacific Ocean via Lake Biwa, Mid 12th to the Mid-20th century.
Source: Author.

Canal Plan	Completed Length km	Instigator	Date
25-km long canal starting from Shiotsu in the north of Lake Biwa towards Tsuruga	12	*Provincial Government—* Taira no Kiyomori, head of a warrior clan in Echizen Province	Mid-12th C
Canal from Oura on Lake Biwa to Tsuruga	12	*Provincial Government—* Toyotomi Hideyoshi ordered the owner of Tsuruga lands, Ōtani Yoshitsugu to build the canal	Late-16th C
Lake Biwa to Tsuruga	0	Kyōto *merchants* lobby Tokugawa *bakufu*	1722
Route survey from Tsuruga to Lake Biwa	0	*Provincial Government—* Maeda Yoshiyasu, *Daimyō* of the Kaga domain	Mid-19th C
Ōsaka to Tsuruga via Lake Biwa	0	Lobbying of National Government by Yoshida Kozaburo, an army captain; Ministry of Construction allocated money for survey	1923

Canal Plan	Completed Length km	Instigator	Date
130 km canal joining Ise Bay with the Sea of Japan	0	Private initiative—Baron Ono Tomochika, businessman, and Mayor of Yokkaichi (*local government*)	1961

From the mid-12th century the key players in these canal proposal and construction attempts have been the war lords controlling the necessary territory, Taira no Kiyomori, Toyotomi Hideyoshi and Maeda Yoshiyasu, merchant associations from Kyōto, military strategist, Yoshida Kozaburo, and a business entrepreneur, Baron Ono Tomochika, together with local government support from the Mayor of Yokkaichi. Table 9 summarises those canals that were constructed in the study area for the purposes of water transport, although the Lake Biwa Canal was built also for irrigation and electricity generation. In the case of the canals built in Ōsaka and Edō they were part of land reclamation on marshy ground to provide access to warehouses and commercial properties. The table lists the names of the key individuals responsible for these initiatives, noting that it was first the merchant class that were responsible for canal building in the Edō period, then the local government of Kyōto in the construction of the Lake Biwa Canal in the late 19th century.

Table 9. Japanese Canal Construction During the Early Modern and Modern Periods—Key Agents.
Source: Author.

Canal Constructed	Date	Key Agents
Ōsaka port and commercial district	Early 17th C	*Merchants*—Doton Nariyasu, Suminokura Ryōi
Kyōto Takase River Canal (9.7 km) from Nijō-Kiyamachi to Fushimi Port,	1611	*Merchants*—Suminokura Ryōi, Chaya Shirōjirō and Gotō Shōzaburō
Edō port and commercial areas around Nihonbashi	Early 17th C	*Shōgun*—Tokugawa Ieyasu
Lake Biwa Canal (20 km)	1885	*Local Government*—Kyōto Prefecture Mayor, Kitagaki Kunimichi

The key players in these successful canal developments came both from the institutions of government and from merchant organisations. In Ōsaka and Kyōto, the prime movers of commercial canal developments were local merchants including Doton Nariyasu, Suminokura Ryōi, Chaya Shirōjirō and Gotō Shōzaburō. The canals that formed the core of 17th century Edō commercial developments on the banks of the Sumida River were under the direction of the *Shōgun* Tokugawa Ieyasu and his successors. The multi-functional Lake Biwa Canal, undertaken in the late 19th century at the initiative of the Kyōto Prefecture Mayor, Kunimichi Kitagaki, and funded by the national and prefecture governments and the Meiji Emperor, represents Japan's best example of a formerly important transport canal—now a tourist attraction.

References

Aoyama, Toshiki (1999) "The River Law with Commentary by Article: Legal Framework for River and Water Management in Japan—A Word of Recommendation". *IDI Water Series No. 4, Supervised by River Bureau, Ministry of Construction, Japan, Compiled and Commented by Toshikatsu Omachi*. Infrastructure Development Institute, Tokyo, n.p., http://www.idi.or.jp/wp/wp-content/uploads/2018/05/RIVERE.pdf

Atsumi, Masahiro (2009) "River Management in Japan—With Focus on River Levee". River Bureau, Ministry of Land, Infrastructure, Transport and Tourism, Japan, powerpoint.

Australia, Bureau of Meteorology (2019) "Japan Japan-10: Shinano-gawa Japan-11: Tone-gawa Japan-12: Yoda-gawa", http://www.bom.gov.au

Barker, T. C., and C. I. Savage (1974) *An Economic History of Transport in Britain*. Hutchinson University Library, London.

City of Kyoto (n.d.) "Japan Heritage—The Lake Biwa Canal", https://biwakososui.city.kyoto.lg.jp/en/story/

Hadfield, C. (1968) *The Canal Age*. David & Charles, Newton Abbot, Devon.

Hashiguti, Yumi, Rika Hirabayashi and Motoya Yamazaki (2009) "High-standard Levee about which it Thinks from Viewpoint of City Planning", *Reports of the City Planning Institute of Japan*, 7, February, 73–76.

Hashizume, Shin'ya (2019) "A History of Osaka, Japan's City of Water", https://www.nippon.com/en/japan-topics/g00681/a-history-of-osaka-japan's-city-of-water.html

Infrastructure Development Institute (1999) "The River Law with Commentary by Article: Legal Framework for River and Water Management in Japan". *IDI*

Water Series No. 4, Supervised by River Bureau, Ministry of Construction, Japan, Compiled and Commented by Toshikatsu Omachi. Infrastructure Development Institute, Bunkyo City, Japan, http://www.idi.or.jp/wp/wp-content/uploads/2018/05/RIVERE.pdf

Japan, Ministry of Land, Infrastructure, Transport and Tourism (2019) *White Paper on Land, Infrastructure, Transport and Tourism in Japan, 2017*. Ministry of Land, Infrastructure, Transport and Tourism, Chiyoda-ku, Tokyo, https://www.mlit.go.jp/common/001269888.pdf

Kato, Shuichi (1997) *A History of Japanese Literature from the Man'yōshū to Modern Times—New Abridged Edition Translated & Edited by Don Sanderson*. Japan Library, Imprint of Curzon Press, Richmond, Surrey.

Kato, Takashi (2000) "Edo in the Seventeenth Century: Aspects of Urban Development in a Segregated Society", *Urban History*, 27 (2), 189–210.

Kawanabe, Hiroya, Machiko Nishino and Masayoshi Maehata (eds) (2012) *Lake Biwa: Interactions between Nature and People*. Springer, Dordtrecht.

Kawanabe, Hiroya, Machiko Nishino and Masayoshi Maehata (eds) (2019) *Lake Biwa: Interactions between Nature and People*. 2nd ed., Springer, Dordtrecht.

Kitagaki, Kunimichi (2010) *Diary of Kitagaki Kunimichi "Jinkai"*. Shibunkaku Shuppan, Tokyo.

Kuroishi, Izumi (2019) "Archaic Water: The Role of a Legend in Constructing the Water Management Heritage of Sanbonkihara, Japan", in C. Hein (ed.) (2019) *Adaptive Strategies for Water Heritage: Past, Present and Future*. Springer Cham, Switzerland, 152–171, https://doi.org/10.1007/978-3-030-00268-8_8

Lake Biwa Comprehensive Preservation Liaison Coordination Council Office/Metropolitan Areas Development Division, City and Regional Development Bureau, Ministry of Land, Infrastructure and Transport (2003) *Lake Biwa Comprehensive Preservation Initiatives—Seeking Harmonious Coexistence with the Lake's Ecosystem*, Ministry of Land, Infrastructure and Transport, Chiyoda-ku, Tokyo.

Naito, Akira, illustrated by Kazuo Hozumi (2003) *Edo, the City That Became Tokyo: An Illustrated History*. Kodansha International, Tokyo.

Nakamura, Hitoshi, Takaaki Kato and Yuto Shiozaki (2013) "Super Levees along the Arakawa River in Tokyo: Evaluation from the Viewpoint of Spatial Planning in a Low-Lying Area", *International Conference on Flood Resilience: Experiences in Europe and Asia, held in Exeter, UK, 5–7 September*, poster paper (one page).

OECD (2015) *Water Resources Allocation: Sharing Risks and Opportunities*. OECD Studies on Water. OECD Publishing, Manila, http://www.oecd.org/japan/Water-Resources-Allocation-Japan.pdf

Osborne, R. (2013) *Iron, Steam and Money: The Making of the Industrial Revolution*. The Bodley Head, London.

Pearson, R. (2016) *Ōsaka Archaeology*. Archaeopress Publishing Ltd., Oxford.

Reith-Banks, T. (2019) "A City Built on Water: The Hidden Rivers under Tokyo's Concrete and Neon", *The Guardian*, 13 June 2019, https://www.theguardian.com/cities/2019/jun/13/a-city-built-on-water-the-hidden-rivers-under-tokyos-concrete-and-neon

Sadler, A. L. (1937) *Shogun: The Life of Tokugawa Ieyasu*. George Allen and Unwin, London. With a new foreword by Stephen Turnbull (1978), published by Tuttle Publishing, London.

Sakura, Kosuke (2014) "The Relationship between Urban Structure and Waterways in Edo, Old Tokyo", in C. Sanchis-Ibor, G. Palau-Salvador, I. Mangue Alférez and L. P. Martínez-Sanmartín (eds) (2014) *Irrigation, Society, Landscape. Tribute to Thomas F. Glick*. Universitat Politècnica de València, València.

Sakuro, Tanabe (1894) "The Lake Biwa-Kioto Canal", *Proceedings of the Institution of Civil Engineers*, 117, 353–359.

Seidensticker, E. (2019) *A History of Tokyo 1867–1989: From EDO to SHOWA—The Emergence of the World's Greatest City*. Tuttle Publishing, Tokyo.

Tabayashi, Akira (1987) "Irrigation Systems in Japan", *Geographical Review of Japan*, 60, Ser. B (1), 41–65.

Tokyo Reporter (2008) "The Canals of Edo", *Tokyo Reporter*, 18 July 2008, https://www.tokyoreporter.com/japan-news/special-reports/the-canals-of-edo/

Uemura, Yoshihiro (2012) "Geomorphology of Lake Biwa and the Surrounding Region", in Hiroya Kawanabe, Machiko Nishino and Masayoshi Maehata (eds) (2012) *Lake Biwa: Interactions between Nature and People*. Springer, Dordtrecht, 3–8.

Van Gasteren, L. A. (2001) "East Meets West: Lake Biwa Canal, Kyoto, Japan". *International Journal on Public Works, Ports and Waterways Development*, 84, 3–7.

Wasan Institute (2000) *Jinkouki*. Wasan Institute, Tokyo.

Willan, T. S. (1936) *River Navigation in England 1600–1750*, Oxford University Press, Oxford.

Yoda, Masaharu (2012) "4.3.2. The Long-Held Idea of a Lake Biwa Canal", in Hiroya Kawanabe, Machiko Nishino and Masayoshi Maehata (eds) (2012) *Lake Biwa: Interactions between Nature and People*. Springer, Dordtrecht, 293–294.

5. Roads

Kono michi ya
Yuku hito nashi ni
Aki no kure[1]

Bashō, 1694, quoted by Bamhill, 2004: 150

Introduction

This chapter describes the institutional arrangements for ancient and modern roads and the organisations that emerged to administer roads and to transport goods around the country. Unless there was river access, the transfer of people and goods to and from the ports into their hinterlands required rudimentary tracks for porters and for horses. As in many countries, documentary evidence on early road administration is sparse but from Chapter 2 it is clear that the local ruling elites directed slaves or coerced peasants into repairing sections of ancient highways or tracks damaged by natural disasters such as earthquakes, typhoons and floods.

The *sengoku-daimyō* made extensive capital works improvements in their domains including road improvements. However, a major obstacle to the development of a modern capitalistic system in Japan was the problem of access to a free, national road network. For example, in the Edō period the *bakufu* administered road policy by regulating barrier stations and post stations and issuing passports to the population of artisans, farmers and merchants. An enduring government policy instrument has been barrier stations (*sekisho*) and a long section describes their policy objectives drawn from the research by Vaporis (1994).

---

1 A haiku of 5-7-5 syllables translates as: "this road—/ with no one on it / autumn dusk"

The subject is covered in the Japanese language by Takebe (2015). Barriers on roads were first established as a government instrument in the Yamato State then expanded into a system of government-controlled barrier stations established after the Taika Reform of 645 that were finally abolished in the 19th century. With the transfer of the capital of the Tokugawa *bakufu* to Edō at the beginning of the 17th century, Tokugawa Ieyasu understood the military objective of gaining greater political control of the country and authorised five designated highways (gokaidō), as part of Tokugawa domains radiating from Edō and a set of interrelated controlling policy instruments that unfolded during the first half a century of Tokugawa rule. The *Shōgunate*-controlled post stations on the gokaidō were an additional means of reinforcing national security as well as providing revenue to the central government.

With the collapse of the Tokugawa government in 1868 the Meiji Restoration saw the importation of western approaches to the administration of public works. With the rise of mechanised vehicle transport for the movement of people and goods, modern road authorities have been established as government institutions by acts of parliament in their respective jurisdictions. For example, in the U.S.A., the aim was to get the farmers out of the mud, and state road authorities were established in Australia from the 1920s onwards.

In the case of Japan, such developments have occurred only in relatively recent times following the Allied bombing of civil and military infrastructure during the Second World War. The postwar reconstruction of the road sector was greatly influenced by the Americans following the adoption of recommendations in the World Bank-sponsored Watkins Report (1952). Today, there is a large, modern bureaucracy within the Ministry of Land, Infrastructure, Transport and Tourism that administers the highway sector of the Japanese economy.

Ancient Roads in Japan

From time immemorial in the Jōmon period, people tramping narrow paths forged local communication networks amongst small tribes. Japanese archeological scholars have traced the diffusion of the later Yayoi paddy culture from the Itazuka region of Kyūshū to Lake Biwa and then to the northeast by an inland route so as to avoid Jōmon coastal settlements. This route was the precursor to the Tōsandō (Barnes, 2019:

35 and Figure 2, p.35) that was to become part of the gokaidō road system in later Edō times.

There is clear reference to roads (or circuits) by the 10th legendary Emperor, Sujin (c. 3–4th century), who sent his son to the twelve circuits to quell rebellions in adjacent kingdoms of the *Emishi* (Ainu), as recorded in the *Kojiki* (Chamberlain, 1981, Vol.23, Section LXVI, p. 216, footnote 2). A "road" had the same sense of a "circuit" or a "province" at that time (Chamberlain, 1981, Vol. 22, section LX, p. 194, footnote 20). These tracks would have been reinforced and widened by horse riders on Imperial business to the provinces and by troop movements. Chapter 3 has also described the diplomatic and economic importance of roads in the hinterland of ports facilitating the movement of taxation goods and enabling pilgrimages to take place to famous shrines and temples.

From at least the 5th century A.D. roads linked settlements, palaces, tombs, craft production areas and ports (Pearson, 2016: 49). Japanese scholars are confident in their speculation that road infrastructure (and, by implication, some embryonic road administration) was established in the Kōfun period (about 300–538 A.D.). For example, archeological excavations in 1983 of the Ōtsu Road built in the late 5th century to link Kōfun burial mounds showed that the road formation was 1.7 metres wide and 0.3 metres deep (Pearson, 2016: 50). The "most imposing of all was the Naniwa Great Road" connecting Shitennōji Temple and Naniwa Palace that had a width of 17 metres with one metre ditches on the side. It was in use by the end of the fourth century A.D. (Pearson, 2016: 50). This suggests the deployment and direction by some authority (*institution*) managing the slave labour that constructed the road.

In what the Japan Heritage Portal Site (2019) claims as the oldest "national highway" in Japan, the "Road of the Sun" was a straight road, over 20 metres wide, connecting Naniwa and Nara. Sections of this east-west road, the Tajihi Kaidō (road) or Take no uchi Kaidō, linked the important burial tombs at Konda Gobyōyama kōfun and at Daisenryō kōfun with the Nara Basin (Pearson, 2016: 50). The road's strategic significance to the development of Japan is that Chinese missionaries arrived in Naniwa and travelled to Asuka along this road introducing Buddhist culture and Chinese technology. These various roads connected the great burial tumuli of the Kinai Region to the East Asian continent through ports in Sakai and Naniwa, facilitating the movement of goods, flows of information, and international exchange. Ong (n.d.) suggests that the Take no uchi Kaidō—a 26-km long highway that linked Sakai with the Nara basin—is "the oldest major road in Japan".

The Taihō Reforms (702 A.D.) introduced national administration—the *Ritsuryō* system—and this formed the basis of an institution responsible for a national highway network, including the planting of road-side trees for shade in summer. The country was divided into seven major regions plus the five 'home provinces' (*Kinai*) that immediately surrounded the capital of Nara (Heijo-kyō was established in 710). Japan was further divided into 58 provinces (*kuni*), each administered from a provincial capital (*kokufu*). The roads (circuits) facilitated good communications and the efficient movement of Imperial troops in times of unrest. Rice tax was gathered in these provincial capitals before shipment by road to the Imperial capital.

Initially, the design of this highway system was a direct copy of the road system in China established during the Chou dynasty (1122–1222 B.C.), and subsequently improved in the Chin dynasty (222–207 B.C.). Chin highways were 50 paces wide, paved or well compacted, and lined with "shade trees" with each tree located at an interval of every 10 metres. Post stations at intervals of every 30 *ri* (approximately every 112 km) provided fresh horses for those travelling on official business. The Taihō Code stipulated similar dimensions for the Japanese highway system, but, given the different mountainous topography, modifications were made with Japanese roads being narrower, and the post stations were placed at an average interval of 5 *ri* (20 km).

The seven "official" highways were ranked according to three grades: the principal highway (San'yodō), where regulations stipulated the availability of 20 horses at each post station; two secondary highways (Tōkaidō and Tōsandō) with post stations that provided 10 horses; and four lesser highways (*shoro*) with post stations providing five horses. Virtually no other services, such as the provision of food and lodging, were available at post stations. The San'yodō was awarded prominence in this road hierarchy because it connected the Kinai region with the port of Dazaifu to the west that was an important provincial capital in northern Kyūshū—a point of arrival for Chinese and Korean emissaries and skilled craft workers at that time.

In addition to supporting the national institutions of the Court and the military or the local government institutions, the other major participants in overland transport were teamsters or carters using either carts (*shariki*) or horses (*bashaku*) that were located in the ports and satellite towns around Kyōto. Merchants also provided services and organised themselves into caravans—typically tens to hundreds of merchants when travelling long distances. Itinerant peddlers (*renjaku*) travelled shorter distances with wares carried on their shoulders.

Medieval Roads in Japan

From the late 12th century, the ancient highways—the coastal Tōkaidō and the Tōsandō (renamed as the Nakasendō), that was a more difficult inland alternative route when lower reaches of rivers flooded on the Tōkaidō—provided the necessary Imperial and military government communication to and from the Emperor's Court in Kyōto and Kamakura—a distance of about 430 km that could be covered by relays of fresh horses in about 76 hours. The Tōkaidō in the 12th century from Kyōto to Kamakura is described by Tyler (2012, Book 10: 6, pp. 537–541) as having one wooden bridge and post station inns along its route.

As Imperial control weakened, especially during the Heian period (as discussed in Chapter 2), control over the roads fell to local interests, and travel became even more difficult. Roads and barriers (*sekisho*) were either under the control of the propriety lords (*ryoshū*) of *shōen* estates, or, under the control of the regional warlords (in essence, the institution of local government). Some warlords reintroduced the ancient practice of planting shade trees. There was little incentive to improve road communication in Japan because of the medieval structure of largely self-sufficient domains. The institution of barriers, that endured to the modern period, are described next.

The Institution of Barriers (*sekisho*)

Reference has already been made to the role of barriers (*sekisho*) but their enduring nature from ancient times until 1868 requires careful exposition. The institution of *sekisho* was first established as a government instrument in the Yamato State. Toll barriers failed to discourage trade either because of the corruption of local officials responsible for their operation or because the barriers were circumvented by alternative routes. Nevertheless, the government installations (*sekisho*) at strategic points along traffic routes, where travellers were stopped for inspection, were one unique, and enduring policy (apart from a brief lapse) in Japan lasting from the 7th century to the mid-19th century.

Importantly, for later policy developments in the road sector, was this system of government barrier stations for defence purposes established after the Taika Reform of 645 (Kodansha, 1993: 1496–1497). The so-called *sankan* (three barriers) were located at Suzuka (now Mie Prefecture), Fuwa (Gifu Prefecture) and Arachi (Fukui Prefecture) were regarded as of special importance being on strategic routes in case of state dissidents or incursions from the *ara-emishi* (wild-emishi[2]) from the north eastern provinces of Mutsu and Dewa. Since the 7th century, frequent uprisings by the indigenous *Emishi*, who were enemies of the Yamato State, were a constant source of irritation: state control of the frontier remained tenuous (Matsuda, 2019). Another example of the strategic military value of barrier stations is the barrier station at Fuwa (Sekigahara) that was erected in 673 following the Jinshin Rebellion[3] and the Battle at Seta Bridge a year earlier (Kodansha, 1993: 685).

During the mid-Heian period (794–1185), by when the *Emishi* had been pushed further north-east onto the island of Hokkaidō, government *sekisho* fell into disuse. In their place, propriety lords (*ryoshū*) of the *shōen* estates established their own private barrier stations that levied tolls (*sekisen*) in one form or another. Under the *shōen* system of a self-sufficient economy the *ryoshū* controlled the manufacture of luxury and special products, the construction and service trades and the exchange of goods. Goods were as yet not freely produced for a general market nor freely traded for commercial profit. By the end of the Heian period, institutions of government and of religion had erected barriers. The Imperial government levied tolls on travellers and commerce to compensate from the reduction of income as tax-free estates (*shōen*)

---

2   A stanza by Kūkai (Matsuda, 2019: 27), written around 815 A.D., describes the conflicts between the aboriginal *Emishi* and Japanese colonists:

   "They are like the man-eating Raksasa devils, they are not human
      They frequently come to our settlements,
      Where countless people and oxen are massacred and eaten
      Their galloping horses and brandished swords are
      like flashes of lightening"

3   Following the death of Emperor Tenji (626–672) there was a war of succession where Prince Ōama, Tenji's younger brother, supported by local rulers who resented the Taika Reforms of 645, defeated the nominated heir, Prince Ōtomo.

spread across the country. Likewise, local military powers (*jitō*) and religious organisations erected barriers on their estates to raise revenues.

Barrier stations proliferated during the Kamakura and Muromachi periods. For example, the Ashikaga family were intimately involved both in the development of a commercial economy and in the patronage of new commercial and service groups. The economy was then fundamentally transformed during the Muromachi period because of the *ryoshū* control over the *shōen* estates weakened and because of the new demands placed upon the economy by the military aristocracy in the provinces. Commerce developed as a separate activity within the national economy. In turn, the Muromachi *bakufu* become more and more dependent on the services of commercial tax contractors. Most trading and artisan activities moved into the intermediate status of guilds and monopoly *organisations* (*za*) that depended either for protection on the aristocracy or on support from powerful religious institutions. Nevertheless, the continued existence of commercial tolls and barriers meant that trade remained highly regulated.

During the Warring State period (1477–1567) the military function of the barrier re-emerged. Most *daimyō* were preoccupied by erecting barriers (*bansho*) to defend the borders of their domains—even during the period of national unification (1568–1600). Warlords constructed armed outposts with high walls and deep moats on sites that offered natural defences, or structures on strategic mountain passes. Striving for the unification of the country, both Oda Nobunaga and Toyotomi Hideyoshi endeavoured to promote economic growth and to assert their political power authority over territories by pulling down these barriers to free trade.

The full story of barrier stations—"a curious institution"—is thoroughly documented by Vaporis (1994, Chapter 3: 99–133) and only the salient points of this complex policy instrument, vigorously implemented by the Tokugawa *bakufu* from the early 17th century, are summarised here.

> The creation of a sekisho network must be seen as the act of a nascent political power to establish and extend its authority over the other daimyo and over a society that had been experiencing tremendous upheaval... The bakufu gave and took land at will, built up and maintained military superiority over its likely opponents, prohibited the construction of new castles and required authorisation for the repair of old ones. It also maintained a system of direct surveillance of the domains through

centrally appointed inspectors, assumed direct control of key commercial cities, and supervised both domestic and foreign trade (Vaporis, 1994: 101–102).

The mature network of Tokugawa *sekisho* consisted of 53 barriers in 9 provinces of which 24 were classified by the *bakufu* government as *ōmaki* (very important). The distribution of barriers (see Vaporis, 1994, Map 2 and legend, pp. 106–107) reflects the political concerns of the Tokugawa *bakufu* attentive to the potential military threat of the *daimyō* in the north and northwest of Honshū.

The physical size of the barrier was in proportion to its strategic military importance with one or two simple buildings each with a number of rooms serving various functions (Vaporis, 1994: 112–114). For example, at Hakone, and its five branch stations, there were in total 51 guards (in 1688) comprising of head guards (*banshi*), who inspected the surrounding areas, regular guards (*joban*), who inspected authorised travel permits (see next section), foot soldiers (*ashigaru*) and attendants (*chūgen*). The arsenal at Hakone contained 10 *teppo* (matchlock guns modelled on those brought to Japan by the Portuguese in the mid-16th century), five Japanese native long bows made of bamboo, 15 long-handled spears and halberd and 12 staves (Vaporis, 1994: Table 6: 117). Several barrier stations employed a peasant reserve (*go ashigaru*) where the government used commoners as "an apparatus of the state" (Vaporis, 1994: 118).

Today, travellers in Japan can see what Lord Redesdale called a "curious institution" at the Hakone barrier station (Redesdale, 1915: 406; Vaporis, 1994: 99). A restoration of this strategically located *sekisho* on the Tōkaidō between Lake Ashi and an adjacent mountain range may be inspected today (The Association for Japanese History and Travel, n.d.; and AllAboutJapan, 2017). In addition, Vaporis (1994: 112) describes these structures and provides a diagrammatic plan of their layout (Vaporis, 1994: Table 4, p. 113) that housed 22 guards (in 1688). In addition, the British painter Nigel Caple travelled along the Tōkaidō Road between 1998 and 2000 and made artistic drawings of the fifty-five barrier stations (*sekisho*).

Roads in the Early Modern Period

Edō Roads

In Japan, a national approach to administering a road network emerged again from the middle of the 17th century. Although it took more than half a century before the Tokugawa *bakufu* formally introduced road administration it was essentially the vision of one man—Tokugawa Ieyasu as the 'policy entrepreneur'—who reinforced the strategic importance of the road sector as an attempt to secure peace and to control society's spatial mobility. In 1603, when the court appointed Tokugawa Ieyasu as *seii taishōgun* ("Barbarian-Subduing Generalissimo") he established the Edō *Shōgunate*, and created a "centralised Feudalism" (Vaporis, 1994: 32) where previous territorial tensions were balanced between the national government and the regional *daimyōs*. Parochialism was superseded by an embryonic national economy that emerged during the Edō period.

The facilitation of economic progress owed much to a national network of roads (and also to coastal shipping). There was a strategic requirement to gain greater political control of the country. The *bakufu* promptly embarked on the construction of a nationwide transport system, including a highway network, secure barrier stations and post station towns that supplied lodgings, labour and horses. The government authorised five designated highways radiating from Edō and set up barriers at strategic points to regulate the movement of people across the country through the issue of travel permits. Four major thoroughfares radiated from Nihonbashi (now the symbolic centre of Japan) and a fifth branched off from one of the four (for a map, see https://en.wikipedia.org/wiki/Tōkaidō_(road)#/media/File:JP_-Gokaido.png).

For the most part, these roads passed through domains held by the *fudai daimyō*, the hereditary vassals of the Tokugawa family, thus ensuring safe communications for government officials across the country. Eight branch roads were also part of the national road system (Vaporis, 1994, Map 1, p. 20). Typically, road widths varied from 5.5 metres to 7.3 metres (Vaporis, 1994: 36).

Table 10 summarises the important characteristics of the gokaidō that largely conformed to the natural contours of the land and required numerous river crossings by boat and, in the case of the Tōkaidō, an open sea-crossing between Miya and Kuwana. The table also gives the number of post stations along each route. The Kōshu dochū's main function was an escape route for Tokugawa forces from Edō. A retreating party could pick up the road at the Hanzomon of Edō Castle and be protected by a 100-man musket unit stationed on the western outskirts of the city at Naitō Shinjuku (a post station town). Further west at Hachioji, a 1,000-man samurai unit was strategically located to cover the escape route. *Fudai daimyō* controlled the castle town of Kōfu and this provided even more protection. Here, the escaping party could continue northwards to the Nakasendō or to travel by boat down the Fuji River to a *bakufu*-controlled stronghold on the Tōkaidō, Sumpu (Shizuoka), where Tokugawa Ieyasu had ordered the construction of a three-moated castle in 1607.

Table 10. Strategic Importance of the Tokugawa Shōgunate Gokaidō System of Roads.
Source: based on Vaporis, 1994: Table 1, p. 23 and pp. 32–34.

Road	Length (km)	Stations (no.)	Strategic Importance
Tōkaidō	539	57	Coastal link to commercial centre of Ōsaka after Tokugawa military power increased with the fall of Osaka Castle in 1615
Nakasendō	527	67	Links to Imperial Court at Kyōto as the alternative inland route although mountainous had cheaper transport-related services
Kōshu dochū	211	45	Connects with the Nakasendō at Shimo-suwa where the entire road was lined by *fudai daimyō* estates (with standing armies) and provided escape route for *Shōgunate* if attacked in Edō; also, of great economic value providing access to gold on Takeda family domains
Nikkō dochū	145	21	A direct line of communication to counter any attacks by any north eastern *daimyō*
Ōshū dochū	396	10	Branches off the Nikkō dochū at Utsunomiya towards Shirakawa—a *fudai* castle town designed to repel any attacks by the north eastern *daimyō*

Another example of the internal control of movements by the *bakufu* is the shallow ford of the Seta River regarded as a strategic point for transporting an army across this river. The government was naturally reluctant to dredge the riverbed despite its obvious commercial advantages for river trade between Ōsaka and its hinterland. The Tokugawa *Shōgunate* government formally allowed dredging only five times in 200 years. As with any edict there were cases of law breakers: the farmers around the lake (a loose coalition of interests) occasionally dredged the riverbed themselves, pretending that they were collecting clams. This opened up a narrow channel and faster water flow for small boats to ply the river thus facilitating the movement of rice harvests and goods by water.

Edō Period Road Maps

Considerable details on roads are contained in documents and woodblock prints that have survived together with guidebooks, maps, and other travel-related materials published during the Edō period. An atlas of the Tokaidō highway between Edō and Ōsaka, compiled by Ochikochi Dōin and illustrated by the famous *ukiyo-e* artist, Hishikawa Moronobu (1618–1694), was first printed in 1690. It was published as a set of five volumes that form a route map of the highway. The atlas is in the album format; this consists of a number of narrow sheets carefully pasted together to form a continuous sheet that can be laid flat or open at any section.

Another important publication from 1810 is the *ryokō yōjin shu* (*Travel Precautions*). This shows the highway system (including point-to-point distances) and the locations of barrier stations, rivers, mountains, famous places, hot springs and temples that issued amulets. The book offered descriptions of travel equipment and medical remedies for sea sickness, falling off a horse and poisonous insect bites. Other publications included picture books such as Utagawa Hiroshige's woodblock print compilation *Tokaidō gojusan tsugi* (*Fifty-three Stations of the Tokaidō*); and publications that introduced specific places, such as *Tokaidō meisho zue* (*Pictures of Famous Places along the Tokaidō*), *Edō meisho zue* (*Pictures of Famous Places in Edō*) and *Dochū sugoroku* (a board game with a picture map).

Road-Related Policies During the Edō Period

In 1601, Tokugawa Ieyasu dispatched Okubo Nagayasu (1545–1613)—a Senior Councillor in the *bakufu* and Hikosaka Motomosa—the Chief Intendant—to survey the Tōkaidō, including the facilities and services offered at each post station. Based on this investigation, designated post stations on the Tōkaidō were granted official status by *the bakufu* with a policy directive to maintain 36 horses at each post station. Within a few years this decree was extended to post stations on all gokaidō roads. In 1637, a decree was applied to a limited number of post stations on the Tōkaidō and Nakasendō for the requisition of "assisting horses" (*sukeuma*) from nearby villages.

This facilitated the speediest of communication of state business with the Emperor's court in Kyōto. A system of a relay of horse riders (*roppara hikyaku*), first established when the *Shōgunate* was based in Kamakura, allowed the journey to be completed in 72 hours (Moriya, 1990). During the Edō period the number of courier services (*hikyaku*) proliferated, such as the *tsugi-bikyaku*—only available high-ranking *bakufu* officials— the *hikyaku tonya*—commercial message-carrying services available to everyone else—and the *tōshi-bikyaku*—a single runner, without relay, who carried a message or parcel from the sender to the addressee. Each *daimyō* established his own communication network with couriers (*daimyō-bikyaku*) taking messages between the domain and the *daimyō* residence in Edo and their rice warehouses in port towns.

Subsequent policy initiatives and directives in the Edō era are summarised in Tables 11 to 14. In 1612, road maintenance on the gokaidō was sheeted home as a local government (*han*) responsibility. Four years later, in order to keep road surfaces in good shape, a load limit for horses transporting goods was imposed at 40 *kan* (150 kg)—a figure that remained constant during the Tokugawa era. Major policy directives on maintaining control of movements are associated with the third *Shōgun*, Tokugawa Iemitsu (1604–1651). In 1625, the government issued an edict on instructions as to how travellers passing through *sekisho* barriers should behave and what information must be presented. Ten years later, the enactment of the Laws of the Warrior Houses prohibited *sekisho* being erected on *daimyō* domains.

Table 11. Summary of Road Policies and Regulations, 1601–1661.
Source: Based in Vaporis, 1994: 17–174, and Notes pp. 269–331; and on Kodansha, 1993: 1577.

Year	Shōgun	Policy Initiative/Regulation
1601	Tokugawa Ieyasu	Dispatched Okubo Nagayasu (Senior Councillor) and Hikosaka Motomosa (Chief Intendant) to grant official status in designated post stations on the Tōkaidō with requirements to maintain 36 horses at each post station (within a few years decree extended to all roads on the gokaidō)
1612	Tokugawa Ieyasu	Directive to *bakufu* intendants: 1. Maintenance of road surface and digging of drainage ditches by sides of the road; 2. No removal of grass on road embankments; 3. Repair of all bridges—large or small by authority of intendant. Directive to *bakuhan*: allocation of corvée extracted from villages along the road to repair and clean assigned sections of the road.
1616	Tokugawa Ieyasu	Regulations Concerning Ferry Crossings (*fune watashi sadame*) primarily to enforce designated crossing points. Load limit for horses transporting goods fixed at 40 *kan* (150 kg)—a figure that remained constant during Tokugawa era.
1625	Tokugawa Iemitsu	Edict on instructions to travellers passing through *sekisho* barriers
1635	Tokugawa Iemitsu	Laws of the Warrior Houses prohibited *sekisho* being erected on *daimyō* domains bur circumvented by erection of *bansho* barriers[#]
1637	Tokugawa Iemitsu	Decree for a limited number of post stations on the Tōkaidō and Nakasendō that "assisting horses" (*sukeuma*) be requisitioned from nearby villages
1659	Tokugawa Ietsuna	Magistrate of Road Affairs (*dochū bugyō*)—overseeing of the upkeep of road infrastructure and processing of petitions; communication policy with *bakufu* intendants (*daikan*) who reported on all matters pertinent to roads under their jurisdiction. *Bakufu* officials periodically checked to ensure approved road and bridge maintenance had been completed satisfactorily to orders. Apart from a few large bridges repaired at *bakufu* expense, most others were maintained as a cost to the local communities.

Year	Shōgun	Policy Initiative/Regulation
1661	Tokugawa Ietsuna##	Standardisation of travel permits (*sekisho tegata* or *kitte*) that had existed from the 1620s and specified personal details on females when applying for a permit

\# For example, Tosa had 86 *bansho* in the 1780s of which 62 (*sakaime bansho*) were located on its borders with Sanuki, Awa and Iyo provinces (Vaporis, 1994: 129). Early in the Tokugawa era their purposes were military defence guarding potentially hostile borders and to apprehend criminals, but as peace and stability was established their prime purpose was to control (and tax) commodity flows and to prevent peasants running away.

\#\# Vaporis (1994: Table 7, p. 140) lists the 22 issuing authorities for each province, or region, for female travel permits for passage through *bakufu sekisho*.

In 1659, a major reform to the road sector is associated with the fourth *Shōgun*, Tokugawa Iesuna (1641–1680). The position of Magistrate of Road Affairs (*dōchū bugyō*) was created to oversee the upkeep of roads. This involved the processing of petitions about issues on the state of roads, barriers and post stations and on communication policy with *bakufu* intendants (*daikan*) who reported on all matters under their jurisdiction. *Bakufu* officials periodically checked to ensure approved road and bridge maintenance had been completed satisfactorily to orders. In 1661, there was a standardisation of travel permits (*sekisho tegata* or *kitte*) that had existed from the 1620s and the permit contained specified personal details on females when they made an application (Table 12).

Table 12. Summary of Road Policies and Regulations, 1687–1720.
Source: Based in Vaporis, 1994: 17–174 and Notes pp. 269–331; and on Kodansha, 1993: 1577.

Year	Shōgun	Policy Initiative/Regulation
1687	Tokugawa Tsunayoshi	Legal documents recognise the names on the gokaidō
Late 17th C	Tokugawa Tsunayoshi	Magistrate of Finance (*kanjo bugyō*)—previously involved with administration of *bakufu* lands that included the gokaidō and all roads not administered by the Magistrate of Road Affairs—joint administration with Magistrate of Road Affairs

Year	Shōgun	Policy Initiative/Regulation
1694	Tokugawa Tsunayoshi	Genroku Reforms with universal *sukego* taxation administered by Magistrate of Road Affairs; post stations were ordered to provide a specified number of porters and horses from designated assisting villages (*josukego*—regular assisting villages; *osukego*—auxiliary villages)
1697	Tokugawa Tsunayoshi	Decree that "assisting horses" (*sukeuma*) be requisitioned from nearby villages to a post station
1712	Tokugawa Ienobu	Shotoku no Chi conservative fiscal policy—Five weigh stations on Tōkaidō and Nakasendō (additional weigh stations on Nikkō dochū, Koshu dōchu and Hokkoku established in 1743—to enforce regulations regarding load limits by appointing Weight Verification Officers (*kanme aratamesho shutsuyaku*)
1720s	Tokugawa Yoshimune	Centralisation of administration with all intendants under the responsibility of the Magistrate of Road Affairs who was assisted by auxiliary officers (*doshin* and *yoriki*) and creation of new categories of villages to support post stations

From the late 17th century onwards, institutional arrangements changed with a joint administration involving the Magistrate of Road Affairs and the Magistrate of Finance. The Genroku Reforms of 1684 ensured that the *sukego* taxation was administered by the Magistrate of Road Affairs. In the 18th century, weigh stations were introduced to regulate loads carried on major roads. In 1720, there was a centralisation of road administration with all intendants under the responsibility of the Magistrate of Road Affairs, who was assisted by auxiliary officers.

In practice, during the first six decades of the Edō period, there were widespread discrepancies until a notice issued in 1821 by the Magistrate of Road Affairs reproached post stations for such breaches in regulations, such as non-compliance in the number of horses and porters. *Bakufu* officials periodically checked to ensure approved road and bridge maintenance had been completed satisfactorily to orders by the local governments. Apart from a few large bridges (across the Yahagi, Yoshida and Seta rivers), repaired at *bakufu* expense, most others were maintained at a cost to the local communities.

From the early 19th century, many of the travel restrictions were eased and actions by government made road transport more enjoyable. Maps were produced and sold to travellers using the gokaidō (Table 13). The roadside environment was improved through horticultural measures such as tree planting. By mid-century, man-powered carts were allowed between sections of the Nakasendō. In 1862, The free use of wheeled vehicles and small carts on all roads was legal. With the restoration of the Meiji Emperor in 1868, both post stations and *sukego* fees were abolished.

Table 13. Summary of Road Policies and Regulations, 1800–1868.
Source: Based in Vaporis, 1994: 17–174 and Notes pp. 269–331; and on Kodansha, 1993: 1577.

Year	Shōgun	Policy Initiative/Regulation
1803	Tokugawa Ienari	Survey of gokaidō for the purpose of making road maps.
		Magistrate of Road Affairs orders replanting of old or dying road-side trees with seedlings and removing roots and vines from roadway.
Early 19th C	Private initiatives	Introduction of alms huts (*segyo-sho*) on difficult stretches of road
1849	Tokugawa Government	Man-powered carts (*ita guruma*) allowed between Tarui and Imasu on Nakasendō but size and number were regulated. By 1860 there were about 3,500 carts.
1862	Tokugawa Yoshiyori	Free use of wheeled vehicles and small carts on all roads
1868	Meiji government	Abolition of post stations and *sukego* systems

Institution of Edō Post Stations

The Tōkaidō had 53 post stations between Edō and Kyōto: a metaphor for the pilgrimage journey that the Indian Buddhist acolyte Sudhana took on his quest for enlightenment and studies under 53 guidance of "good friends" who directed him towards the Way to Enlightenment. Today, any traveller in Japan can gain an appreciation of the streetscapes of the Edō period and buildings in post stations because the Japanese government has provided financial aid for the preservation and maintenance of *koedō*—a designated "town retaining old townscapes with the feeling of Edo" (Sato *et al.*, 2011).

The Preservation Districts for Groups of Traditional Buildings system is designated by any municipality based on the national Law for the Protection of Cultural Properties (implemented in 1975). Similarly, the Ministry of Land, Infrastructure, Transport and Tourism established the Historical Street Projects in 1982 with subsidies to maintain districts and roads as urban planning projects in designated areas where distinct historical townscapes and sites remain. The broad aims of these policies are to increase tourism and generate money for the local economy.

One good example of such a town is Kawagoe City, located about 30 km north-west of central Tōkyō, with its development of a *kurazukuri* (traditional storehouse) street landscape. Soon after the Great Fire of Kawagoe in 1893 merchants paid for the construction of storehouses with thick, fire-resistant clay mortar walls, and historical street landscapes gradually were created. In the Taishō period (1912–1926), many western-style buildings for merchant houses and banks were developed to create a street landscape in which *kurazukuri* buildings are in harmony with western-style buildings. In 1990, Kawagoe City began its historical district environment development project. Its historical townscape (Ichibangai-dōri, Kanetsuki-dōri, Kyushigimachi-dōri, Kashiya-yokochō) was designated in 1999 as an "Important Preservation District for Groups of Traditional Buildings".

Post stations were a Tokugawa government business monopoly where their operating costs were borne by the *han* provincial government and the taxation income provided an important source of revenue to the Tokugawa coffers. Post stations were officially designated so as to limit their proliferation. Most post station managers were of warrior lineage and were often heads of villages and/or operators of the *honjin* inns that were reserved for travellers on official government business. *Honjin* inns were the largest and the most impressive building in the post station (Vaporis, 1994: footnote 14, p. 273). Stipends to post station managers, and to the messenger relay service, were paid by local intendants out of local taxation rice.

Tokugawa government-sanctioned post stations on major highways provided refreshments, lodgings for different classes of traveller, food and other places a traveller may visit. Regulations issued in 1637, and again in 1694 (*sukegō*), specified the number of horses and porters to be provided at each post station. For example, at the Oiwake post station (at the intersection of the Nakasendō and the Hokkoku-Kaidō, today Karuizawa) the annual number of porters and horses used for official transport in 1702 were 2,310 and 4,335, respectively, rising to 14,741 and 18,197 in 1830 before reaching a peak in 1858 of 19,648 porters and 17,324 horses (Vaporis, 1994, Table 3, p. 73).

After the early 1640s, regulations fixed the resources of the post stations so that no expansion of the system was possible, and, indeed, some post stations failed to provide the stipulated number of horses and porters. Instead, *sukegō* levies involved "assisting villages" who provided additional post station horses and porters during times of high traffic demand[4] and this caused contention and confrontation that was resolved by the Magistrate of Road Affairs (Vaporis, 1994: 82–97).

Post towns had inns and taverns well-staffed with *meishimori*, the rice serving waitresses allotted to individual male customers. After bathing the customer on arrival, *meishimori* served food, enjoyed banter over dinner then offered sex for a fee (Bornoff, 1991: 149). Inns at the relaying post stations had become indistinguishable from houses of prostitution. For example, at Shinagawa post station in 1844 the regulations permitted five hundred prostitutes, but eye-witness accounts suggest that there were almost three times that number of women offering sexual services (Vaporis, 1994: 81). During the Edō era, there were short periods when the Tokugawa government outlawed prostitution on moral grounds, but it was difficult to enforce, and, importantly, was a source of revenue to the government so regulations became lax. The *bakufu* taxed prostitutes' incomes: in the mid-19th century, this taxation amounted to about 7 per cent of the post station incomes along the Tōkaidō (Vaporis, 1994: 81).

Whilst such services at the government-sanctioned post stations represented the emergence of a service economy under a national government monopoly, there was one organisation that did attempt to control the moral behaviour of those lodging in post stations. An organisation called *Naniwa Kō* established a chain of inns with a brand

---

4   The contribution from assisting villages for horses and porters increased from about 3 per cent and 31 per cent, respectively, in 1819 to about 18 per cent and 83 per cent in 1861 using the post station of Shinagawa as an example (Vaporis, 1994: 83).

advertising that its member inns did not provide prostitutes so as to ensure "tired travellers got a good night sleep" (Sheldon, 1958: footnote 50, p. 15).

Constraints on Travel

The most restrictive policy involving the road system on the movement of *daimyō* and samurai was the *sankin-tōkai* (alternate year attendance system)—introduced in 1635 as part of the Law of Warrior Houses reform that required the *tozama* ("outside" *daimyō*) and their household retainers (typically 150 to 300 people) to spend an equal time in Edō and in their domains (Vaporis, 1997). Female members of a *daimyō* family were kept hostage in Edō. Thus, the lords had to maintain two households and this expenditure amounted to 70–80 per cent of their income (Kodansha, 1993: 1311). The designated route from the domain followed a road on the gosendō and the overnight stays of a large number of retainers at the post stations were an additional expense, and a source of revenue to the *bakufu*.

In order to control the movement of peasants, the Tokugawa *bakufu* issued strict regulations and implemented the issue of travel permits in association with the regional *daimyōs* (provincial government) that had to be shown at the toll barriers. The provincial *daimyōs* also had an economic reason to impose travel restrictions on their peasants: absenteeism, especially during the harvest season. It meant a loss of productivity and hence income to the *daimyōs*. Even when travel was permitted transport services were in short supply and it was expensive.

The *bakufu* could have generated more income by raising transport fees, but it remained unwilling to close the gap between the fixed rates that remained below the negotiated rates at market value. As of 1711, fees became the base rate and subsequent government directives were expressed as a percentage increase. Derived from data in Vaporis (1994, Table 4, p. 82), Table 14 shows the indicative changes in transport costs in *mon* during the Edō period for the hire of one horse, for one porter and for a light load for a pack horse (either for a rider with up to 20 kilos luggage, or, for 71 kilos of luggage without a rider). Hire of a horse was twice as expensive as the hire of a porter.

Table 14. Indicative Costs (in *mon**) of Transport From 1606 to 1868—The Oikawa Post Station.
Source: based on Vaporis, 1994, Table 4, p. 82; and author's calculation.

Year	One Horse	One Porter	Light Load
1606	42	N/a	N/a
1643	32	16	23
1666	38	19	24
1681	55	N/a	N/a
1690	41	21	27
1711	49	25	32
1815	71	36	46
1863	100	49	62
1868	379	191	248

*—Inflated to 2020 prices, the value of 1 *mon* in 1868 was approximately 0.0000048 cents

Coins denominated in *mon* were cast in copper or iron and circulated alongside silver and gold ingots (with denominations of 4,000 *mon* = 16 *shu* = 4 *bu* = 1 *ryō*). The financial system in early-modern Japan is known as *sanka seido* (the triple standard system) where different types of coin of varying quality were in circulation along with gold, silver and paper money (Ohkura and Shimbo, 1978; Tagaki, 2018). With the *New Currency Act* of 1871, the official rate in Japan was expressed as 1 yen equalling 10,000 *mon*. On international markets, the yen was valued at U.S. $0.048 (0.97 cents in 2020 prices).

Samurai travelled on horseback. Members of the upper classes travelled by a covered palanquin (*kago*) suspended from a long pole that was carried on two men's shoulders. The standard method of travel for peasants was on foot, as wheeled carts were almost non-existent. Women were forbidden to travel alone: men had to accompany them. Other restrictions were also put in place for travellers, but, whilst severe penalties existed for violating various travel regulations, and many women disguised themselves as men, *bakufu* enforcement remained haphazard. Gradually, transport services developed with increased personal safety for walkers, and the adoption, even by commoners, of palanquins and rental horses.

Coastal shipping, rivers and canals were the main means to transport heavy cargoes as road haulage was far too expensive. Some commodities, such as woven silk and sake, could be transported easily in a cart. However, most crops, such as taxation rice, were harvested in such great volumes that a caravan of packhorses or carts across the rough and dangerous roads was impractical.

Pilgrimages

The only feasible way for ordinary people to travel was for them to obtain a travel permit and to go on a pilgrimage. Pilgrimages to famous temples and shrines have a long history in Japan. Of the countless temples and shrines scattered throughout the country, Ise (Mie Prefecture), with its inner shrine (constructed in the 3rd century) and its outer shrine (constructed in the 5th century) has been a premier pilgrimage destination from the 10th century onwards. Ise Shrine is mentioned in the Man'yoshu, an 8th century anthology of poems. The shrine is etched into the Japanese psyche because, according to legend, the daughter of the Suinin (the 11th legendary Emperor), Princess Yamatohime, searched throughout Japan for a site to house the sacred mirror (*yata no kagagami*) until the voice of the spirit Amaterasu Ōmikami instructed her to locate the shrine at Ise.

During the 15th century, and in what may be classed as advertising by a religious institution, lower ranking clerics of Ise Shrine (*ōshi*— literally, master) went around provinces proselytising, collecting funds, and emphasising that seven pilgrimages to Ise Shrine guaranteed eternal salvation (Kodansha, 1993: 628). In the Muromachi period, an organisation of special guides (*sendatusu*) began leading masses of pilgrims to Ise, resulting in lodgings springing up along the roads to the shrine.

However, it was only during the Edō period that mass tourism exploded as a social phenomenon. The desire to make a pilgrimage to Ise Shrine, at least once in a lifetime, was universal amongst Japanese men of the day. Upon returning home from their long trip, the pilgrims passed out souvenirs to their fellow villagers, and, no doubt, bragged about the things they had seen and heard on the journey. By the early 19th century, nearly every village in Japan had confraternities that annually sent pilgrims to Ise. Separate associations were organised for each of the most popular deities, such as Jizō (a bodhisattva known as the saviour of children), Fudō Myōō (an incarnation of Buddha tasked with saving those resistant to Buddhist teachings) and Inari (a fox deity associated with the harvest). In addition, private businesses were established that specialised in helping pilgrims find lodging throughout Japan.

Inns that took in commoners sprouted up. At Ise, people engaged in this business were known as *onshi*. The meals served to the guests at *onshi* houses were lavish and were washed down with high-quality sake. They provided lodgings, hosted pilgrims at prayers, conducted ceremonies and played Shintō music and organised dancing. After paying their respects at Ise Shrine, pilgrims headed off to the pleasure quarters of the Furuichi district, where banquets known as *shojin otoshi* were held for them. Afterwards, for a fee, the pilgrims were entertained with singing, dancing and prostitutes. According to Susuki (n.d.: n.p.) "this blend of spirituality and entertainment, of the sacred and the worldly, was a defining feature of travel in the Edo period."

Private enterprise soon exploited the business opportunities from pilgrims (Suzuki, n.d.). Located on the road that ran between the Inner Shrine and Outer Shrine areas, the village of Furuichi grew mainly as a result of the demand from pilgrims for places to eat meat following long periods of abstinence, to drink and to stay the night. Beginning in the early decades of the Edō period, there developed a small *yūkaku* (red light district), consisting of six teahouses, which grew larger and more prominent over the course of the Edō period. By the Hōei era (1704–1711), there were 162 courtesans and 60 teahouses. This grew to 70 prominent teahouses and 1,000 courtesans, and three or four playhouses, by the Kansei era (1789–1801).

Data compiled by Suzuki (n.d.) suggests Ise Shrine drew on average from 200,000 to 400,000 pilgrims annually, each staying 4–5 days, with that pilgrimage total reaching about a million in some years. Mass pilgrimages by men and women of all ages occurred in Japan roughly once every sixty years and were usually triggered by news of miraculous events such as "amulets falling from the sky" (Suzuki, n.d.). Participants received alms along the way. The first *okage mairi* took place in 1650, and the tradition carried on for roughly the next two hundred years, dying out with the last *okage mairi* in 1867. Mass pilgrimages are known to have taken place in 1705, 1771 and 1830, when the shrine received concentrated bursts of 3 million, 2 million, and 5 million visitors, respectively.[5]

Highway Administration in the Modern Period

The Home Ministry (*Naimushō*) was established in November 1873 (abolished in December 1947 by the Allied Occupation Forces). A Department of Public Works was included within this portfolio. The Japanese Government did not see roads as an investment priority given the public works priorities of railway construction and industrialisation (Ministry of Land, Infrastructure, Transport and Tourism, 2021). When Yamagata Aritomo was appointed in 1883 as Head of the Home Ministry, he created bureaux for general administration and budget, local government, police, public health, topographical surveys, census, religious institutions and public works.

The first general regulation for roads is found in the 1876 *Law on Road Classification*, although its enforcement was sporadic. In 1909 (Japan's population was 45.5 million), there were only 61 motor cars registered with the Home Ministry. In comparison, in 1911 (population 49.8 million), there were approximately 1.8 million goods wagons, 172,000 horse-drawn carts, 144,000 *jinrikisha*, 36,000 ox carts and 9,000 horse-drawn carriages (Moulton with Ko, 1931: 87). A census of motor cars and trucks taken in 1920 (population 55.5 million) showed there were still only 7,912 motor cars and trucks throughout the country (Steele, 2016: 88).

The road classification of 1876 specified national, prefectural, town and village roads where road widths were specified for the latter two categories. From 1881 to 1900, the annual public expenditure on roads amounted to 7 million yen and from 1901 to 1916 expenditure increased three-fold (Moulton with Ko, 1931: 87). The *Highway Law* of 1919 established regulations for roads and a classification scheme on the respective widths, gradients and curvatures, and regulations for bridge construction. Data from the Department of Home Affairs, Public Works Bureau, reveal that in 1920 the government authorised 282.8 million yen over a 30-year period for road improvements (Moulton with Ko, 1931:

---

5   In 2013, the number of visitors to Ise Shrine passed 10 million—the first time since 1896 when counts were first taken (Japan Times, 20 December 2013).

87). The plan involved the construction of new highways and bridges, specifically for motorised vehicles, and the paving of national and prefectural roads.

In 1932, the First Five-Year Highway Construction Plan was published calling for the construction of 9,809 km of national highways by 1936. The Second Plan for 1937 to 1941 proposed the construction of an additional 13,268 km. By 1939, only 37 per cent of the planned national road network had been constructed (Table 15). The concept of expressways first appeared in a government document in 1943, when the Ministry of Internal Affairs published a National Automobile Highway Plan of 5,490 km, influenced by the concept of German Autobahns, but the plan was abandoned in 1944 (Shibayama, 2017).

Table 15. Road Network Length in Kilometres by Classification and by Year, Japan 1925–1939.
Source: based on World Engineering Congress, Publications Committee, 1929: 87; and Steele, 2016, footnote 27, p. 99.

Road Classification	1925	1933	1939
National Roads	8,228	8,146	8,617
Prefectural Roads	93,094	99,257	114,466
Municipal Roads	17,648	n/a	n/a
Town and Village Roads	920,220	n/a	n/a

By 1940, less than 2 per cent of all roads were paved. On the national highway system only 18.6 per cent of the network of 8,600 km was paved (Steele, 2016: 90). Steele (2016: 90–95) suggests several reasons for this shortfall in construction and points the finger at the rise of the military influence in government circles and the dream of a Japanese-dominated pan-East Asia. Japanese bureaucrats and military advisors placed priority on improving railways in Taiwan, Korea and Manchuria, including the grandiose scheme of building a high-speed railway, *dangan ressha* (bullet train), connecting Tōkyō with Shimonoseki (the westernmost tip of Honshu on the Kanmon Straits that separate Kyūshū), then, by way of an under-sea tunnel, to South Korea and finally onto other destinations in China and Southeast Asia.

Highway Administration Post-1945

As part of Japan's post-Pacific War reconstruction, a memorandum from the Supreme Commander for the Allied Powers (SCAP) in 1948 introduced a five-year road plan to replace the German Autobahn-style highway planning in vogue during the early 1940s (Muto, 2008). The state of the highway network can be judged from the following statistics. In the 1950s, of the 140,657 km of national highways and prefectural roads, only 15 per cent had two or more lanes and only 5.4 per cent were paved; and 47 per cent of all the bridges were wooden (David, 2014: 18). At the 1952 census, less than 6 per cent of the national highways and prefectural roads in Japan were paved; bicycles accounted for 87 per cent of registered vehicles, other slow modes of transport (horse and ox-carts and handcarts) accounted for 7 per cent and private motor cars accounted for only 6 per cent (Black and Rimmer 1981: 30).

In 1952, the *Law Concerning Special Measures for Highway Construction* (SMHC Law) was enacted which provided loans from a Trust Fund in the Ministry of Finance to construct roads and it authorised the collection of tolls from users to repay the loan. This also gave rise to a new road administration with the *Road Law* (as amended in 1952). The *Law for Temporary Measures Concerning the Source of Funds for the Improvement of Roads 1953* was passed into legislation and this prescribed that the government should establish five-year road improvement programs from 1954 onwards. In 1953, a petrol tax of 54 per cent of its retail price was also introduced to accelerate the road construction program. Earmarked funds for road improvement were also introduced in 1954 and expanded as a major fund-raising channel for road construction and maintenance at both national and regional levels.

As noted by Black and Rimmer (1981), the first five-year plan had a strong American influence due to the involvement of specialists led by Dr Ralph Watkins who had been invited by the Japanese government to consider the economic feasibility of an expressway linking Nagoya with Kōbe. In his report, Watkins commented on "the sorry state of roads" in Japan—referring in part to the fact that only about a quarter of even first-class national roads, and only two-thirds of the National Highway Route 1 connecting Tōkyō and Ōsaka, were paved. The Watkins Report stressed the importance of roads as social overhead capital and their crucial role in economic growth. It also introduced the concept of road traffic demand analysis and methods of estimating traffic diversion from existing roads to newly-constructed roads.

The *Nihon Doro Kodan* (Japan Highway Public Corporation) was established by law in April 1956. The Japan Highway Public Corporation was legally a non-profit government corporate entity established for the purpose of construction and management of expressways and ordinary toll roads that covered national motorways, regional motorways, including toll tunnels and toll bridges, car parks and service areas. The Corporation was neither directly within the government nor completely outside state control.

Such institutional positioning worked effectively to maintain consistency with nationwide development strategies. The Japan Highway Public Corporation also enjoyed some privileges offered by the national government that included: exemption from corporation tax; compulsory collection of tolls and other charges related to expressway operations; power of compulsory purchase of land and of administrative enforcement through the *Land Acquisition Law*; and loans from the government, bond placement to government funds and government guarantee of bonds.

One of its first tasks was to review the Watkins' study and it published its own report (Japan, Nihon Doro Kodan, 1957) that formed the foundation of an International Bank for Reconstruction and Development (World Bank) appraisal of toll roads (Kapur *et al.*, 1997). The revised *Special Measures for Highway Construction Law* was repealed with the Japan Highway Public Corporation taking over responsibility from the Ministry of Construction to construct a national highway tolled network and to collect the road user revenues. These developments, and the start of the International Bank for Reconstruction and Development funding for highway projects,[6] allowed American engineers to influence highway design and construction in Japan—albeit scaling back road widths. This led to the creation of a Japanese version of the *Highway Capacity Manual* (U.S. Bureau of Public Roads, 1950) that was used to standardise expressway design.

---

6   The International Bank for Reconstruction and Development (World Bank) has lent funds to numerous JHPC projects since the 1960s: all repayments were made by 1990.

National motorways have developed steadily and rapidly since 1957 when the Japan Highway Public Corporation (JHPC) received authorisation from the national government to construct its first expressway, the Meishin (Nagoya—Kōbe) Expressway. The Meishin Expressway was the first to open in 1963, linking Rittō (Shiga Prefecture) with Amagasaki (Hyōgo Prefecture)—a distance of 71 km. The Japan Highway Public Corporation undertook surveys, designed expressways and toll roads and oversaw their construction. The Tōmei Expressway was the second to open with partial service in April 1968, with the completed route between Tōkyō and Nagoya (347 km) being operational on 26 May 1969.

The Watkins Report also triggered a flurry of additional highway legislation providing for national expressways, national toll roads, revised funding arrangements (government bonds, grants to prefectures) and metropolitan expressways, such as the *National Development Longitudinal Expressway Construction Law*—the *National Expressway Law* enacted 1957; the *Metropolitan Expressway Public Corporation Law (1957)*; and the *Hanshin Expressway Public Corporation Law (1959)*.

The activities of the Japan Highway Public Corporation expanded in 1966 when the *National Development Arterial Expressway Construction Law* was enacted to provide a comprehensive construction plan covering 7,600 km of national expressways. In 1972, the Consultative Council on Roads for the Minister of Construction implemented a nation-wide toll pool, whereby revenue was pooled from all expressways to provide a single source of operating funds.

In 1987, the *National Development Arterial Expressway Construction Law* was revised, where the Japanese government approved expanding the expressway network (through the Fourth Comprehensive National Development Plan) to 11,520 km together with 2,480 km of access-controlled national highways, where a map of this system as of April 2018 may be found at https://www.mlit.go.jp/road/road_e/images_n/policies/p1_1_1.jpg. With the revision of the Law came inefficiencies, welfare loss and a mounting debt, because the newly planned routes of 3,920 km incurred high construction costs and only low projected traffic volumes to provide revenue (Kimura and Maeda 2005: 9). The tolls were revised in 1989 and again in 1994. The redemption principle was re-organised by extending the redemption period, initially from 30 years to 40 years, and, eventually, to 50 years.

Prime Minister Koizumi Junchirō established the Committee for Promoting Privatization of Four Highway-related Public Corporations that were responsible for the construction and management of highways in Japan: the JHPC (1956); the Metropolitan Expressway Public Corporation (1959); the Hanshin Expressway Public Corporation (1962); and the Honshū—Shikōkū Bridge Authority (1970). In December 2002, the committee's final opinion report recommended an organisational reform based on the principle of vertical unbundling, where highway service companies would provide services to an infrastructure holding organisation.

The Privatization Bill was passed in the *Diet* in June 2004. Privatisation of highways was based on the following acts: *the Expressway Company Law*; the *Japan Expressway Holding and Debt Repayment Agency Law* (JEHDRA); the *Law Regarding the Development of Highway-Related Laws in Connection with the Privatization of the Japan Highway Public Corporation*; and the *Act for Enforcement of Acts Related to Privatization of the Japan Highway Public Corporation Road Bureau, Ministry of Land Infrastructure* (Road Bureau, Ministry of Land, Infrastructure, Transport and Tourism, 2018: 7).

There are two key elements to the Privatization Bill (Mizutani and Uranishi, 2006). First, six specific joint-stock highway corporations (one-third government owned) would have the power to veto highway construction, although the Panel on Infrastructure Development would make the final decision on whether to proceed or not. Secondly, an independent administrative agency, the Japan Expressway Holding and Debt Repayment Agency (JEHDRA) was established to function as an asset-holding and debt-servicing public organisation with a sunset clause. The JEHDRA took over both the assets and the debts held by the former highway-related public corporations, and then leased the assets to the six expressway companies that would then collect tolls from each expressway and pay back the JEHDRA with the agreed lease fee such that once the repayment is completed by 2050, the agency would be dissolved.

With a recognition of a declining national population, and that land transport networks were largely mature, road administration was placed within a new "super" ministry, the Ministry of Land,

Infrastructure, Transport and Tourism (MLIT). It was established as part of administrative reforms on 6 January 2001 with the merging of the Ministry of Transport, the Ministry of Construction, the National Land Agency and the Hokkaidō Development Agency. Of all Ministries in Japan, it has the greatest number of employees. It is in charge of the comprehensive and systematic use of national land, development and conservation, infrastructure development, implementation of transport policies and maritime safety and security. In addition to its policy functions, the Ministry contains transport departments for ports and harbours, maritime, roads, railways and civil aviation.

Together with regional public corporations, NPOs and other citizens' groups, the Japanese government aims to enhance the administrative management of roads. In order to achieve more effective, efficient and transparent road administration, Japan has promoted a result-oriented administrative management for roads (Road Bureau, Ministry of Land, Infrastructure, Transport and Tourism, 2018: 19).

Today, bicycles are ubiquitous in urban areas and country towns and villages. Growing steadily from a base of about 3 million bicycles in 1920 (Koike, 1991: Figure 1, p. 41), Koike points out that the bicycle ownership rate has always been higher than the car ownership rate and laments that, in 1988, the length of exclusive bicycle paths represented only 0.13 per cent of the road network. The revised *Road Traffic Act of 1981* permitted bicycles to share the sidewalk with pedestrians. Writing in the early 1990s, Koike (1991: 44) suggests that the bicycle "has not been accepted as a legitimate mode of transport in the Japanese transport hierarchy".

It was not until December 2016 that the *Bicycle Use Promotion Act* was adopted with the establishment of the "Bicycle Use Promotion Headquarters" within the Ministry of Land, Infrastructure, Transport and Tourism (Road Bureau, Ministry of Land, Infrastructure, Transport and Tourism, 2018: 25). In 2020, there were some 69.1 million bicycles registered (the registration fee is approximately 500 yen) in Japan.

The principles underpinning this institutional interest in bicycles as a transport mode are that they contribute to the reductions in car dependency, in traffic congestion and in emissions. Bicycles improve mobility in a time of disaster and have health benefits. The main responsibility of the national government is to promote bicycle use in an integrated and systematic manner. The role of municipal governments is to implement realistic measures through a proper role sharing with the National Government. Public transport operators should aim for a symbiotic relationship between bicycle and public transport. Citizens are urged to support various bicycle-use measures implemented by the National and municipal governments (Road Bureau, Ministry of Land, Infrastructure, Transport and Tourism, 2018: 25).

Conclusions

A 'national' *institution* for roads in Japan has existed from ancient times, and, on occasion, policies have been copied from overseas experience. In the first place, the Yamato kings and queens learnt from the Chinese about road administration, especially the importance of locating post stations and planting shade trees. Security on the roads—initially on the borders with indigenous tribes, and, later, for internal control—was facilitated by erecting barriers that became a long-standing institution associated with the road network.

Barriers on roads were first established as a government instrument in the Yamato State then expanded into a system of government-controlled barrier stations established after the Taika Reform of 645 that were only abolished in the later part of the 19th century. They were essential components of road administration during the Edō period when Tokugawa Ieyasu designated five radial highways from Edō and used them to ensure firearms were not smuggled into the capital nor the wives of *daimyō* held captive smuggled out of Edō, and that the movement of ordinary people was controlled through the issue of travel permits.

The government controlled post stations had an equally long history. Their prime purpose was to provide horses and porters to relay messages and packages. During the Edō period, accommodation and food services were added primarily for the *daimyō* and their retainers who travelled as part of the system of alternate year attendance in Edō. The costs of the operations of post stations were born by the *daimyō* domains and obligations on local villages. In addition, the *bakufu* levied taxes on each post station, including revenue derived from prostitution.

The first formal recognition of an institution to manage roads can be traced to the establishment in 1659 by Tokugawa Ietsuna of a Magistrate of Road Affairs. The role was the overseeing of the upkeep of road infrastructure, the processing of petitions and communication policy with the *bakufu* intendants who reported on all matters pertinent to roads under their jurisdiction. *Bakufu* officials periodically checked to ensure approved road and bridge maintenance had been completed satisfactorily to orders at a cost borne by local communities.

The modern era brought about the modernisation of government along Western lines. The Home Ministry was established in November 1873 (abolished in December 1947) and public works was included within this portfolio. However, the Japanese national government did not see the importance of investment in roads given other priorities and it was not until the post-Pacific War, and the modern democratic era, that highway administration mirrored countries such as the U.S.A.

The American, Dr Ralph Watkins, was invited by the Japanese Government to consider the economic feasibility of the Nagoya—Kōbe Meishin Expressway. The Watkins Report triggered a flurry of highway legislation providing for national expressways, national toll roads, revised funding arrangements (government bonds, grants to prefectures) and metropolitan expressways. For example, in 1956, the Japan Highway Public Corporation was established and took over responsibility from the Ministry of Construction to construct the national toll highway network and to collect road user tolls.

By the beginning of the 21st century, land transport networks were largely mature and road administration was placed within a new "super" ministry: the Ministry of Land, Infrastructure, Transport and Tourism (MLIT). Administrative reforms of 6 January 2001 merged the Ministry of Transport, the Ministry of Construction, the National Land Agency and the Hokkaidō Development Agency. The Ministry is in charge of the comprehensive and systematic use of national land, development and conservation, infrastructure development, implementation of transport policies and maritime safety and security.

Prime Minister Kozumi Junichiro (1942–) established a committee on highway privatisation that recommended, in December 2002, organisational reform based on the principle of vertical unbundling, where highway service companies would provide services to an infrastructure holding organisation. The Privatization Bill was passed in the *Diet* in June 2004. Six joint-stock highway corporations (one-third government owned) were created and an independent administrative agency (Japan Expressway Holding and Debt Repayment Agency) was established to function as an asset-holding and debt-servicing public organisation.

Government policies direct the services these authorities deliver, including budget allocations for road planning, construction and maintenance. The regulatory framework for the highway sector determines the rules that affect the everyday actions and decisions of businesses and citizens when going about their work, personal business or leisure activities. Therefore, the regulatory framework is a critical determinant of how the government delivers its services effectively (Australia, NSW Regulatory Policy Framework Review Panel, 2017). The functions of national and prefecture road authorities and the responsibilities of local government—and the way they are structured—are not static over time but have evolved with regulatory and policy reform. This will continue to be a challenge for Japan as discussed in the final chapter to this book.

References

AllAboutJapan (2017) "Hakone Sekisho: Historical Checkpoint", https://allabout-japan.com/en/article/6114/

Australia, NSW Regulatory Policy Framework Review Panel (2017) *NSW Regulatory Policy Framework: Independent Review—Final Report*. NSW Treasury, Sydney, https://www.treasury.nsw.gov.au/sites/default/files/2018–02/Independent%20Review%20of%20the%20NSW%20Regulatory%20Policy%20Framework%20final%20report.pdf

Bamhill, D. L. (2004) *Bashō's Haiku: Selected Poems of Matsuo Bashō*, translated and with an Introduction by David Landis Bamhill. University of New York Press, Albany, New York.

Barnes, G. L. (2019) "The Jōmon-Yayoi Transition in Eastern Japan: Enquiries from the Kantō Region", *Japanese Journal of Archaeology*, 7, 33–84.

Black, J. A., and P. J. Rimmer (1981) "Japanese Highway Planning: A Western Interpretation", *Transportation*, 11, 29–49.

Bornoff, N. (1991) *Pink Samurai: Love, Marriage & Sex in Contemporary Japan*. Pocket Books, New York.

Chamberlain, B. H. (1981) *The Kojiki: Records of Ancient Matters*, translated into English in 1906 with annotations in the Second Edition by W. G. Aston. Tuttle Publishing, Tokyo.

David, D. (2014) "The Japanese Experience with Highway Development", *Journal of Infrastructure Development*, 6 (1), 17–42.

Japan Heritage Portal Site (2019) "Takenouchi Kaido /Yokooji: Japan's Oldest National Highway with a History of 1400 Years—Story 44", https://japan-heritage.bunka.go.jp/en/stories/story044/

Japan, Nihon Doro Kodan (1957) *Evaluation of the Kobe-Nagoya Expressway Survey: A study of the Report Submitted to the Japanese Government by a Group of Experts Headed by Ralph J. Watkins*. Nihon Doro Kodan, Tokyo.

Kapur, D., J. P. Lewis and R. Webb (eds) (1997) *The World Bank: Its First Half Century, Volume 2: Perspectives*. Brookings Institute Press, Washington D. C.

Kimura, Fukunari and Mitsuhiro Maeda (2005) "Transport Infrastructure Development in Japan and Korea: Drawing Lessons for the Philippines - Summary", https://citeseerx.ist.psu.edu/viewdoc/download?doi=10.1.1.691.3815&rep=rep1&type=pdf

Kodansha (1993) *Japan: An Illustrated Encyclopedia*. Bunkyo-ku, Tokyo.

Koike, Hirotaka (1991) "Current Issues and Problems of Bicycle Transport in Japan", *Transportation Research Record*, 1294, 40–46.

Matsuda, W. (2019) "Poets on the Periphery: Kūkai's Vision of Frontier Governance", *Journal of Asian Humanities at Kyushu University (JAH-Q)*, 4, 21–37.

Ministry of Land, Infrastructure, Transport and Tourism (2015) *Priority Plan for Infrastructure Development: The Cabinet Decision on September 18, 2015*. Ministry of Land, Infrastructure, Transport and Tourism, Tokyo.

Ministry of Land, Infrastructure, Transport and Tourism (2021) "History: Age of Modernisation", https://www.mlit.go.jp/road/road_e/q1_history_2.html

Mizutani, Fumitoshi and Shuji Uranishi (2006) "Privatization of the Japan Highway Public Corporation: Policy Assessment", *European Regional Science Association Conference Papers*, Volume 6, 229, https://citeseerx.ist.psu.edu/viewdoc/download?doi=10.1.1.738.6905&rep=rep1&type=pdf

Moriya, Katsuhisa, translated by T. Ronald (1990) "Urban Networks and Information Networks", in Chie Nakane and Shinzaburō Ōishi (eds) (1990) *Tokugawa Japan: The Social and Economic Antecedents of Modern Japan*. Tokyo University Press, Tokyo, 97–114.

Moulton, H.G. with the collaboration of Junichi Ko (1931) *Japan: An Economic and Financial Appraisal*. The Brookings Institute, Washington, D.C.

Muto, Hiromi (2008) *Doro Gyosei [Road Administration]*. Tokyo University Press, Tokyo.

Ohkura, Takehiko and Hiroshi Shimbo (1978) "The Tokugawa Monetary Policy in the Eighteenth and Nineteenth Centuries", *Explorations in Economic History*, 15 (1), 101–124.

Ong, Daina (n.d.) "Takenouchi Kaido, the Oldest Recorded Road in Japan", https://www.japan-guide.com/ad/takenouchikaido/

Redesdale, A. B. F. M., Lord (1915) *Memoirs, 2 Volumes*. Hutchinson & Co., London.

Road Bureau, Ministry of Land, Infrastructure, Transport and Tourism (2018) *2018 Roads in Japan*. Ministry of Land, Infrastructure, Transport and Tourism, Tokyo, http://www.mlit.go.jp/road/road_e/pdf/ROAD2018web.pdf

Sato, Tetsuji, Jun Nakamura, and Kenta Shimizu (2011) "Comprehensive Evaluation Index for Redevelopments of Historical Streets in Japanese Koedo Cities", *Proceedings of the Eastern Asia Society for Transportation Studies*, 8, n.p.

Sheldon, C. D. (1983) *Merchants and Society in Tokugawa Japan*, Cambridge University Press, Cambridge.

Shibayama, Takeru (2017) "Japan's Transport Planning at National Level, Natural Disasters, and their Interplays", *European Transport Research Review*, 9 (44), https://doi.org/10.1007/s12544-017-0255-7

Steele, M. W. (2016) "Roads, Bridges, Tunnels and Empire: Highway Construction and the Great East Asian Co-Prosperity Plan", *Asian Cultural Studies*, 87–101,

Suzuki, Shousei (n.d.) "The Ise Pilgrimage: A 'Must' Once in a Lifetime", https://web.archive.org/web/20180421093301/http://web-japan.org/tokyo/know/pilgrimage/ise.html [accessed 2 July 2019].

Takagi, Hisashi (2018) "Recent Studies of Bronze Coin Integration at the Beginning of Early-modern Japan," 安田女子大学紀要, 46, 11–18.

Takebe, Kenichi (2015) 道路の日本史―古代駅道路から高速道路へ [*History of Roads in Japan: From Ancient Station Roads to Highways*]. Chuko Shinsho, Tokyo.

The Association for Japanese History and Travel (2018) "Past and Present of Hakone Barrier Station", 14 July 2018, http://japan-history-travel.net/?p=5743

Traganou, J. (2004) *The Tokaido Road: Traveling and Representation in Edo and Meiji Japan*. Routledge Curzon, New York.

Tyler, R. (2012) *The Tale of the Heike*, translated by Royall Tyler. Viking Penguin, London.

U.S. Bureau of Public Roads (1950) *Highway Capacity Manual, First Edition*. U.S. Bureau of Public Roads and Highway Research Board, Washington, D.C.

Vaporis, C. N. (1994) *Breaking Barriers: Travel and the State in Early Modern Japan*. Harvard University Press, Cambridge, Mass.

Vaporis, C. N. (1997) "To Edo and Back: Alternate Attendance and Japanese Culture in the Early Modern Period", *The Journal of Japanese Studies*, 23 (1), 25–67.

World Engineering Congress, Publications Committee (1929) *Industrial Japan: A Collection of Papers by Specialists on Various Branches of Industry in Japan*. International Publishing and Printing Company, Tokyo.

6. Railways

> Just like horse-drawn carriages and sailing ships
> were taken over by trains and steamships in the
> beginning of the 19th century the latter half of the
> 20th century is the age of automobiles and airplanes,
> and now the railway is on the road to extinction
>
> Nishida, 1977, quoted by Strobel and Straszak, 1981: 56

Introduction

In the 19th century, railways were a significant marker in the industrialisation of Japan with the Meiji government introducing Western ideas and technologies. Great Britain had been keen to exploit new markets for its mature domestic railway industry, and in 1869, the British Minister to Japan, Harry Parkes, advocated to the Japanese Government that railways should be constructed as a matter of urgency (Aoki, 1994: 28). The first line opened between Shimbashi (Tōkyō) and Noge Kaigan, Yokohama, on 14 October 1872 under the control of the Ministry of Public Works. Other routes were completed in the 1870s until a cash strapped government allowed for the private sector to build and operate lines.

At the turn of the 20th century, and during the First Sino-Japanese War and the Russo-Japanese War, the Japanese Government realised the strategic functions of military transport, and, in 1906, enacted the *Railway Nationalization Act* and purchased 17 leading private railway companies. Japan Government Railways became a virtual monopoly of railway business until the Allied Occupation Forces instructed the Japanese Government to reorganise Japanese Government Railways as a public corporation (Japanese National Railways). Upon declaration of bankruptcy in 1987, Japanese National Railways was privatised and broken up into geographical divisions over a network of 23,474 km (Imashiro, 1995).

Whilst the institutional trajectories of railway administration in Japan has mirrored international trends this chapter also places emphasis on high-speed rail developments (Hayashi et al., 2020). A new age of inter-city passenger transport was heralded by the Japanese with the opening in 1964 of the Tōkaidō Shinkansen to the extent that its success encouraged several nations to change their minds about the role of railways—"a so called 'railway renaissance' began in a number of nations" (Straszak, 1981: 49)—an international story that has been updated by Loo and Comtois (2015).

The chapter summarises the external events leading to the roll out of early government narrow gauge railways and the role of the Japanese private sector in the expansion of this network. From the time that the main trunk railways were nationalised in 1906, the market was dominated by the government until 1987, when Japan National Railways was privatised, and the major changes in administration and their reasons are described. The story of private-railway development on even narrower gauges (782 mm) from the 1910 *Light Railway Act* is also pursued, including innovative business practices. The administration of municipal horse-drawn and electric tramways systems, from the late 19th century, and urban subway systems from 1920, where both private and public sectors were involved, are also explained. The greatest technological achievements—coming almost 100 years after the Russians demonstrated the steam engine in Japan—has been the development and deployment of high-speed rail and magnetic levitation rail, and the final sections of this chapter describe their driving forces.

Early Modern Period

Early Railways

British players dominated the early history of Japanese railways and its institutional arrangements, despite a number of other international players' attempts at gaining influence by gifting steam engines to some regional *daimyō* late in Edō era (Free, 2008). The first railway equipment seen in Japan arrived with a Russian naval squadron lead by Admiral E.

V. Putiatin in 1853 (Kodansha, 1993: 1244). Foreigners had suggested to the Tokugawa *Shōgunate* the construction of concession railways between Tōkyō and Yokohama, Ōsaka and Kōbe and between concession ports and large cities (Aoki, 1994), but no action was taken with the regime in chaos.

With the establishment of the Meiji government, the British Minister to Japan stepped in and convened a meeting on 7 December 1869 with government leaders represented by Iwakura Tomomi (Vice Premier), Sawa Nobuyoshi (Minister of Foreign Affairs), Ōkuma Shigenobu (Vice Minister of Finance) and Itō Hirobumi (Assistant Vice Minister of Finance). Minister Parkes argued that railways were a symbol of centralised power and that railways could carry rice quickly from other areas to Tōhoku (then suffering from another poor year for the rice harvest) thereby minimising the effects of famine (Aoki, 1994: 28).

A decision was reached to build a priority line between Tōkyō and Kōbe and a branch line to Tsuruga, skirting Lake Biwa. The British Minister Parkes introduced to the government Horatio Nelson Lay, who sold railway bonds in London and who also began hiring British engineers to design and build railways in Japan. Lay signed a contract with the Meiji government at an interest rate of 12 per cent per annum over 10 years but the contract was abruptly terminated when the Japanese government discovered that Lay would make a 3 per cent margin on each bond sold (Aoki, 1994: 28). Instead, the Japanese Government decided to construct the first railway with a terminus in Tōkyō (Shimbashi) and the other at Noge Kaigan in Yokohama—a distance of 29 km.

In April 1870, the Japanese Government hired Edmund Morel (1841–1871) as its first Engineer-in-Chief. On his advice, in August 1871, the Ministry of Public Works was established, whose major role was introducing Western technology to Japan. He advised the government on engineering education and administration and, in April 1871, an engineering college (later, the Tōkyō Imperial Technical University) opened. The Ministry of Public Works administered the railway expansion program with Masaru Inoue, who had studied railway and mining at University College London, as its first Director of Railways in Japan.

The technical advice from British engineers was that the locomotives should run on the 3' 6" (1,067 mm) narrow-gauge tracks built in

British colonies, such as South Africa and Australia, where the density of traffic was relatively low. Morel's role was to guide and supervise construction, to screen engineers working on the project and to provide guidance on the screening of foreign equipment imports. The hiring of foreigners for railways began in 1870 and it is of little surprise that the majority were British working in civil engineering, machinery for manufacturing, rolling stock repair and train scheduling and operations. The peak number of 119 in June 1874 fell afterwards, especially when the curtailment policy was put into effect in 1881 by the Japanese Government (Aoki, 1994: 30). The first shipment of ten tank locomotives and 58 two-axle passenger carriages manufactured in Britain arrived in Yokohama in September 1871. On 12 June 1872, two daily train services started between Shimbashi and Yokohama, with six daily services beginning two days later. On 14 October 1872 the Meiji Emperor attended the opening ceremony at Shimbashi and Yokohama stations.

On 25 August 1870, surveying work began between Ōsaka and Kōbe. Construction included the first wrought-iron bridge and tunnel in Japan (running under a raised-bed river). Regular service started on 11 May 1874. Two years later, the line had been extended to Kyōto and reached Ōtsu on Lake Biwa in 1880. This section included the 670 metre-long Osakayama Tunnel that was designed and built by a British engineer, T. R. Shervinton (Rhymer-Jones, 1881: 316). By 1890, it was possible to travel by rail from Kōbe, Ōsaka, Kyōto and Nagoya to Shimbashi then transfer in Tōkyō crossing by road to Ueno Station then on to Sendai in the north east. There were also short sections of railway on the islands of Hokkaidō, Kyūshū and Shikōku (Figure 4).

Early Private Railways

Private companies were major players in the early stages of railway development in Japan because the government faced a financial crisis from the rapid introduction of Western technologies (Shindo, 1954), such as the construction of government-run plants and factories and compensation for *daimyō* deprived of feudal privileges. Japanese private railways were governed by the *Railway Construction Act of 1892* that recognised the distinction between inter-city private railways and government-owned railways. This legal framework for private railways promulgated in their articles of association that their business be confined to moving people. After the mid-1880s, the apparent profitability of railways was sufficient to attract a flood of entrepreneurs with 60 per cent of revenue derived from passenger traffic.[1] Between 1887 and 1906, private companies laid down 5,253 km of track compared to the 1,880 km by the government (Moulton with Ko, 1931: 69)—a ratio of 2.8 to one.

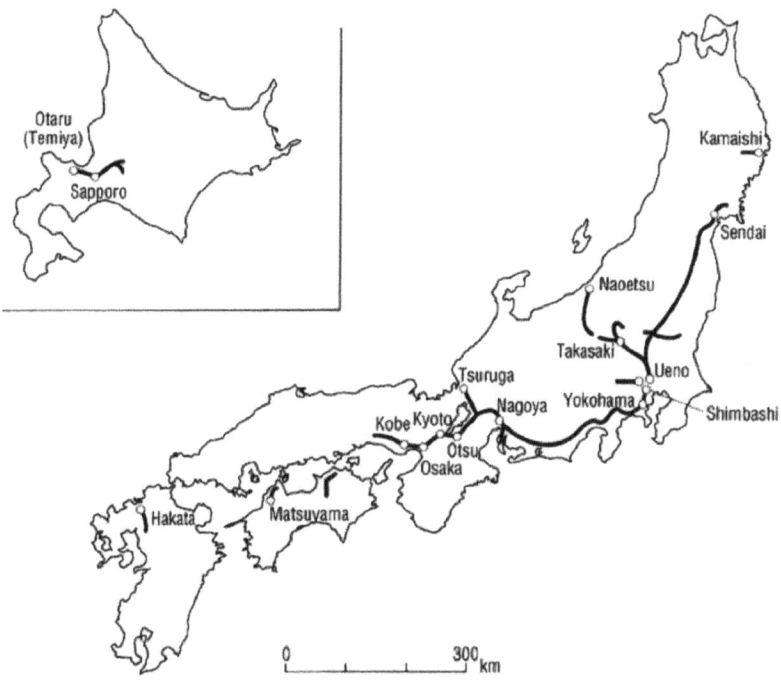

Figure 4. Extent of Japanese Railway Network by 1 January 1890.
Source: Aoki, 1994: 30, reproduced with permission.

Private operators were not constrained in introducing innovative methods to encourage patronage (Saito, 1997). For example, the Iyo Railway on Shikōkū island opened in October 1888 between Matsuhama

---

1   From the fiscal year 1917–1918 to 1928–1929, railway earnings as a percentage of total capital ranged from 7.8 per cent to 11.6 per cent annual on government railways and from 6.1 per cent to 9.8 per cent on private railways (Moulton with Ko, 1931: 73–74).

Bay and Matsuyama (Kishi, n.d.)—a distance of about 12 km—operating on a 762 mm gauge. It was the first private railway company in Japan to involve itself in the development of bathing resorts. From the 1890s, the company offered generous fare reductions during the summer season because it considered summer bathers to be its most valuable customers. The company formed the Baishinji Bathing Association in June 1899, developed a new bathing resort by the Setō Inland Sea, opened a summer station and started operating special trains for bathers. Soon, it provided related facilities, including hot baths and inns (Ogawa, 1998: 29).

Another example of early railway entrepreneurship also occurred on Shikōkū. When Otsuka Koreaki (1864–1928) became the manager of the Sanuki Railway and the Nankai Railway, he took guidance from then current U.S.A. management practices and installed a tearoom in the first-class carriage, employed young women as waitresses, introduced a train supervisor system and transferred much of the authority to the train supervisor. Financed with the help of local capital, Otsuka built the Takamatsu Hotel at the Takamatsu Railway terminus, and aquariums and other recreational facilities at both the Takamatsu and Kotohira terminus (Ogawa, 1998: 30). Around the same time, railway companies in the Kansai area grew their business by transporting tourists during the spring and autumn sightseeing seasons. So powerful was this railway branding that the region has been named the "Empire of Private Railways" (Miki, 2003).

Private railway companies operated excursion trains and built temporary facilities on leased, publicly-owned land, such as beaches and riversides. For example, in August 1901, the Kyōto Railway Company (the present JR Sagano Line) operated a special evening train, with on-board performances of court music, to Arashiyama, one of Japan's most famous scenic spots about 5 km from Kyōto, to catch cool breezes, to view a full harvest moon and to enjoy firework displays (Ogawa, 1998: 29). Excursion trains became a fashion in the Kansai area after the success of the Kyōto Railway Company.

The technological influence of American railways played a role during the establishment of both the Hankyū and the Hanshin Railways in the Kansai region. Key individuals within these corporations had visited cities in the U.S.A., such as New York, and decided that electric railways would be a good example of the power traction to adopt in Japan. In June 1899, the Settsu Electric Railway Company was founded under the guidance of Sotoyama Shuzō. The company applied to the Japanese Government for permission to open a railway line between Kōbe and Amagasaki (about 22 km), and, on approval one month later, changed its trading name to the Hanshin Electric Railway Company. The transfer of American-style, wide-gauge high-speed technology to build this inter-city electric railway (construction began in 1900), was directed by Misaki Shozō—an engineering graduate of Purdue University in the U.S.A.—who devised a diversified model of private railway business, influenced by early private railways that were active in land speculation in Western countries (Semple, 2009: 213–214).

After the 17 major trunk-line railway companies disappeared after nationalisation, the private, short-distance electric railway companies in the Kansai area, such as Hanshin and Hankyū, changed their articles of association to start the management of amusement parks to attract more patronage. In October 1907, the board of directors at Hanshin Electric Railway Company permitted leasing of land and buildings and the management of recreational facilities. Other companies soon followed.

Management practices quickly evolved with railway companies first risking their own capital in the facilities that they leased to professional operators then making direct investments and managing their own permanent facilities. A good example of this is the Hanshin Amusement Park. This trend towards more business diversification occurred in metropolitan areas, where the number of individual shareholders on railway boards declined gradually and institutional investors, such as banks and insurance companies, emerged as the major shareholders, and put more pressure on increasing revenues and earnings, as detailed by Ogawa (1998, Table 1, p. 31). Private railway companies developed and operated 37 major amusement complexes between 1899 and 1924.

One of the key innovators in the diversification of railway businesses was Kobayashi Inchizō (1873–1957). He is widely regarded in Japan and his story is documented in an autobiography (see Semple, 2009: 219–226 and 410). He joined Mitsui Bank Ltd. in 1893 and helped establish the Minō Arima Railway Company (now Hankyū Corporation) in 1907, becoming its President in 1927 and chairman in 1934 (Kodansha, 1993: 801). After the nationalisation of the Hankaku Railway (now JR Takarazuka Line), the board of directors took advantage of the permit for Hankaku to run on to Umeda in Ōsaka. The planned destinations were Minō and the famous Arima Hot Spring. On the route to the hot spring terminus, Takarazuka was then a modest place with only a few small inns and a cold spring. Kobayashi purchased reclaimed land at Mukogawa and opened a fashionable indoor swimming pool: it was a financial failure. Kobayashi covered the closed pool with planks and rebuilt it into a general amusement hall with 10 attractions and organised a performing girls chorus that has evolved into the present-day Takarazuka Operetta Troupe.

Regarded as the origin of large-scale suburban housing development by corporations in Japan, Kobayashi initiated the development of Ikeda New Town (Shuntaro and Lintonbon, 2016), about 16 km from central Ōsaka. In addition, the Hankyū markets, located near the railway terminus in Umeda (Ōsaka), were opened in 1925. It eventually became a modern, major department store with a food basement that would be familiar today to any traveller to a major Japanese town.

Kobayashi's innovative management techniques had a significant effect on railway companies throughout Japan: his ideas spread to the Mekama Railway and Tōkyū Railway and to many other railway companies. In 1918, Den-en Toshi Company built a "garden city" (Den'en chōfu) west of Tōkyō (Watanabe, 1980) and it was laid out by Busawa Eiichi along the format of an English Garden City, such as Letchworth that was founded in 1903. It was quickly realised that providing transport to its residents, who wanted to commute to central Tōkyō, was a necessity. The Tōkyū Group began as the Meguro-Kamata Electric Railway Company in 1922.

Government Railways

During the First Sino-Japanese War (1894–1895) and the Russo-Japanese War (1904–1905) the government recognised the strategic functions of transport and the undesirability of the private-sector control of national assets. Support grew for the government to control a unified railway network. The Chambers of Commerce in Tōkyō and in Kyōto were strong advocates for railway nationalisation. In 1906, the *Railway Nationalization Act* was introduced to nationalise railway trunk lines, where the government purchased, at generous prices for the private sector (479,320,000 yen), 17 leading railway enterprises. From the time of railway nationalisation onwards, government railways became the major player on the railway network that had suddenly expanded its route kilometres from 2,500 km to 7,150 km (mainly narrow 1,067 mm gauge), and a market share of less than half growing to 90 per cent. Japan Government Railways was a government-owned monopoly business. However, this investment, in the period just before the First World War, resulted in the government not having the funds to further expand the railway network into the countryside.

Only 20 private steam railway companies continued operating (Terada, 2001). Generally, these companies operated short lines, and only four had a network of more than 50 km. In passing the *Light Railway Act 1910* (amended 1921) the government encouraged smaller, private operators into the market. The government subsidised these railways with 5 per cent each year of their construction costs for the first 10 years of their operations (Moulton with Ko, 1931: 70). The government retained the right to purchase these railways at any time.

In 1920, as the railway network expanded, the Ministry of Railways was established (absorbed in 1943 under the Ministry of Transport and Telecommunications). Route kilometres grew at an even annual rate reaching about 20,000 km by 1935 (Strobel and Straszak, 1981: Figure 4.3, p. 57). In the late 1920s, railways in Tōkyō were being electrified and the technology spread rapidly to the main lines. Development planning for an urban railway network in the Tōkyō metropolitan area began in 1925. The first government approved urban railway network plan (five lines, 82.4 km) was published in 1925 in conjunction with plans for reconstruction after the great Kantō earthquake disaster of 1923. After that, including the latest plan of 2000, there have been nine rounds of planning for this urban railway network (Morichi *et al.*, 2001).

The Japanese Government also made a shrewd allocation of research and development resources in an institution that returned spectacular results fifty years after its establishment. In 1907, when it was called the Imperial Railway Agency, the government formed the Railway Technical Research Institute. In the mid-1930s it developed a blueprint for a standard gauge line (1435 mm) between Tōkyō and Kyūshū and undertook research and development for a high-speed steam locomotive project (Genser and Straszak, 1981: 147–148).

Resources for civil purposes diminished as pressures for military leaders curtailed railway investment, although a unified railway system was recognised as an essential aspect of Japan's growing militarisation (Aoki *et al.*, 2000). Nevertheless, passenger and freight traffic almost tripled between 1935 and 1945 (Genser and Straszak, 1981: 148). The Pacific War imposed obvious constraints on civilian passenger movements. From 1943, the national railway reduced its civilian passenger services, giving priority to military transport. In 1944, it abolished all the limited express trains, first-class carriages and dining and sleeping carriages. Under the *Ordinance for Collection of Metals* some railway operators were forced to remove one track from double-track lines, and others were forced to discontinue their business entirely, in order to satisfy the military demand for steel.

Railways became obvious strategic targets for Allied bombing raids over Japan. The damaged tracks were quickly repaired and made operational. For example, some lines on the national railway network resumed services one-day after Tōkyō was bombed, and the San'yo Main Line, in extraordinary circumstances, resumed services two days after the atomic bomb was dropped on Hiroshima. However, the aftermath of war left material shortages throughout the economy, including a lack of bunker coal for steam engines, and, inevitably, rail services were disrupted.

Urban Tramways

In addition to this national railway network, there were other railways operating electric, horse-drawn and man-powered trains, running mainly on tramways (Aoki, 1995; Yuzawa, 1985). The first horse-drawn tramway was constructed in Tōkyō in 1880 and within a few years most cities had a tramway. In 1890, an electric tramway experiment was conducted in Tōkyō, although the municipal government of Kyōto was the first to operate an electric streetcar on 1 February 1895 using electricity generated by the Lake Biwa Canal. Electric trams gradually replaced horse drawn and steam and gas propelled tramways in all cities. Table 16 summarises the tramway systems in the study area defined for this book that exist today, their date of opening and their network lengths.

Under the *Tramway Law of 1921*, the national and local governments had the option to purchase tramways from the private sector. By 1932, 83 tramways, with a total route length of 1,480 km, were operating in 67

Japanese cities (Utsunomiya, 2004: 10)—with the horse-drawn systems earning twice as much from their freight business as from receipts from passengers (Moulton with Ko, 1931: 79).

Table 16. Urban Tramways in the Study Area in the Modern Period.
Source: based on Utsunomiya, 2004, Table 1, p. 1.

Tram System	Opened	Length (km)	Operator
Tōkyō, Den'en chōfu	1907	5.0	Tōkyū Corporation
Kyōto, Arashiyama	1910	7.2	Arashiyama Electric Tram Railway
Tōkyō, Arakawa	1911	12.2	TMG Transportation Bureau
Ōsaka	1911	18.7	Hankai Tramway
Gifu	1911	23.9	Meitetsu
Matsuyama	1911	9.6	Iyō Railway
Ōtsu	1912	21.6	Keihan Electric Railway
Tōyama	1913	6.4	Tōyama Chiho Railway
Kyōto, Kitano	1925	3.8	Kyōto Dento
Toyohashi	1925	5.4	Toyohashi Railway
Fukui	1933	21.4	Fukui Railway

Urban Subways

In August 1920, a private venture—the Tōkyō Underground Railway Company—was established. Construction between Ueno and Asakusa—a distance of 2.2 km—commenced. This first subway line in Japan opened on 30 December 1927. In 1939, a through service from Asakusa to Shibuya commenced, with arrangements made with the Tōkyō Rapid Railway Company. Two years later, the Teito Rapid Transit Authority (*Teito Kōsokudo Kōtsū Eidan*) was created (Tokyo Metro, 2020). Ōsaka City was the first municipal government in Japan to manage an underground railway—the Midosuji Line between Umeda and Shinsaibashi.

Modern Democratic Period

Governance Model—Government Railways

The Ministry of Transport and Telecommunications was reorganised in 1945 when the Ministry of Transport was re-established. Japan's government railways were operated by the Ministry of Transport's Railway Department up until June 1949 when an entirely new institution for railway governance was imposed on the Japanese. Post-war Japan was run by the Allied Occupation Forces. A letter from General MacArthur dated 22 July 1948 instructed the Japanese Government to reorganise Japanese Government Railways as a public corporation called Japanese National Railways (JNR) which commenced business on 1 June 1949 (Imashiro, 1995).

The public corporation model was little understood by railway managers and it did not suit Japanese business culture. According to Okada (2010: 1), "rampant capital expenditure and irresponsible management" caused Japan National Railways to sink further into debt, with the inevitability of railway privatisation. Upon declaration of bankruptcy in 1987 (Saito, 1989), JNR was privatised and broken up into the West Japan Railway Company, the Central Japan Railway Company, the East Japan Railway Company, the Kyūshū Railway Company, the Shikōkū Railway Company and Hokkaidō Railway Company. All these companies operated narrow gauge and international standard gauge railways (Shinkansen, high-speed rail except on Shikōkū) over a network of 23,474 km.

While the division of operations began in April of 1987, privatisation was not immediate: initially, the government retained ownership of the companies. Privatisation of some of the companies began in the early 1990s (Mizutani, 2000). By 2006, all of the shares of JR East, JR Central and JR West had been offered to the market, and, today, they are publicly traded. On the other hand, all of the shares of JR Hokkaidō, JR Shikōkū, JR Kyūshū and JR Freight are still owned by the Japan Railway Construction, Transport and Technology Agency, which is an independent administrative state institution. Another nearly 3,400 km of routes are operated by the major private railways. These are known in Japan as "third sector railways"—new companies, financed with private and local government funds that absorbed some of Japanese National Railways' rural lines.

The structure of a typical railway governance model, in the form of a hierarchical flow diagram, can be ascertained from company reports (Central Japan Railway Company, 2019: 40). JR-Central's Board of Directors is composed of 18 members (including three outside directors) and chaired by the company chairman. JR Central also employs an auditor system, and its Audit and Supervisory Board consists of five members (four of whom are outside auditors). JR-Central has appropriate accounting audits made by an audit corporation and by Deloitte Touche Tohmatsu LLC. A Management Meeting is held ahead of the monthly Board of Directors meeting for in-depth discussion of important management issues. Chaired by the president, the Management Meeting is attended by all full-time directors, Audit and Supervisory Board members and some corporate officers.

Whereas the separation of the ownership of infrastructure and operations has become common in Europe, in Japan, railway companies develop rolling stock, structures, track, electrical and signalling, manage operations and maintenance. The companies promote many affiliated businesses through its subsidiaries to maximise operating and flexibility, such as coach transportation, merchandise and food, real estate and other services such as hotels and travel tours.

Taking the JR-Central railway network (Figure 5) as an example as it covers most of this book's study area, its market area represents 23.7 per cent of the country's land area but contains, in 2019, about 60.6 per cent of national population and almost two thirds (65.5 per cent) of prefectural GDP. The railway network is comprised of the 552.6 km Tōkaidō Shinkansen and twelve narrow-gauge lines of 1,418.2 km. For the year ended 31 March 2012, 85.4 per cent of revenue comes from the high-speed line, 8.2 per cent from other railways, 5.7 per cent from other railway revenues (track usage fees, land leasing fees at stations, usage fees from store operators at stations and advertising) with less than one per cent coming from other businesses (Central Japan Railway Company, 2012: 4). As would be expected during the Covid-19 global pandemic, its *Annual Report* ending June 2020 showed "comprehensive income" as 87 per cent of the previous year—and with a stability in the revenue streams similar to 2012 as reported above (https://global.jr-central.co.jp/en/company/ir/brief announcement/2020/_pdf/2020_08.pdf).

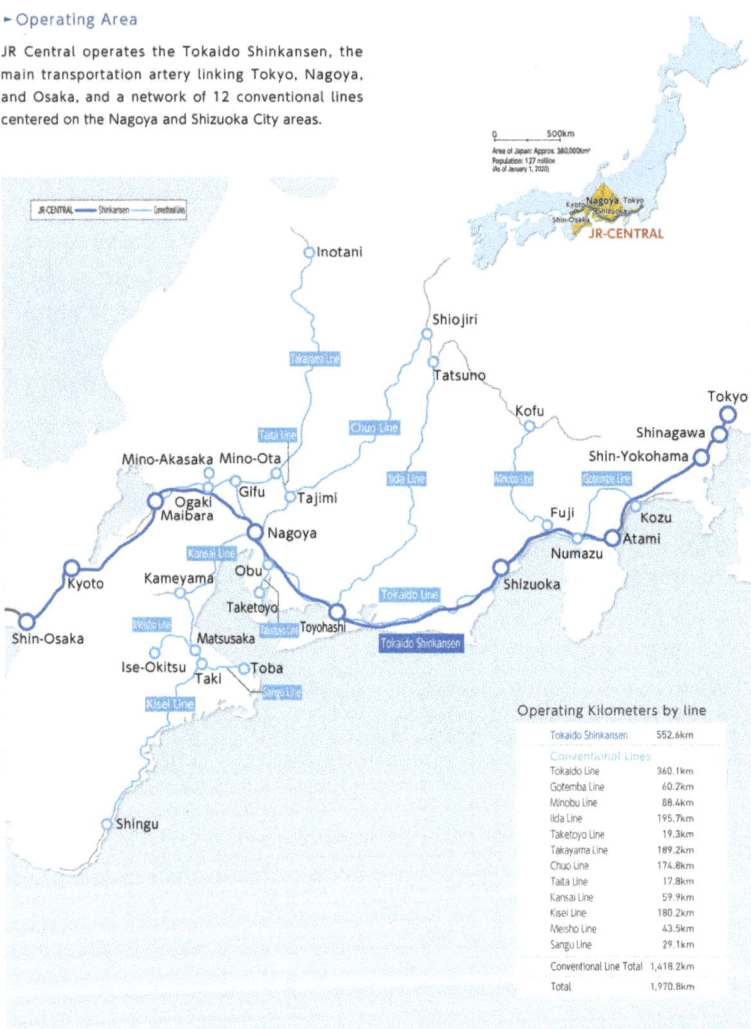

Figure 5. Central Japan Railway Network of Shinkansen and Other Lines, June 2019.
Source: Central Japan Railway Company, 2019: 48. All rights reserved.

Freight

International competitiveness for freight and logistics is a pressing issue for Japan. In 2011, the Ministry of Land, Infrastructure, Transport and Tourism formulated its policy on international container port strategy that promotes international competition through the creation of tactical ports (for example, the "Keihin" ports of Kawasaki, Tōkyō and Yokohama and the "Hanshin" ports of Ōsaka and Kōbe). Much of the freight volume passes through ports on the Sea of Japan side that entails expensive domestic landside transport costs (together with road traffic incidents and the declining numbers of long-distance truck drives where the average age has exceeded 50 years).

To make ports in Eastern Japan more competitive, a more efficient nation-wide feeder transport system (road and rail) is required (Yamaguchi, 2011). For example, between 1998 and 2010, JR Freight (Yoshizawa, 2012) operated a dedicated rail service for sea containers between Yokohama Honmoku Station (on the Kanagawa Coastal Rail Line Company) and Sendai Port station (on the Sendai Coastal Rail Line Company). Foreign trade and inter-modal freight to selected regions of Japan involves JR 12-foot containers and international 20-foot and 40-foot containers. With rail freight operations running to schedule, it is possible to adhere to the loading program for export vessels in ports. With rail and sea modes integrated there is an environmental benefit with reduced carbon dioxide emission compared to air cargo. Furthermore, government reforms of domestic container distribution have allowed JR Freight to develop a business model for the feasibility of transporting bonded containers on round trips (Yoshizawa, 2012).

Governance Model—Private Railways

The Ministry of Land, Infrastructure, Transport and Tourism classifies private railways into different groups. Fifteen of the most important companies are classified as major private railways. One serves Nagoya, one serves Fukuoka and the rest are all in Tōkyō and Ōsaka. Some other railways operating in or near large metropolitan centres are classified as quasi-major private railways but there are no clear distinctions between these railways and major private railways (Terada, 2001).

It is instructive to compare the governance structures of private railways during the period that JNR ran at a loss and were privatised in the 1980s. The managements of Hanshin and Hankyū railways have been studied in detail by Semple (2009) and it is somewhat fortuitous that when identifying a suitable case study railway company, the management of Hankyū Holdings, Inc. and Hanshin Electric Railway Co., Ltd. were integrated to establish Hankyū Hanshin Holdings, Inc in October 2006 (Hankyu Hanshin Holdings, 2019). It is important to point out that another major private railway company—the Tōkyū Group, operating in the Tōkyō region—demonstrates leadership in sustainability, corporate responsibility and local community development (Tokyu Corporation, 2019).

Hankyū Hanshin Holdings is structured with a Board of full-time (five) and part-time (four) Directors who have a two-way conversation with the President and the Chairman of the Group Management Committee (Hankyu Hanshin REIT, Inc., 2020: 21). The Group Management Committee itself is represented with the Heads of the various business divisions of the company and independent advisors. The group companies are also represented on the Group Management Committee. The company is guided by a Medium-Term Management Plan—a concrete action plan, extending over the period from the fiscal 2019 to 2022. Actions include enhancing the value of the Umeda area; activating the railway line-side land uses; improving the transport networks with new lines; facilitating inbound tourism; and expanding the scale of the condominium businesses (Hankyu Hanshin Holdings, 2019: 17 details 25–23).

Hankyū Hanshin Holdings operates the following divisions: railway, bus and taxi operations in the Kansai region through its Hanshin Electric Railway; Hankyū Travel provides Japanese travel arrangements for foreign visitors; Hankyū-Hanshin-Daiichi Hotel Group operates about 45 hotels, mostly in Tōkyō and Ōsaka; the Takarazuka Revue Company stages theatrical revues; and Hankyū Express imports and exports cargo, provides logistics and handles international shipping. A breakdown of its revenue streams in 2019 is provided in Table 17. It illustrates the diversity of the company business, and that railway income is similar to earnings on real estate development (about 30 per cent).

Table 17. Hankyū Hanshin Holdings Breakdown of Revenue Streams, 2019.
Source: calculated by author from Hankyū Hanshin Holdings, 2019: 5–6.

Business Activity	Annual Revenue (billion yen)	Percentage
Urban Transport	238.6	30.0
Real Estate	237.3	29.9
International transport	90.0	11.3
Entertainment	74.5	9.4
Hotels	64.9	8.2
Information & Communication Technology	53.5	6.7
Travel Services	35.5	4.5

The services offered by Japanese public- and private-sector railways (and airports) represent excellent examples of transport modal integration. All major economic activity areas in the Kantō, Kansai and Nagoya regions have international air services with the urban core areas connected by express rail services, with convenient interchange to the high-speed rail network. Passengers can transfer easily between the Shinkansen and conventional lines by simultaneously touching the ticket gates with an "EX-IC" card and a conventional line card such as TOICA (Tokai IC card) or PASMO. For example, JR Central has a special discount membership service—"Express Reservation" and "EX-IC"—which enables passengers to make reservations on the Tōkaidō and San'yo Shinkansen from mobile phones or personal computers, and to board the train directly from the entry gates without waiting in line at the ticket office window.

Urban Subways

There were only two subway systems in Japan—one in Tōkyō; the other in Ōsaka—before the modern democratic period. To keep pace with the commuter travel demands in the post-Second World War period, subways were constructed in a number of cities throughout Japan and Table 18 shows those subways in the study area. The table identifies the lines, network length and the year opened. The ownership structures are privately managed or a partnership between government and the private sector.

Table 18. Subway Lines and Network Length in the Study Area, 2020.
Source: Japan Subway Association, 2020; Japan Visitor, https://www.japanvisitor.com/japan-travel/japan-transport/japan subway#kysu.

City	Lines	Network Length (km)	Year Opened
Nagoya	6 Main Lines	93.3	1957
Tōkyō	Asakusa Line, Mita Line, Shinjuku Line, Ōedo Line	109.0	1960
Yokohama	Blue Line, Green Line	53.4	1971
Kōbe	Seishin-Yamate Line, Kaigan Line	38.1	2002
Kyōto	Karasuma Line, Tōzai Line	31.2	1981

The Shinkansen Program

In the modern democratic period, the government of Japan was not burdened with a defence budget, had a long tradition of investing in education, had a strong engineering culture and, significantly for railway development, had a surplus of experienced military and aeronautical engineers at its disposal for peace-time research and development in the Japan Railway Research Institute. They were fully aware of developments in France and in West Germany on technical matters related to high-speed rail and magnetic levitation technologies. Furthermore, there was a strong tradition that private industry (construction, machine-building, electrical and electronics industries) be contracted by governments to execute railway designs (Genser and Straszak, 1981: 160).

These factors proved vital in the modernisation of the Japanese railway network, and for planning of high-speed rail systems. On May 10 1956, Japan National Railways Head Office set up the "Investigation Committee for Enhancement of Traffic Capacity on the Tōkaidō Line". Fifteen months later the Ministry of Transport established the "Trunk Line Investigation Committee" that recommended, in July 1958, the need to construct an entirely new route for the Tōkaidō railway line. The JNR President Sogō Shinji (1864–1981) appropriated money in the company's 1959 budget.

Construction of the line with 10 approved stations, including platforms at Tōkyō and a new station in Ōsaka (Shin-Ōsaka), started in April 1959 (a loan of U.S. $80 million was secured from the World Bank in 1961). In 1960, high-speed test operations with continuous mesh catenary were conducted on the JNR Tōhoku line, and, in November 1962, a prototype train topped 200 km/h. By mid-1964, tests were running on the completed section of the Tōkaidō track near Maibara (Shiga Prefecture) before full commercial services between Tōkyō and Shin-Ōsaka started on 1 October 1964 (Straszak, 1981, Table 1, pp. 29–32). This timing was to catch the world's attention as the 1964 Summer Olympic Games opened ten days later in Tōkyō, signalling that Japan had "been welcomed back" into the international (Western) community (Hood, 2006).

This highly successful completion of the "Tōkaidō Shinkansen" (Straszak and Tuch, 1977) was "due to the President of the JNR, Mr.

Sogo..." (Straszak, 1981: 7), and it opened the way for the Shinkansen program that was an exemplary international example of a national government development program as part of a national socio-economic system (Shima, 1994). In 1969, the New Comprehensive National Development Plan stated "...with the advanced information and rapid transport system...we can expect that all of Japan...will be integrated into a single unit" (Straszak, 1981: 5). To illustrate this, JNR prepared a series of iso-chrone maps from 1971 to 1985 to demonstrate the shrinking of journey times by rail from Tōkyō to the rest of the Japanese archipelago (Srazsak, 1981, Figure 2.9, p. 21).

Development of the Shinkansen network was a key part of the 1969 Second Comprehensive National Development Plan and led to the *Diet* promulgating on 18 May 1970 *Law Number 71 "Law for Construction of Nation-Wide High-Speed Railways"* with the Minister of Transport as the authority to implement the Shinkansen Program. Originally, the Shinkansen lines were seen as a way to solve the problem of insufficient capacity on JNR's conventional lines, but the passage of the Development Law meant that Shinkansen lines had become part of the national strategy to achieve balanced development nationwide and to revitalise the more peripheral regions of Japan (Takatsu, 2007: 9).

In response, JNR set up its Network Planning Department that was reorganised in 1977 as the Planning Division in the Shinkansen Construction Department (Straszak, 1981: 7). A map of the early high-speed railway network to integrate the "whole of Japan into a single unit" is printed in Straszak (1981, Figure 2.5, p. 13). Details on the procedural process as to how the Minister of Transport approves the basic plan and construction approval can be found in Strazsak (1981, Figure 2.6, p. 15) who also provides a description of the roles played by actors in civic and civil society in the planning for high-speed rail (Gensher and Straszak, 1981: 154–162).

High-speed railways continued to be constructed across Japan, but the expansion forced JNR further into debt. With high labour costs (the administration of the Shinkansen Program employed 13,369 people in March 1976) and expenses outstripping revenues, JNR accumulated annual deficit mushroomed from about 800,000 million yen in 1971 to 3,160 thousands of millions of yen in 1975 (Gensher and Straszak, 1981, Table 5.1, p. 151)—approximately a four-fold increase in four years. To compound its financial problems, JNR also lost its share in ton-kilometres of domestic freight carried by the national rail network from about 30 per cent in 1965 to 13 per cent ten years later (Gensher and Straszak, 1981, Figure 5.18, p. 196).

The 1987 railway reforms transferred responsibility for operations of the Tōhoku and Jōetsu Shinkansen lines to JR East, the Tōkaidō Shinkansen to JR Central and the San'yo Shinkansen to JR West. The September 1987 *Law on the Transfer of Construction Projects for Shinkansen Lines Overseen by Passenger Railway Companies to the Japan Railway Construction Company* (JRCC) transferred responsibility for constructing Shinkansen lines to the JRCC (Takatsu, 2007: 9).

The Shinkansen Railway Holding Organization, established as part of the JNR privatisation process, owned the four existing Shinkansen lines (Tōkaidō, San'yo, Tōhoku and Jōetsu) and leased the infrastructure facilities to the operating companies. However, this arrangement was abandoned in 1991 when the operators complained that they could not easily draw-up long-term business plans because they could not depreciate Shinkansen assets. The role of the Shinkansen Railway Holding Organization was taken over by the Railway Development Fund (RDF) with responsibility for transferring all Shinkansen assets and liabilities to the railway operators in the JR group.

The Shinkansen Program has had extraordinary impacts (Hayashi *et al.*, 2017). The Tōkaidō Shinkansen has carried about 6.4 billion passengers since its inaugural commercial service in 1964 (Central Japan Railway Company, 2019:18). Journey times between Tōkyō and Shin-Ōsaka have dropped from 3 hours 10 minutes on the *hikari* service to 2 hours 33 minutes on the *nozomi* service. This has been facilitated by the construction of additional platforms and the installation of additional draw-out tracks at Shin-Ōsaka Station. Timetable changes in the Spring of 2020, introduced a "12 Nozomi Timetable," allowing all Nozomi 700A type services to run at the same highest speed of 285 km/h and reduce the journey time to 2 hours 30 minutes (Central Japan Railway Company, 2019: 8).

Magnetic Levitation Railways

Japan National Railways initiated research on a linear propulsion railway system in 1962. In July 1972, the JNR Technical Research

Institute ran a prototype called ML-100 using a superconducting magnet linear synchronised motor at 60 km/h. This represented a world's first. Germany followed with its maglev test track in Emsland. In 1977, testing of vehicles of speeds up to 500 km/h moved to a new track of length 7 km in Hyūga, a port-city on Kyūshū Island.

When JNR was privatised in 1987 the development of the maglev system was taken over by the Central Japan Railway Company. It decided to build a better testing facility in Yamanashi Prefecture to the west of Tōkyō with a longer track length of 18.4 km, including tunnels, steeper gradients and curves. From 1997, MLX01 trains were tested there, followed by long-distance running tests by alternately operating two trainsets with rolling stock and facilities for commercial use.[2] Cumulative running distance was 2.76 million km, as of February 28, 2019 (Central Japan Railway Company, 2019:12). Running tests were started with the Series L0 rolling stock, based on commercial specifications, and covered 4,064 km in one day reaching a top speed in 2015 of 603 km/h (Central Japan Railway Company, 2019: 25). In total, investment in the Yamanashi line was 170.6 billion yen; for its extension to 42.8 km there was an additional 339.1 billion yen. The investment in proprietary superconducting maglev technological developments was 197.1 billion yen (Central Japan Railway Company, 2019: 24).

When JR Central announced the decision of building the Maglev Chuō Shinkansen, and opening it in 2045, its stock price plunged. In May 2011, the Ministry of Land, Infrastructure, Transport and Tourism reported that it was appropriate to utilise the maglev technology on the inland Southern-Alps route and designated JR Central as the construction authority between Tōkyō and Ōsaka (and to finance the construction) and also to be the railway operator (Central Japan Railway Company, 2012: 24). The development concept for a service with a maximum speed of 505 km/h cost of 9,030 billion yen. The inland route avoids the coastal areas along the Tōkaidō route that are vulnerable to the risk of

---

2 In 2015, Professor Yoshitsugu Hayashi (Nagoya University) kindly arranged a site briefing and a test ride with JR Central Railway at the Yamanashi Test track. To illustrate the seamlessness of travel in Japan, that morning I took the JR Hokkaidō rapid transit from Sapporo to the New Chitose Airport, an ANA flight to Tōkyō Haneda Airport, followed by rail to the newly opened Shinagawa to Tōkyō Station—a short journey that few people would ever make by Shinkansen. At Tōkyō Station, I met up with Professor Hayashi and we took the JR Chuō line to Ōtsuki Station arriving mid-morning.

earthquakes and tsunami inundation. The environmental assessment, and the two-stage Construction Implementation Plan were approved in 2014 and 2018, respectively.

The first phase of the project is the extension of the Yamanashi line for a distance of 286 km that would link the stations at Shinagawa and Nagoya (Figure 6). The estimated cost for construction and rolling stock is 5,523.5 billion yen. As of 2020, construction contracts for the most time-consuming and most difficult construction work, such as the construction of the Southern Alps tunnel and the Shinagawa and Nagoya Terminal Stations, have been let. Work is proceeding towards a 2027 completion date (Central Japan Railway Company, 2019: 22). The *Act on the Japan Railway Construction, Transport and Technology Agency, Independent Administrative Agency*, was revised in November 2016. The Agency provides JR Central with the loans for part of the funds required for the construction of the Chuō Shinkansen. Japan Central Railway borrowed a total of 3 trillion yen before July 2017 (Japan Central Railway Company (2020: 73).

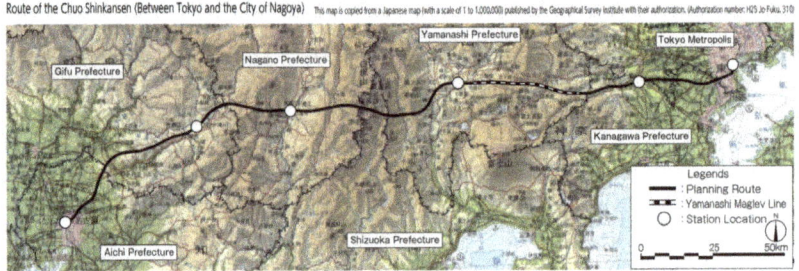

Figure 6. Proposed Route for the Chuō Shinkansen between Shinagawa, Tōkyō, and Nagoya (Approximate Locations of the New Stations are Indicated) and the Current Yamanashi Test Track.
Source: Central Japan Railway Company, 2020: 102. All rights reserved.

Conclusions

The import of railway technology in Japan had a strong British connection (Table 19). The British Minister convened a meeting in late 1869 with the Vice Premier, the Minister and Vice Minister of Foreign Affairs and the Assistant Vice Minister of Finance. Railways were perceived as a symbol of centralised political power that would reinforce the legitimacy of the new Meiji government. The Japanese Cabinet began hiring British engineers to design and build railways in Japan and appointed Edmund Morel as its first Engineer-in-Chief. On his advice, the Ministry of Public Works was established in 1871 to administer the railway expansion program with Masaru Inoue (who had studied railway and mining at University College London) as its first Director of Railways. British engineers determined that the locomotives should run on the 3' 6" (1,067 mm) narrow gauge tracks. The first railway, with a terminus in Tōkyō (Shimbashi) and the other at Noge Kaigan (Yokohama), opened in 1872.

The private sector entered into railway construction also at an early date, until the government privatised all major trunk lines in 1906. The government promoted railway construction in regional areas on an even narrower gauge (782 mm) through the 1910 *Light Railway Act* (revised 1921). The dominance in ownership of railways by the government lasted until 1987 when Japan National Railways was privatised and divided into the regional operations that exist today. Municipal governments were largely responsible for the introduction of horse-drawn and electric trams from the late 19th century, and urban subway construction was initiated in Tōkyō by the private sector, although subsequent developments in other cities involved both sectors.

Table 19. Summary of Major Events in Japanese Railway Development—
Institutions and Organisations.
Source: Author.

Major Event	Date	Key Players
Introduction of steam engine	1853	Russian government
Lobbying to introduce railways	1869	British Minister to Japan
British railway expert, Edmund Morel hired as Engineer-in-Chief.	1870	Japanese Cabinet
Establishment of Ministry of Public Works Masaru Inoue appointed as first Director of Railways in Japan	1871	Japanese Cabinet
Shimbashi to Yokohama railway opens	1872	Ministry of Public Works
Ōsaka to Kōbe railway opens	1874	Ministry of Public Works
First horse-drawn tramway, Tōkyō	1880	Municipal Government
Railway Construction Act	1892	Private companies

Major Event	Date	Key Players
Railway Nationalization purchase of 17 private railway companies.	1906	Japanese Government *Diet*
Railway Technical Research Institute formed	1907	Imperial Railway Agency
Light Railway Act 1910 encouraged narrower gauge 762 mm railways	1910	Japanese Government *Diet*
Ministry of Railways established	1920	Japanese Government *Diet*
Urban railway network plan approved	1925	Japanese Government *Diet*
First Subway opens, Tōkyō	1927	Private company
Japanese National Railways (JNR) formed	1948	Allied Occupation Forces
High-speed rail opens Tōkyō and Shin-Ōsaka	1964	Japanese National Railways
Privatisation of JNR	1987	Japanese Government *Diet*
Company assumes responsibility for maglev	1987	Central Japan Railway Company
Construction of Chūō maglev approved	2018	Ministry of Land, Infrastructure, Transport and Tourism

By international standards, the post-Second World War technological developments in high-speed rail and in magnetic levitation systems have been impressive. The Railway Technical Research Institute (established in 1907) and the Japan Railway Research Institute (established 1948), together with research and development (R&D) expertise from industry and the military, provided the platform for this railway expertise.

Although derided at the time, the vision of a national network of high-speed rail provided by the JNR President, Mr. Sogo, has been spectacularly realised. The New Comprehensive National Development Plan of 1968 foresaw that the technology would integrate the economy and society into a single unit—a policy aspiration that has been highly successful. The opening of the Maglev Chūō Shinkansen later this decade will further speed up the flow of people, information and new ideas in the study area.

Possibly the greatest challenge is how best to maintain the vast railway system against a context of an ageing population, reduced government income from taxation and a lack of central and local government capacity to provide the required subsidies. One way is to separate the owner of the infrastructure from the rail operator (the franchise model), as in the European Union, but policy reform and transitions from existing arrangements to new ones have proved to be difficult in the Japanese cultural context. Most profitable lines are owned by private entities and the new model would force operators into an internal subsidy of the less lucrative services with the beneficiary being the government with reduced subsidies. Whatever the institutional arrangements in the future, there is the problem of maintaining ageing infrastructure such as tunnels and bridges where the average age of these infrastructure maintained by governments is 32 years (Okajima Gen[3] pers. comm.). The collapse, in early December 2012, of the Sasago motorway tunnel highlights the risks of under-investing in the maintenance of infrastructure.

References

Aoki, Eiichi (1994) "Dawn of Japanese Railways", *Japan Railway & Transport Review*, 1, 28–30.

Aoki, Eiichi (1995) "Japanese Railway History 5—Construction of Local Railways", *Japan Railway & Transport Review*, 5, 34–37.

Aoki, Eiichi, Mitsuhide Imashiro, Shinichi Kato, and Yasuo Wakuda (2000) *A History of Japanese Railways, 1872–1999*. East Japan Railway Culture Foundation, Tokyo.

Central Japan Railway Company (2012) *Central Japan Railway Company: Annual Report 2012 For the Year Ended March 31, 2012*. Central Japan Railway Company, Shinagawa, Tokyo.

Central Japan Railway Company (2019) *Central Japan Railway Company: Annual Report 2019*. Central Japan Railway Company, Shinagawa, Tokyo.

Central Japan Railway Company (2020) *Central Japan Railway Company: Annual Report 2020*. Central Japan Railway Company, Shinagawa, Tokyo.

Free, D. (2008) *Early Japanese Railways, 1853–1914: Engineering Triumphs That Transformed Meiji-era Japan*. Tuttle, Tokyo.

Genser, R., and A. Straszak (1981) "The Shinkansen and Railway Issues", in A. Straszak (ed.) (1981) *The Shinkansen Program: Transportation, Railway, Environmental, Regional, and National Development Issues*. International Institute for Applied Systems Analysis, Laxenburg, 147–207.

---

3   At the time, Gen Okajima was the Manager of the Sydney Office of the Central Japan Railway Company.

Hankyu Hanshin Holdings (2019) *Hankyu Hanshin Holdings Integrated Report 2019*. Hankyu Hanshin Holdings, Osaka, https://www.hankyu-hanshin.co.jp/upload/irRelatedInfoEn/247.pdf

Hankyu Hanshin REIT Inc. (2020) *Hankyu Hanshin REIT: Sustainability Report, May 2020*. Hankyu Hanshin REIT Inc., Osaka.

Hayashi, Yoshitsugu, K. E. Seetha Ram and S. Bharule (eds) (2020) *Handbook on High-Speed Rail and Quality of Life*. Asian Development Bank Institute Press, Manila.

Kodansha (1993) *Japan: An Illustrated Encyclopedia*. Kodansha, Bunkyo-ku, Tokyo.

Loo, B, P. Y. and C. Comtois (2015) *Sustainable Railway Futures: Issues and Challenges*. Ashgate Transport and Mobility Research Monograph, Farnam, Surrey.

Miki, Masafumi (2003) "Cities in Kinki Region", *Japan Railway & Transport Review*, 36, 56–63.

Mizutani, Fumitoshi (2000) "Japan", in D. M. Van De Velde (ed.) (2000) *Changing Trains—Railway Reform and the Role of Competition: The Experience of Six Countries*. Ashgate Publishing Limited, Aldershot, Hants.

Morichi, Shigeru, Seiji Iwakura, Toshiya Morishige, Makato Itoh and Shio Hayasaki (2001) "Tokyo Metropolitan Rail Network Long-Range Plan for the 21st Century", paper presented at the Transportation Research Board 80th Annual Meeting, 7–11 January, Washington, D.C.

Moulton, H. G., with the collaboration of Junichi Ko (1931) *Japan: An Economic and Financial Appraisal*. The Brookings Institute, Washington, D.C.

Nishida, M. (1977) "History of the Shinkansen", in A. Straszak and R. Tuch (eds) (1977) *The Shinkansen High-Speed Rail Network of Japan—Proceedings of an IIASA Conference, June 27–30, 1977*. Pergamon Press, Oxford, 11–20.

Ogawa, Isao (1998) "History of Amusement Park Construction by Private Railway Companies in Japan", *Japan Railway & Transport Review*, 15, 28–34.

Okada, Mitsuji (2010) "Japanese Case Study: Planning, Implementing and Operating a Successful HSR Network", in *High Speed Rail World Australia 2010: Conference Proceedings—24–25 August 2010, InterContinental Hotel, Sydney, Australia*. Terrapinn, Sydney.

Rhymer-Jones, T. M. (1881) "Imperial Government Railways of Japan—The Osaka-yama Tunnel, Otzu, Lake Biwa", *Minutes of the Proceedings of the Institution of Civil Engineers*, 64, 316–318.

Saito, Takahiko (1989) "Transport Coordination Debate and the Japanese National Railways Problem in Postwar Japan", *Transportation Research Part A: General*, 23 (1), 13–18.

Saito, Takahiko (1997) "Japanese Private Railway Companies and Their Business Diversification", *Japan Railway and Transport Review*, 10, 2–9.

Semple, A-L. (2009) "The Influence of Hankyu and Hanshin Private Railway Groups on the Urban Development of the Hanshin Region, Japan", unpublished PhD thesis, School of Biological Earth and Environmental Sciences, University of New South Wales, Sydney.

Shindo, Motokazu (1954) "The Inflation in the Early Meiji Era—History of Inflation in Japan", *Kyoto University Economic Review*, 24 (2), 39–59.

Shima, Hideo (1994) "Birth of The Shinkansen—A Memoir", *Japan Railway & Transport Review*, 3, 45–48.

Shuntaro, Nozawa, and J. Lintonbon (2016) "Suburban Taste: Hankyu Corporation and its Housing Development in Japan 1910–1939", *Home Cultures*, 13 (3), 283–311.

Straszak, A. (ed.) (1981) *The Shinkansen Program: Transportation, Railway, Environmental, Regional, and National Development Issues*. International Institute for Applied Systems Analysis, Laxenburg.

Straszak, A., and R. Tuch (eds) (1977) *The Shinkansen High-Speed Rail Network of Japan—Proceedings of an IIASA Conference, June 27–30, 1977*. Pergamon Press, Oxford.

Strobel, H. and A. Straszak (1981) "The Shinkansen and Transportation", in A. Straszak (ed.) (1981) *The Shinkansen Program: Transportation, Railway, Environmental, Regional, and National Development Issues*. International Institute for Applied Systems Analysis, Laxenburg, 49–146.

Takatsu, Toshiji (2007) "The History and Future of High-Speed Railways in Japan", *Japan Railway & Transport Review*, 48, 6–21.

Terada, Kazushige (2001) "Railway Operators in Japan 1: Railways in Japan—Public & Private Sectors", *Japan Railway & Transport Review*, 27, 48–55.

Tokyo Metro (2020) "History", Tokyo Metro, Tokyo, https://www.tokyometro.jp/lang_en/corporate/profile/history/index.html

Tokyu Corporation (2019) *Tokyu Corporation Integrated Report 2019*. Tokyu Corporation, Shibuya, Tokyo, https://www.tokyu.co.jp/ir/english/upload_file/m002-m002_09/Tokyu_Integratedreport_2019E.pdf

Utsunomiya, Kiyohito (2004) "When will Japan Choose Light Rail Transit?", *Japan Railway & Transport Review*, 38, 10–16.

Watanabe, Shunichi (1980) "Garden City Japanese Style: The Case of Den-en Toshi Company Ltd., 1918–28", in G. E. Cherry (ed.) (1980) *Shaping an Urban World*. Mansell, London, 129–143.

Yamaguchi, Seiichi (2011) "International Strategic Freight Ports Policy and Yokohama Port's Approach" *Cargo Handling JAPAN*, 56 (3), 1–10.

Yoshizawa, Jun (2012) "JR Freight Company's Quest for Intermodal Freight Transport", *ICHCA'S Cargo World 2011/12*.

Yuzawa, Takeshi (1985) "The Introduction of Electric Railways in Britain and Japan", *The Journal of Transport History*, 6 (1), 1–22.

7. Civil Aviation and Airports

The Japanese people appear to be quite as air-minded as those of any other country, and a steady development of the aviation industry is expected

Moulton with Ko, 1931

Introduction

The Japanese aviation industry dates from the late Meiji era and its early development heavily involved the military, especially in the period leading up to the Second World War. In June 1912, the navy formed The Committee for Naval Aeronautic Research (海軍航空術研究会 *Kaigun Kōkūjūtsu Kenkukai*) (Sagen, 2004: 76). By 1916, the Japanese Imperial Navy had initiated the land-based *kōkūtai* system (naval air station and the flying unit stationed there) and, by the Spring of 1918, three Maurice Farman and Curtis seaplanes flew non-stop from Yokosuka (Kanagawa Prefecture) to Sakai (Ōsaka Prefecture)—a distance of 391 km.

Japan was a signatory to the international Convention Relating to the Regulation of Aerial Navigation dated 13 October 1919. In December of that year, a Special Aeronautical Committee was set up as an advisory organ to the Ministry of War in order to study the ways and means of directing, promoting and regulating all civil aviation enterprises. This Committee drafted Japan's *Air Navigation Law* of April 1921 (Kataoka, 1936: 95). The first year of civilian flights took place in the same year. The private enterprise company, Japan Air Transport Institute, pioneered seaplane passenger services from the Ohama shore near Sakai to nearby Kizugawa Airfield, Ōsaka, and then on to Tokushima City at the eastern end of Shikōkū Island (63 km).

The Japanese Government stepped in as an airline operator when, on 30 October 1928, it established the Japan Air Transport Corporation (JAT) as the national flag carrier. JAT absorbed the Japan Air Transport

Institute and two other small companies and began scheduled passenger services in 1929. In current prices, the national government subsidised JAT annually by about U.S. $1 billion. Its aircraft were frequently chartered (for free) by the military for missions in Asia, especially during the 1931 invasion of Manchuria. The military role in Japanese aviation history expanded during the 1930s (Peattie, 2013), but with the country's defeat in 1945 its airfields were taken over by Allied occupying forces until they were returned to Japan for civilian aviation that recommenced from 1952 onwards.

In the modern democratic period, aviation is strongly regulated by international and bilateral agreements and technical innovation through the International Civil Aviation Organisation (Cronin, 2013). This chapter will demonstrate the strong regulatory role that the Japanese Government exercises over the private-sector organisations providing civilian airline services. From 1929, the Japanese Government has also been an airline operator (JAT then JAL) until its privatisation in 1987.

In the post-war era, the national government has been the sole planner for airports, the major operator of major airports and the primary source of funds for major airport construction. Somewhat unusual is the fact that legislation allows airport terminals and associated parking to be operated by the private sector. Under private finance initiatives (PFI), the government is increasing the opportunity for the private sector to be involved with operating airports under concession agreements with the Japanese Government (Sato and Okatani, 2016: 2). All of the above themes are illustrated in detail with airports in the Chūbu, Ōsaka and Tōkyō regions and with the historical development of airline companies and airport terminal operators. We start with the early stages of Japanese aviation in the modern period.

Modern Period

The early development of aviation is closely tied to the Japanese military, especially a few individuals in the Imperial Navy who argued against the then prevailing doctrine of land-based warfare (Sagen, 2004). In 1903, Lieutenant Commander Akiyama Saneyuki lectured at the Naval Staff College in Tōkyō on the advances in aviation technology. However, enthusiasts in the navy were marginalised from decision-making officers despite expressing their views in various fora. Lieutenant Commander

Yamamoto Eisuke presented a written statement on aviation to his superiors in March 1909 (in April 1927, he was appointed chief of the Naval Aviation Department). By July 1909, the army and navy jointly established The Provisional Committee for Research on Military Air Balloons (臨時軍用気球研究) and in June 1912 the navy formed The Committee for Naval Aeronautic Research (海軍航空術研究会), sending officers abroad for flight training and gathering strategic information on aviation.

Melzar (2020) argues that the successive reshaping of Japan's aviation has happened under French, British, German, and American influence with technological transfer a key element. The first experiments in naval aviation in Japan took place in early November 1912, when the Navy purchased and tested the French-manufactured Maurice Farman and Curtis float biplanes off Oppama in Yokosuka (Kanagawa Prefecture) before unveiling them at the 1912 Naval Review held off the coast at Yokohama (Suzuki and Sakai, 2005). Equipment and planes were imported from the Netherlands, the UK and the U.S.A., and planes were also produced under international licencing agreements. Japanese manufacturers developed their own planes such as the Mitsubishi shipboard attack plane Model 13 (1924) and the Kawasaki reconnaissance plane Model 88 (1928) but these were based predominantly on Western manufacturing designs.

Japanese aeronautical engineering advanced quickly and introduced distinctive innovations. In 1936, the Mitsubishi Aircraft Company produced the A5M1 shipboard fighter plan that went into service a year later and the more powerful engine A5M2 that entered service with the Imperial Navy early in 1937. This plane was highly successful in securing Japanese air supremacy over China after the outbreak of the Second Sino-Japanese. The success of this aircraft created a new awareness of the potential of strategic air power, which increased when a new fighter, the A6M2 (known as the "Zero" fighter), designed by Mitsubishi Heavy Industries in Nagoya, was accepted by the Navy in July 1940. This fighter aircraft out-performed Allied military aircraft in the early stages of the Pacific War.[1]

---

1   Designed by Horikoshi Jirō (1903–1982), the Zero was the first all-metal, low-wing monoplane with an enclosed cockpit produced by any world power outside of the U.S.A. or Europe. It possessed unparalleled advantages of speed, handling, manoeuvrability and an impressive range of 3,000 km. In the conflict with China

Civilian aircraft were mainly imported from the Netherlands (Fokker) and the U.S.A. (Douglas DC-2). Together with the Japanese Nakajima aircraft (Mikesh and Abe, 1990) they were deployed in the 1920s when civilian aviation started up. Data from the Japanese Department of Communications, Bureau of Aeronautics, *Manual on Aeronautics*, show that in the first year of civilian flights in 1921 civilian planes flew a total of about 50,000 km (Moulton with Ko, 1931: 89). In 1922 and 1923, three small companies—the first being the Japan Air Transport Institute—launched air transport service in Japan on a modest scale, covering limited routes between domestic cities. The inaugural service took place on 3 November 1922 with a flight off the Ohama Coast near Sakai to Tokushima City on Shikōkū Island. These private companies struggled to maintain their operations through the 1920s.

The Japanese Government was a strong supporter of commercial aviation. On 30 October 1928, in order to promote civil aviation, the Japanese Government established a national flag carrier, Japan Air Transport Corporation (JAT), which absorbed the three private airline companies and expanded services. JAT was officially controlled by the government's Ministry of Communications. It received the equivalent of U.S. $1 billion (in today's currency) from the Japanese Government during its first 11 years of operations. JAT began its first regular passenger service the following year, initially sharing the Imperial Japanese Army air base at Tachikawa (about 41 km west of Tōkyō Railway Station) as its Tōkyō terminal. The majority of the civilian flying fields were small and poorly equipped so the formation of JAT spurred the construction of Haneda Airport to serve Tōkyō.

In 1930, the Ministry of Communications purchased a 48-hectare piece of private land in the town of Haneda on Tōkyō Bay (the direct distance from Tōkyō Station is 15 km) for the purpose of constructing an airfield. Operations of the new civilian Haneda Airfield began in 1931. Through the 1930s, Haneda Airfield handled flights to and from various airfields in Japan, in Korea and in the puppet state of Manchuria. The

---

in July 1940, the Zero achieved an impressive kill ratio against outdated Russian, American, and Chinese designs, although many of these were antiquated biplanes. During the latter half of 1940, the Zero gained complete air superiority for Japan, destroying 59 Chinese aircraft in the air without losing a single fighter (Warfare History Network, 2019).

military gradually took over aviation operations at Haneda Airfield: in 1939, its runway was extended to the length of 800 metres and a second runway of the same length was constructed. During the war, civilian flights in and out of Haneda became extremely rare.

In exchange for the subsidy to JAT, the government had free use of the aircraft and facilities, and, importantly, the Japanese military, especially the Japanese army, played a substantial role in its governance. Noguchi and Boynes (2012) analyse the role of the state in determining the use of budgets within Japan Air Transport (1928-1938) and Japan Airways (1938–1945). Through the decade of the 1930s, as the Japanese Empire began to expand, the military made full use of JAT's airplanes for various conflicts overseas. JAL's aircraft were used in the invasion of Manchuria but this military transport role decreased as the army and JAT helped to establish the Manchukuō Aviation Company in 1932 (a consortium of the puppet government of Manchuria, the South Manchurian Railway Company and Sumitomo *zaibatsu*), the Huitong Airways (1936)—in preparation for Japan's invasion of north China—and China Airways (1938), which later absorbed Huitong Airways (Century of Flight, n.d.).

These military imperatives allowed JAT to shift its focus to the civilian passenger market and begin using its new 14-passenger Douglas DC-2s on more commercially profitable routes between Japan and Manchuria in 1936. JAT benefitted from a resurgence in military passenger traffic with the start of the Second Sino-Japanese War of 1937. In 1938, JAT carried nearly 70,000 passengers, representing 2.6 per cent of the world's passenger traffic (Century of Flight, n.d.). The same year, Kizugawa Airport in Ōsaka handled 8,800 departures and arrivals and 10,000 passengers (equivalent of a mean passenger occupancy per aircraft of 1.14).

At the end of the year, the Japanese Government established a new airline, Greater Japan Airways (GJA), as a monopoly business for all civil aviation when JAT was merged into the new company. GJA was originally an independent private company when the Japanese Government bought out half of the company's net worth. GJA was primarily an international operator, and it used a combination of foreign and domestic aircraft for its services. These planes included the eight-passenger Nakajima AT-2 airliner, the 11-passenger Mitsubishi MC-20 transport aircraft, and the domestically built version of the 21-passenger seat Douglas DC-3. The Japanese had signed a licensing agreement with the Douglas Company in February 1938 to build domestic versions of the DC-3.

The beginning of the war in the Pacific in December 1941 substantially affected Japanese commercial aviation. One month after the start of hostilities, the Japanese Government suspended all commercial operations of GJA. Instead, the airline's services were completely geared to support the military's operations in the Pacific. Japanese airfields were heavily bombed by Allied forces, and, with the occupation of Japan, its airfields were under the control of Allied air commands that lasted until the end of the Korean War. Civilian air services in Japan did not resume until 1952.

Modern Democratic Period

With the defeat of Japan in 1945, Allied forces occupied many airfields. Japan was prohibited from producing or using airplanes, and all facilities for the manufacture of aircraft and for aeronautical research were either dismantled or converted to other purposes. This directive by the Allied Occupying Forces lasted until April 1952 when Japanese civil aviation activities resumed following the conclusion of the San Francisco Peace Treaty (Kodansha, 1993: 86).

The modern commercial aviation industry in Japan, as we understand it today,[2] emerged after the end of the Pacific War with the resumption of international and domestic flights. The industry is highly regulated internally, and greatly influenced both by bilateral agreements on international air services (the first with the U.S.A. in 1952, then the

---

2   The key policies of the Japanese Government in the 21st century have been: "Basic Policy on Economic and Fiscal Management and Structural Reform 2002" approved by Cabinet on 25 June 2002; report of the Aviation Subcommittee of the Transportation Policy Council (21 June 2007) "Measures for Future Development and Operation of Airports and Aviation Security Facilities—A Strategic New Aviation Policy Vision"; Cabinet decision on Asia Gateway Concept "Basic Policy for Economic and Fiscal Management 2007" approved on 19 June 2007; review of legal system related to airport maintenance and operation (promulgation of law on 18 June 2008, partial enforcement); Ministry of Land, Infrastructure, Transport and Tourism growth strategy (17 May 2010) formulated six strategies in the aviation field and approved by Cabinet on 18 June 2010 as "New Growth Strategy"; and Cabinet decision on Japan Revitalization Strategy (31 July 2012 (Civil Aviation Bureau, Ministry of Land, Infrastructure, Transport and Tourism, 2012).

United Kingdom, and now there are agreements with 55 countries and one region) and by the International Civil Aviation Organisation (ICAO), established in 1947 in Montreal, Canada, whose core function is to research new air transport policy and standardised innovations (https://www.icao.int/about-icao/Pages/default.aspx).

Nowadays, in Japan, air carriers are predominantly private-sector organisations, airports are operated primarily by national and local governments (with a few major airport hubs now operated on concessions from the government), terminals and parking are contested by both sectors and aviation policy is formulated by the Ministry of Land, Infrastructure, Transport and Tourism. Air traffic control is a government function provided by the Air Traffic Services System within the Civil Aviation Bureau of the Ministry of Land, Infrastructure, Transport and Tourism.

Government Airlines and Private-Sector Airlines

When civilian air transport resumed, Japan Air Lines (JAL) was established in 1953 as a major private company to service domestic and international markets. In order to foster the company as a national flag carrier, a new bill in the *Diet* was passed to make JAL a special corporation. The government invested in JAL the equivalent of the value of the capital stock that the company originally sold in starting its business (Yamauchi and Ito, 1996, footnote 1, p. 4; Ito and Yamauchi, 1996). Around the same time, several small private airline companies were founded, but the domestic market was in its early stage of development and their business conditions were unstable with bankruptcies and consolidations occurring.

By 1957, All Nippon Airways (ANA) had become the second major airline. The remaining private companies underwent various consolidations, and by the mid-1960s, there were four airline companies operating in Japan: JAL; ANA; Japan Domestic Airlines (JDA); and Toa Airways (TA). In the second half of the 1960s, TA formed cooperative arrangements with ANA, whilst JDA associated with JAL. This flagged possible company mergers but the buoyant passenger demand lead to TA and JDA merging with each other in 1971 to form Toa Domestic Airlines—later the Japan Air System (JAS).

The Japanese Government kept a watchful eye on these business practices. A Cabinet Meeting Resolution of 1970 "Concerning Airline Operations" approved a restructuring of the airline industry. The reform resulted in a change from a two-company (JAL and ANA) regime to a three-company (JAL, ANA, JAS) regime. There were specific rules ("The Aviation Constitution") issued in 1972 that segmented the industry into different markets. JAL would service international routes and domestic trunk routes; ANA would serve domestic trunk and local routes plus short-distance international charter flights; and JAS would serve local routes and a portion of domestic trunk routes. JAL and JAS merged in 2002. A new carrier could enter the international air cargo market if threshold demand was established. Strict economic rules to all aspects of the Japanese airline industry were introduced where the three main airlines were required to follow the Ministry of Transport's (MOT's) 'administrative guidelines' as to their business plans and domestic and international routes flown.

In the 1970s, the annual growth rate of revenue-passenger kilometres in the domestic markets was 12.2 per cent, and, in international markets, the figure was an astounding 42.4 per cent when airline networks expanded (Yamauchi and Ito, 1996: 4). However, the aviation sector of any domestic economy cannot be isolated from international market trends and the deregulation of the United States airline industry that occurred in 1978 (Williams, 2017; Miyoshi, 2015; and Sinha, 2019) proved an important external influence on Japanese government policy. Subsequent quantitative analyses demonstrated the success of deregulation to consumers in Japan (Kanda *et al.*, 2006) although this claim of success is disputed by Ito (2007).

In September 1985, the Minister of Transport consulted the Council for Transport Policy (an official advisory committee to the Minister) about the future of airline services in Japan. Their reports advocated for greater competition in both domestic and international markets: (1) international routes would be served by multiple carriers; (2) competition on domestic routes would be promoted by new entry into particular city pair markets; and (3) JAL would be completely privatised (the government held a 34.7 per cent equity share when it was privatised in November 1987). Interestingly, the Council for Transport Policy Report argued that "an American style of deregulation does not suit circumstances in Japan" because of the capacity limitations of

Tōkyō International (Haneda) Airport and Ōsaka International (Itami) Airport, and because of the different competitive strengths of the airlines (Yamauchi and Ito, 1996: 6–7).

This partial deregulation enabled the three carriers to make their own decisions on matters such as capacity increases, introduction of new types of fares and routes to fly. The *Civil Aeronautics Law* was revised at the end of 1994 to relax the conditions for introducing and setting discount fares in domestic markets. In 1995, JAL introduced a new discount fare which was 25 to 35 per cent lower than the regular fare, with restrictions similar to the U.S. discount ticketing system. Another example was in 2000, when, to compete with high-speed rail, JAL, ANA, and JAS introduced the 'shuttle' service in the Tōkyō—Ōsaka (Itami) market to standardise the airfare, make the tickets interchangeable amongst the three companies and speed up the boarding process (Ito, 2007: 5–7).

In 1997, the Japanese Government further deregulated the business by allowing new entrants into the domestic market. In 1998, Skymark started operations on the second busiest domestic route—Haneda (Tōkyō) to Fukuoka—and Air Do started flying between Haneda and Sapporo (Hokkaidō) on the busiest domestic route. Described as "no frills" airlines with cheaper fares, Skymark and Air Do were the first new entrants since JAS began operations in 1945. By 2021, there were eight domestic and international carriers (Table 20), two cargo carriers (ANA Cargo and Nippon Cargo Airlines, owned by Nippon Yuson) and 14 domestic airlines that commenced operations between 1983 and 2010.

The list of Japanese domestic airlines and their commencement date are as follows: Air Do (1998); Amakusa Airlines (2000); All Nippon Airways Wings (2010); Fuji Dream Airlines (2009); Hokkaido Air System (1998); Ibex Airlines (2004); Japan Transocean Air (1993); New Central Airlines (1978); New Japan Aviation (2011); Oriental Airbridge (2001); Ryukyu Air Commuter (1985); and Solaseed Air (2011). Their ownership structure is varied reflecting ANA and JAL support of regional airlines, local government and business interest in investing in air transport, corporate investors and the encouragement of ordinary investors.

For example, Air Do started up with 26 shareholders, owners of small- and medium-sized Hokkaidō-based companies, plus professional individuals. The main shareholders are now Kyoto Ceramics, Reikei Co.,

Tokyo Marine and Fire Insurance and Hokkaido Electric. The company made a direct appeal to the citizens of Hokkaidō to support Air Do and bring more affordable fares to the region. Some 7,000 shares were sold at 50,000 yen each (U.S. $450)—mostly on a one share per person basis that has created a useful market of loyal passengers (Aviation Strategy, 1999: 14). However, the airline has had a checked history with bankruptcy and periodic restructuring (Ito, 2007).

Table 20. Ownership of Japanese Domestic and International Airlines.
Source: Author based on Airline Company Websites.

Airline Company	Commenced Operations	Ownership
All Nippon Airways (ANA)	1952	ANA Holdings
Japan Airlines (JAL)	1951	Japan Airlines Co., Ltd.
Jetstar Japan (JJP)	2012	Qantas (33.3%), JAL (33.3%), Mitsubishi Corporation (16.7%) & Century Tokyo Leasing Corporation (16.7%)
Peach Aviation (APJ)	2011	ANA, FEIG, and the Innovation Network Corporation of Japan
Skymark Airlines (SKY)	1998	Low-cost carrier Integral Corporation (50.1%), with minority investments from ANA (16.5%), Sumitomo Mitsui Banking Corporation and the Development Bank of Japan (33.4%)
Spring Airlines Japan (SJO)	2014	Low-cost carrier owned by Spring Airlines, China (33%) and various Japanese investors.
StarFlyer (SFJ)	2006	ANA (19.0%) stake, and TOTO, Yasakawa Electric Corporation, Kyushu Electric Power Company and Nissan Motor Company
ZIPAIR Tokyo (TZT)	2020*	Subsidiary of JAL

* Due to Covid-19 passenger services have been delayed but cargo flights to Bangkok commenced in June 2020

Amongst these regional airline companies, the ownership patterns are diverse. J-Air is a wholly owned subsidiary of JAL, whereas Ibex Airlines is a regional airline with a collaborative arrangement with ANA. Solaseed Air's major shareholders are the Development Bank of Japan (22.4 per cent), Miyazaki Kotsu Co., Ltd. (17.0 per cent) and ANA Holdings Inc. (17.0 per cent). Fuji Dream Airlines is a wholly owned subsidiary of Suzuyo & Co., Ltd. (core businesses include domestic and international logistics) and New Central Airlines is owned by Kawada Industries.

There is a long history of the Japanese Government formulating policies on inbound travellers (Soshiroda, 2005), although the current population decline and the Covid pandemic of 2019 has forced the government to re-think ways of attracting tourist business. In the 1990s, there was a further decentralisation of charter flights to regional airports in Japan when, from 1989 to 2010, the number of airports servicing charter flights increased from 18 to 32. The share of charter flights handled by regional airports increased from 75 per cent to 92 per cent (Wu and Peng, 2014: 51).

Japan deregulated its airline market in 2000 by implementing a new *Airline Act* that applied equally to both scheduled service and charter airlines. Japan lifted the restrictions regulating the number of charter flights operated by foreign carriers in an attempt to attract more foreign carriers. Suffering from an ageing and shrinking population, Japan began to vigorously promote inbound tourism in 2003 by launching the "Visit Japan Campaign".

On 16 May 2007, the Japanese Government launched the Asian Gateway Initiative to achieve "Asian Open Skies", especially to promote outbound tourism. Under the Asian Open Skies policy, Japan signed open skies treaties with Korea and the U.S.A. in 2010, with Hong Kong, Macau, Singapore, Malaysia and Taiwan in 2011, and with China in August 2012. The Ministry of Land, Infrastructure, Transport and Tourism progressively liberalised air charter services: in December 2008, it introduced measures to allow foreign airlines to operate charters between Japan and a third country without the permission of Japanese airlines.

In particular, the Ministry announced its intent to promote the air charter business at Narita International Airport by allowing charter flights to be operated on routes serviced by scheduled flights. In 2010, as part of the Asian Gateway Initiative, the Ministry further deregulated Haneda by allowing this airport to service long-haul charters (Wu and Peng, 2014: 54). In the entire Japanese market, charters are operated on more routes and reach more airports than regular airlines (Wu, 2016: 263).

The year 2012 heralded the low-cost carrier (LCC) era in Japan when the first LCC-dedicated terminal was opened at Kansai Airport (Terminal 2) in October (Civil Aviation Bureau, Ministry of Land, Infrastructure, Transport and Tourism, 2012: 37–39). Terminal 2 marked the launch of an airport-airline collaboration, giving birth to the first Japanese based LCC, Peach Aviation. As shown in Table 20, three more Japanese low-cost carriers have entered the aviation market since 2020.

Airport Policy and Planning

The Japanese Government plays a dominant role in airport planning, funding and construction of aviation facilities. The *Aerodrome Development Law* (1952) stipulated that, of various aerodromes in Japan, those serving civil aviation routes are to be designated as "airports". These airports are regulated by the *Aeronautical Law (1952)* with regard to safety, *the Noise Prevention Law (1967)* with regard to environmental noise and the *Airport Development Law (1956)* with regard to airport developments (Shibata, 1999: 125).

The law classifies airports that offer scheduled commercial flights as: Category One—those required for international routes; Category Two—those required for major domestic routes; and Category Three—those required for regional domestic routes. Table 21 has been updated with a footnote and classifies the 94 Japanese airports into these three categories (Kōbe Airport had not been constructed at the time this table was prepared) and describes those airports that now have been privatised.

Table 21. Classification of Japanese Airports, as of 1999.*
Source: reproduced from Shibata, 1999, Table 1, p. 127, and updated by the Author.

Airport Category	Operator or Ownership	Name of Airport/ Aerofrome	Number of Airports
ONE	Ministry of Transport	Tōkyō International, Ōsaka International	4(5)
	Public Corporation	New Tōkyō International (Narita)	
	Stock Corporation	Kansai International, (Chūbu International)	
TWO	Ministry of Transport	New Chitose, Wakkanai, Kushiro, Hakodate, Sendai, Niigata, Nagoya, Yao, Hiroshima, Takamatsu, Matsuyama, Kochi, Fukuoka, Kita-Kyushu, Nagasaki, Kumamoto, Oita, Miyazaki, Kagoshima, Naha.	20
	Municipality	Asahikawa, Obihiro, Akita, Yamagata, Yamaguchi-Ube.	5
	Defense Agency or Defense Facilities Administration Agency	Tokushima Aerodrome, Sapporo Aerodrome, Komatsu Aerodrome, Miho Aerodrome.	4
THREE	Municipalities	(Medium and smaller regional airports)	59
		Total Number of Airports Subject to Application of Airport Development Law	92(93)

*As of 2021: Chūbu, Kansai, Kōbe & Ōsaka (Itami) Airports are privatised; Tōkyō International Airport (Haneda) is operated by the Civil Aviation Bureau, Ministry of Land, Infrastructure, Transport and Tourism; Sendai Airport, after the 2011 Northeast Japan Earthquake and tsumami was rebuilt for U.S. $21.1 million by a consortium led by the Tōkyū Corporation on a 30-year public service concession scheme; and Hiroshima Airport was privatised from mid-2021.

Airport development plans had been formulated by the Ministry of Transport every five years. The first plan was for the period 1967 to 1970 where the policy objective was to increase the capacity of Haneda and Ōsaka (Itami) Airports (Table 22). From 1971 to 2002 Airport Development Plans focused first on the construction of Narita Airport and from the 4th Plan onwards the focus was on the development of Kansai Airport.

The central government is responsible for building large international airports (the so-called Category I airport), and the objectives of the 5-Year Airport Development Plans between 1967 and 2002 make the focus on major international airports clear (Table 22). Because of shortages of funding in the national treasury the 7th Plan was over 7 years. There is no reference to subsequent airport development plans and the government of Japan introduced legislation on private finance initiatives (PFI) that permit the private sector to form consortia that can bid for concessions to operate major airports.

Table 22. Policy Objectives Japanese 5-Year Airport Development Plans.
Source: reproduced from Shibata, 1999, Table 2, p. 131.

Airport Development Five Year Plans	Period	Policy Objectives
First Airport Development Plan	1967–1970	To develop Ōsaka International Airport and Tōkyō International Airport (Haneda Airport) due to lack of overall capacities.
Second Airport Development Plan	1971–1975	Development of New Tōkyō International Airport (Narita Airport), improvement of Ōsaka International Airport, and development of regional airports.
Third Airport Development Plan	1976–1980	Promotion of works related to development of airport surrounding areas, development of Narita Airport.
Fourth Airport Development Plan	1981–1985	Ultimate completion of Narita Airport (the first phase of development of which was completed in 1978 development of Kansai International Airport, and of Haneda Airport towards the Tokyo Bay.
Fifth Airport Development Plan	1986–1990	Promotion of developing Narita Airport and Kansai International Airport, continuation of the Fourth Airport Development Plan.

Airport Development Five Year Plans	Period	Policy Objectives
Sixth Airport Development Plan	1991–1995	Further promotion of the Fifth Airport Development Plan.
Seventh Airport Development Plan	1996–2002	Further promotion of the Sixth Airport Development Plan (both Narita Airport and Kansai International Airport were commissioned but have not ultimately been completed).

Major airports (except for Narita and Kansai) are funded through the Airport Development Special Account. The main feature of this funding mechanism is that most of the money for building airports is accumulated from passengers' fares (and not from the general taxpayer). Passengers pay aviation fuel tax and airport charges which are included in airfares. This account is funded by airport charges—landing fees, special landing fees, navigation charges, aviation fuel tax, subsidies from the General Account of the national government and borrowing from government investment and loan program (Yamauchi and Ito, 1999, Figure 7, n.p.). Funds borrowed from the government will be also repaid by passengers in the future. Another characteristic of the funding mechanism is its revenue pooling. The revenue received at each airport is brought together into the special account and allocated according to the central governments planning.

As noted by Hayashi (2021: 1.1.B) a unique aspect is that Japanese airport terminals and car parks were constructed and are owned and managed by a private entity or a 'third sector' entity (a company jointly owned by a local government and private entities). Most of the airports in Japan were established and operated by the Ministry of Transport. Other modes of ownership involving the private sector have developed (as detailed later) because of the shortage of national funding. Funding problems have also caused landing charges to be increased to the highest level in the world.

In 2013, the *Act for the Operation of Government Controlled Airports by Private Sector Entities* was enacted to enable the central and local governments to privatise airports through concession. The Ministry of Land, Infrastructure, Transport and Tourism announced the Basic Policy on the Operation of Government Controlled Airports by Private Section Entities (Basic Policy for Airports), which provides for the basic framework for all concessions of national airports (TMI Associates, 2020).

Airports in Metropolitan Tōkyō

Three civilian airports serve the Tōkyō metropolis (population in 2020 of about 37.4 million). The oldest is the Ministry of Communications' Haneda Airfield that dates from 1931. After the Second World War, the airfield was used solely by the occupying forces before being partially returned to Japan in 1952 and fully by 1959. The other international airport is located at Narita in Chiba Prefecture and commercial flights started there in 1978. Ibaraki Airport started as a military airfield, and is a minor regional airport that, today, offers services on a limited number of domestic and international routes.

Ibaraki Airport

Prior to March 2010 Ibaraki Airport (98 km north of Tōkyō Station) was known as Hyakuri Airfield. It was first developed by the Imperial Japanese Navy in 1937, with much of the land claimed from local farmers under the direct orders of Emperor Hirohito. After the end of the Pacific War, the locals reclaimed the land and resumed farming. The military base was re-opened in 1956 by the Japan Air Self-Defence Force. In March 2010, after a 22 billion yen (U.S. $243 million) local and national government investment, the airfield was renamed as Ibaraki Airport, offering only two routes—an Asiana service to Seoul (Asiana Airlines) and to Kōbe (Skymark Airlines)—with only 203,070 travelling passengers that year. The Ibaraki Airport website (http://www.ibaraki-airport.net/en/flight.html) lists domestic flights to Fukuoka, Kōbe, Naha and Sapporo (Skymark) and international flights to Shanghai and Xi'an (Spring Airlines) and to Taipei (Tiger Air Taiwan).

Haneda Airport

On 13 September 1945, Haneda Airfield was taken over by the U.S. Army Air Forces and renamed the Haneda Army Air Base. Projects to expand the air base were quickly formulated, with families from neighbouring areas being evicted from their homes. After a construction period that lasted from October 1945 to June 1946, Haneda Army Air Base had expanded to 257.4 hectares. In 1952, a portion of Haneda was returned to the Japanese Government, and that portion was named Tōkyō International Airport so as to establish the first international gateway. By 1959, all of Haneda had been returned to the Japanese Government.

The impoverished state of public finances in post-war Japan allowed only the paving the taxiway and apron at Haneda from the national budget. To restore the airport as an international gateway, Japan urgently had to expand the facilities to be suitable for an airport capable of serving Japan's capital of Tōkyō. The Japanese Cabinet decided to build a terminal with private capital, and in 1953 Japan Airport Terminal Co., Ltd. (JAT) was established through the cooperation of major Japanese businesses with capital of 150 million yen. The terminal opened in May 1955.

From that date, 64 significant airport developments (including some associated national and global developments) are listed on the Haneda Airport Website , where the details of each development can be found at https://tokyo-haneda.com/en/enjoy/history_of_haneda_airport/index.html. Images of the staged development of Haneda Airport between 1955 and 2010 can be found in Yamaguchi (2013, Figure 3, p. 11). In 1984, Haneda Airport "Okiai-tenkai" expansion project was initiated and a pair of parallel runways (A and C) and a single crosswind runway (B) were built in stages into Tōkyō Bay. In order to create the airport islands, dredged clays were used on these offshore expansion projects (1984–2007) and the D-runway project (2007–2010) (Watabe and Sassa, 2016).

With extra runway capacity, the international network expanded significantly from 18 flights a day to 4 cities to 55 flights a day to 17 cities, including the opening of new routes to Europe and to the U.S.A. With the opening of the International Passenger Terminal (TIAT) in 2011, the number of annual international passengers increased to 7.25 million. As a twenty-four-hour international hub, the number of passengers connecting from Japanese regional airports to international flights at Haneda increased about four-fold. In addition, an international cargo terminal (TIACT), which has advanced functions, was opened. The desirability of increasing flights to and from Haneda is now under discussion. According to the Ministry of Land, Infrastructure, Transport and Tourism's website, the number of international flights of 60,000 per year in 2015 are projected to increase to 99,000 per year in 2020. Due to the Covid-19 pandemic and international travel restrictions, the total passenger traffic dropped from 86.9 million in 2019 to 31.2 million in 2020 (Gorka, 2021).

Narita International Airport

Projections of traffic growth and landing slots at Haneda Airport in the 1960s indicated there was a need for a second airport to serve the Tōkyō metropolis. However, the planning and delivery of Japanese airports was no longer confined to a dialogue amongst the three tiers of government. From the time that the Japanese Government made a formal decision on 16 November 1962, and the Ministry of Transport planned the "New Tōkyō International Airport" of about 2,300 hectares some 70 km from Tōkyō Railway Station, organised community opposition has dogged airport development up to the present day.

The example of the location of Narita Airport represents the most extreme case, probably in its history, of civil disobedience against a Japanese government, from within a society that is traditionally respectful of hierarchical authority (Andrews, 2016). Whilst community consultation on major infrastructure projects was not common practice by all governments in the 1960s, the lack of government transparency and the failure to address land acquisition adequately have been factors that have fuelled trenchant opposition to the development of Narita Airport (Bowen, 1975). Aspects of this story still resonate in this third decade of the 21st century.

After investigations of alternative sites in the prefectures of Chiba and Ibaraki, The Aviation Council Report to the Minister of Transport recommended the Tomisato site (southwest of the finally selected site) that was unexpectedly announced by the Chief Cabinet Secretary, Tomisaburo Hashimoto, at a press conference. Opposition movements had already risen in each of the potential airport sites, such as the Tomisato-Yachimata Anti-Airport Union formed in 1963. Local farmers expressed outrage at the one-sided nature of the decision and allied with political opposition parties—the Japanese Communist Party and the Social Democratic Party of Japan. By 1966 opposition to the proposal of building an airport still remained strong.

The secretive side of Japanese politics emerged with the Satō Cabinet (Satō Eisaku, Prime Minister 1964–1972) colluding with the Transport Vice-Minister, Wakasa Tokuji, the Liberal Democratic Party Vice-President, Kawashima Shōjirō and the Chiba Prefectural Mayor, Tomonō Taketo, to move the construction site 4 km to the northeast onto the Goryō Farm—a state-owned tract of land that once had been in the ownership of the Imperial Family. The Cabinet anticipated—incorrectly as events turned out—that the impoverished farming communities of Sanrizuka would sell their land and be compensated with a "fair" price as was the law (Lemay-Fruchter, 2021). As it transpired, the Goryō Farmland comprised less than 40 per cent of the area needed for the airport plan so a major program of land acquisition from the public was still required.

On 22 June 1966, the Liberal Party Prime Minister, Satō Eisaku, after briefing prefectural officials, held a broadcast conference with Mayor Tomonō Taketo regarding the Sanrizuka plan. As no public consultation had taken place, Sanrizuka and Shibayama residents learnt of the decision from the broadcast. Furious opposition broke out amongst frustrated communities, as had previously occurred in Tomisato. The opposition was led by the Sanrizuka-Shibayama United Opposition League against Construction of the Narita Airport (三里塚芝山連合空港反対同盟), which locals formed under the leadership of government opposition parties.

At its height, the 'union' mobilised 17,500 people for a general rally, while thousands of riot police were brought in on several occasions. The "union" became increasingly radicalised and the struggle resulted in significant delays in the opening of the airport, as well as deaths on both sides (known as the Tōhō Jūjiro Incident). The government originally tried to purchase land with the landowners' agreement. However, as a substantial number of landowners refused to sell their land, the government decided in 1971 to legally evict residents which only prompted more protests. As of 2020, there remain five households on the airport property with one owner recently reported to have turned down U.S. $1.6 million for the purchase of his land (Leff, 2020).

Narita Airport finally opened on 20 May 1978. The opening day attracted a union rally estimated at 22,000 people who declared a continuing campaign of resistance against the airport. Over 500 guerrilla actions have taken place against Narita airport since its opening in 1978 (Leff, 2020). For instance, there were clashes between riot police and protesters, and numerous attempts of arson targeted at fuel pipelines. However, with Narita Airport operational, and the chance of closing it remote, the defiance of the union movement gradually eroded, and internal fractures split the union movement, severely damaging its credibility and influence. In addition, the government started adopting a more conciliatory approach in the 1990s, commencing with a stakeholder symposium on various airport issues. In 1995, the (then) Prime Minister, Murayama Tomiichi (June 1994–January 1996 as Head of Japanese Socialist Party), issued an apology to the affected residents.

The final site area of Narita International Airport was reduced to 1,040 hectares that meant that the northerly runway had to be reduced to 2,600 metres in length. In March 2012 the introduction of the simultaneous parallel takeoff and landing system, together with two runways of length 2,500 metres, increased the number of annual aircraft slots to 250,000. In 2003, the Japanese Government passed the *Narita International Airport Corporation Act* (成田国際空港株式会社法) that privatised the airport. On 1 April 2004, the New Tōkyō International Airport was officially renamed Narita International Airport. Its site plan can be found at Civil Aviation Bureau, Ministry of Land, Infrastructure, Transport and Tourism (2012: 23).

According to the Civil Aviation Bureau website the aim of Narita International Airport is to strengthen the international aviation network to make the airport a major hub in Asia by expanding domestic feeder lines, offering more aviation services, such as low-cost carriers (Jetstar Japan and AirAsia Japan) and business jets, and increasing terminal and parking capacity. The airport handled 44.3 million passengers in 2019, dropping to 10.5 million in 2020 (Gorka, 2021).

The Japanese Government is in the process of boosting Narita International Airport as an international hub. The actions by Narita International Airport Corporation (2021) include from the winter of

2019: curfew restrictions were removed to allow aircraft to take off and land up to midnight; 146 additional slots between 21.00 and 24.00 hours; and reconfiguring rapid exit taxiways to allow four more flights each hour. The current short runway is to be lengthened to 3,500 metres. The construction of this third runway, at a cost of some U.S. $4.6 billion, is expected to be completed by 2030 (Ellis, 2019: 1). The new runway increases the annual number of airport slots from the current 300,000 to 500,000 or from 72 hourly slots to 98 hourly slots.

Airports in the Ōsaka Region

There are three major airports in the Ōsaka region located in Kōbe, Ōsaka Itami and Kansai that collectively handled about 47 million passengers in 2019. Today, they are managed and operated by a private-sector consortium led by VINCHI airports (Headquarters in Paris) but the historical path of each airport has differed. Itami (Ōsaka No. 2 Airfield) was a compromise location involving the city governments of Ōsaka and Kōbe, but, from the late 1930s, it was predominantly a military facility—first by the Japanese armed forces then by the U.S. occupying forces until being returned to the Japanese Government in 1959 and then used for civilian flights.

Kōbe and Kansai are relatively new airports constructed in Ōsaka Bay (Yukawa and Matsubara, 2019, Figure 1, n.p.). The introduction of jet aircraft, and the associated noise, prompted community action that ultimately led to the construction of Kansai airport built in Ōsaka Bay that was operational from 1994. The City of Kobe continued to lobby for its own airport and the Japanese Government stimulus packages following the Great Hanshin Earthquake of January 1995 provided an opportunity to construct a single runway airport on an artificial island in Ōsaka Bay.

There are two other airports in the Ōsaka region to consider: the first because of its association with the early years of civil aviation in Japan; the second because it is one example of the numerous small airports scattered across the Japanese archipelago. Seaplanes took off from the waters off Ohama Coast, near Sakai, and offered passenger services through Kizugawa Airfield (at the mouth of the Kizu River that empties into Ōsaka Bay) then onto Shikōkū Island. Yao Airport is a small general aviation airport that offers some scenic and charter flights.

Kizugawa Airfield

From 1923, seaplanes started taking off and landing in the waters at the mouth of the Kizu River with flights to and from Tokushima, Takamatsu, Matsuyama (Shikōkū) and Beppu (Kyūshū). With the growing demand for mail and cargo in the Ōsaka region, a private airfield on land was required. The Ministry of Communications Aviation Bureau selected the wetland at the mouth of the Kizu River for the site to construct the 39-hectare airfield that was 14 km south of Ōsaka Railway Station (Wikipedia Japan, https://ja.wikipedia.org/wiki/木津川飛行場).

The airfield, built by the Ministry of Communication as its first aerodrome project in Japan, was put into service in 1929 when Japan Air Transport opened flights to the Tachikawa Army Airfield (Tōkyō) and the Tachiarai Army Airfield in Fukuoka. In 1938, Kizugawa was equipped with a runway length of 720 metres, and the airport was, at the time, the largest aviation base in Japan. Civil flight operations were moved to Ōsaka No. 2 Airfield (Itami) as the surrounding area had become industrialised, with chimneys causing obstacles to flight manoeuvres, and problems with heavy fog. The Japanese military continued to use the airfield.

Ōsaka No. 1 Airfield (Yamato River Estuary)

In 1931, the City of Ōsaka formulated a landfill plan on the estuary of the Yamato River for a new airfield site (Ōsaka No. 1 Airfield), and, two years later, construction started. It was completed in 1939. However, the chairman of the Kōbe Business Association objected on the grounds that it was too far away to serve Kōbe. The Ōsaka Chamber of Commerce and Industry defended its locational decision until finally the Japanese Government stepped in, arguing that the location was unsuitable for an international airfield and prone to thick fog. The City of Ōsaka abandoned its plan in 1942 (Hashizumi, 2004), and national and prefectural governments worked collaboratively on a more suitable airfield location.

Ōsaka No. 2 Airfield (Itami)

As a compromise solution brokered by the Japanese Government, construction on Ōsaka No. 2 Airfield (Itami) began in July 1936 on a 53-hectare site that was about 10 km north of Ōsaka Railway Station and 36 km east of Kōbe city centre. It opened as No. 2 Ōsaka Airfield (第二大阪飛行場) in 1939. Most of the land is located in Hyōgo Prefecture (Itami City) but the remaining portion is in Ōsaka Prefecture (cities of Toyonaka and Ikeda). The terminal complex is located today in all three of these cities. Initially, the airport was used primarily by the Imperial Japanese Army. Its military function continued when occupation forces took over the airfield in 1945, expanding it to 221 hectares, and renaming it the U.S. Itami Air Base. The airfield was used extensively by U.S. forces during the Korean War (June 1950–July 1953).

Following its return to Japanese control in March 1959 it was renamed Ōsaka Airport. The Japanese government planned an airport expansion project with an additional 82.5 hectares of land so that the runways could accommodate the landing and take-off of jet aircraft. Despite some protests from locals, the plan was approved by the three neighbouring local government assemblies between 1960 and 1961 with strong backing from local business groups. The aviation industry was also supportive because it was anxious to compete with the high-speed rail services that opened between Tōkyō and Shin-Ōsaka in 1964.

Jet flights began on 1 June 1964 and that immediately triggered more complaints from nearby residents about jet aircraft noise (Yukawa and Matsubara, 2019, n.p.). Further protests occurred in 1966 when the government compulsorily purchased land to extend the runway. The main runway at Ōsaka Airport was completed in 1970 and served major international airlines such as Pan Am, British Airways, Cathay Pacific and Air India. With the rapid growth of the Japanese economy, the areas around Ōsaka Airport had become a residential commuter-belt to Ōsaka.

Dissatisfied local residents became organised and sued the managing airport organisation—the national government—demanding compensation for aircraft noise-related damage (exacerbated by the U.S. Armed Forces using the airport for aircraft maintenance and re-fuelling) and the suspension of night-time flights. In addition to this lawsuit, over 20,000 local residents wanted the closure of the airport on grounds of 'environmental pollution'. The injunction of night flights was not granted by the Supreme Court after 6 years of deliberations, but the national government voluntarily restricted the airport operating hours to between 07.00 and 21.00 hours.

By the mid-1970s, the airport was subject to extensive slot restrictions, with operations limited to 200 jets and 170 propeller aircraft per day, and no take-offs or landings allowed after 21.00 hours. These restrictions led the major domestic airlines to adopt more widebody aircraft that caused additional concern amongst locals who protested against the increased aircraft noise and the greater danger of a crash event.

Plans were mooted to close Ōsaka Itami Airport following the opening of Kansai Airport in 1994, but nearby communities opposed such a move because of the likely job losses. The Japanese Government proposed downgrading Ōsaka Itami Airport's status to a second-class airport. However, that would have imposed on local governments the payment of one-third of the airport's operating costs and this generated more protests from the surrounding local governments. The proposal to close Ōsaka Itami Airport was withdrawn.

Kansai International Airport

In the late 1960s, the Kansai region was losing trade, development, and firms to the rapidly growing Tōkyō region. To help make Ōsaka and Kōbe more attractive, both city governments proposed the construction of a new international airport to rival the then second airport for Tōkyō at Narita. Ōsaka Itami Airport was facing capacity constraints as air traffic boomed along with economic growth. At first, developers, and some government officials, wanted to build the new airport near Kōbe but the City of Kōbe Government rejected a plan for a large international airport.

In 1971, the Ministry of Transport commissioned a study into the location of a new airport to accommodate growing passenger demand from Ōsaka and to eliminate the noise issue at Ōsaka Itami Airport. The planning objective of Kansai Airport was to resolve the environmental noise problem at Ōsaka Itami Airport. Out of the five feasible sites in the Ōsaka Bay area, Senshu, the most southern location, was selected but opposition from residents forced the airport site 5 km offshore on reclaimed land (Yamaguchi, 2013: 16). The plan was for an artificial island that would be 4,000 metres long and 2.5 km wide (1,000 hectares). Innovative engineering was required for solid foundations for the runways and the built structures, and building structures to withstand typhoons, waves and earthquakes.

The airport cost over U.S. $20 billion to build. Construction started in 1987, and, once the island had been completed and the compacted soils allowed to settle, the airport construction began, taking an additional four years. The airport has two parallel runways (built by 1994 and 2007, respectively), two terminals and a cargo facility. To connect the island with the mainland, a 3-km long bridge was built at a cost of U.S. $1 billion (Cummins, 2020). It is worth noting that advances in aircraft engine technology had shrunk the footprint of the noise contours by the time Kansai Airport was opened in 1994 so that it would have had been possible to have built it closer to the shore, thereby reducing the costs of ground transport access.

The financial scheme to construct Kansai Airport involved not only central and local governments but also the private sector. This reflected Japanese Government economic policy during 1980s to endorse "Minkatsu"—private finance initiative (PFI)—in building social infrastructure, such as city halls. By international comparisons, Japan was slow to extend PFI to economic infrastructure such as airports. In 2012, in order to slash the size of government debt, the Japanese Government passed a law to establish the *New Kansai International Airport Corporation* (*NKIAC*) and to integrate Kansai Airport and Ōsaka Itami Airport in order to pool the cash-flows together, to increase corporate value by strategic investment, and to market the operational right of the two airports to competing consortia. In September 2013, NKIAC announced that it would acquire Ōsaka Airport Terminal Co. for 27.8 billion yen (about U.S. $262 million).

As pointed out by Freshfields Bruckhaus Deringer (2021), a change in the PFI Law made the concession-style public-private partnership (PPP) possible but a tailoring of the PFI framework was required to comply with international investors' expectations. NKIAC conducted a public tender to sell the operating rights for the two airports in May 2015. The sole bidder for the two airports on a 45-year concession was a consortium led by VINCI Airports (40 per cent), with ORIX Corporation, a Japanese integrated financial services company (40 per cent) and the remaining

20 per cent by Hankyū Hanshin Holdings and Panasonic (www.vinci-concessions.com) and other investors.[3] The contract was signed on 15 December 2015. According to a press release by VINCI Airports (2017), the consortium was the preferred bidder for the 42-year Kōbe Airport concession contact—a bid that was also successful.

Kōbe Airport

The history of Kōbe Airport is a story of local lobbying for an airport closer to Kōbe as the need for an alternative to Ōsaka Itami Airport became apparent, as discussed above. In 1971, the Kōbe City Government proposed an airport adjacent to Port Island—an artificial island constructed south of Sunnomiya Station in Ōsaka Bay between 1966 and 1984 for maritime, educational, commercial and recreational uses. The plan called for six runways more than 3,000 metres in length built on a 1,100-hectare artificial island. However, the Mayor of Kōbe, Miyazaki Tatsuo, declared his opposition to building such a large airport that was located so close to the city.

He was re-elected mayor in 1973 by defeating a candidate whose manifesto supported the airport development. Kōbe businesses were strong supporters of an airport and pressed the city government for a smaller facility with only one 3,000-metre long runway. This plan was submitted to the Ministry of Transport in 1982 as an alternative to the Kansai Airport proposal that was being supported by the Ōsaka and Wakayama prefectural governments. After the national government rejected the Kōbe proposal, the Hyōgo Prefectural Government switched its support in 1984 for the Kansai Airport proposal.

---

3   The full list of investors are: ASICS Corporation; Iwatani Corporation; Osaka Gas Co., Ltd.; Obayashi Corporation; OMRON Corporation; The Kansai Electric Power Company, Incorporated; Kintetsu Group Holding Co., Ltd.; Keihan Holdings Co.,Ltd.; Suntory Holdings Limited; JTB Corp.; Sekisui House, Ltd.; Daikin Industries, Ltd.; Daiwa House Industry Co., Ltd.; Takenaka Corporation; Nankai Electric Railway Co., Ltd.; Nippon Telegraph and Telephone West Cerporation; Panasonic Corporation; Hankyu Hanshin Holdings, Inc.; Rengo Co., Ltd.; The Senshu Ikeda Bank, Ltd.; Kiyo Holdings, Inc.; The Bank of Kyoto, Ltd.; The Shiga Bank, Ltd.; The Nanto Bank, Ltd.; Nippon Life Insurance Company; Mizuho Bank, Ltd.; Sumitomo Mitsui Trust Bank, Limited; MUFG Bank, Ltd.; Resona Bank, Limited; and the Private Finance Initiative Promotion Corporation of Japan (http://www.kansai-airports.co.jp/en/company-profile/about-us/).

In 1985, the city and prefecture decided to independently fund the construction of its own airport, but its construction was stalled by a lack of funding. On January 1995, a 7.2 magnitude (Richter scale) earthquake with an epicentre at nearby Awaji Island hit the region causing loss of life, with deaths amounting to 4,571 in Kōbe alone (The City of Kōbe, 2009: 1). There was substantial damage to buildings, infrastructure (Chung, 1996, Chapter 4) and the three major airports in the region (Chung, 1996: 260–266). To aid the recovery of a devastated local economy the Japanese Government used infrastructure spending as a stimulus package.

Despite ongoing opposition from sections of the community, there remained support for the airport plan. At the 1997 mayoral election, the pro-airport coalition won a narrow victory over the anti-airport coalition. Construction began in September 1999, but the political controversy continued: 87,000 signatures were collected in a petition to dismiss the Mayor in 2000. A citizen lawsuit to cancel the project was dismissed in 2004. The airport finally opened on 16 February 2006 at a cost of U.S. $3 billion.

In 2013, the Kōbe mayor, Yada Tatsuo, endorsed a proposal to consolidate the management of the three Kansai region airports by adding Kōbe Airport to the planned sale in 2014 of operating concessions at Ōsaka Itami and Kansai airports. Accordingly, VINCI Airports added Kōbe Airport to its management and operations portfolio in April 2018. Agreement on the gradual expansion of domestic flight slots and operating hours at Kōbe with a maximum daily aircraft movement of 80, and operation hours were extended from 7:00 to 23:00 hours from May 2019.[4]

Yao Airport

Yao airport started as the Hanshin Aviation School in 1938. Two years later, the airfield was seized by the army as the Taishō Airfield and was expanded. After the Second World War, the occupation forces called it the Hanshin Airfield before it was returned to Japanese control. Yao airport, operated by the Ministry of Land, Infrastructure, Transport and Tourism, is located 15 km southeast of Ōsaka Railway Station and it

---

4   http://www.kansai-airports.co.jp/en/company-profile/about-airports/kobe.html

functions both as a general aviation airport and as a base for the Japan Ground Self-Defence Force (JGSDF Camp Yao). Several small airline carriers offer sightseeing and charter flights, including Asahi Airlines and Hankyū Airlines (owned by Hankyū Electric Railway Company). Established in 1966, the First Flying Co., Ltd. is an air carrier based at Yao Airport. It operates inter-island passenger services in Okinawa and irregular passenger services to the Hiroshima-Nishi airport.

Airports in the Nagoya Region

Nagoya's first airport, constructed in 1944, was the Komaki Airport used by the Imperial Japanese Army Air Service. It was heavily damaged by allied bombs during the Pacific War, rebuilt by the allies as their military base before being returned to the Japan Government in 1957. It was Nagoya's main airport until the opening of Chūbu Centrair International Airport in 2005, located in Ise Bay some 47 km south of Nagoya Railway Station.

Komaki Airfield/Nagoya Airfield/Nagoya Airport

In 1944, Komaki Airfield was developed 12 km north of Nagoya Railway Station for the Imperial Japanese Army Air Service, but, during the Pacific War, it was bombed heavily that year and also during the first half of the next year. The airfield was taken over by the American occupation forces and renamed Nagoya Air Base when it was reconstructed. In May 1946, the base became the Headquarters of the Fifth Air Force that controlled air force occupation units throughout Japan. Nagoya Air Base was returned to the Japanese Government in July 1957.

Nagoya Airport served as the main airport for Nagoya until the opening of Chūbu Centrair International Airport in 2005. During the 1980s and early 1990s, Nagoya Airport was a busy international airport because of the overflow from Japan's other international airports. The airport was constrained by its location in a residential area of Aichi Prefecture that restricted the number of daily flights and imposed a night-time curfew. It lost some business in 1994 with the opening of Kansai Airport that was some 210 km away.

On 17 February 2005, nearly all of Nagoya Airport's commercial transport flights moved to Chūbu Centrair International Airport and it was renamed Nagoya Airfield. Today, Aichi Prefecture manages the airport facilities and regularly handles international business flights (with a dedicated business aviation terminal), regional services, general aviation and the Japan Air-Self-Defense Force.

Chūbu Centrair International Airport

The Nagoya region has a population of about 10 million and is a major manufacturing centre, with the headquarters and production facilities of the Toyota Motor Corporation and production facilities for Mitsubishi Motors and Mitsubishi Aircraft Corporation. Local business groups lobbied government for a new airport, especially for 24-hour cargo operations. The airport's operator is a consortium comprising the national and local governments and over 200 Japanese companies. The consortium, known as the Central Japan International Airport Company (CJIAC), was appointed by the Japanese Government in July 1998 to be the constructing and managing body of Centrair airport. There were extensive protests over the project's necessity by local environmentalists and fishermen. Airport construction started in August 2000.

Functioning as a new air gateway to the central region of Japan, the airport was built as an artificial island (the land-reclamation scheme started in 2001 and was completed by the Spring of 2003) in shallow water located off the eastern shore of Ise Bay near Tokoname. The project was delivered 100 billion yen under the budget of U.S. $7.3 billion and was opened, on schedule, in March 2005. The island, constructed by Penta-Ocean Construction Co, was initially designed to allow for one large runway. The airport occupies an area of 4.3 km by 1.9 kim on the island (817 hectares), leaving the remaining space for local wildlife. A second runway was added later (Airport Technology, 2021).

The passenger terminal was designed by a joint venture consortium. CJIAC commissioned four construction companies to participate in the planning, design and survey of the passenger terminal area. The four companies were two Japanese companies, Nikken Sekkei Ltd and Azusa Sekkei Co., Hellmuth, Obata and Kassabaum Inc of the U.S.A. and Bovis Program Management Japan Inc. The English civil engineering firm, Arup, was responsible for structural and faced engineering of the buildings.

Chūbu Centrair International Airport achieved its policy objectives with the transfer of flights from Nagoya Airport and a new airport with no curfew restrictions that has allowed the passenger business to grow. The sharp downturn in airline patronage in 2020 was a result of the Covid-19 global pandemic that curtailed domestic and international travel with governments of countries imposing lockdowns, quarantines and travel restrictions and airlines substantially cutting passenger services (ICAO, 2021; OECD, 2020). In Japan, in the week 10–16, 2020, the air travel sales volume registered a decline of 93 per cent compared to the equivalent weeks of the previous year. This constituted a decline of over 90 per cent for eleven weeks in succession since the global outbreak of the coronavirus pandemic (Statistica, 2020).

Japanese Airport Terminals

The laws on airport development in Japan specify that the private sector may be involved in the planning, construction, management and operations of terminals and car parking. This private entity, or a 'third sector' entity (a company jointly owned by a local government and private entities). One example of this is at Haneda Airport where the Japan Airport Terminal Company (JAT) has been active since 1953, and, at other major airports, since 1973. The major developments that have been initiated by JAT at Haneda are summarised in Table 23. Major capital works projects include the international terminal (1970), its extension (2002), terminal 2 (2004), its extension (2010), a new international terminal (2010) and the P4 parking structure (2010).

Table 23. Major Developments of Terminals and Parking, Haneda and Narita Airports by Japanese Airport Terminals (JAT).
Source: based on Japan Airport Terminal Co, Ltd, https://www.tokyo-airport-bldg.co.jp/company/en/corporate_profile/history/history.html.

Date	Airport Terminal Development
July 1953	JAT was established with ¥ 150 million in private capital and started planning for terminal building projects
May 1955	Completed and opened terminal building and started rental and merchandise sales operations
May 1970	Completed new international arrival terminal building

Date	Airport Terminal Development
Feb. 1973	Started commissioned management and maintenance of terminal building at Narita International Airport
Mar. 1978	Opened Narita Office at Narita International Airport
May 1978	Started duty-free and other merchandise sales, hotel reservation services and other operations at newly opened Narita International Airport
Sep. 1993	Started operation of Terminal 1
July 1994	Opened Ōsaka Office at Kansai International Airport
Mar. 1998	Started operation of Haneda International (passenger) Terminal
May 2002	Completed extension work on Haneda International (passenger) Terminal
Dec. 2004	Started operation of Terminal 2
Feb. 2005	Opened Chūbu Office at newly opened Central Japan International Airport. Started wholesale of duty-free goods at newly opened Central Japan International Airport
Feb. 2007	Started operation of South Pier in Terminal 2
Aug. 2010	Started operation of complete P4 parking structure
Aug. 2010	Completed extension of Haneda Terminal 2 in Phase III plan
Oct. 2010	Started operation of extended south part of Haneda Terminal 2
Oct. 2010	Started operation of new International Terminal (PFI project)
Nov. 2011	Completed renovation of Haneda Terminal 1
Apr. 2013	Started operation of extended South Pier in Haneda Terminal 2

Terminal management has demonstrated its ability to respond to external events. For example, Tokyo International Air Terminal Co., Ltd. introduced a safety measure for the Covid-19 outbreak for international departure process at Haneda/Terminal 3—an automated facility where passengers can scan their boarding passes by themselves and pass through the gate to the aircraft in accordance with the digital sign or flapper doors (https://tokyo-haneda.com/site_resource/whats_new/pdf/000008004.pdf).

The privatisation of the three airports in the Kōbe-Ōsaka region gave VINCHI Airports the responsibility for developing terminal space and other functions at those airports. Details of the seven Kansai Airports' companies involved in terminal operations are listed on the airport website (Table 24). They include retail, security, firefighting, passenger information, car park management, construction and maintenance, heating and cooling and hotels.

Table 24. Kansai Airports and Group Companies and the Business Scope of Terminal Services.
Source: reproduced from http://www.kansai-airports.co.jp/en/company-profile/about-us/file/group.pdf.

	Name of group companies	Business scope
1	[New company] Kansai Airports Retail & Services	Retail: duty-free, other retail, F&B Services: currency exchange, advertising, insurance, lounge operation
2	[New company] Kansai Airports Operation Services	Security, fire fighting, passenger information, car park management, cleaning, baggage cart service, daily maintenance
3	[New company] Kansai Airports Technical Services	Maintenance, construction projects, IT services
4	CKTS Co., Ltd. *No change to company name; Business scope changed	Passenger, ramp & cargo handling, aircraft maintenance support, vehicle maintenance
5	KIA Heating & Cooling Supply Co., Ltd. *No change to company name & business scope	Heat supply
6	World Air Passenger Service Co., Ltd. *No change to company name; Business scope changed	Hotel (ITAMI), temp staffing
7	Kansai Airports Kobe *No change to company name & business scope	Operation, maintenance and management of Kobe Airport

Airport Ground Transport Access

The international airports located in the three major conurbations of the case study area—Chūbu, Ōsaka and Tōkyō—are well connected by ground access to their hinterlands, with the exception of Ōsaka Itami Airport. The Chūbu Centrair Airport station is owned by Central Japan International Airport Line Company, Ltd. and leased to the private railway operator, Meitetsu, whose services connect to the Tokomane railway line then on to Jingu-mae in Nagoya. The airport is also connected to Nagoya Station by the Nagoya Railroad. The fastest train takes 29 minutes (using μ-SKY).

Kansai Airport has two railway company services: JR West that connects to Ōsaka Station (about 70 minutes) via Tennōji; and the short Nankai-Kūkō line to Izumisano Station operated by the Nankai Electric Railway Company. The Port Liner rail connects Kōbe Airport to Sannomiya Station, Kōbe, in 18 minutes. Ōsaka Itami Airport access by rail is complicated and depends on the destination. The airport is connected by a monorail to Hotarugaike Station that has a plethora of railway companies serving the Ōsaka, Kōbe and Kyōto areas (https://www.osaka-airport.co.jp/en/access/train).

There are two rail options to get to and from Narita International Airport. There are the railway services to Tōkyō Station on the JR East Narita Express which takes about an hour. The alternative route to Tōkyō is to take the Keisei Electric Railway Express Skyliner to Ueno Station (with connecting Shinkansen services) which takes forty-one minutes (https://www.uenostation.com/keisei-skyliner-for-narita-airport/). Haneda Airport is directly connected to the Keikyū Line and from Terminal 3 to Shinagawa (where there is a Shinkansen station) which takes thirteen minutes on the limited express service. Also from Terminal 3 the Tōkyō Monorail Line takes thirteen minutes to Hamamatsu-chō Station (https://tokyo-haneda.com/en/access/train/index.html).

Conclusions

Civil aviation is subject to international technical and safety standards such as those issued by the International Civil Aviation Organisation (ICAO) and to bilateral agreements on air services; Japan is no exception. The country was a signatory to the 1919 International Convention Relating to the Regulation of Aerial Navigation and signed its first bilateral airline agreement with the U.S.A. in 1952, followed by similarly structured agreements with other countries. Today, the manufacture of passenger jet aircraft is dominated by two overseas companies—Boeing and Airbus. In the early years of aviation in Japan, civilian aircraft were imported from France (Maurice Farman and Curtis float biplanes), the Netherlands (Fokker) and the U.S.A. (Douglas DC-2). Later, the Douglas DC-3 was manufactured in Japan under licence and local companies—Mitsubishi and Nakajima—made small civilian planes.

The Japanese governments and the military jointly promoted aviation in the late 1910s to the late 1930s. The navy formed The Committee for Naval Aeronautic Research and, in 1916, the Japanese Imperial Navy initiated the land-based, naval air stations and flying units. Three years later, the Ministry of War established a Special Aeronautical Committee to promote and regulate all civil aviation enterprises through the Air Navigation Law of April 1921.

Three private-sector airlines offered domestic, regional services until they were nationalised in late 1928 as the national flag carrier, the Japan Air Transport Corporation, under the control of the Ministry of Communications. The route network grew along with the territorial expansion of the Japanese Empire. With the defeat of Japan in the Pacific War civilian air transport did not resume until 1952 with the national carrier re-branded as Japan Airlines (JAL), which operated domestically and international until its privatisation in 1987.

The U.S. Occupation Forces used Japanese airfields in the 1940s and 1950s and promoted to the Japanese Government the concept of airline competition. By the mid-1960s, there were four Japanese airline companies: JAL; ANA; Japan Domestic Airlines (JDA); and Toa Airways (TA). A Cabinet Meeting Resolution of 1970 "Concerning Airline Operations" restructured the industry, and, in September 1985, the Minister of Transport introduced partial deregulation of the industry and further deregulation in 1997. The impacts of these policies on new entrants into the airline business are summarised in Table 25.

Table 25. Summary of Institutions and Organisations—Japanese Aviation and Airports.
Source: Author.

Industry Function	Institution	Organisation
International Convention Regulation of Aerial Navigation	Government of Japan (1919)	
Air Navigation Law	Ministry of War (1921)	
Aeronautical Law	Ministry of Transport (1952)	

Industry Function	Institution	Organisation
Aerodrome Development Law / Airport Development Law	Ministry of Transport (1952; 1956)	
Airlines	Japan Air Transport Corporation (1928–38), Greater Japan Airways (1938–45), Japan Airlines (1951–1987); Manchukuō Aviation Company (1932–45)	Japan Air Transport Institute (1921–29); All Nippon Airways (1952–) ; Low-cost carriers, e.g. Skymark Airlines (1998–); Jetstar Japan (2012–)
Airports	Ministry of Communications; Ministry of Transport; MLIT, e.g. Haneda (1931–); Narita Airport (1978–); Ōsaka Itami (1959–2015); Kōbe (2006–2017); Nagoya Airport (1957–2005); Kansai (1994–2015)	Chūbu Centrair (2005–); Kansai (2015–); Ōsaka Itami (2015–); Kōbe (2017–); Hiroshima (2021–)
Airport Terminals and Parking	Prefecture/City Governments and private sector at most terminals	Japan Airport Terminal Co. (1953–); VINCHI Airports (2015–)

Japan signed open skies treaties with Korea and the U.S.A. in 2010, with Hong Kong, Macau, Singapore, Malaysia and Taiwan in 2011, and with China in August 2012. The Ministry of Land, Infrastructure, Transport and Tourism progressively liberalised air charter services. In December 2008, it introduced measures to allow foreign airlines to operate charters between Japan and a third country without the permission of Japanese airlines. This spawned low-cost carriers (LCC) that has driven domestic and international passenger demand that then required more airport capacity.

Airport planning and construction have been in the hands of governments in Japan. Pre-1945, the airfields were shared between the military and civilian airlines. In 1930, the Ministry of Communications purchased a 48-hectare piece of private land in Haneda on Tōkyō Bay and constructed a new civilian airfield that handled flights to and from various airfields in Japan, in Korea, and in the puppet state of Manchuria. With the resumption of civilian aviation the Japanese Government enacted the *Aerodrome Development Law (1952)* with Japanese airports being regulated by the *Aeronautical Law (1952)* with regard to safety, the *Noise Prevention Law* (1967) with regard to environmental noise and the *Airport Development Law (1956)* with regard airport ownership and airport funding.

The specific details of airport construction, development and funding (in more recent years, using a concession model of financing from the private sector) have been explained using a range of airport classifications in the Chūbu, Ōsaka and Tōkyō metropolitan regions (with a combined population of about 82 million).

The unique aspect of the *Airport Development Law of 1956* is that Japanese airport terminals and car parks were constructed and are owned and managed by a company jointly owned by a local government and private entities. The case study of the Japan Airport Terminal Company (JAT) describes how the private company has been active since 1953 at Haneda Airport and at other major airports since 1973.

A theme throughout this book has been the relative role of the state institutions when compared with private-sector organisations in the planning, construction and operations of transport infrastructure and services. In the case of aviation and airports, Table 25 has summarised some of the main events in Japanese aviation and airport history and classifies the main actors as institutions or organisations. Araki (n.d.: 3) has explained, for all Japanese airports, the ownership—whether government or private sector—of facilities (runways, taxiways and aprons), terminals and air traffic control. The aviation industry has always been regulated, and policies are formulated by committees so there is less opportunity for individuals to make substantial contributions to the historical evolution of Japanese airports and air services.

The characteristics of Japanese airport rail connections are that train services are integrated into airport design and layout and furthermore these services provide convenient transfers onto the high-speed railway network that now covers a large portion of the main Japanese islands. The integration of transport with land uses (for example, express rail services and airports) is a policy issue that has tested governments in developed countries since the late 1960s. The next chapter of this book will examine how Japanese governments have approached the challenges of such integration with particular reference to the Tōkyō metropolis.

References

Airport Technology (2021) "Centrair (NGO/RJGG)", https://www.airport-technology.com/projects/central_asia/

Andrews, W. (2016) *Dissenting Japan: A History of Japanese Radicalism and Counterculture from 1945 to Fukushima*. Hurst & Co., London.

Araki, Emiko (n.d.) "Current Approaches Toward Further Enhancement of Airport Management in Japan". Japan Civil Aviation Bureau, Ministry of Land, Infrastructure, Transport and Tourism, Tokyo.

Aviation Strategy (1999) "Japanese Deregulation: Skymark and Air Do Jolt JAL, ANA and JAS." *Aviation Strategy*, 17, March, 14–17.

Bowen, R. W. (1975) "The Narita Conflict", *Asian Survey*, 15 (7), 598–615.

Century of Flight (n.d.) "Early Japanese Civilian Aviation", *Airlines and Airliners*, http://www.century-of-flight.freeola.com/new%20site/commercial/Japanese%20civil%20aviation.htm

Chung, R. (ed.) (1996) "The January 17, 1995 Hyogoku-Nanbu (Kobe) Earthquake: Performance of Structures, Lifelines and Fire Protection Equipment". *National Institute of Standards and Technology, Special Publication 901*. U.S. Government Printing Office, Washington, D. C.

Civil Aviation Bureau, Ministry of Land, Infrastructure, Transport and Tourism (2012) これまでの航空政策について [About Aviation Policy so far], Document 3, October, Civil Aviation Bureau, Ministry of Land, Infrastructure, Transport and Tourism, Tokyo.

Cronin, P. M. (2013) "Taking Off: Civil Aviation, Forward Progress and Japan's Third Arrow Reforms", *Center for New American Security, Working Paper, September*. Center for New American Security, Washington, D. C.

Cummins, N. (2020) "The History Behind Osaka Kansai International Airport", *Simple Flying*, 17 August, https://simpleflying.com/osaka-kansai-history/

Ellis, P. (2019) Airport Development International News—Focus Region Asia-Pacific-1", *Momberger Airport Information*, 10 December 2019, 1110, 1–10.

Feldhoff, T. (2003) "Japan's Capital Tōkyō and its Airports: Problems and Prospects from Subnational and Supranational Perspectives", *Journal of Air Transport Management*, 9, 241–254.

Freshfields Bruckhaus Deringer (2021) "Infrastructure Privatisation in Asia: The New Kansai Airport 'Mega-Concession'", https://www.freshfields.com/en-gb/what-we-do/case-studies/new-kansai-case-study/

Gorka, D. (2021) "Total Passenger Traffic at Haneda Airport in Tokyo, Japan, from 2011 to 2020", https://www.statista.com/statistics/226462/passenger-traffic-at-tokyo-airport/

Hashizume, Shinya (2005) "あったかもしれない日本―幻の都市建築" [*Japan that May have been—A Phantom History of Urban Architecture*]. Kinokuniya Publishing, Shibuya, Tokyo.

Hayashi, Hiromi (2021) "Japan: Aviation Laws and Regulations 2021", in *ICLG Aviation Laws and Regulations*, February.

ICAO (2021) "Economic Impacts of COVID-19 on Civil Aviation", https://www.icao.int/sustainability/Pages/Economic-Impacts-of-COVID-19.aspx

Ito, Takatoshi (2007) "Political Economy of Competition Policy in Japan: Case of Airline Services", *GraSPP-DP-E-07–001*, April. Graduate School of Public Policy, University of Tokyo, Tokyo.

Ito, Takatoshi and Hirotaka Yamauchi (1996) "Air Transport Policy in Japan", in G. Huffbauer and C. Findlay (eds) (1996) *Flying High*. Institute for International Economics, Washington, D. C., 33–61.

Kanda, Yusuke, Shigeru Morichi and Naohiko Hibino (2006) "我が国における航空規制緩和政策の影響分析"[Analysis of the Impact of Airline Deregulation Policy in Japan], *Japan Society of Civil Engineers, Works on Civil Engineering Planning*, 23, 771–777.

Kataoka, Naomichi (1936) "Japanese Air Navigation Regulations", *Journal of Air Law and Commerce*, 7 (1), 95–107.

Kodansha (1993) *Japan: An Illustrated Encyclopedia*. Kodansha, Bunkyo-ku, Tokyo.

Leff, G. (2020) "One Man Lives—and Farms—in the Middle of Tokyo Narita Airport", *View from the Wing*, 23 August, https://viewfromthewing.com/one-man-lives-and-farms-in-the-middle-of-tokyo-narita-airport/

Lemay-Fruchter, L. (2021) "Sanrizuka Struggle", Institute for Youth in Policy, https://www.yipinstitute.com/articles/sanrizuka-struggle

Melzer, J. P. (2020) "A New Perspective on Japanese Aviation History", in Melzer, J. P. (ed.) (2020) *Wings for the Rising Sun: A Transnational History of Japanese Aviation*. Brill, New York, 1–7.

Mikesh, R. C., and Shorzoe Abe (1990) *Japanese Aircraft, 1910–1941* (Putnam Aeronautical Books). U.S. Naval Institute, Annapolis, Maryland.

Miyoshi, Chikage (2015) "Airport Privatisation in Japan: Unleashing Air Transport Liberalisation?", *Airport Management*, 9 (3), 210–222.

Moulton, H. G., with Junichi Ko (1931) *Japan: An Economic and Financial Appraisal*. Brookings Institution, Washington D. C.

Narita International Airport Corporation (2021) "Functionality Enhancement at Narita International Airport", https://www.naa.jp/en/b2b/enhancement/

Noguchi, Masayoshi, and T. Boynes (2012) "The Development of Budgets and their Use for Purposes of Control in Japanese Aviation, 1928–1945: The Role of the State", *Accounting, Auditing & Accountability Journal*, 25 (3), 416–451.

OECD (2020) "COVID-19 and the Aviation Industry: Impact and Policy Responses", OECD Policy Responses to Coronavirus (COVID-19), October, http://www.oecd.org/coronavirus/policy-responses/covid-19-and-the-aviation-industry-impact-and-policy-responses-26d521c1/

Peattie, M. (2013) *Sunburst: The Rise of Japanese Naval Air Power, 1909–1941*. Naval Institute Press, Annapolis, Maryland.

Sagen, J. (2004) "A Battle Against Tradition: The Rise of Naval Aviation in Modern Japan", 国際基督教大学学報 3-A, アジア文化研究 [*International Christian University Academic Bulletin 3-A, Asian Cultural Studies*], 71–85.

Sato, Masanori, and Shigeki Okatani (2016) "Recent Developments in Public-Private Partnerships in Japan", *IFLR1000/ Energy and Infrastructure 2016*, 1–4, https://www.iflr1000.com/NewsAndAnalysis/Recent-developments-in-public-private-partnerships-in-Japan/Index/5487

Shibata, Isaku (1999) "Japanese Laws Related to Airport Development and the Need to Revise Them", *Journal of Air Law and Commerce*, 65 (1), 125–136.

Sinha, D. (2019) *Deregulation and Liberalisation of the Airline Industry: Asia, Europe, North America and Oceania*. Routledge, London.

Soshiroda, Akira (2005) "Inbound Tourism Policies in Japan from 1859 to 2003", *Annals of Tourism Research*, 32 (4), 1100–1120.

Statistica (2020) "Change in Air Travel Transaction Volume During the Coronavirus (COVID-19) Pandemic in Japan from January 1 to June 16, 2020, by Type", https://www.statista.com/statistics/1112134/japan-coronavirus-covid-19-impact-air-travel-transactions-by-type/

Suzuki, Shinji, and Masako Sakai (2005) "History of Early Aviation in Japan", *43rd AIAA Aerospace Sciences Meeting and Exhibit, 10 January 2005–13 January 2005, Reno, Nevada*, https://doi.org/10.2514/6.2005-118

The City of Kobe (2009) *The Great Hanshin-Awaji Earthquake Statistics and Restoration Progress—January 1, 2009*. The City of Kobe, Kobe.

The Japan Times (2019) "Narita Airport to Apply for Permission to Start Runway Extension Plan", *The Japan Times*, 2 November 2019.

TMI Associates (2020) "A General Introduction to Public-Private Partnerships in Japan", *The Law Review*, https://www.lexology.com/library/detail.aspx?g=f48372fb-da82–4295-acdf-f82fa11c8af9

VINCI Airports (2017) "The VINCI-ORIX-Kansai Airports Joint Venture is Named Preferred Bidder for the Kobe Airport in Japan", 25 July 2017, press release.

Warfare History Network (2019) "Japan's World War II Zero Fighter Terrified the Allies", *The National Interest*, 8 May, https://nationalinterest.org/blog/buzz/japans-world-war-ii-zero-fighter-terrified-allies-56647

Watabe, Yoichi, and Shinji Sassa (2016) "History of Land Reclamation using Dredged Soils at Tokyo Haneda Airport", *Japanese Geotechnical Society Special Publication*, 2 (51), 1784–1789.

Williams, G. (2017) *The Airline Industry and the Impact of Deregulation*, 2nd Edition. Routledge, London.

Wu, Chun Tao (2016) "How Aviation Deregulation Promotes International Tourism in Northeast Asia: A Case of the Charter Market in Japan", *Journal of Air Transport Management*, 57, 260–271.

Wu, Chun Tao, and Lei Peng (2014) "Changes in Air Charter Market Operations in Japan: Airlines, Airports and Aviation Policies", *Asia Pacific World*, 5 (2), 44–62.

Yamaguchi, Katsuhiro (2013) "Evolution of Metropolitan Airports in Japan: Airport Development in Tokyo and Osaka", *OECD Roundtable on Expanding Airport Capacity under Constraints in Large Urban Areas, 21–22 February, Discussion Paper No. 2013–13*. OECD, Paris.

Yamauchi, Hirotaka, and Takatoshi Ito (1996) "Air Transport Policy in Japan", *Working Paper No. 124, Center on Japanese Economy and Business Columbia Business School*, Columbia University, New York, September.

Yukawa, Yoshiyasu and Kenji Matsubara (2019) "Noise Control Measure at ITAMI", *Proceedings of InterNoise, Madrid, 16–19 June 2019, INTER-NOISE and INTER-CON Conference Proceedings, Inter-noise 19*, Madrid, Spain, 624–631.

8. Urban Planning Institutions and the Integration of Land Use and Transport

> Transport planning and land-use planning are not separate activities but should be performed by a single department as an ongoing process.
>
> Sharp, 1970

Introduction

In previous chapters, institutional and organisational transformations were examined from a perspective of the historical delivery of infrastructure and services for ports, canals, roads, railways and airports. In contrast, this chapter is about institutions and organisations that plan for future transport together with their adjacent land uses. For long-term future transport infrastructure development, there is a need to consider land use and transport as an "integrated planning process" (Buchanan, 1963; Sharp, 1970). Therefore, this chapter explores some examples of how Japan has responded to this challenge of a comprehensive approach to land-use and transport developments and the planning institutions that have guided such developments.

Watanabe (1980: 63) points out the importance of developing planning systems that are based on specific socio-historical conditions and cites Japan as important case studies, where, in a short space of time, feudal castle towns were supplanted by steel and skyscrapers. From ancient times, Japanese rulers had knowledge transmitted from China as to the main principles in the layout of capital cities (Hein, 2016), and, during the early Edō period, Tokugawa Ieyasu drew on geomancy in developing his new castle town with its distinctive arrangement of functional areas, largely to control the different classes in society (Hamp, 2019: 2–4). However, it was not until the modern period following the Meiji Restoration that government institutions to control, and direct, urban development were established based on overseas experiences.

The early institutional initiatives were confined to the new capital of Tōkyō. Institutional arrangements had also to cope with the reconstruction of cities, especially after the 1923 Kantō Earthquake (Hammer, 2011), and after the bombing of most major cities during the Second World War, such as Tōkyō (see Hein, 2016, Fig. 7, p. 9). Two levels of the Japanese planning system are described: at the metropolitan level with Tōkyō as an example because it provides the genesis of the contemporary Japanese land-use planning system; and the national system that subsequently evolved in the modern democratic period following the end of the Pacific War.

Within these planning frameworks, there are three topics that are examined in detail—which all would be familiar today to urban planners across many parts of the world: the land adjustment mechanism and value capture; transport-oriented development; and 'smart cities'. One of the most successful policies associated with the post-war reconstruction of Japanese cities is the land-readjustment program that has been promoted in many Asian cities by Japanese consultants (Archer, 2000). Murakami (2011: 1) points out that "Tokyo is one of the most advanced cases of the transit-oriented megalopolis model" and he estimates the monetary potential to finance new railways through the value capture mechanism. Transit-oriented development is illustrated along with the Japanese new town program.

The Japanese Government has also been proactive on what might a future society and its urban form and function take (James, 1990). For example, the "multi-function polis (MFP)" was an urban development concept developed by the Ministry of International Trade and Industry (MITI) and explored for implementation in Australia (Australian and Japanese Governments Joint Steering Committee to Oversee a Major Study Investigating the Feasibility of the Multifunction Polis Concept, 1990; Smith et al., 1993; Hamnett, 1997). More recently, Japanese Government policies to promote 'smart cities' have been initiatives in many countries since the early 21st century and specific Japanese examples are described in this chapter.

Planning Tōkyō in the Modern Period

The purpose of this section is not to repeat the history of urban planning in Tōkyō as there exists a substantial literature in English on its planning (for example, Hall, 1966; Cybriwsky, 1998; Hein, 2010). Also, the history of planning legislation in Ōsaka-Kōbe is described by Perez (*et al.*, 2019). The Meiji government took the initiative to restructure Edō from a medieval castle town into a modern capital city. This "modernisation" of Tōkyō was in conformance with a "Western image" as the prime objective (Funo, 2005: 246). It is important to note that, before the Meiji Restoration, the spatial layout of Edō was arranged by class: ordinary people lived to the east of the castle primarily on the banks of the Sumida River and Edō Bay.

Commercial Edō was designed for the traffic movements on water and on foot. Although there was some reliance on forms of land transport, such as ox-drawn carriages, the conveyance of goods into and out of Edō depended on complex network of canals (Hamp, 2019: 3). Despite these logistical efficiencies, writings by Westerners were scathing of the dismal and dilapidated state of many buildings in the new capital (Hein, 2016: 3), for example, around Nihonbashi (The Far East, 1872). Therefore, the Meiji government focused on adapting the new capital Tōkyō to worldwide development standards.

With regard to urban planning, Coaldrake (cited by Hamp, 2019: 6) states:

> At the beginning of the new era one of the most urgent tasks facing the Meiji leaders [...] was the construction of a new built environment for the conduct of the affairs of state and the development of modern industry, commerce and education. The 'accepted practices of the world' meant the creation of Western-style urban plans and buildings, particularly for the newly designated capital city of Tōkyō

The Emperor Meiji commissioned the 50-person Iwakura Mission (led by statesman Iwakura Tomomi, 1825–1883) who travelled to North America and Europe in 1871–1873 (Kodansha, 1993: 640–641). In a friendship mission, they sought to promote the "civilisation and cultural renewal" of Japan in accordance with Western models of development, that included urban planning practices (Hamp, 2019: 6).

The risk of fire was well understood in Edō times with unambiguous Tokugawa Government directives on managing the outbreak of fires. There were 91 fires that burned 15 blocks or more over a period of 234 years (Sand, 2017: 88). After the Great Ginza Fire of 1872, the Meiji government issued a statement advocating the building of a fireproof city, and Shin-ryōgae-chō (Ginza) was reborn as a Westernised *rengagai* or 'bricktown' (Tokyo Ginza Official, 2021). The Ginza Brick Quarters Project (1872–1877) was promoted by the Minister of Finance, Ōkuma Shigenobu, and was symbolic of modernisation launched to refashion the entire district with European highlights fashioned in red brick buildings. The English architects—the Waters Brothers—were invited to prepare plans for the area. A decade later, 2,855 buildings had been completed in a Georgian style with streetscape of maples, willows and gaslights (Sorensen, 2002).

The origin of city planning legislation in Japan—the *Tōkyō Town Planning Ordinance*—was formulated in 1888. Hibiya Park, Ueno Park, and the road that runs along the Imperial Palace moat, are physical legacies of that time. The *Tōkyō Town Planning Ordinance* was superseded by the *City Planning Act of 1919*, which, in turn, was short lived because of the 1923 Great Kantō Earthquake. On 1 September 1923, a magnitude 7.9 earthquake struck the Kantō region. Approximately 3,465 hectares (44 per cent of the Tōkyō's area) was subsequently destroyed by the fires that were triggered by the earthquake. About three-quarters of households were affected by the disaster.

The following day, the Cabinet of Prime Minister Yamamoto Gonbe established the Bureau for Reconstruction of the Imperial Capital—an institution under the direct control of the Prime Minister. The Minister of Home Affairs and former Mayor of Tōkyō, Goto Shinpei, was appointed as President of the Bureau for Reconstruction of the Imperial Capital. He led the planning and reconstruction of the city, incorporating modern planning methods. The original budget request to implement the plan was 1.5 billion yen but this was cut by about a third to 468 million yen (Metro Tokyo, 2021). The main mechanism for government intervention was land readjustment (described in more detail in a later section) to rezone land over significant parts of the devastated areas.

Both the national and the Tōkyō metropolitan governments have continuously been involved in trying to regulate urban growth and renewal with their planning institutions evolving with time. From 5

April 1919 and 15 July 2018, a total of 235 Tōkyō City planning laws and regulations, and numerous Cabinet orders, were issued so what follows by necessity is a cursory examination of the interactions between governments, the private sector and the broader community of interested stakeholders in the processes of urban development in the modern democratic era. The details of these laws and regulations are listed in a document that is regularly updated on the Metro Tokyo, and the reader can readily access them (http://www.toshiseibi.metro.tokyo.jp/eng/pdf/index_06.pdf?1503).

Planning Tōkyō in the Modern Democratic Period

With changing socio-economic circumstances in the chaotic period after 1945, the Comprehensive National Land Development Act of 1950 was promulgated by the Japanese Government. The first substantial step towards post-war reconstruction was made under the Tōkyō Special City Plan (e.g. land readjustment for reconstruction). By the beginning of 2013, land readjustment projects had been completed in 593 areas (approximately 21,312 hectares) and they are ongoing in 23 areas (approximately 520 hectares) in the Tōkyō ward areas, and in 36 areas (approximately 1,055 hectares) in the Tama district (Tokyo Metropolitan Government, n.d.: 74). In June 1950, the *Capital Construction Law* was established as a national project to construct Tōkyō as a national showcase. Given the high population growth and the rapid suburbanisation, this law proved ineffective in controlling urban development in the Tōkyō region.

As a result, the *National Capital Region Development Act* of April 1956 was introduced to control development over the greater metropolitan region.[1] Under this act, the Tōkyō Metropolitan Government promoted an all-out revision of urban plans: parks and green spaces in 1957; expressways in 1959; and high-speed railways in 1962. The partial revision of the *Building Standards Act* of May 1950 in January 1963 resulted in zoning to secure open spaces, to redress the imbalance between the over-concentrated population and urban facilities. The formulation

---

1 Yokohama, Kawasaki, Atsugi, Hachioji, Tachikawa, Oume, Kumagaya, Urawa Saitama, Tsuchiura, Ushiku, Tsukuba, Narita, Chiba, Kisarazu, Tama, Sagamihara, Machida, Kawagoe, Kasukabe, Koshigaya, Kashiwa.

of these land-use plans at the ward level opened up new avenues for skyscraper development. Green spaces that had been designated under earlier policies gave way to land readjustment projects enabling further comprehensive, high-rise residential development.

The Second and Third National regional capital plans (1976 and 1986) both addressed the formulation of policies for "suburban development areas" around the existing built-up areas of Tōkyō in order to develop balanced and well-designed hierarchical urban centres and to preserve some green areas but on a much smaller scale than before. Notably, the plans were not only limited to industrial and satellite cities but also to academic, recreational and cultural facilities.

This transformation from a mono-centric city to a poly-centric employment structure was anticipated by Lewis Mumford (1895–1990) who made substantial contributions to the history of technology, the history of cities and urban planning practice. Writing in 1937, he predicted the emergence of a new form of the metropolis called the "poly-nucleated city", suggesting that even without planning and "intelligent public control" the de-centralisation of urban functions would accelerate. However, over the years, despite the substantial efforts to promote a multi-nucleus urban pattern, Tōkyō continued to preserve its strong centralised structure (Alpkokin et al., 2007a).

The Fourth and Fifth Plans firmly designated "business core cities"[2] defined as the high-density core settlements within the Tōkyō central area; and "bases for large cooperation" defined as the large centres outside the Tōkyō central area. Urban re-generation plans have also been applied for non-core city development and one good example is the re-development of Roppongi, where a multi-use, 54-floor tower has been constructed near subway rail stations. The Plans state their primary aim as polycentric spatial re-structuring with a circular development of stronger urban nodes outside the Tōkyō central area to ensure self-reliant regions, to strengthen the regional network and co-operation, and also to mitigate the stress on the central area.

Despite these top-down national and metropolitan government policy interventions, the high economic growth from the mid-1950s onwards caused a further intensification of population and industry

---

2   Mito, Maebashi, Takasaki, Utsunomiya, Kofu.

in Tōkyō resulting in a confused mixture of land uses and further suburban sprawl. A new *City Planning Act* was promulgated in June 1968 and put into force a year later as a strategic land use planning tool to prevent housing shortages, to reduce long journey-to-work commuting travel and to tackle environmental pollution. Significantly, there was a devolution of powers to prefectural governors and municipalities to ensure greater citizen participation in the land-use development process (Tōkyō Metropolitan Government, n.d.: 3–4).

In 1980, the "district planning system" was established where municipalities—the local governments that are closest to residents—were given decision-making powers. In June 2013, the *City Planning Act* was partially revised, in association with the enforcement of the *Decentralization Law* (the third package bill), that abolished the requirement to send a copy of relevant documents to the Minister of Land, Infrastructure, Transport and Tourism following a decision on city planning.

Railway improvements and linking land-use development has a long history in Japan. For example, even before the 1940s, when the railway enterprises invested in new rail lines, they also owned and developed the land parcels around the major stations. Since the 1960s, Tōkyō has developed its rail network (Morichi *et al.*, 2001: 3), not only its central subway system but also suburban railways connecting the centres designated in the land-use plans. In the 1970s and onwards, new rail lines have connected the business core cities and the centre of Tōkyō (the Musashino-line in 1973; the Hokuso-line in 1979; and the Tsukuba express connecting Tsukuba and Akihabara in 2005).

Another important feature of railway development is that local councils responsible for transport policy assist in the development the railways in their metropolitan areas; they give recommendations about certain construction and upgrading projects. Only if listed in the Council's report, can construction commence on new railway lines. The ninth report by the Tōkyō Metropolitan Council in 1966 was the first document to address transit-focused development.

Figure 7 identifies the main policy areas located within the Tōkyō Capital Region. The existing urban area of Tōkyō is indicated in light brown. The lightest of the shading shows the suburban development areas. The areas shown in black are designated for green conservation.

The dark brown areas are the nodes identified for new urban development such as Utsunomiya (connected to central Tōkyō Station by high-speed rail) and Kōfu (a station on the Chuō maglev Shinkansen linking Shinagawa Station). The extensive rail and subway networks in Tōkyō facilitate public transport connections from all of the development locations in Figure 7 into core activity areas, as can be demonstrated by consulting the interactive rail service MiniTokyo3D website (https://minitokyo3d.com).

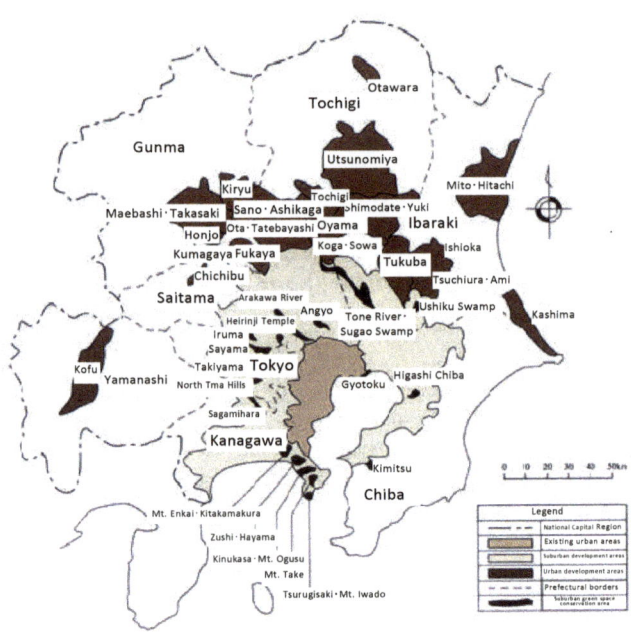

Figure 7. Map of the Tōkyō Capital Region Policy Areas.
Source: Tokyo Metropolitan Government, n.d., Figure 2–4, p. 12, http://www.toshiseibi.metro.tokyo.jp/eng/pdf/index_02.pdf?1503.

Institution for National Land-Use Planning

At the national level, the Japanese Government has, in theory, the necessary institutional arrangement to achieve integrated approaches, where all modes of transport and land development are located in one ministry. The most recent organisational structure (as of 2015) for the Ministry of Land, Infrastructure, Transport and Tourism (MLIT) is found at https://www.mlit.go.jp/common/000026153.pdf. In addition to mode specific bureaux covering maritime and ports, waterways, roads, railways and civil aviation, there is also a bureau devoted to spatial planning and regional policy to complement a top-down approach to integrated planning. There is a hierarchy of land-use plans that flows from the top downwards from the national level, to the regional level, to the prefectural level and finally to the municipal level as illustrated by the Tokyo Metropolitan Government (n.d.: 7).

Land Readjustment Program

Land readjustment is such an important component in understanding the processes of urban development in major Japanese cities that a description of its institutional arrangements is worth outlining. Category 1 Urban Redevelopment Projects are executed by the method called "right conversion". The right conversion is a method of equivalent exchange between rights (original assets), such as the ownership, lease right and rented house right of land and building prior to the project execution and a right to land and building after the project execution (resultant assets = "entitled" floors). Amongst the building floors that are constructed by the project (including pieces of land corresponding to the floors), floors that exceed "entitled" floors are called reserved floors that are sold to obtain the funds to cover the costs of launching a project. Those people in the affected area who do not accept the "right conversion" may make a request compensation from the project executor to move out and relocate somewhere else (Tokyo Metropolitan Government, n.d., Figure 3–9, p. 74).

The land readjustment program usually functions through the collaborative activities of civil society, although sometimes the program is in partnership with local government. A private citizen—a landowner, or a land lease right holder or a group of them—within the designated project area may become an executor or executors by preparing a constitution and a project plan. The unanimous consent of right holders within the area are first obtained and then permission from the prefectural governor is obtained to proceed for implementation of the development. Those other than right holders within the area may also become executors by obtaining unanimous consent of the right holders.

To explain how private organisations can be involved in the urban development process, redevelopment associations of landowners, or land-lease right holders, are formed as follows. If the founders are at least five in number within the project area, and they have prepared the articles of incorporation and a project plan with the consent of at least a two-thirds majority of members, then they may become executors by obtaining the authorisation from the prefectural governor to establish a partnership that becomes the urban redevelopment association. Specified architectural consultants carry out the project in cooperation with the executors through their provision of funding or design technology.

A more commercial organisation is formed in the following way. Business corporations, or limited liability companies, that share at least two-thirds of the land parcels within the project area and hold more than half of voting rights, prepare the articles of incorporation together with a project plan. Once they obtain consent of a two-thirds majority of the landowners and the land lease right holders within the project area, and if the right area of consenters constitutes two thirds or more of the total right area, then they become executors of a development by obtaining authorisation from the prefectural governor.

There is a provision in the program that the Tōkyō Metropolitan Government and municipalities may become executors in land readjustment schemes by obtaining project approval from the Minister of the Ministry of Land, Infrastructure, Transport and Tourism and the prefecture governor. Also, the Urban Renaissance Agency and the Tōkyō Metropolitan Housing Supply Corporation may become executors by obtaining project approval from the Minister of Land, Infrastructure, Transport and Tourism.

Land Readjustment Mechanism

The mechanism of the land readjustment program and local government planning is illustrated in Figure 8. This mechanism has proved to be a highly successful policy for the redevelopment of station precincts. It has allowed existing landowners to share in some of the profits that arise from re-zoning to higher densities, for developers to consolidate lots to allow imaginative higher density buildings to be erected and to return land for public purposes around railway station pedestrian access points. This provision in the planning act is illustrated with a case study of Shibuya in Tōkyō that reveals the complexity of such an integrated urban redevelopment project.

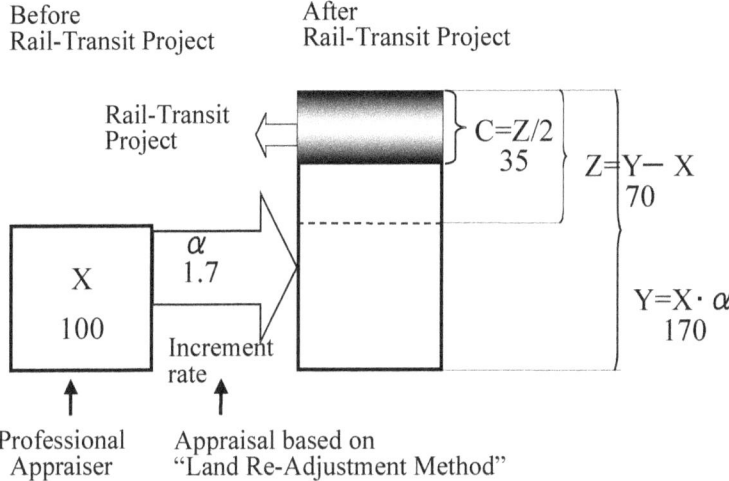

Figure 8. Mechanism of the Land Re-adjustment Program in Japan.
Source: Professor Kazuaki Miyamoto, pers. comm.

Shibuya Station in Tōkyō has posed difficulties for passengers in finding how to change trains due to its complicated structure that was formed through its repeated extension and reconstruction since the Taishō era. In addition, it has suffered problems in terms of safety and convenience, such as a station square crowded with pedestrians and buses. In order to resolve these problems, a plan promoted drastic improvement of safety and convenience by reorganising and improving the station square plaza and re-developing its adjacent areas in an integrated manner together with railway improvements.

The conceptual vision was a strengthening of the international competitiveness of the locality by introducing cultural, exchange and information-transmission functions, advanced business functions (such as creative content industries, and industrial development functions). The Shibuya Station improvement project involved public-private cooperation, based on two documents: the development policy for Special Urban Renaissance Urgent Development Areas; and the Policy on Infrastructure Development in the Shibuya Station Central Area. The project timeline from 2007 to 2013 involved land readjustment projects, railway improvement projects, a national road project under the direction of the Ministry of Land, Infrastructure, Transport and Tourism is summarised in Table 26.

Table 26. Land Readjustment and the Timeline for the Recent Redevelopment of Shibuya Station, 2007–2013.
Source: Author.

Date	Activity
September 2007	Formulation of the 2007 Town Development Guidelines for Shibuya Station Central Area
June 2008	Opening of the Tōkyō Metro Fukutoshin Line; formulation of the Policy on Infrastructure Development in Shibuya Station Block
June 2009	City planning decisions on projects for roads, traffic square, land readjustment, etc.
March 2011	Formulation of the 2010 Town Development Guidelines for Shibuya Station Central Area
October 2012	Formulation of the Policy on Infrastructure Development in Shibuya Station Central Area
March 2013	Underground installation of the Tōkyū Tōyoko Line; Start of its mutual direct operation with the Fukutoshin Line
June 2013	City planning decisions on the special urban renaissance districts (Shibuya Station area, Shibuya 3, Chōme 21 area)

"Transit-Oriented Development"

The phrase "transit-oriented development" (TOD) is a give-away to its American origin. Before describing, with examples, the Japanese characteristics of TOD, the U.S. concept is first explained. In the international Western literature, transit-oriented development is a concept where a rail, bus, or ferry public transport can anchor a more environmentally and socially responsible urban form to achieve more sustainable urban development outcomes. For example, in the U.S.A. transit-oriented development has been promulgated by leading architects and planners, with support from the development industry (Calthorpe Associates, 1990; Calthorpe, 1993), as part of the 'new urbanism' (which in itself is an American term).

Transit-oriented development "is viewed by many as a promising tool for curbing sprawl and the automobile dependence it spawns" (Cervero *et al.*, 2004: 3). A synthesis of the literature suggests that the U.S. transit-oriented developments include the following ten characteristics.

1. Development that lies within a five-minute walk of the transit stop, or about a quarter of a mile from stop to edge. For major stations offering access to frequent high-speed service this pedestrian catchment area may be extended outwards to a 10-minute walk.

2. A balanced mix of uses of residential and commercial space located adjacent to a major transit stop with a 24-hour ridership.

3. A place-based zoning code at, or near, transit stops that generates buildings that shape and define memorable streets, squares and plazas, while allowing uses to change easily over time.

4. A built form with public transit included that presents an average block perimeter limited to no more than 1,350 feet (411 metres). This generates a fine-grained network of streets, dispersing traffic and allowing for the creation of quiet and intimate thoroughfares.

5. Minimum parking requirements are abolished since the goal is to reduce private motor vehicles and make them more, and not less, convenient for pedestrians and users of public transport.

6. Maximum parking requirements are instituted as a counter to the usual notion of providing parking for every peak demand. For every 1,000 workers, no more than 500 spaces and as few as 10 spaces are provided.

7. Parking costs in TOD are "unbundled," and full market rates are charged for all parking spaces to promote less car use.
8. Major stops provide bike stations, offering free attended bicycle parking, repairs and rentals. At minor stops, secure and fully enclosed bicycle parking is provided.
9. Transit service is fast, frequent, reliable and comfortable, with headways of 15 minutes, or less. Roadway space is allocated to different users and traffic signals timed primarily for the convenience of walkers and cyclists.
10. Traffic is calmed, with roads designed to limit speed to 30 mph (50km/h) on major streets and 20 mph (30km/h) on lesser streets.

Even before the 1940s in Japan, when the railway enterprises invested in new rail lines, they also owned and developed the land parcels around the major stations along the route. As noted in Chapter 6, Ichizō Kobayashi introduced the concept of combining railway development and suburban development (Kato, 1996: 45) in an attempt to persuade bankers about the feasibility of his business (Tokyo Kyukou Dentetsu Kabushiki Kaisha, 1973; Park *et al.*, 2011).

The essence of station area transit-oriented developments in Japan are high-rise mixed-use buildings above, and adjacent to, the station platforms with the streets on one side of the railway tracks modern redevelopments and the other side a more traditional mix of bars, cafes and small businesses. Based on field observations in the neighbourhoods surrounding railway stations (Kōbe, Kyōto, Nagoya, Shizuoka, Yokohama, Kawasaki and Tōkyō) a study by Black (*et al.*, 2016) identified five key elements that produce high-quality design outcomes that can be adapted and applied in any cultural setting for transit-oriented developments: accessibility; amenity; axis; affordability; and ancestry.

Table 27 summarises selected transit-oriented developments built during the first decade of the 21st century on 11 railway lines (with the different rail technologies shown) in Tōkyō. The table also reveals the lead agency in the station development whether a government project, a private enterprise project or a public-private sector partnership.

Table 27. Selected Tōkyō Railways Developed Post-2000 by Governments,
Private Companies and Public-Private Partnerships.
Source: Murakami, 2011: 1.

Name	Opened	Length (km)	Technology	Ownership
Shinagawa HSR station	2003	N/a	HSR	Private
Ōedo Line	2000	27.8	MRT	Public
Mita Line	2000	4.0	MRT	Public
North-South Line	2000	5.7	MRT	Private
Hanzamon Line	2003	6.0	MRT	Private
Tōkyō Bay Line	2001	7.3	CRT	Public-Private
Tsukuba Xpress	2005	58.3	CRT	Public-Private
Hokusō Line	2000	3.8	CRT	Public-Private
Saitama Xpress	2001	14.6	CRT	Public-Private
Minatō-Mirai Xpress	2004	4.1	MRT	Public-Private
Tama Monorail	2000	16.0	LRT	Public-Private

Legend: HSR—high-speed rail; MRT—mass rapid transit;
CRT—commuter heavy rail; LRT—light rail transit (tram).

Murakami (2011: 1) also analysed land-value changes (adjusted to 2000 prices) for the period 2000 to 2007, and found the ability of the new Shinagawa HSR station, the MRT and CRT stations, and high-rise office property redevelopments at stations to stimulate local economic development were considerable in central Tōkyō. However, in outer Tōkyō, the ability of the new railway extensions (and car-dependent commercial property developments at highway interchanges) was found to be insignificant for value capture. The conclusion is that transit-oriented developments are only successful in stimulating the value of land and properties where the location is suitable and where suitable planning instruments are in place.

Nagoya Station

Railway stations in Japan are important for local communities because as transport hubs with integrated mixed land uses, they serve as a focal point and are modern attractive environments where people gather. This is recognised by JR Central who have cooperated with requests from local municipalities to improve stations by building over-tracks, including installing handicap accessible passages, promoting railway elevators, developing plazas in front of stations for pedestrian, cycling, bus and taxi access (Central Japan Railway Company, 2020: 52).

Currently, in terms of floor space, Nagoya Station is the largest in the world. When the Chūo Shinkansen enters service, Nagoya Station will be the world's first to conveniently transfer passengers amongst all forms of public transport: maglev, high speed rail, conventional rail, air express rail, subways, city buses, long-distance coaches and taxis. The progressive expansion of Nagoya Station as a "transit-oriented development" started with JR Central Towers, opened in 2000, and JR Gate Tower, opened in 2017 (Central Japan Railway Company, 2020: 42).

The station attracts large numbers of passengers and visitors—almost one-quarter of a million people each day. The land-use activities in the buildings make a significant contribution to the region's economy. The merchandise section manages department stores and provides sales services for goods and food in stations and trains. The real estate section develops commercial facilities in stations and areas under elevated tracks, and also leases real estate such as station buildings. Another section manages hotels, travel agencies, and advertising agencies. The building characteristics and functions of JR Towers, JR Gate Tower and Takashimaya Gate Tower Mall are summarised in Table 28 below.

Table 28. Nagoya Station—Associated Buildings and Services, 2020.
Source: based on Central Japan Railway Company, 2020.

Building	Height (metres)	Area (sq. m.)	Function
JR Towers	245	417,000	Department store, hotel and offices
JR Gate Tower	220	260,000	Commercial facilities, 160 fashion stores, electronics, JR Gate Tower Hotel, together with Nagoya Marriott Associa Hotel and offices

The businesses represent a major commercial / retail destination in the Nagoya region in addition to its function as a major transport hub. The operating revenues of these consolidated Central Japan Railway Company's business subsidiaries, excluding JR Central railway business, totalled 636.6 billion yen in the financial year ending in 2019 (Central Japan Railway Company, 2020: 42). Other examples of transit-oriented developments are contained in Japanese new towns.

Japanese New Towns

To fully understand such examples of transit-oriented development, such as Tama New Town and Tama Garden City, they need to be placed within the context of the Japanese New Town Policy. The growth of the Japanese economy from the 1960s onwards resulted in a rapid influx of population into Tōkyō, and other major cities, resulting in skyrocketing land prices. Therefore, many households settled on the outskirts of the city where land was cheaper. This uncontrolled expansion of the urban fringes of large Japanese cities by private-sector property speculators led to poorly planned communities with poor access to amenities and transport and inadequate infrastructure to service the population.

Japan's New Town program consisted of a many diverse projects, most of which aspired to the creation of all-inclusive urban environments. The program was heavily informed by the Anglo-American Garden City tradition (Grant, 2014) initiated in 1898 by Sir Ebenezer Howard in the UK (Welwyn, Letchworth), American neighbourhood design (Radburn), as well as Soviet strategies of industrial development (Hein, 2003). Some 30 new towns have been built all over Japan. Most of these constructions were initiated during the period of rapid economic growth in the 1960s, but construction continued into the 1980s of which Tama New Town is a good example of the institutional approach taken.

Tama New Town

Conceived in 1965 to ease the growth pressure in Tōkyō, Tama New Town (多摩ニュータウン) provided hundreds of thousands of housing units in a planned, pleasant urban environment that was once the former green belt encircling Tōkyō. The planning and development were carried out jointly by The Housing and Urban Development Corporation, Tōkyō, the Metropolitan Housing Supply Corporation and Tōkyō Metropolitan Government. Construction began in 1966 and the first phase opened in 1971. Construction continued in phases for the next four decades,

Tama New Town has a population of approximately 200,000 making it the largest housing development in Japan in an area of 2,892 hectares. Tama New Town is approximately 14 km long stretching east-west, and between 1 and 3 km wide, located in an expanse of hills known as Tama Hills about 15 km west of central Tōkyō (Takayama et al., 2019, Figure 2, p. 2316). It straddles the municipalities of Hachiōji, Tama, Inagi and Machida cities, and, administratively, each area is governed by its respective municipal authority, although they all come under the jurisdiction of the Tōkyō Metropolitan Government.

Tama New Town is divided into 21 neighbourhoods, each with about 3,000 to 5,000 houses and flats, each with two elementary schools and one junior high school as well as a neighbourhood centre with shops, police station, post office, medical clinics and so on. Several neighbourhoods form one district, each of which are centred around a commuter rail station. Tama New Town is served by more than ten railway stations, most of them on the Keiō Sagamihara Line and Odakyū Tama Line, both of which provide a direct service to Shinjuku Station in central Tōkyō. JR Nambu Line and Tama Toshi Monorail Line also serve the area.

The area surrounding the Tama Center Station complex, in the municipality of Tama, is the designated centre of Tama New Town. The station complex also includes shopping arcades and a bus terminal. The surrounding area is separated into business, commercial and leisure zones. Some of the negative issues identified with this program have been longer commuting times into Tōkyō, high housing costs and relatively poor access to a range of urban functions (Tanabe, 1978). In 2002, Prime Minister Koizumi Junichirō (1942–) announced the end of new town construction, although the towns continue to receive government funding for redevelopment.

Tama Garden City

In contrast, Tama Garden City (the Den'en Toshi Development Project)[3] has achieved a more satisfactory outcome with the integration of land

---

3   The GREAT project that was funded under the Australian Indonesian Governance Reform Program that allowed the author to visit Japan to undertake research into

use and transport planning. The problem context is as follows. In 1956, the first comprehensive plan for national and capital region development was established—first defining the Tōkyō metropolitan area to be within a 100-km radius from the core of old Tōkyō. At the time, there was an essentially mono-centric urban structure with its associated high commuting stresses on the city centre, caused especially by the congestion on the centrally focused railways (Alpkokin *et al.*, 2007b).

Governments formulated policies to promote controlled decentralisation, to avoid over centralisation and to introduce a "green belt" to preserve large-scale green areas very similar to County of London Plan prepared in 1943 by J. H. Forshaw and Patrick Abercrombie. Powerful lobby groups in Japan, including private railway companies, helped to torpedo the plan. The "Tokyo greenbelt plan" failed, and the subsequent plan of 1968 completely abolished the green belt concept that allowed the Den'en Toshi Development Project to proceed. There are nine defining characteristics of this development:

1. One enterprise has developed both land and the railway.
2. There has been a complete internalisation of the external economy of the Railway Development.
3. There has been a well-planned land-use and land readjustment.
4. Infrastructure development and acquisition of land for the railway and public use has been coordinated in stages.

TOD, to conduct fieldwork in Tama New Town, and to study the land adjustment program. The following people were interviewed and provided valuable information: Ir. Eddi Santosa, Director, MRT Jakarta, Balai Kota DKI Jakarta; Dr Masafumi Ota, Manager, Project Coordinating Secretariat, Planning and Administration Division, Railway Headquarters, Tokyu Corporation, Tokyo; Mr Dongkun Oh, Assistant Manager, Residential Realty Division, Residential (Development) Headquarters, Tokyu Corporation, Tokyo; Professor Yoshitsugu Hayashi, Dean, Graduate School of Environmental Management, Nagoya University; Professor Kazuaki Miyamoto, Musashi University of Technology, Yokohama; Dr Hiroshi Mori, Chief Consultant, Social-System Policy Department, Mitsubishi Research Institute, Inc, Otemachi 2—Chome, Tokyo; Dr Masaki Arioka, Kumagai Gumi Company, Iidabashi, Tokyo; Dr Hiroshi Mr Yoneda Gen, Deputy Director, Division 2 and Division 1, Development Assistance Department, Japan Bank for International Cooperation, 4–1, Ohtemachi 1-chome, Chiyoda-ku, Tokyo; Mr Michihiko Ogawa, Program Officer, Division 2, Indonesia, Japan Bank for International Cooperation, 4–1, Ohtemachi 1-chome, Chiyoda-ku, Tokyo; Mr John Hart, Multi-modal Transport Manager, NSW Roads and Traffic Authority; Professor John Renne, University of New Orleans, New Orleans.

5. The extension of the railway has been in accordance with settlement development.
6. Well-coordinated feeder service to the station.
7. This has provided a stable revenue from fares.
8. Shopping complexes have been developed by the same enterprise.
9. Overall there is a high level of accessibility to public transport.

Ishibashi and Taniguchi (2005) have analysed development of Tama Garden City pointing out that it began as the development of a low-density residential area but gradually shifted to high-density developments. Planning relating to this development was undertaken with appropriate revisions being made in the preparation process to ensure there was a response to the changing socio-economic conditions of escalating land prices. Instead of regarding the master plan as a fixed plan that determined the final shape of the new town, its continuous review processes have introduced flexibility. The apparent success of the planning of Tama Garden City is a factor that has encouraged the National Government in the late 1990s to speculate on the nature of future urbanisation in Japan, including 'smart cities'.

Smart Cities

The literature on 'smart cities' is extensive. A search was made in February 2022 of the Google Scholar® database by entering the key words 'smart cities' that retrieved some 1.24 million citations. This is not surprising given that the roots of the smart city movement can be traced back to the beginning from the late 1960s when the Community Analysis Bureau in Los Angeles used computer data bases, cluster analysis and infrared aerial photography to gather data, produce reports on neighbourhood housing quality and demographics, and made recommendations to governments on resource allocation to tackle urban poverty (Vallianatos, 2015). This sub-section focuses on the policy context for smart cities in Japan and gives examples of smart city initiatives in Kashiwa (Chiba Prefecture), Yokohama (Kanagawa Prefecture) and Tōyama (Tōyama Prefecture). Examples of initiatives for travel mobilities in smart cities are drawn from Toyota's "Woven City" (Shizuoka Prefecture) and Maebashi (Gunma Prefecture).

Global and Japanese Smart Cities

Today, with advances in information and communication technologies, and the plethora of data collection devises, common attributes of a 'smart city' are sensor networks that collect information to be stored and analysed in order to improve services. The Japanese government, and the country's industrial and technology companies, have been pioneers in developing an integrated approach to energy and sustainability issues in smart cities with eco-town projects in 1997, followed in 2008 by the Eco Model City program.

At the United Nations Conference on Sustainable Development (Rio+20), the Japanese Government made an announcement on promoting the "FutureCityInitiative" which creates human-centred "new value" to resolve the challenges of the environment and ageing. In June 2010, the Japanese Government identified the "FutureCity Initiative" as one of 21 national projects in its "New Growth Strategy". Japan for Sustainability, launched in 2011 and promoted by the Cabinet Office, designated as "Future Cities" eleven cities. As three of these eleven cities—Kashiwa, Tōyama and Yokohama—all fall within the study area defined for this book, the smart city components of each city are described in some detail (https://www.japanfs.org/en/projects/future_city/index.html).

Kashiwa City—Smart City

Kashiwa City is located some 40 km north-northeast of Tōkyō Railway Station. Formerly, Kashiwa-no-ha, was a famous horse-breeding area in the Edō era directly under the control of the Tokugawa *Shōgunate*. With the establishment of prefectures, the Japanese government promoted settlement and agriculture with Mitsui's Hachiroemon Takayoshi (the 8th head of the Mitsui clan) as president of a land reclamation company. During the Korea War, the United States Air Force built a communications base there on an area of 188 hectares that was returned to Mitsui Fudosan Co., Ltd. in 1979. In 2001, Kashiwa City began a Land Readjustment Project based on an urban planning project at the 273-hectare Kashiwa-no-ha area.

In December 2011, the Cabinet Office selected Kashiwa-no-ha as a "Comprehensive Special Zone for Regional Revitalization and an Environmental Future City". The city builders were the private-sector company Mitsui Fudosan Co., Ltd., who attracted some of the brightest academic minds to set up facilities in the area, including the University of Tōkyō Kashiwa Campus, Chiba University Kashiwa-no-ha Campus and the National Cancer Center Hospital East. This academic infusion was coupled with the creation of the Urban Design Center Kashiwa-no-ha (UDCK), a consortium to design and implement a long-term, multi-decade "master plan" (https://kashiwanoha-smartcity.com/en/). Since its genesis in 2001, Kashiwa-no-ha has tackled ways to improve citizen's health and set up one of Japan's biggest co-working areas (Kashiwa-no-ha Open Innovation Lab, or KOIL) to stimulate idea exchange amongst entrepreneurs and professionals. Initiatives during Covid-19 include the simulation of ventilation in offices.

Yokohama—Smart City

The City of Yokohama proposed activities on the "civil power" of the city's population of 3.69 million: the historical background of the opening of its port to international trade; and the accumulated knowledge about the environment and energy. The proposal featured implementation of the Yokohama Smart City Project (YSCP)—solar power, electric vehicles, CEMS (Severe Environmental Memory System) and the domestic and international dissemination of innovative water supply and sewerage technologies. The smart city project is founded on mutual support in the local area through NPOs and major support networks for a super-ageing society. This includes the implementation of life-support functions to renovate housing for the elderly, making transport barrier free, and the creation and transmission of culture and art.

The city established the Yokohama Smart Business Association in 2015 in order to prepare for the practical application of the technologies verified through the smart city program. The city installed a co-generation system to share energy from the Yokohama City University Medical Centre to the adjacent Minami-ku Government Building. In one of the sustainable residential model districts (Tōkaichiba-chō), town development for residents, companies, government and others using city land will be carried out as a model case to resolve social challenges. These include residential suburbs based on the proposals by private companies such as the supply of a diversity of homes with energy conservation and carbon reduction devices.

Tōyama—Smart City

Tōyama City is a major urban area on the Sea of Japan coast with a population of about 420,000 on flat terrain that has rapidly suburbanised and become car dependant. In order to address the above issues, as well as a rapidly ageing population and falling birth rates, the city has set its basic policy to develop a compact city focused around public transport. The vision is to create an elderly-friendly, low-carbon, sustainable city by promoting the use of public transport and attracting residents back into the urban centre.

On 29 April 2006, Tōyama opened a new light rail transit (LRT) tramway using innovative tram-train technology. The current network of light rail and heavy rail can be viewed on a website (http://www.urbanrail.net/as/jp/toyama/toyama.htm). The evolution of this passenger network is complex. The City Government has converted the JR Tōyamakō Line (1067 mm gauge, single track of 7.6 km, also known as Portram) into a light rail transit (LRT) system in 2006. The Tōyama Chihō Tetsudō's Kamidaki Line was opened in 1907 as a tram system and on 14 March 2015 the 300-metre spur to Tōyama Railway Station was completed to coincide with the inauguration of the Hokuriku Shinkansen services. On 21 March 2020 the Tōyama Chihō Tetsudō's Kamidaki Line was also connected to Portram at Tōyama station.

The Tōyama prefectural and municipal governments and local economic groups jointly set up a third-sector company, the Tōyama Light Rail Co., capitalised at 498 million yen (U.S. $4.4 million). It took over a 6.5-km section of railway from the West Japan Railway Co. and extended it through the city's streets by 1.1 km. The LRT system cost the company 5.8 billion yen (U.S. $51.4 million) as it had to buy rollingstock and lay additional tracks. The Tōyama City Government covered about half of the cost with the Prefectural Government and the Ministry of Land, Infrastructure, Transport and Tourism providing the remainder of the loan (Light Rail Now, 2006).

Mobility in the Smart City—the Toyota Company

The City of Toyota, with a population of 420,000, has a target to reduce emissions by 30–50 per cent by 2030. As the home of the Toyota Motor Company, the city is, unsurprisingly, focusing on transport and mobility issues for its smart city initiative, including a plug-in hybrid car-sharing system and the development of solar power-based charging infrastructure. Japan's largest car manufacturers and technology firms are involved in autonomous driving vehicles and data collection, dissemination and analysis.

However, the company's venture into sustainable cities is the announcement in January 2020 of a new town "Woven City,"—a reference to the Toyoto Company's origins in 1933 as a division of the Toyoda Automatic Loom Works established in Nagoya by Toyoda Kiichirō (https://global.toyota/en/newsroom/corporate/31171023.html). On 23 February 2021, the Toyota Motor Corporation and Woven Planet Holdings, Inc. (Woven Planet) held a ground-breaking ceremony for the construction of Woven City at the old vehicle yard adjacent to the former Higashi-Fuji Plant site of Toyota Motor East Japan, Inc in Susono City.

This initiative is to be built on the 71-hectare site of the car factory that closed in late 2020 (Kyodo, 2021). The new city will begin with 2,000 residents, including Toyota employees, during the first few years and will also serve as a home base for researchers. Residents will have in-home robotics to assist their daily lives, with sensor-based AI systems monitoring their health. Only fully autonomous, zero-emission vehicles will be allowed to travel on the main streets. Woven City will have three types of streets interwoven with each other on the ground level: one dedicated to automated vehicle driving; one to pedestrians; and one to pedestrians using personal mobility vehicles. Underground there will be roads used to transport goods and waste (Global Toyota, 2021).

Mobility in Maebashi City

In April 2019, the Ministry of Economy, Trade and Industry (METI) and the Ministry of Land, Infrastructure, Transport and Tourism jointly started a "Smart Mobility Challenge" project aimed at implementing new mobility services. The ministries selected 28 areas and projects of which Maebashi was a successful applicant. It is Japan's most car-dependent locality with 0.67 vehicles per person (Japan BRANDVOICE, 2019) and, with an ageing population, older residents do not want to give up their driving license for fear of a loss of independence—a problem in most developed countries (Nakanishi and Black, 2015).

Maebashi, with a population of about 332,999 in its core (in October 2019), and a surrounding metropolitan region with approximately 1.26 million people, embarked on the "Smart Mobility Challenge," aiming to create an urban traffic environment where all citizens can move freely. The city is one of a select number in Japan starting to pioneer Mobility as a Service (MaaS) that aims to integrate local buses, trains, taxis and other modes of transport into a single on-demand app. The MaaS project captures in digital format all traffic flow in the Maebashi area and the various mobility options will be synced and organised inside a common platform. For the user, this means that upon selecting a destination the app will compose the best multi-transport route and accept payment for all parts of the travel as one transaction. Commercial facility managers and advertising firms are getting involved in this grand mobility vision allowing such things as activity information and pre-paid bookings using the app.

A consortium of private and public sector partners and a university are involved: the traffic planning firm Jorudan; data analysis by NTT Data; telecom giant NTT DoCoMo and its partner in AI bus services, Mirai Share. The transport operators are 6 local bus firms (for example, Nippon Chuō Bus), 10 local taxi firms and rail operators (JR East—Jōetsu and Ryōmō lines; and Jōmō Electric Railway Company). Japan's leading autonomous driving research hub with a fleet of 18 self-drive test vehicles (including buses, trucks and a taxi) is the Center for Research on Adoption of NextGen Transportation Systems (CRANTS), part of Gunma University's campus in Maebashi City. Technological solutions could also be applied to act as "last-mile" solutions, connecting people's homes and public transport stops.

Conclusions

Since antiquity, rulers of empires and ancient states have laid out their cities according to some formalised plan. The Japanese Emperors followed the layout principles of Chinese capital cities, such as Chang'an (Xian), when developing Heijo-kyō (Nara) and Heian-kyō (Kyōto) in the 8th century. Medieval castle towns in Japan had their own characteristic morphology. Similarly, the Tokugawa Government based in Edō developed one of the world's largest cities of that time with an obvious spatial structure that segregated the designated strata of society. With the Meiji Restoration of 1868, the capital of Japan was transferred from Kyōto to Tōkyō (Edō), where Western principles of planning and design were introduced.

The institutions charged with urban development were modernised and Japanese delegations undertook overseas missions to determine the best way to manage urban growth and renewal. The Emperor Meiji commissioned a 50-person mission to travel to North America and Europe in 1871–1873 seeking "Western models of development" that included urban planning practices. The early institutional initiatives were confined to the new capital of Tōkyō. After the Great Ginza Fire, the Meiji government issued a statement advocating the building of a fireproof city—the Ginza Brick Quarters Project (1872–1877) that was promoted by the Minister of Finance, Ōkuma Shigenobu, and based on British concepts.

The first city planning legislation in Japan—the *Tōkyō Town Planning Ordinance* (1888)—derived from this project was soon superseded by the *City Planning Act* of 1919, which, in turn, was short lived because of the 1923 Great Kantō Earthquake. The day after the earthquake, the government established the Bureau for Reconstruction of the Imperial Capital—an institution under the direct control of the Prime Minister.

The main mechanism for government intervention into the land market was land readjustment that rezoned land over significant parts of Tōkyō. The institutions dealing with urban planning underwent gradual transformations: from 5 April 1919 to 15 July 2018, 235 Tōkyō City planning laws and regulations, and numerous Cabinet orders, were issued. In June 1950, the *Capital Construction Law* was established as a national project to construct Tōkyō as a national project. The first substantial step towards the post-war reconstruction was made under the Tōkyō Special City Plan using the land readjustment mechanism for reconstruction.

The *National Capital Region Development Act* of April 1956 aimed to control development over the greater metropolitan region. Under this Act, the Tōkyō Metropolitan Government promoted an all-out revision of urban plans: parks and green spaces in 1957; expressways in 1959; and high-speed railways in 1962. The partial revision of the *Building*

Standards Act of 1950 in January 1963 resulted in zoning to secure open spaces to redress the imbalance between the over-concentrated population and urban facilities.

The Second and Third National Capital Region Development Plans (1976 and 1986) both addressed the formulation of policies for "suburban development areas" around the existing built-up areas of Tōkyō in order to develop balanced and well-designed hierarchical urban centres and to preserve some green areas but on a much smaller scale than before. The Japanese Government has the necessary institutional arrangement to achieve integrated approaches, where all modes of transport and land development are located in one ministry—the Ministry of Land, Infrastructure, Transport and Tourism. In addition to mode specific divisions covering maritime and ports, waterways, roads, railways and civil aviation, there is also a division devoted to national spatial planning and regional policy.

Policy outcomes from these institutional arrangements include transit-oriented developments (of which Nagoya Station represents a world-leading example of integrated land-use and transport), often facilitated through the mechanism of land readjustment, and new towns, such as Tama Garden City. The Japanese Government has also promoted more sustainable cities. Launched in 2011, and promoted by the Cabinet Office, eleven Japanese cities were designated as "Future Cities", including Kashiwa, Tōyama and Yokohama. In April 2019, the Ministry of Land, Infrastructure, Transport and Tourism and the Ministry of Economy, Trade and Industry jointly promoted the "Smart Mobility Challenge" for cities to implement new mobility services (for example, Maebashi). Finally, Toyota's Woven City initiative promises to be one model for a city based on sustainable road transport.

When the 5th Science and Technology Basic Plan was endorsed by Cabinet in 2016 it introduced Society 5.0 as the sort of society that Japan should aspire towards (Government of Japan, Cabinet Office, n.d.). Society 5.0 is premised on the broad transitions that have historically occurred in Japanese society from archaic to the present when the vision for the future is driven by the institution of the national government with details of implementation being left to local government, businesses and the community. These future challenges for both institutions and organisations are explored in the final chapter on Conclusions and Speculations.

References

Alpkokin, P., J. Black, Hirokazu Kato and V. Vichiensan (2007a) "Polycentric Employment Formation in Mega-cities: Analysis from APEC-TR Collaborative Research", *Journal of the Eastern Asia Society for Transport Studies*, 7, 1446–1459.

Alpkokin, P., N. Komiyama, H. Takeshita and Hirokazu Kato (2007b) "Tokyo Metropolitan Area Cluster Employment Formation in Line with its Extensive Rail Network", *Journal of the Eastern Asia Society for Transport Studies*, 7, 1403–1416.

Archer, R. W. (2000) "Urban Redevelopment with Landowner Participation using the Land Pooling/Readjustment Technique", in Anthony Gar-On Yeh and Mee Kam Ng (eds) (2000) *Planning for a Better Urban Living Environment in Asia*, Ashgate, Aldershot, Hants, 252–277.

Australian and Japanese Governments Joint Steering Committee to Oversee a Major Study Investigating the Feasibility of the Multifunction Polis Concept (1990) *MultiFunction Polis Feasibility Study*. Joint Steering Committee, Australian Government Publishing Service, Canberra.

Black, J., K. Tara and P. Pakzad (2016) "Planning and Design Elements for Transit Oriented Developments/ Smart Cities: Examples of Cultural Borrowings", *Procedia Engineering*, Proceeding of Sustainable Development of Civil, Urban and Transportation Engineering, Ho Chi Min City, Vietnam, April 2016, 142, 2–9.

Buchanan, C. D. (1963) *Traffic in Towns: A Study of the Long Term Problems of Traffic in Urban Areas*. Her Majesty's Stationery Office, London.

Calthorpe Associates (1990) *Transit-Oriented Development Design Guidelines*. Calthorpe Associates for Sacramento County Planning & Community Development Department, Sacramento, California.

Calthorpe, P. (1993) *The Next American Metropolis: Ecology, Community and the American Dream*. Princeton Architectural Press, Princeton, New Jersey.

Central Japan Railway Company (2020) *Central Japan Railway Company: Annual Report 2020*. Central Japan Railway Company, Shinagawa, Tokyo.

Cervero, R., et al. (2004) *Transit Oriented Development in America: Experiences, Challenges, and Prospects*. National Academy Press, Washington, D.C.

Cybrinsky, R. (1998) *Tōkyō—The Shogun's City at the Twenty-First Century*. John Wiley & Sons, New York.

Funo, S. (2005) "Tokyo: Paradise of Speculators and Builders", in P. J. M. Nas (ed.) (2005) *Directors of Urban Change in Asia*, Taylor and Francis Inc. London, 245–265.

Global Toyota (2021) "Toyota Breaks Ground for "Woven City": Construction of the Prototype City of the Future where all Ecosystems are Connected Begins at the Higashi-Fuji Site (Susono City, Shizuoka Prefecture)", https://global.toyota/en/newsroom/corporate/34827717.html

Government of Japan, Cabinet Office (n.d.) "Society 5.0", https://www8.cao.go.jp/cstp/english/society5_0/index.html

Grant, J. L. (2014) *Garden City Movement*. Springer, Dordrecht.

Hall, P. (1966) *The World Cities*. McGraw-Hill, New York.

Hammer, J. (2011) "The Great Japan Earthquake of 1923", *Smithsonian Magazine*, May.

Hamnett, S. (1997) "The Multi-Function Polis 1987–199", *Australian Planner*, 34 (4), 227–232.

Hamp, M. (2019) "From Edo to Tokyo—Birth of a Global City", https://medium.com/@hamp.mathias/from-edo-to-tokyo-birth-of-a-global-capital-c9effafada34

Hein, C. (2003) "Visionary Plans and Planners: Japanese Traditions and Western Influences", in N. Fiévé and P. Waley (eds) (2003) *Japanese Capitals in Historical Perspective*. Routledge Curzon, New York, 309–343.

Hein, C. (2010) "Shaping Tokyo: Land Development and Planning Practice in the Early Modern Japanese Metropolis", *Journal of Urban History*, 36 (4), 447–484.

Hein, C. (2016) "Introduction—Special Section on Japanese Cities in Global Context", *Journal of Urban History*, 42 (3), 1–14.

Ishibashi, Noboru, and Hirokuni Taniguchi (2005) "多摩田園都市開発の計画プロセスに関する研究 ―土地区画整理事業の組み合わせによって作られた郊外住宅地計画に関する研究 その1" [Study on the Planning Process for the Development of Tama Garden City: Study on the Planning of Suburban Residential Area Developed Through a Combination of Land Readjustment Projects (1)], *Journal of Architecture and Planning (Transactions of AIJ)*, 70 (598), 129–136.

James, P. (ed.) (1990) *Technocratic Dreaming: Of Very Fast Trains and Japanese Designer Cities*. Left Book Club Cooperative, Melbourne.

Japan BRANDVOICE (2019) "Japan Sparks New Life in Local Communities with Human-centric Smart Cities", 23 December, https://bq-magazine.com/japan-brandvoice-japan-sparks-new-life-in-local-communities-with-human-centric-smart-cities/

Kachi, Noriyasu, Hirokazu Kato, Yoshitsugu Hayashi and J. Black (2005) "Making Cities More Compact by Improving Transport and Amenity and Reducing Hazard", *Journal of the Eastern Asia Society for Transportation Studies*, 6, 3819–3834.

Kato, Shinichi (1996) "Progress in Railway Transportation", *Japan Railway & Transport Review*, September, 44–48.

Kodansha (1993) *Japan: An Illustrated Encyclopedia*. Kodansha Ltd, Bunkyo-ku, Tokyo.

Kyodo, Jiji (2021) "Toyota Begins Building Smart City Near Mount Fuji", https://www.japantimes.co.jp/news/2021/02/23/business/corporate-business/toyota-smart-city-construction/

Light Rail Now (2006) "Toyama: 'Tram-Train' Streetcar Line is 'Model' for Japan's Light Rail Revival', Light Rail Now Production Team, May 2006, https://www.lightrailnow.org/news/n_toy_2006–05a.htm

Metro Tokyo (2021) "Reconstruction Following the Great Kanto Earthquake", https://www.toshiseibi.metro.tokyo.lg.jp/keikaku_chousa_singikai/pdf/tokyotoshizukuri/en_2_02.pdf

Morichi, Shigeru, Seiji Iwakura, Toshiya Morishige, Makato Itoh and Shio Hayasaki (2001) "Tokyo Metropolitan Rail Network Long-Range Plan for the 21st Century", paper presented at the Transportation Research Board 80th Annual Meeting, 7–11 January, Washington, D. C.

Murakami, Jun (2011) "The Transit-Oriented Megalopolis: Rail Transit Technologies, Urban Regeneration Programs & Land Value Redistributions in Tokyo", poster paper presented at the Transportation Research Board 90th Annual Meeting, January, Washington, D. C.

Nakanishi, Hitomi, and J. A. Black (2015) "Travel Habit Creation of the Elderly and the Transition to Sustainable Transport: Exploratory Research Based on a Retrospective Survey", *International Journal of Sustainable Transportation*, 10 (7), 604–616.

Park, Naesun, Quynh Anh Dao and Hitoshi Ieda (2011) "What Makes TOD Success?: Analysis of Japanese Suburban Center TOD by Comparison of Tachikawa Station and Machida Station", *Proceedings of the Eastern Asia Society for Transportation Studies*, 8, n.p.

Perez, J., A. Araldi, G. Fusco and Takashi Fuse (2019) "The Character of Urban Japan: Overview of Osaka-Kobe's Cityscapes", *Urban Science*, 3 (4), 105, https://doi.org/10.3390/urbansci3040105

Sharp, E. A., Lady (1970) *Transport Planning: The Men for the Job—A Report to the Minister of Transport*. Her Majesty's Stationery Office, London.

Smith, M., J. Black and J. Gilchrist (1993) "Prototype Transport and Urban Development Concepts for the Australian Multi-Function Polis", *Selected Proceedings of the Sixth World Conference on Transport Research., Lyon '92, Volume III Transport Policies*. L'imprimerie Chirat, St-Just-La-Perdue, France, 2129–2140.

Sorensen, A. (2002) *The Making of Urban Japan*. Routledge, London.

Takayama, Koki, Yuichiro Watanabe, Hsiang-Chuan Chang and Akinori Morimoto (2020) "Study on the Characteristics of Japanese Transit Oriented Development as Seen from Long-term Land-use Changes", *Transportation Research Procedia*, 48, 2313–2328.

Tanabe, Hiroshi (1978) "Problems of the New Towns in Japan", *Geojournal*, 2 (1), 39–46.

Tokyo Ginza Official (2021) "History", https://www.ginza.jp/en/history

Tokyo Kyukou Dentetsu Kabushiki Kaisha (1973) *Tokyo Kyukou 50 Nenshi*. TKDKK, Tokyo.

Tokyo Metropolitan Government, Bureau of Urban Development (n.d.) "Outline of the City Planning", http://www.toshiseibi.metro.tokyo.jp/eng/

The Far East (1872) "Old Photos of Japan", *The Far East*, July. J. R. Black, Yokohama, https://www.oldphotosjapan.com/en/photos/760/anjincho-in-nihonbashi

Vallianatos, M. (2013) "How LA Used Big Data to Build a Smart City in the 1970s", GIZMODO, https://gizmodo.com/uncovering-the-early-history-of-big-data-in-1974-los-an-1712551686

Watanabe, Shun-Ichi (1980) "Planning History in Japan", *Urban History Yearbook*, 7, 63–75.

9. Conclusions

A state without the means of some change is without the means of its conservation

Burke, 1987: 106

Context to the Analysis of Transport Change

The book has considered the modes of transport in Japan as dynamic governance systems that have responded to ever-changing political, economic, social and security imperatives, and described how these issues have been resolved. These transitions have been interpreted as six major time periods as proposed by Ishii (1980: viii): archaic; ancient; medieval; early modern; modern; and contemporary. The introductory chapter has justified this choice, explained the distinction between institutions and organisations and has defined a study area where the historical evolution of transport institutions and organisations has been described in detail.

History helps us to understand the past and informs us as to what might be relevant for the future. In Japan, a vision of the future—Society 5.0—has been mapped out (Government of Japan, Cabinet Office, n.d.) and is premised on the broad transitions that have historically occurred in Japanese society, where Society 4.0 corresponds to contemporary Japan in the second decade of the 21st century. The issues, and the institutional challenges of Japan Society 5.0, comprise the final parts to this chapter.

To set the socio-political context for this transport history, Chapter 2 commences with a description of migration from continental Asia to the Japanese archipelago, the importation of paddy rice cultivation, embryonic state formation, state expansion across the islands of Honshū, Kyūshū and Shikōku with governance by a succession of powerful clan chiefs, Emperors and Court nobles, and warlords at the regional level. The institution of Emperor has lasted from ancient times but was reduced to ceremonial status under three military governments. The unification of Japan was eventually achieved in 1603 under the Tokugawa *Shōgunate* that was followed by two-and-a-half centuries of peace. This military government was replaced by the institution of Emperor in 1868, heralding in modern systems of national, prefecture and local government that prevail up to the present day.

Along with political transformations have come substantial sociotechnical system transitions. Throughout the history of transport in Japan, innovations and policies that relate to the movement of people and freight—from archaic times to the present—both civic and civil society (mainly from the 16th century)—have been intimately entwined in one way or another to deliver progress, change and technological and managerial innovation. These major transitions that have taken place since archaic times have been covered in detail in Chapters 3–7, where the institutions and organisations responsible for governing and administrating each transport mode—ports and shipping, canals and waterways, roads, railways and airports and civil aviation—have been documented. Integrated land-use planning with transport is only a modern concept and these developments leading to more sustainable urban transport future have been described in Chapter 8.

All of these chapters have concluding summaries that address the key questions raised in the Introduction. In particular, these chapters have addressed the following questions for each transport mode:

- Who were the relevant institutions and organisations in society? What were their respective roles in relation to the movement of traffic on all transport modes especially issues of authority and power relations?
- Who were the key players behind the changes in these institutions and organisations and what tangible things did they achieve in the transport sector?
- To what extent is Japan influenced by overseas ideas in the transformation of its institutions, organisations and transport?

Institutional and Organisation Change in Transport by Mode

Ports and Shipping

Places to dock ships with variable tidal heights are possibly the oldest of man-made elements of transport infrastructure, and it is unsurprising that in two millennia port functions and ownership patterns have changed substantially. Initially, the ports at Suminoe and Naniwa served Imperial purposes for tribute missions and trade. As centralised political power declined other players emerged to fill the vacuum. For example, Watanabe was originally a port on a *shōen* estate, managed by Court nobles, but the port underwent a major transformation in late Heian and Kamakura periods, evolving from a warehousing and transhipment centre to collection of lumberyards and storehouses belonging to religious organisations and rich families. Other examples of organisations owning ports included the merchants of Sakai and the Buddhist religious order's trading network at Ishiyama Honganji.

In the medieval period, warlords usurped the powers formerly associated with the court in Kyōto to establish military governments where *daimyō* ruled their domains and those with coastal waters could use ports to enter into legal and illicit trade and to wage war with other domains. Piracy was rife although it was as much an institution of 'local government' as an illegal organisation. Under the Tokugawa military government that lasted for over 250 years, economic growth was largely driven by merchant organisations who dominated the workings of ports and coastal shipping. When the institution of Emperor was reinstated with the Meiji Restoration of 1868, ports were deemed "government-owned structures", which brought them under national government jurisdiction.

After the Second World War, the *Port and Harbor Act (1950)* dramatically shifted port administration from the central government to local governments with a "port management body". However, with the increasing container shipping in the 1960s, the Ministry of Transport devised a public corporation model that would develop and manage international container terminals in Kōbe, Yokohama and Nagoya. The national government and private companies also invested in these port development authorities (abolished 1977 and replaced by port management corporations (PMC). Later, the Kōbe-Ōsaka International Port Corporation was launched by a consortium of the national government, the City of Kōbe, the City of Ōsaka and city banks.

These changes to port governance and shipping occurred through the actions of individuals. It is less easy in the distant past to consistently identify their names, but some examples can be found. The improved port at Watanabe, protected by stone levees and piers, was developed by Tōdaiji Temple's Abbot, Shunjō Chōgen, to accommodate oceangoing vessels in the transport of building materials for the temples. Piracy organisations flourished until they were largely eradicated by an edict from one of the powerful warlords Toyotomi Hideyoshi, who then incorporated the ships into his own navy for the invasion of Korea. The Tokugawa *bakufu* asked Kawamura Zuiken to plan the secure transport of commodities to Edō and developed coastal shipping routes from the late 17th century.

In the early Edō period, the *bakufu* allowed townspeople to construct canals in the marshes, including Dōtombori that was completed in 1615 by the merchant Doton Nariyasu. Suminokura Ryōi (1554–1614) excavated several canals in Ōsaka including the Hozugawa and the Takasegawa to facilitate economy activities. Sand and soil excavated from these constructions were used in creating the foundations for the expansion of the port town.

Overseas ideas and influences have long been influential in the maritime transport sector. The importation of Chinese culture and administrative systems (for example, the T'ang Dynasty Oceangoing and Marketing Department) were mechanisms for expanding state power in the ancient period. The actions of foreign powers, especially the U.S.A. in the mid-19th century, not only opened up selected Japanese ports for trading, but also had bearing on the events leading up to the Meiji Emperor's Restoration. In the late 19th century, Western models of administering public works were introduced by the Japanese Government and a Dutch engineer, De Rijke, planned the construction of Tempozan in the port of Ōsaka. General McArthur, during the Allied occupation of Japan, implemented port administration based on U.S. practice. Finally, following international trends in port governance (for example, Brooks, 2004; Brooks *et al.*, 2017), Ōsaka port privatised its management.

Canals

The story of canals is much simpler because, unlike in continental Europe, England and the U.S.A., Honshū never developed a network of commercial canals due to its mountainous terrain and fast flowing rivers engorged after snow melt and typhoon rain. The main purposes of canal construction in Japan have been primarily to irrigate agricultural land, to control river flooding, to provide town water and to provide defensive moats around castles, of which the 17th century moats of Edō Castle are an excellent example of Japanese engineering techniques that received no external influences.

From Yayoi times, irrigation channels would have facilitated the local movement of rice and other produce. There have been only three substantial canal achievements for transport in the study area. Dating the 3-km long Horie Canal is difficult but there is no doubt of its importance by the 6th and 7th centuries. The Horie canal was completed by Imperial command. The canals constructed in Kyōto demonstrate the dynamics of the three-way interactions amongst merchant organisations and the *daimyō* and *bakufu*. Although there have been attempts and proposals to link Lake Biwa to the ocean, only the Lake Biwa Canal construction by the Kyōto City Government in the late 19th century has been successful.

In the late 16th century, Toyotomi Hideyoshi revived an ancient plan to connect Lake Biwa with the Sea of Japan and ordered the owner of Tsuruga lands, Ōtani Yoshitsugu, to build a canal from Oura on Lake Biwa to Tsuruga located on the Sea of Japan. These works were aborted because of the difficult mountainous terrain. Between 1605 and 1611, Suminokura Ryōi formed an enterprise with the other two leading merchant families, Chaya Shirōjirō and Gotō Shōzaburō to construct canals and to make the four rivers of Kyōto (Tenryu, Takase, Fuji and Hozu Rivers) more navigable for shipping goods. In 1868, when the national capital was transferred from Kyōto to Tōkyō, there was an inevitable economic decline experienced in the city. The Prefecture Mayor, Kunimichi Kitagaki, commissioned the construction of Lake Biwa Canal. The historical significance of this integrated development project is that it was the first project in the Meiji era that did not involve foreign engineers.

Roads

Road administration also has a long and complex history that has the role of government as the prime agent, although the role of individuals is more difficult to determine with any certainty. Roads served Imperial purposes, such as ceremonial links to ancient Kōfun burial mounds, links to ports for diplomatic missions with overseas nations and, importantly, the means of strategic control over the territorial expansion of the Yamato State, that included setting up road barriers (*sekisho*) guarding the entrances to the Kinai region.

The *sekisho* is one of Japanese oldest institutions, lasting until 1868. They were duplicated on national roads, *shōen* estates and, during the medieval period, on warlord domains—all providing security and a means to raise revenue with a passage toll. The purpose of the *sekisho* reached full fruition under the Tokugawa *Shōgunate* as a government control mechanism when five national main highways (and secondary roads) were designated radiating from Nihonbashi, Edō. The issue of travel permits (passports) was designed to control the movement of people by the government, especially any female members of the *daimyō's* family trying to escape from Edō.

The Tokugawa government edict of an alternative resident system was not only a control mechanism of the regional warlords but a way of draining their incomes because the entourages travelling to and from Edō would have to have stopped both regularly and overnight at post stations, spending money that provided taxes to the *bakufu*. As restrictions were eased in the middle to late Edō era, commers, often on pilgrimages, would too have spent money in post stations.

As with ports, the Meiji Restoration ushered in new forms of government administration and roads. The Home Ministry (*Naimushō*) was established in November 1873 (abolished in December 1947 by the Allied Occupation Forces) and roads were included within this portfolio. The first general regulation for roads is found in the 1876 *Law on Road Classification*. The *Highway Law* of 1919 established regulations for the road and classification scheme on respective widths, gradients, curvatures and bridge construction. As part of Japan's post-Pacific War reconstruction, a memorandum from the Supreme Commander for the Allied Powers (SCAP) in 1948 introduced a five-year road plan to replace the German Autobahn-style highway planning in vogue in Japan during the early 1940s.

Road administration during the modern democratic era can be summarised as follows under government direction. In 1952, the law concerning *Special Measures for Highway Construction* (SMHC Law) provided loans from a Trust Fund in the Ministry of Finance to construct roads and approval for tolls to repay the loan. The Watkins Report triggered a flurry of additional highway legislation providing for national expressways, national toll roads, revised funding arrangements (government bonds, grants to prefectures) and metropolitan expressways. For example, the Japan Highway Public Corporation was established in April 1956—a non-profit government corporate entity established for the purpose of construction and management of expressways and ordinary toll roads.

In recognition that road networks were largely mature, road administration was placed within a new "super" ministry—The Ministry of Land, Infrastructure, Transport and Tourism (MLIT) in 2001. Prime Minister Koizumi Junichirō established the Committee for Promoting Privatisation of Four Highway-related Public Corporations and in June 2004, The Privatization Bill was passed in the *Diet* in June 2004. Six joint-stock highway corporations (one-third government owned) were created and an independent administrative agency, the Japan Expressway Holding and Debt Repayment Agency (JEHDRA) was established to function as an asset-holding and debt-servicing public organisation (the agency will be dissolved once the loan repayment is completed by 2050).

There is plenty of evidence that overseas influences were important to the development of the Japanese road sector. Road design, such as widths, the planting of shade trees by the side of the road and the location of post stations, were influenced by Chinese practice. German Autobahn-inspired planning was popular with governments of the 1930s and 1940s. In the modern democratic era, highway design was derived from the U.S. *Highway Capacity Manual*. Road improvement programs had a strong American influence due to the involvement of economic specialists led by Dr Ralph Watkins whose report triggered a flurry of additional highway legislation.

Railways

The governance of railways has a much shorter history, only from the late 19th century when both public and private sectors were involved. In October 1872, the first line opened between Tōkyō and Yokohama under the management of the Ministry of Public Works. Other government routes were completed in the 1870s until a cash-strapped government allowed the private sector to build and operate railways. Soon, the Japanese Government realised the strategic importance of railways and enacted the *Railway Nationalization Act* (1906) purchasing leading private railway companies. Japan Government Railways became a virtual monopoly of railway business until the Allied Occupation Forces instructed the Japanese Government to reorganise government railways into a public corporation that lasted until 1987 when Japan National Railways was divided into regional operations and privatised. Private railways continued to operate low traffic and largely rural services. Private companies also managed urban subways and light rail.

The greatest government railway achievement, show-cased to the world at the 1964 Tōkyō Summer Olympics, was the successful completion of the "bullet train". It opened the way for the Shinkansen program that was an exemplary international example of a national government development program as part of a national socio-economic system. Japan National Railways initiated research on a linear propulsion railway system in 1962. When Japan National Railways was privatised in 1987, the development of the maglev system was taken over by the Central Japan Railway Company. The Maglev Chūō Shinkansen between Tōkyō and Ōsaka is expected to open in 2045.

In terms of Japanese personalities who influenced railway technology, three names stand out—two from the private sector; the other from the public sector. Kobayashi Inchizō is recognised in Japan as a pioneer of private railway companies and their diversified business model, which includes land-use development along the route of a railway. Otsuka Koreaki, the manager of the Sanuki Railway and the Nankai Railway, followed U.S. management practices and installed a tearoom in the first-class carriage, employed young women as waitresses and transferred much of the authority to the train supervisor. The "Tōkaidō Shinkansen", when it opened for passenger services in 1964 owed much to the vision of the President of the JNR, Sogō Shinji, at a time that railways, worldwide, were in decline. It is a fair assessment to say he helped initiate a global "railway renaissance".

Overseas' pressure, first from the Russians, to introduce railway technology culminated with the British Minister to Japan, Harry Parkes, successfully lobbying that railways using British technology and expertise be introduced to Japan. In April 1870, the Japanese Government hired the British engineer, Edmund Morel, as its first Engineer-in-Chief, who advised on the establishment of the Ministry of Public Works, on engineering education and administration and on the formation of an engineering college (later, the Tōkyō Imperial Technical University). The private railway companies in cities, including Ōsaka and Tōkyō, were especially innovative, including importing U.S. railway technology and developing land and associated land-use activities, such as department stores.

Aviation and Airports

Both the government and the private sectors were initially involved with aircraft design and manufacture and in providing civilian flights at a time when airfields were rudimentary when compared to those of the 21st century. Japanese aeronautical engineering advanced quickly and introduced distinctive innovations, such as the Nakajima aircraft. The Japanese Government stepped in as an airline operator when it established the Japan Air Transport Corporation (JAT) in 1928 as the national flag carrier. JAT absorbed private companies. Military aviation expanded during the 1930s at the expense of civil aviation until 1945 when airfields were taken over by Allied occupying forces. When civilian air transport resumed in 1953, Japan Air Lines (JAL) was established as a major private company servicing domestic and international markets.

In the case of airport development, the Japanese government was cash strapped in the post-war period. The paving of the taxiway and apron at Haneda came from the national budget. However, to restore the airport as an international gateway, the Japanese Cabinet decided to build a terminal with private capital, and, in 1953, The Japan Airport Terminal Co., Ltd. was established through the cooperation of major Japanese businesses. Airports are regulated by the *Aeronautical Law (1952)* with regard to safety, the *Noise Prevention Law (1967)* with regard to environmental noise, and the *Airport Development Law (1956)* with regard to airport developments. Recently, major airports (for example, Kansai) have been funded by private-sector consortia using the private financing initiative (PFI).

The individuals who have shaped the pioneering Japanese aviation sector both came from the military sector. In the first decade of the 20th century, two members of the Imperial Navy argued against the then prevailing doctrine of land-based warfare. They were Lieutenant Commander Akiyama Saneyuki, who lectured at the Naval Staff College in Tōkyō on the advances in aviation technology, and Lieutenant Commander Yamamoto Eisuke, who presented a written statement on aviation to his superiors. Both the military and the civilian government recognised the potential of aviation.

The successive reshaping of Japan's aviation has happened under French, British, German and American influence with technological transfer a key element. In the modern democratic period, aviation is strongly regulated by international and bilateral agreements and technical innovation through the International Civil Aviation Organisation (ICAO). In addition, foreign trends in aviation policy are influential. New airline entrants have been allowed, there have been bankruptcies and mergers, the industry has been de-regulated (for example, the *Civil Aeronautics Law* was revised at the end of 1994 to relax the conditions for introducing and setting discount fares in domestic markets) with, today, eight major carriers in the international passenger, domestic passenger and freight markets.

Integrated Land Use and Transport

From an institutional perspective, spatial planning, and divisions covering all modes of transport, are found within the Ministry of Infrastructure, Land, Transport and Tourism (MLIT). Important characteristics of the Japan planning framework that has allowed integrated developments include a government-directed land readjustment program, government new town initiatives building on the private-sector model of suburban railway developments and transit-oriented developments that have created some stunning architectural spaces, such as Kyōto Station and the world's largest railway (and maglev) station in Nagoya. Whilst the Western literature suggests transit-oriented development is an American planning concept, Chapter 8 has convincingly demonstrated that, for decades, it has been part and parcel of the Japanese private railway business model, as demonstrated by the career described in the autobiography written by Kobayashi Inchizō (Kobayashi, 1989).

Further Research

The methodology and approach described in this book have application to any jurisdiction and any time period, as defined by the researcher. In the case of Japan, there are obvious avenues for further original research to that underpinning this book, especially by researchers, versed in the Japanese written and spoken language, who can access primary historical data and conduct interviews with key informants about contemporary transport modes. Research designs could embrace any, or all, time horizons, any, or all, transport modes, could be locally based, sub-regional or regional, and could be urban or rural in their focus. Higher education thesis work across the country, collectively, could add up to a rich understanding of how transport institutions and organisations have changed over time. Equally, similar approaches to research framing could be applied to any jurisdiction in the world.

Japan Society 5.0—Visions

The fourth question posed in the introduction to this book was: what might the future in Japan look like in terms of institutions, society and transport? Who will be the visionary leaders in transport and organisational change in the Japanese society of the future? The current leaders of Japan envisage a fundamentally different society and have given it a name. "Society 5.0" (Government of Japan, Cabinet Office, n.d.) is premised on the broad transitions that have historically occurred in Japanese society—from the initial society of the hunter gatherers of the Jōmon period (c. 10,000 B.C. to c. 300 B.C.) to Society 2.0 with the paddy rice cultivation during the Yayoi period (c. 300 B.C. to c. 300 A.D.), then Society 3.0 from ancient to medieval times and the early industrialised state to Society 4.0 (the information society) that approximates to contemporary Japan in the third decade of the 21st century.

In November 1995, Japan enacted the Science and Technology Basic Law. The Science and Technology Basic Plan aims to comprehensively and systematically advance science and technology policy. The 5th

Science and Technology Basic Plan was endorsed by a Cabinet Decision on 22 January 2016, covering the 5-year period between the fiscal years 2016–2021. The plan introduced Society 5.0 as the sort of society that Japan should aspire towards. The essential characteristics of Society 5.0 are identified as follows:

> [...] information from sensors in physical space is accumulated in cyberspace. In cyberspace, this big data is analyzed by artificial intelligence (AI), and the analysis results are fed back to humans in physical space in various forms" (Government of Japan, Cabinet Office, n.d.: a).

Information technologies in every industrial sector, and in social activities, will address stagnant economic growth and solutions to emerging social and environmental problems including meeting the United Nations' Sustainable Development Goals (SDGs).

The Japanese Government mentions "smart cities" as a desirable policy goal. Funding for experimental demonstration projects have been completed in various cities, to the extent that the government believes Japan is on the verge of a major transition from the present "Society 4.0" to a future "Society 5.0" that has only been sketchily outlined and, so far, subject to limited academic scrutiny and relevant peer-reviewed publications. Holroyd (2020) explores the conceptual background, rationale, policies and programmes Japan has enacted in pursuit of the visions of Society 5.0. Gladden (2019) investigates the presumed human-centeredness of Society 5.0 by comparing its makeup with that of earlier societies. The frameworks and analyses developed in a research monograph by the University of Tokyo and Hitachi (Hitachi-UTokyo Laboratory, 2020) look at the strengths and weaknesses of the Society 5.0 paradigm and potential benefits and dangers of its implementation.

An initial step towards achieving Society 5.0 was made when, in August 2019, the Japanese Government established the Smart City Public-Private Partnership Platform to promote collaboration to achieve Society 5.0 with more than 100 cities and more than 300 companies and research institutions signed up. As part of the broader Society 5.0 vision, Japan has 229 smart city projects in 157 areas. The platform supports projects with knowledge exchange, business-matching and closer ties between public, private and academia.

The transformation to Society 5.0 is predicated on achieving "smart cities" of the future of which the transport sector is prominent. The

Japanese Government's policy goals are, for an "inclusive" society, to reduce road and public transport congestion; to lower CO_2 emissions; to reduce road traffic accidents; and to stimulate mobility consumption (especially the purchase of autonomous vehicles and "smart", self-driving wheelchairs for the elderly). New "added value" to mobility is generated through the artificial intelligence (AI) analyses of big data in a database spanning diverse types of information that might include sensor data from motor vehicles, real-time information on the weather, road traffic conditions, accommodation, food and drink and an individual's personal history (Government of Japan, Cabinet Office, n.d.: b).

More specific transport challenges being faced in Society 5.0 are contained in the 2020 White Paper issued by the Ministry of Land, Infrastructure, Transport and Tourism (Policy Bureau, Ministry of Land, Infrastructure, Transport and Tourism, 2020). The report outlines a range of challenges facing Japan including climate change, keeping safe from disasters, achieving a sustainable infrastructure maintenance cycle, securing regional transport and making use of new technologies. In order to provide a rationale for speculation on what this means for institutional and organisation change, the next section provides an historical perspective by contrasting Society 4.0 with its predecessor, followed by some ideas on role of the national government in Society 5.0, before analysing institutional and organisational change using four contemporary problems as examples.

Speculations on Society 5.0

First, it is worth reflecting on the key similarities and differences in Japan Society 3.0 and Japan 4.0. with respect to road transport and personal mobility (Table 29). Governments of both societies formulated clear policies for roads, and both societies had mechanisms for maintaining roads. Of course, the vehicle technologies and the power to move those vehicles are dramatically different. Travel is a derived demand from the socio-economic activities in which people are engaged, so it is in these aspects of society that the most profound changes have occurred.

In an agrarian society the majority of the population were farmers and were tied to the land. In addition, both *bakufu* and *han* (provincial) governments restricted the movement of ordinary people unless there were successful applications to obtain a travel permit. Spatial restrictions were in place with little change in inter-generational occupations. Society was very static. The qualitative transitions to Society 4.0 included: a reduction in transaction and travel costs; removal of the Confucian class system; an expansion in occupations; unbounded personal mobility; inter- and intra-regional migration; choice of residential and workplace locations; and expectations, and optimism, that, over time, prosperity and well-being would continue to increase.

Table 29. Characteristics of Societies 3.0 and 4.0—Road Transport and Mobility.
Source: Author.

Characteristic of Society	Society 3.0	Society 4.0
Road Governance	Policies formulated by *bakuhan* system	Policies formulated by national government
Road Funding	Impost by *bakufu* on *daimyō* (*han*) government plus local corvée	National and prefecture governments budget allocations with money raised from taxation
Personal Mobility	Highly regulated market	Intra- and inter-regional migration; unrestricted travel in domestic and international markets
Daily routines	Fixed, and tied to agricultural seasons; barter and markets	Flexible; commuting; shopping malls; on-line shopping
Transport Technology	Horses, carts, *norimono*, *kago*, walking	Motor vehicles, taxis, buses, coaches, trucks, *jinrikisha*, bicycles, walking
Mass Communications	Written edicts nailed on posts; gossip	Newspapers*, radio, cinema, television, internet
Transport Energy Sources	Animals and humans	Petroleum, diesel, batteries, hydrogen fuel-cells
Working Conditions	Every day except festivals	Regulated working hours, paid vacations, public holidays

*The first Japanese daily newspaper that covered foreign and domestic news was the *Yokohama Mainichi Shinbun* (横浜毎日新聞), first published in 1871.

The chapters of this book have demonstrated that transitions are processes that have required continuous adaptations, where the institutions of governments had significant agency. The governance challenges will be negotiations with the changing networks of actors, relationships involving power and resources, understanding new patterns of consumption and determining how shifts in future mobility are regulated, priced and taxed. The primary role of the national government is how this transition will be efficiently and equitably managed, although Docherty (*et al.*, 2017:123) suggest that it is "difficult to be optimistic", based on the failure of all national governments in managing the global problem of car dependency that started in the second half of the 20th century.

It can be speculated that the role of the central government will decline in relative terms. In Japan, the national government is driving Society 5.0 forward, although, in its promise to devolve decision making, the unspecified details of its implementation are left to local government, businesses and the community to work out. Indeed, a key overarching message from the national government is a commitment to work more effectively with all relevant stakeholders than has been the case. Morimoto (2021, Chapter 10) points out one of the most difficult issues in city planning and transport is consensus building with stakeholders and this in itself requires reform in how governments go about their business.

One probable reform that will distinguish Society 5.0 from earlier models used Japanese by governments will be the introduction of "agile governance". Agile governance requires a diverse range of stakeholders, including governments, businesses, individuals, and communities who will carry out ongoing analysis of the social situations they find themselves in, define the goals they seek to achieve, design the various systems for achieving these goals and carry out ongoing dialogue-based assessments of outcomes to make improvements to these systems (Japan, Ministry of Economy, Trade and Industry, 2021: v). Governance-related issues for realising Society 5.0 are wide ranging, from privacy, system security and transparency to the allocation of responsibilities and cyber security. The underlying proposition is that Society 5.0 will be socially fluid in terms of its (yet to be determined goals) requiring governments to be more flexible and adaptable to changing circumstances than is currently the case: solutions are constantly revised to ensure their optimality based on conditions and goals that constantly change.

The implications of this agile governance for future transport policy making is clear. For example, the past goals set for urban transport planning have been primarily solving congestion from growing demand based on economic and environmental considerations (a classic systems approach). In the area of transport and mobility such challenges in Japan include debt-burdened governments' abilities to finance new infrastructure and maintenance, automation and consumer behaviour in the opportunities opening up in an accelerating digital economy. In the future, goals will be designed to continuously and rapidly run cycles of "goal-setting", "conditions and risk analysis", "system design", "operations", "evaluation" (with a full range of economic, environmental and social inputs), and "solutions" (Figure 9) in a closer partnership of the civic and civil spheres of society. Communications will be best described as "two-way symmetrical communication" as opposed to one-way asymmetrical communication (see Black, 1997).

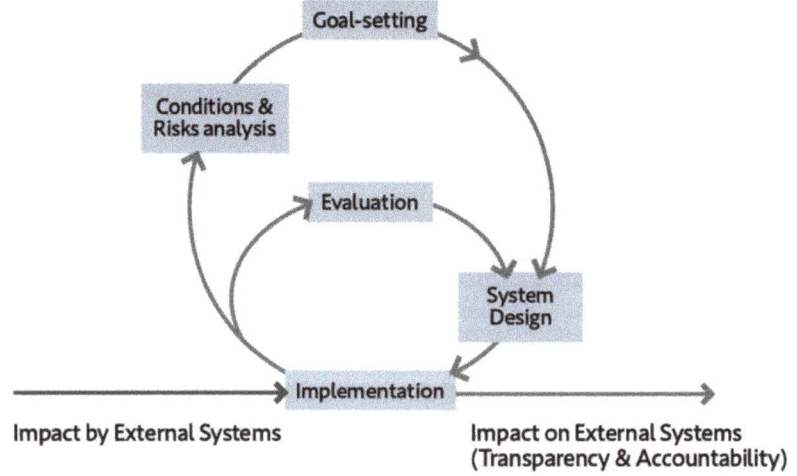

Figure 9. Japanese Concept of Agile Governance.
Source: reproduced from Japan, Ministry of Economy, Trade and Industry, 2021: Fig. 1.2, p. 8.

The rapidity of actions needed to constantly monitor the need to implement the cycles in Figure 9 imply that a greater spatial devolution of decision making is required. Society 5.0 should facilitate "innovation by citizens and for citizens" (Deguchi and Karasawa, 2020: 165) and this suggests that more leadership at the local government level is required. However, more work needs to be done also to engage citizens and users and to prepare a climate that continuously facilitates bottom-up, grassroots initiatives. Local governments must work out how they will gather local data on the physical space such as roads, buildings, people movements and vehicular traffic, and how they will develop platforms that integrate effective Big Data into cyberspace infrastructure.

The aspiration of agile governance is that cyberspace will facilitate citizen-led, community-based planning by allowing citizens to be involved in the gathering and collating of Big Data (e.g., mobile spatial data or real-time people-flow data replacing the periodic person trip surveys conducted by consultants to government) and of the sharing and evaluating future visions (Deguchi *et al.*, 2020b: 94) for local places. This would involve regulatory easing where government data are made available as open data. According to Deguchi and Karasawa (2020: 161), planners must achieve a perspective of harmony between individual and group interests when designing the environment and institutions, as the "principle of honouring human dignity requires no less." All of this seems to be predicated on a substantial shift in values from the current position of a predominantly paternalist government, foe example, in road planning—described by Healy (1977: 205) as "a positivist procedure which has been criticized as technical and elitist"— to genuine co-production in transport planning and implementation and solving mobility problems.

To provide more detail about agile governance in Japan, four specific challenges are selected for analysis from the documentation on Society 5.0: the international competitiveness of the Japanese automotive industry, value added smart applications to mobility and government-industry responses to maintaining the mobility of older citizens with autonomous driving vehicles; an ageing population and the problem of the decline in rural towns and villages; the ever-present threat of natural disasters and building for resilience; and aviation safety and security. Whilst Japan has many more problems where institutional and organisational reforms are required, all four of these challenges are closely related to the movement of people and freight.

Personal Mobility and Autonomous Driverless Vehicles

Organisations will become more dominant in Society 5.0 than has been the case. For example, there is a strong belief in the Japanese vehicle manufacturing sector that technology can help solve personal mobility problems, without over-burdening the energy sector, adding to environmental pollution and solving road safety problems, as has been outlined with the example of Toyota's Woven City Project (Chapter 8). The transition to "green energy" will be complete by mid-century, under government-formulated targets, but implemented by private-sector energy providers.

Digital players, supported by mega-fund investors, are revamping Japan's long-stagnant taxi industry (Agarwal *et al.*, 2018). Japanese car manufacturers are producing hydrogen fuel technology cars (Pollet *et al.*, 2019, Table 1, p. 91), where the role of government might be to give incentives to potential buyers (as in California) to expand the market penetration of this technology. Already local governments are promoting a hydrogen economy with, for example, the City of Tōkyō deploying hydrogen fuel cell buses during the 2021 Summer Olympic Games and setting a longer-term goal of putting 200,000 such buses into service by 2025 (Phillips, 2019).

The third and fourth decades of the 21st century will reveal closer collaboration and cooperation amongst all sections of civil and civic society in Japan. Twenty years ago, Cabinet established the Strategic Headquarters for the Promotion of Advanced Information and Telecommunications, with its roadmap of autonomous vehicle development. The roadmap has been updated annually since 2014, and the Promotion of Advanced Information and Telecommunications (2019: 103–111) illustrates the 2019 version. Distinctive features of the roadmap are the respective scenarios for three types applications: passenger vehicles; logistics services; and public transport services. Developments in information technology and software engineering by the private sector will deliver enhance tools to make supply chains more efficient and reliable.

Examples of leveraging "big data" for supply chain resilience are Toyota's "RESCUE," developed with Fujitsu, and a visualisation system called the Local Economic Driver Index (LEDIX)—a private sector collaboration between the Teikoku Data Bank and Takram (World

Bank, 2020, Fig. 2.4, p. 22). These systems will be applied to map out logistical supply chains in order to understand rapidly the impacts of supply chain disruptions and opportunities for economic development, including post-disaster recovery (World Bank, 2020: 84).

This technological revolution in the transport sector has demanded increased inter-ministerial cooperation. In 2015, Prime Minister Abe Shinzō announced the 2015 revision of the Japan Revitalization Strategy that included, as a strategic item, autonomous driving vehicles, and in doing so established the Panel on Business Strategies in Automated Driving in the Ministry of Economy, Trade and Industry (METI), and in MLIT. The panel was tasked to resolve current problems, and to formulate actions that would secure Japan's competitiveness in the field of autonomous driving systems and would solve various societal problems, such as road congestion, road safety and personal mobility for the elderly (Ki, 2020: 31). The major governmental players in the Japanese autonomous vehicle policy making are the Ministry of Internal Affairs and Communications (MIC), METI, MLIT and National Police Agency. To support this panel, SIP was established as the Japanese government's cross-ministerial research and development program (Ki, 2020: Fig.3.1., p. 33).

Within this institution, the Promoting Committee for SIP Automated Driving Research Project was formed with input from government, industry and experts drawn from universities (Ki, 2020, Fig. 3.4, p. 34). The Project Director is from the Toyota Motor Corporation, with sub-project directors drawn from universities, consultancy and the automotive industry. Other members include the Cabinet Office, the National Police Agency, the Ministry of Internal Affairs and Communication (MIC), the Ministry of Economy, Trade and Industry (METI) and the Ministry of Land Infrastructure, Transport and Tourism (MLIT) together with industry and academic experts. Research and development is outsourced to industry and academic research groups.

Whilst research and development are imperative to transform the transport sector, the major obstacles to the introduction of fully driverless vehicles (Level 5) are legal and regulatory, not technology. Less than six months after the National Police Agency's proposal, the Japanese *Diet* enacted amendments to the Road Traffic Act allowing Level 3 automated vehicles to be used on public roads from May 2020. Level 3 automated vehicles are capable of driving without the need for the driver to monitor the dynamic driving task, or the road and the roadside driving environment, but the law does require the driver be in a position to resume control, if needed. The issue of transfer of control between vehicle and driver has proved controversial, and the Japanese automotive industry is split as to whether this can be done safely. In March 2021, Honda launched the world's most advanced self-driving car using "level 3" autonomous driving technology, with an initial batch of 100 Legend models in Japan (Sugiura, 2021).

Recommendations from a report by a National Police Agency (NPA) on 1 April 2021 on "level 4" self-driving vehicles is that they should be held responsible for following the traffic rules and be operable without the need for a human with a driving license. However, the report did not clarify the primary responsible party for accidents or law violations. Trials with a view to the practical use of "level 4" technology are already underway. The Japanese government aims to start these public transport services (especially targeting the elderly) in some areas in 2022 and hopes to make them commonplace nationwide by 2025. The NPA will conduct studies at the same time with the objective of revisioning the Road Traffic Act (Machida, 2021).

The future challenge is to take experience from the numerous demonstrations and trials undertaken across Japan and convert them into operational systems of automated vehicles, freight vehicles and public transport—with all systems regulated by the national government. All trials have involved multiple actors and the future land transport in Japan will involve more service delivery actors than at present.

To illustrate this complexity, in March 2021, a demonstration experiment of a self-driving bus (with two attendants and space for six passengers) was conducted by the Council for Area Development and Management of Otemachi, Marunouchi and Yurakucho, in Tōkyō. The trial comprised of companies, and others in the neighborhood, and the Japanese telecom giant SoftBank's subsidiary Boldly Inc. (formerly SB Drive), which develops autonomous driving technology (Michinaga, 2021). The bus made five to eight round trips a day on an about 350-metre straight section between the Marunouchi Building and the Marunouchi Park Building at a speed of about 6 km/h. The bus runs on the right side of the street (Japanese drive on the left), and automatically stops when people walk or cross the street in front of it.

Finally, a new industry that adds value to personal mobility in the form of digital applications will emerge and one that will require government regulation over communication security and personal privacy. Given the increasing computational power and miniaturisation of personal devises, such as smart watches, it is easy to imagine a world where access to a "device" through face and voice recognition allows instantaneous access and retrieval of information about any dimension of proposed travel. Required information might be, but is not limited to, about: the journey/destination (mode, time, make bookings for a driverless vehicle, or map out the route for a personal, autonomous vehicle level 5); and, more importantly, through artificial intelligence (AI) get a personalised itinerary for things to do with detailed descriptions at the destination, such as tourist sites, hot springs, shopping, cafes, restaurants, etc, given the Japanese love of taking photographs and videos that are automatically stored on the "cloud", the whole experience of that trip retrieved afterwards and communicated to family and friends if desired.

Ageing Population and Rural Shrinkage

Japan, along with many other countries, is facing a population decline (National Institute of Population and Social Security, 2018; cited in Central Japan Railway Company, 2020: 16) together with an ageing demographic structure that have several implications for transport. These include: a decline in the total amount of daily travel (unless offset by a change in immigration policy or substantial boosts to tourism); marginally less peak-period commuter traffic with working from home; a reduced income taxation base to fund transport infrastructure and maintenance; and a higher proportion of elderly people who have grown up with access to personal transport and a desire to maintain that independence. The value-added mobility system outlined above will assist greatly the future mobility of the elderly. Responses to these challenges are being initiated by local government and the private sector.

A shrinking population, coupled with the outmigration of the young to larger cities, has resulted in a deteriorating economic situation for small towns in Japan. Public projects implemented top-down under the Comprehensive National Development Plans have undermined the rural municipalities' capacity to independently promote context-tailored development (Chang, 2018). The absence of innovation in counter-shrinkage policies stems from several structural factors that need to be addressed: the highly centralised policy-making process; sectionalism in the central bureaucracy; financial independency of rural municipalities; and the nostalgic pro-regrowth mind-set by many conservative politicians.

Champions need to emerge from organisations that can address the problems of rural Japan. Drawing on a case study methodology from four shrinking communities in Minami and Uchikō, Shikōkū Island, Chang (2018) investigated examples of community re-vitalisation. Apathy in the local institutions for change and low resident engagement were identified to be the two main barriers to starting initiatives. Both of them stem from the sense of resignation and powerlessness nurtured in the local people by decades-long decline and policy neglect. Successful local programs were instigated by intermediate organisers who acted as catalysts creating a future vision of the place, building trust-based networks of motivated residents, organising collaborative activities and bringing in external funding and knowledge that created connections with various key actors outside of the communities.

The challenge for governments is to devise policies on the processes of building local capacity that prepare the foundation to implement locally-based approaches to arresting rural decline in Japan. Inspiration for such policy development could come from the Cittaslow (Slow City) approach that is a sustainable development model addressing rural shrinkage and promoting the quality of life in rural communities (Cittaslow, n.d.). Legally established in March 2001 in Greve, Italy, by the General Secretary, Marzio Marini, "Cittaslow—Rete Internazionale delle città del buon vivere", has now grown into a global network of over 272 participating towns (as of February 2021).

Natural Disasters and Resilience

The central government will continue its role in legislation and emergency funding around natural disasters. The resilience of industrial sectors, firms and supply chains is prioritised under national policies (Ebisudani and Tokai, 2017: 81–82), including: the *Basic Act for National Resilience Contributing to Preventing and Mitigating Disasters for Developing Resilience in the Lives of the Citizenry* (2013); the *Fundamental Plan for*

National Resilience (2014, updated in 2018); and the annual *Action Plan for National Resilience* (since 2014). At the subnational level, key industrial areas, such as Aichi Prefecture and Kawasaki City, have integrated resilient industry as one of the key pillars of their Fundamental Plans for Regional Resilience.

It can be said with certainty that Japan will face major natural catastrophes. Japan is highly vulnerable to natural hazards, such as tsunamis and storm surges (The World Bank, 2020, Table 2.3, p. 35). These predicted seismic events are expected to cause significant economic, asset and financial damages, requiring up to 20 years for recovery and reconstruction. Additionally, future massive storm surges and large-scale river floods are expected to cause major impacts to the large metropolises of Ōsaka, Tōkyō and Nagoya—all key manufacturing hubs (World Bank, 2020: 34).

In the past, the public sector has played the leading role in ensuring infrastructure's resilience. These institutional arrangements have now evolved to public-private agreements that have enabled substantial reductions in the length of time that services have been disrupted. For example, highways were reopened six days after the 2011 earthquake and tsunami in Northeast Japan, because of the prearranged contracts between the Ministry of Land, Infrastructure, Transport, and Tourism and local construction companies (Ranghieri and Ishiwatari, 2014). There is going to be a greater role in the future for private-sector enterprises in disaster resilience—all predicted on the development of smart applications and documentation.

Manufacturing industries are often clustered together in industrial estates, making them key sites for collaborative interventions. Industry stakeholders could work together to strengthen zone-wide capacities for disaster risk preparedness and response. Key resilience strategies include promoting mutually beneficial business continuity plans amongst member firms. Industry stakeholders can also help build strategic partnerships between member firms and governments, critical infrastructure providers and operators and financial institutions for disaster contingency planning. Industrial parks may be able to gain collective access to financing for any resilient infrastructure improvements and post-disaster support (World Bank, 2020: 5).

The future institutional arrangements in the aftermath of disasters is for national and local governments to establish greater cooperation with private firms to develop prearranged agreements for recovery work. Private firms and industry associations have an incentive to cooperate in the quick recovery of the critical infrastructure essential to business continuity, economic loss minimisation and industry competitiveness. By minimising the disruption time to infrastructure services, such as transport, industries remain connected to their supply chains.

Aviation Safety and Security

Governments have a responsibility to ensure aviation safety and security against terrorism. The Civil Aviation Bureau of the Ministry of Land, Infrastructure and Transport is the competent authority in aviation security, sets the standards for security measures to be implemented by air carriers, airport operators and other organisations concerned and therefore will continue to be a major transport agent in the future. Safety measures are being actively introduced in Japan on the basis of new technology and in accordance with international standards, through the activities such as: aircraft inspections; competence certification for airmen; and supervision of the operation and maintenance systems of the air carriers.

On the basis of the new CNS/ATM plans of the ICAO, the installation of next-generation aviation safety systems is being promoted in Japan (Civil Aviation Bureau, Ministry of Land, Infrastructure, Transport and Tourism, 2021). Multifunctional transport satellites (MTSAT) both for aeronautical missions, including air traffic control, and for meteorological missions, including weather observation, have been launched, and an important challenge for aviation will be the continuous update of this technology.

The Centre for Asia Pacific Aviation (CAPA Centre for Aviation, 2010) considered whether the leadership of Prime Minister, Kan Naoto (in office, 2010–2011) would bring with it any change in aviation policy and, importantly, the report looked at the forces of inertia in the bureaucracy that needed overcoming. The Government of Japan has continued to maintain tight control over its aviation market, creating barriers for both domestic firms and foreign competitors through tolerating political coordination, protectionist policies and limiting landing slots and airport access. "Current regulations are incongruous with facilitating increased exposure and competitiveness for the Japanese aviation market in the international arena" (Cronin, 2013: 1).

In fact, there are some within the Ministry of Land, Infrastructure, Transport and Tourism who "desire fair and transparent allocations" of landing slots (Cronin, 2013: 13). Whether these opaque and uncompetitive regulatory frameworks surrounding the Japanese aviation industry have been redressed remains uncertain, but what is certain is that post-Covid 19, as with all counties, Japan will have to resurrect its domestic and international airline industry. Challenges also arise in formulating airspace regulations of drones delivering parcels, and in managing the emerging industry of commuting by small autonomous driving aircraft.

Final Note

In *Blue Ocean Strategy*, Kim and Mauborgne (2005) describe how to create uncontested market space that will render the existing competition irrelevant, imaginatively telling the reader to picture a market universe composed of two sorts of oceans: red oceans and blue oceans. Red oceans represent all the industries in existence today (and, *inter alia*, all of the institutions and organisations dealing with transport). In contrast, blue oceans represent all of the industries *"not* in existence today" (Kim and Mauborgne, 2005: 4). This requires, for any jurisdiction in the world, imagining, and strategically mapping out, an entirely new infrastructure planning and transport sector for both institutions and organisations. This is clearly beyond the scope of this book, but the historical survey contained in it might give inspiration to those willing to take up the challenge. The framework of the new institutional economics, and the general questions posed about institutional and organisational change in the first chapter of this book, will provide the starting points for such an ambitious investigation.

For example, an in-depth institutional analysis of contemporary transport institutions and organisations (the agents) needs undertaking, and interviews with key players must be conducted to gain a deeper understanding of challenges and issues. This type of brief would normally be undertaken by domestic or international consultancy organisations. Creative solutions for institutional and organisational reform need to be designed. Stakeholder and community input to this process will be essential with transparency in the way options are framed. A business case must be presented to decision makers where options are given together with estimates of costs and the identification of benefits on quantitative and qualitative scales. When there truly is a need to change, and it is widely supported in Japan, in the words of Andressen (2002: 149–150), "the system can alter course relatively quickly and effectively".

References

Agarwal, S. D. Luczak, R. Mathis, Ichiro Otobe, and Yoshishige Shiota (2018) "Rebooting Japan's Mobility Market", *McKinsey & Company Automotive and Assembly*, 28 November, https://www.mckinsey.com/industries/automotive-and-assembly/our-insights/rebooting-japans-mobility-market#

Andressen, C. (2002) *A Short History of Japan: From Samurai to Sony*. Allen & Unwin, Crows Nest, New South Wales.

Black J.A. (1997) "Policy Processes and Noise and Air Quality Management Plans at Sydney Airport: The Value of Research into Organisational Communication Strategies", *21st ATRF, Adelaide, September 1997, Papers of the Australasian Transport Research Forum*, 21 (2), 663–676.

Brooks, M. (2004) "The Governance Structure of Ports", *Review of Network Economics*, 3 (2), 168–183.

Brooks, M. R., K. P. B. Cullinane and A. A. Pallis (2017) "Revisiting Port Governance and Port Reform: A Multi-Country Examination", *Research in Transportation Business & Management*, 22, 1–10.

CAPA Centre for Aviation (2010) "Japan Aviation Policy under a Kan-do Government: Bureaucracy the Stumbling Block to a New Future", CAPA Centre for Aviation, https://centreforaviation.com/analysis/reports/japan-aviation-policy-under-a-kan-do-government-bureaucracy-the-stumbling-block-to-a-new-future-29151

Central Japan Railway Company (2020) *Central Japan Railway Company: Annual Report 2020*. Central Japan Railway Company, Shinagawa, Tokyo.

Chang, Heuishilja (2018) "The Resilience of Shrinking Communities in Rural Japan", unpublished DPhil thesis, University of Oxford, Oxford, https://ora.ox.ac.uk/objects/uuid:c3bc0358-b025-4368-af95-a6e828bfd0b8

Cittaslow (n.d.) "Cittaslow International" Charter, http://www.bastamag.net/IMG/pdf/newcharter_1_-1.pdf

Civil Aviation Bureau, Ministry of Land, Infrastructure, Transport and Tourism (2021) "Bilateral Aviation Safety Agreement", https://www.mlit.go.jp/koku/15_hf_000018.html

Cronin, P. M. (2013) "Taking Off: Civil Aviation, Forward Progress and Japan's Third Arrow Reforms", *Center for New American Security, Working Paper, September*. Center for New American Security, Washington, D.C.

Deguchi, Atsushi and Kaori Karasawa (2020) "Issues and Outlook", in Hitachi-UTokyo Laboratory, *Society 5.0: A People-centric Super-smart Society*. Springer Nature Singapore Pte Ltd., Singapore, 155–173.

Deguchi, Atsushi, Chiaki Hirai, Hideyuki Matsuoka, Taku Nakano, Kohei Oshima, Mitsuharu Tai and Shigeyuki Tani (2020a) "What Is Society 5.0?", in Hitachi-UTokyo Laboratory, *Society 5.0: A People-centric Super-smart Society*. Springer Nature Singapore Pte Ltd., Singapore, 1–23.

Deguchi, Atsushi, Yasunori Akashi, Eiji Hato, Junichiro Ohkata, Taku Nakano and Shin'ichi Warisawa (2020b) "Solving Social Issues Through Industry—Academia Collaboration", in Hitachi-UTokyo Laboratory, *Society 5.0: A People-centric Super-smart Society*. Springer Nature Singapore Pte Ltd., Singapore, 85–115.

Docherty, I., G. Marsden and J. Anable (2017) "The Governance of Smart Mobility", *Transportation Research A: Policy and Practice*, 115, 114–125.

Ebisudani, Maiko and Akihiro Tokai (2017) "The Application of Composite Indicators to Disaster Resilience: A Case Study in Osaka Prefecture, Japan", *Journal of Sustainable Development*, 10 (1), 81–91.

Gladden, M. E. (2019) "Who Will Be the Members of Society 5.0? Towards an Anthropology of Technologically Posthumanized Future Societies", *Social Sciences*, 8 (148), https://doi.org/10.3390/socsci8050148

Government of Japan, Cabinet Office (n.d.) "Society 5.0", https://www8.cao.go.jp/cstp/english/society5_0/index.html

Healey, P. (1977) "The Sociology of Urban Transport Planning: A Socio-political Perspective", in D. A. Hensher (ed.) (1977) *Urban Transport Economics*. Cambridge University Press, Cambridge, 199–227.

Hitachi-UTokyo Laboratory (2020) *Society 5.0: A People-centric Super-smart Society*. Springer Nature Singapore Pte Ltd., Singapore.

Holroyd, C. (2020) "Technological Innovation and Building a 'Super Smart' Society: Japan's Vision of Society 5.0", *Journal of Asian Public Policy*, https://doi.org/10.1080/17516234.2020.1749340

Ishii, Ryosuke (1980) *A History of Political Institutions in Japan*. The Japan Foundation, Tokyo.

Japan, Ministry of Economy, Trade and Industry (2021) *Governance Innovation Ver. 2: A Guide to Designing and Implementing Agile Governance*. Ministry of Economy, Trade and Industry, Tokyo.

Ki, Jeehoon (2020) "A Comparative Analysis of Autonomous Vehicle Policies among Korea, Japan, and France", *FFJ Discussion Paper Series #20–02*, April, hal-02562482, Fondation France-Japon de l'EHESS (FFJ), Paris, https://hal.archives-ouvertes.fr/hal-02562482/document

Kim, W. C. and R. Mauborgne (2005) *Blue Ocean Strategy: How to Create Uncontested Market Space and Make Competition Irrelevant*. Harvard Business School, Boston, Mass.

Kobayashi, Koji (1989) *Rising to the Challenge: The Autobiography of Koji Kobayashi* (English Text). Harcout Brace Jovanivich Japan, Tokyo.

Machida, Noritake (2021) "'Level 4' Self-driving Transit Cars in Japan Won't Require Licensed Passengers: Expert Panel", *Mainichi Japan*, 2 April 2021.

Michinaga, Tatsuya (2021) "Autopilot Bus Test Underway on 350-Meter Section in Central Tokyo", *Mainichi Japan*, 10 March 2021.

Morimoto, Akinori (2021) *City and Transportation Planning: An Integrated Approach*. Routledge, London.

Nakanishi, Hitomi and J. Black (2018) "Implicit and Explicit Knowledge in Flood Evacuations with a Case Study of Takamatsu, Japan", *International Journal of Disaster Risk Reduction*, 28, June, 788–797.

National Institute of Population and Social Security Research (2018) "Regional Population Projections for Japan: 2015–2045 (2018)", http://www.ipss.go.jp/pp-shicyoson/e/shicyoson18/t-page.asp

Phillips, S. (2019) "Japan is Betting Big on the Future of Hydrogen Cars", NPR Daily Newsletter, https://www.npr.org/2019/03/18/700877189/japan-is-betting-big-on-the-future-of-hydrogen-cars

Policy Bureau, Ministry of Land, Infrastructure, Transport and Tourism (2020) "Summary of the White Paper on Land, Infrastructure, Transport and Tourism in Japan", 2020, https://www.mlit.go.jp/hakusyo/mlit/r01/hakusho/r02/pdf/English%20Summary.pdf

Pollet, B. G., S. S. Kocha and I. Staffe (2019) "Current Status of Automobile Fuel Cells for Sustainable Transport", *Current Opinion in Electrochemistry*, 16, 90–95.

Promotion of Advanced Information and Telecommunications (2019) "Public-Private ITS Initiative/Roadmaps 2019", Strategic Conference for the Advancement of Utilizing Public and Private Sector Data, Strategic Headquarters for the Advanced Information and Telecommunications Network Society, July 2019, https://japan.kantei.go.jp/policy/it/2019/2019_roadmaps.pdf

Ranghieri, F. and M. Ishiwatari (2014) *Learning from Megadisasters: Lessons from the Great East Japan Earthquake*. World Bank, Washington, D. C.

The Japan Times (2021) "Toyota Begins Building Smart City near Mount Fuji", *The Japan Times*, https://www.japantimes.co.jp/news/2021/02/23/business/corporate-business/toyota-smart-city-construction/

Sugiura, Eri (2021) "Back-seat Driver: How Honda Stole the Lead in Autonomous Cars—A Legal Revolution Paved the Way for an AI Breakthrough—But Rules are Still Vague", *Nikkei Asia*, 24 February 2021, https://asia.nikkei.com/Spotlight/The-Big-Story/Back-seat-driver-How-Honda-stole-the-lead-in-autonomous-cars

World Bank (2020) *Resilient Industries in Japan: Lessons Learned in Japan on Enhancing Competitive Industries in the Face of Disasters Caused by Natural Hazards*. World Bank, Washington, D. C.

List of Figures

Chapter 3

1	Screen Painting of Takamatsu Castle and its Port During the Edō Period.	83

Chapter 4

2	Major Buildings in Modern Tōkyō Superimposed on the Original Canal System of Ginza, c. 1900 (Scale: from Higashi Ginza Station in the south to Shin-Sukibashi in the north = approximately 1 km).	108
3	Photograph of the Lake Biwa Canal at Ōtsu on Lake Biwa, 2018.	111

Chapter 6

4	Extent of Japanese Railway Network by 1 January 1890.	159
5	Central Japan Railway Network of Shinkansen and Other Lines, June 2019.	168
6	Proposed Route for the Chuō Shinkansen between Shinagawa, Tōkyō, and Nagoya (Approximate Locations of the New Stations are Indicated) and the Current Yamanashi Test Track.	176

Chapter 8

7	Map of the Tōkyō Capital Region Policy Areas.	230
8	Mechanism of the Land Re-adjustment Program in Japan.	233

Chapter 9

9	Japanese Concept of Agile Governance.	270

List of Tables

Chapter 1

1	Time Periods—Analysis of Institutions and Organisations.	6

Chapter 2

2	Institutional Shifts in the Administration of Itami, Settsu Province, from the Mid-14th century to the Mid-19th century.	38
3	Dominant Japanese Institutions from Ancient Times to 2022.	56
4	Major Factors Explaining Institutional Change in Japan.	57
5	Selected Key Players in National Institutional Change in Japan from Archaic Times to the Present Day.	58

Chapter 3

6	Dominant Players Controlling International Trade, Japan, from 600–1868.	90
7	Early Ōsaka Ports in History—Institutional and Organisational Analysis.	91

Chapter 4

8	Canal Plans to Link the Sea of Japan with the Pacific Ocean via Lake Biwa, Mid 12th to the Mid-20th century.	116
9	Japanese Canal Construction During the Early Modern and Modern Periods—Key Agents.	117

Chapter 5

10	Strategic Importance of the Tokugawa Shōgunate Gokaidō System of Roads.	130
11	Summary of Road Policies and Regulations, 1601–1661.	133
12	Summary of Road Policies and Regulations, 1687–1720.	134
13	Summary of Road Policies and Regulations, 1800–1868.	136
14	Indicative Costs (in *mon**) of Transport From 1606 to 1868—The Oikawa Post Station.	140
15	Road Network Length in Kilometres by Classification and by Year, Japan 1925–1939.	144

Chapter 6

16	Urban Tramways in the Study Area in the Modern Period.	165
17	Hankyū Hanshin Holdings Breakdown of Revenue Streams, 2019.	170
18	Subway Lines and Network Length in the Study Area, 2020.	171
19	Summary of Major Events in Japanese Railway Development—Institutions and Organisations.	177

Chapter 7

20	Ownership of Japanese Domestic and International Airlines.	192
21	Classification of Japanese Airports, as of 1999.*	195
22	Policy Objectives Japanese 5-Year Airport Development Plans.	196
23	Major Developments of Terminals and Parking, Haneda and Narita Airports by Japanese Airport Terminals (JAT).	212
24	Kansai Airports and Group Companies and the Business Scope of Terminal Services.	214
25	Summary of Institutions and Organisations—Japanese Aviation and Airports.	216

Chapter 8

26	Land Readjustment and the Timeline for the Recent Redevelopment of Shibuya Station, 2007–2013.	234
27	Selected Tōkyō Railways Developed Post-2000 by Governments, Private Companies and Public-Private Partnerships.	237
28	Nagoya Station—Associated Buildings and Services, 2020.	238

Chapter 9

29	Characteristics of Societies 3.0 and 4.0—Road Transport and Mobility.	268

Index

ageing society 54, 178, 243–245, 247, 271. *See also* Society 5.0: ageing population
agricultural practices 18–19, 99, 102, 243
airfields 184, 186, 188, 198, 204–205, 209–210, 216–218, 263
  Haneda Airfield 186–187, 198–199
  Hanshin Airfield 209
  Kizugawa Airfield 183, 203–204
  Komaki Airfield 210
  Nagoya Airfield 210–211
  Ōsaka No. 1 Airfield 204
  Ōsaka No. 2 Airfield 203, 205
airline companies 10, 184, 186, 189, 192–193, 216. *See also* international air carriers
  Air Do 191–192
  All Nippon Airways (ANA) 175, 189–193, 216–217
  All Nippon Airways Wings 191
  Amakusa Airlines 191
  bilateral agreements 184, 188, 215, 264
  Fuji Dream Airlines 191, 193
  Greater Japan Airways (GJA) 187–188, 217
  Hokkaido Air System 191
  Ibex Airlines 191, 193
  Japan Airlines (JAL) 184, 187, 189–193, 216–217, 263
  Japan Air System (JAS) 189–191
  Japan Air Transport Corporation (JAT) 183–184, 186–187, 199, 212, 216–218, 263
  Japan Transocean Air 191
  New Central Airlines 191, 193
  New Japan Aviation 191
  Oriental Airbridge 191
  Ryukyu Air Commuter 191
  Solaseed Air 191, 193
air passengers 10
  early passenger flights 183–184, 186–187
  post-Second World War growth rates 10, 189
airport ground transport access 207, 214
  Chūbu 214
  Ōsaka 214
  Tōkyō 214
airports
  Chitose Airport 175
  Chūbu Centrair International Airport 195, 210–212, 214, 217
  Haneda Airport xv, 175, 186, 199–200, 212, 215, 218
  Ibaraki Airport 198
  Kansai International Airport 4, 10, 171, 194–197, 203, 206–210, 213–215, 217, 264
  Kōbe Airport 194–195, 198, 203, 208–209, 215, 217
  Nagoya Airport 210, 212, 217
  Narita International Airport 193, 196–198, 200–202, 206, 212–213, 215, 217

Ōsaka International (Itami) Airport 88, 93, 191, 195–196, 203–209, 214–215, 217, 258
Yao Airport 203, 209–210
airport terminals
  Haneda 199–200, 212–213, 215, 218
  Kansai 194, 207, 214
  Narita 186, 202, 213
alternate year attendance system 139
ancestral worship 47
Anglo-Japanese Treaty of Commerce and Navigation 50
Anti-Monopoly Law 52
aviation policy 189, 264, 278
  Act for the Operation of Government Controlled Airports by Private Sector Entities 197
  airline deregulation 190–191, 216
  airport classification 195, 218
  airport financing 10, 218
  airport privatisation 194–195, 198, 202, 214
  airport terminal financing 184, 189, 197, 199, 207, 212, 214, 217–218, 263–264
  airport terminals 184, 197, 199, 207, 212, 217–218, 263–264
  air traffic control 189, 206, 218, 278
  Civil Aeronautics Law 191, 264
  Council for Transport Policy Report 190
  low-cost carriers 192, 194, 202, 217
  military aircraft 10, 185
  private finance initiatives (PFI) 184, 196, 207, 213. *See also* private finance initiatives (PFI)
  regional airlines, ownership of 191–193

bakufu 25–29, 32, 34–47, 57, 59–60, 77–78, 81–82, 92, 101, 105, 108, 116, 121–122, 127–135, 138–140, 150–151, 258–260, 267–268
  Kamakura. *See* Kamakura *bakufu*
  Muromachi. *See* Muromachi *bakufu*

Tokugawa. *See* Tokugawa *bakuhan*
battles 23, 28, 31, 33–34, 58, 78, 80, 126
  Hakusukinoe 23
  Ichi no Tani 78
  Iwai Rebellion 72
  Mongol invasion 27
  Sekigahara 28, 33–34, 58
  Seta Bridge 126
bicycles 4, 145, 149–150, 236, 268
black ships 44, 93
bubble economy 54
bugyō 26, 35, 37, 80–81, 92, 133–134
buke 25, 31, 58, 90
bureaucratic style 55
bushi 25–27

canal evacuation 115
canals and integrated development
  electricity generation 117
  Keage Power Station 112
  water for irrigation 112, 115, 117. *See also* irrigation systems
canal transport 9, 82, 99, 101, 108–109, 111, 115, 117
  Asaka Canal 110, 115
  Great Lake Biwa Canal 113
  Kanda Canal 107
  Kyōto 100, 105, 109–110, 112, 115, 117
  Lake Biwa 9, 13, 19, 71, 100, 102–103, 108–118, 122, 157–158, 164, 259. *See also* Lake Biwa survey
  Lake Biwa Canal 100, 109–113, 115, 117–118, 164, 259
  Ōsaka 100, 103, 106, 109, 112–113, 116–117
  Shiotsu towards Tsuruga 103, 116
  Takase River Canal 105, 117
  Tatsumi Canal 105
  Tōkyō 107–108
capital cities 15, 21, 23–24, 41
  Heijo-kyō 21, 76, 79, 124, 248
  Nara 76–78, 90, 123–124, 248
  Takatsu no Miya 21
choki 99, 107
Chōshū Five 45

civic society 11, 55, 272
civil society 2, 115, 173, 231, 256
coastal shipping routes 81, 258
coinage 42, 140
Committee for Naval Aeronautic Research 183, 185, 216
container shipping 8, 86, 257
Customs Department 85
Customs Law 84
Customs Tariff Law 84

daimyō 9, 16, 28–29, 32, 34–45, 47, 60–61, 75, 78, 80, 90–91, 93, 103–107, 109, 121, 127–128, 130, 132–133, 139, 150, 156, 158, 257, 259–260, 268
Daoism 18, 20, 57
diplomatic missions 72, 76, 260
disaster prevention programs 114, 267, 271, 276–277
  environmental conservation 7, 104, 114–115, 149, 151, 229, 235, 243–244, 266, 270
  flood control 9, 75, 81, 84, 99, 103, 114–115, 259
  levees and sluice gates 79, 114, 258
Dōjima Rice Exchange 41–42, 59–60, 82
dugout canoes 71, 99, 102

economic development
  role of governments in 7
Edō Castle 36, 106, 130, 259
Edō period 28, 33, 39–40, 42, 47, 50, 59, 70, 75, 80–81, 90–93, 102, 104–109, 117–118, 121, 129, 131–132, 136, 138–139, 141–142, 150, 156, 223, 243, 258, 260
Edō port administration 117
Emishi (Ainu) 17, 23, 57, 123, 126
evolutionary paths 11, 57
expressway construction 145–147, 151, 248, 261

Far Eastern Commission 51
female sea-deities 72

guilds 30–31, 35, 40, 59–60, 74, 81, 127

highways. *See also* premodern highways
highway administration: modern era 143
  Department of Public Works 143
  First Five-Year Highway Construction Plan 144
  Law on Road Classification 143, 260
  vehicle registrations 145, 149
highway administration post-1945 145
  Committee for Promoting Privatization 148
  creation of Ministry of Land, Infrastructure, Transport and Tourism 148
  expressways in Kinki/Kinai region 145, 147
  Hanshin Expressway Public Corporation Law 147
  Japan Highway Public Corporation 146–148, 151, 261
  Land Acquisition Law 146
  Law Concerning Special Measures for Highway Construction 145–146, 261
  Law for Temporary Measures Concerning the Source of Funds for the Improvement of Roads 145
  Metropolitan Expressway Public Corporation Law 147
  National Development Arterial Expressway Construction Law 147
  National Expressway Law 147
  national motorways 146–147
  petrol tax 145
  Privatization Bill 148, 151, 261
  Road Law 145
  Watkins Report 122, 145, 147, 151, 261
Home Ministry 49, 143, 151, 260

industry research 17, 163, 172, 174, 178, 189, 262, 273
insei system 25
institution, definition of 15, 26

integration of land use and transport 10, 223, 230, 233, 240, 247, 249
international air carriers 10, 171, 188, 190, 192, 205
International Container Terminal Corporation Act 86
irrigation systems 9, 19, 24, 99, 102, 104, 112, 115, 117, 259
Itami governance 37–39, 61

Jardine, Matheson & Company 45
jitō 26, 28, 79, 127
Jōmon 8, 15, 17–18, 57, 71, 101–102, 122, 265
jōri system of land division 102

kabane system 22
Kamakura *bakufu* 25, 27. *See also* military government: Kamakura
  Council of State 26
  Formulatory of Adjudications 26
  Kemmu Restoration 27
  Three Regulations for Great Crimes 27
kanpaku 25, 90
Kantō method of flood management 104
knowledge transfer 2, 11
  American railway technology 160
  bokumin texts 36, 49
  British railway technology 1, 177, 263
  Chin dynasty highways 124
  Chinese culture 21, 258
  Chinese *Zhenguan Zhengyao* 21
  Collected Statutes of the Great Qing Dynasty 37
  Confucianism 23, 26, 36, 40–41, 43, 57, 268. *See also* Neo-Confucianism
  European legal theory 48
  geomancy 106, 223
  German Autobahns 144–145, 261
  Iwakura Mission to U.S.A. and Europe 225
  legal-bureaucratic state 23
  military aircraft (French, British, German, and American) 185, 264

ritsuryō codes 23, 48, 57, 76, 124
Shi Bo Si (Oceangoing and Marketing Department) 73
Taihō Code 24, 57–58, 124
T'ang-style taxes 24
U.S. *Highway Capacity Manual* 146, 261
Zen Buddhism 38–39, 74
Kōfun period 20, 71–72, 123, 260
koku 34, 41, 75, 81–82
Korean Bronze Age culture 19
Korean War 53, 188, 205
  special procurements 54
kuge 25

Lake Biwa survey 109, 116. *See also* canal transport: Lake Biwa
land administration 24
land readjustment program. *See* national land-use planning: land readjustment program
land reclamation 8, 69–71, 81, 88–89, 92, 106, 117, 243
land use and transport integration vii, 10, 223, 238, 240, 264
land-use planning system. *See* national land-use planning
land-value capture 10, 224, 237

magnetic levitation railways 1, 156, 172, 174, 178
Marine Transportation Bureau 85
maritime ports 72
  Dazaifu 5, 72, 124
  Dejima 44, 80
  Hakodate 46
  Hanshin 4, 9, 70, 86–88, 93–94, 168
  Hyōgo 8, 74–75, 78, 83
  Ishiyama Honganji 8, 70, 75, 79–80, 91–92, 257
  Kōbe 9, 70, 78, 83–88, 93
  Nagasaki 36, 40, 44–46, 80
  Nagoya 86
  Naniwa 8, 21, 69–71, 73, 75–77, 81, 89, 91, 123, 257
  Niigata 46

opening-up of ports to foreign trade 45
Ōsaka 69–71, 75, 86, 89
Sakai 8, 29, 70, 75, 77–79, 86, 91–92, 123, 257
Shimoda 71, 82
Suminoe 73, 77, 89, 91, 257
Sumiyoshi 73
Takamatsu 82–83
Uraga Harbour 44, 58
Watanabe 8, 70, 75, 79, 89, 91, 257–258
Yokohama 44–46, 70, 85–86
maritime regulations 74
Marxian history 16
Meiji government 39, 48, 50, 61, 83–84, 94, 136, 155, 157, 177, 225–226, 248
  constitution 48–49, 113
  Diet 49
  importing Western technology 50
  legislative assembly 48
  policy of industrial promotion 83
  prefectures 48–49, 243, 256
  public works 50, 122, 143, 151, 258
  regional integration 49
  Sinified legal system 48
  state-owned enterprises 50
Meiji Restoration xiv, 8, 10, 28, 42–43, 45–48, 59–60, 93, 122, 224–225, 248, 257, 260
  Charter Oath 47–48
  kokutai 48
  seitaishō 48
Memorandum on the Japan Customs System 85
merchants 9, 16, 29, 31, 35, 37, 39–43, 46, 48, 50, 59–61, 70, 75–78, 81–82, 90–93, 100, 103, 105–108, 116–118, 121, 125, 137, 257–259
  caravans 125, 141
  family constitution 40
  financial influence 41
  itinerant peddlers 125
  moneylenders 27, 82
  Ōsaka 10-wholesale group 82

Ōsaka 24-wholesale group 82
rice trade 41
teamsters 124
migration routes 15, 17, 57, 89, 255
military aircraft. *See* aviation policy: military aircraft
military government 8, 16, 22, 90, 256–257
  Kamakura 16, 22, 25–27, 56–58, 90, 127. *See also* Kamakura *bakufu*
  Muromachi 16, 22, 27–30, 37, 56–58, 60, 77, 90, 92, 127, 141. *See also* Muromachi *bakufu*
  Tokugawa 16, 33, 57, 256–257. *See also* Tokugawa *bakuhan*
Minatogawa Man 17
Ministry of Communications 186, 198, 204, 216–217
Ministry of Finance 84–86, 145, 261
Ministry of Home Affairs 85
Ministry of Land, Infrastructure, Transport and Tourism xv, 4, 87, 114–115, 122, 137, 143, 148–151, 168–169, 175, 178, 188–189, 193–195, 198, 200, 202, 209, 217, 231–232, 245–246, 249, 261, 267, 278–279. *See also* national land-use planning
Ministry of Transport 10, 86–87, 149, 151, 163, 166, 172, 190, 196–197, 200, 206, 208, 216–217, 257
Mito School of Thought 43
modern government 56, 59
  American aid budget 53
  Japanese Constitution (1946) 16, 52–53, 56, 59
multi-function polis (MFP) 224
Muromachi *bakufu* 29, 32, 77–78, 127. *See also* military government: Muromachi
  dual peasant system 30
  hanzei tax 28
  kokujin lordship 28, 30
  nihonkokuō shi. *See nihonkokuō shi*
  status of merchants 29
  tansen tax 28

tributary trade 29
myōshu 30

National General Mobilization Act 51
National Government Rice Agency 42, 60
national land-use planning 223, 224, 228–231, 256. See also new towns; See also Ministry of Land, Infrastructure, Transport and Tourism; See also transit-oriented development
  land readjustment program 10, 231–232, 264
  Nagoya Station 214, 238, 249
  smart cities 11, 224, 242–244, 246, 266
    mobility in smart cities 246–247, 249
  Tama Garden City 239–240, 242, 249
  Tama New Town 239–241
Neo-Confucianism 26, 40, 41. See also knowledge transfer: Confucianism
new institutional economics (NIE) 6, 59, 90, 279
new towns 11, 107, 162, 224, 239–242, 246, 249, 264. See also national land-use planning
nihonkokuō shi 32

Ōsaka Stock Exchange 61

Pacific Ocean 9, 100–101, 103, 116
Pacific War. See war: Pacific War
path dependency 59
pilgrimages 79, 123, 136, 141–142, 260
  accommodation 142
  entertainment 142
  Ise Shrine 101, 113, 117, 141–143, 210–211
piracy 31–33, 58, 77–78, 80, 90–91, 257–258
  anti-piracy regulation 33, 58
  eradication 32–33, 80
  smuggling 32–33, 37
  sword-hunt edict 33, 58
planning Tōkyō 225, 227

Building Standards Act 227, 248
Bureau for Reconstruction of the Imperial Capital 226, 248
Capital Construction Law 227, 248
City Planning Act 226, 229, 248
Decentralization Law 229
Ginza Brick Quarters Project 226, 248
National Capital Region Development Act 227, 248
Tōkyō Special City Plan 227, 248
Tōkyō Town Planning Ordinance 226, 248
political parties 1, 51
Port and Harbor Act (1950) 85, 93, 257
Port Customhouse 84
Port Development Authority 86, 258
port management bodies 85–87, 257
Port Management Corporation 87
post stations 9, 121–122, 124–125, 129–130, 132–139, 150, 260–261
  abolition 136
  assisting horses 132–133, 135
  courier services 132
  honjin inns 137
  locations 124
  Naniwa Kō 138
  prostitution 138–139, 142, 150
  provision of horses 124, 129, 132–133, 135, 138, 150
  services 124, 132, 150
  taxation 137–138
premodern highways
  bansho 127, 133–134
  circuits 123–124
  Edō escape route 130
  gokaidō 122–123, 129–130, 132–134, 136
  Kōshu dochū 130
  load limits 132–133, 135
  Magistrate of Road Affairs 133–136, 138, 150
  maintenance 132–135, 137, 151
  man-powered carts 136
  maps 131, 136

Naniwa Great Road 123
Nikkō dochū 130
Ōtsu 123
road widths 129
Take no uchi Kaidō 123–124
Tōkaidō 104, 109, 124–125, 128–130, 132–133, 135–136, 138
Tōkaidō survey 132
Tokugawa policy 7, 9, 132–139
Tōsandō (Nakasendō) 109, 122, 124–125, 130, 132–133, 135–136, 138
weigh stations 135
Preservation Districts for Groups of Traditional Buildings 137
private finance initiatives (PFI) 7, 184, 196, 207, 213, 264
private sector 4, 7, 88, 155–156, 162, 164, 171, 177, 184, 189, 196–197, 203, 207, 212, 216–218, 227, 236, 239, 244, 262, 264, 272, 275, 277
　airlines 184, 186, 189, 216–218
　buses 4, 170, 247
　light rail 237, 262
　railways 4, 155, 158–161, 166, 169–172, 174, 177–178, 214, 241, 262–263
　subways 156, 165, 171, 178, 262
public sector 87, 247, 262, 277
　airlines 183–184, 186–187, 189, 199, 212, 216, 218, 263
　buses 4, 238, 272
　light rail 237, 245
　railways 10, 157, 159, 162, 166, 171–172, 177, 238, 262
　subways 156, 171, 238

Queen Himiko 20, 58, 73

railways 4, 9–10, 49–50, 83, 144, 149, 155–164, 166–167, 169, 171–173, 177–178, 218, 223–224, 227, 229, 231, 241, 248–249, 256, 262–263
　British technology 155, 157, 263
　Central Japan Railway Network 168
　Den-en Toshi Company 162
　foreign expertise 10, 263
　freight 164–166, 168–169, 174
　governance models: public and private 166–167, 169–171
　government railways 10, 159, 162, 166, 262
　Japanese National Railways 155, 166–167, 169, 172–175, 178, 262
　narrow gauge tracks 177
　private operator innovations 156, 159, 161–163
　private railway companies 4, 155, 160–163, 167, 177–178, 215, 241, 262–263
　privatisation 155–156, 166, 169, 175, 177, 262
　Railway Nationalization Act 155, 162, 262
　Railway Technical Research Institute 163, 178
　Tramway Law of 1921 164
　urban subways 156, 165, 171, 177–178, 228–230, 262
　urban tramways 156, 164–165, 177, 245
River Act (1896) 100, 113–114
River Act (1964) 100, 114
River Cooperative Organization System 115
rivers. *See* topography and rivers
road barriers 9, 121–122, 125–129, 131, 150, 260
　auxiliary villages 135
　guards 128, 260
　locations 126, 131
　passenger inspections 125, 128
　strategic military value 126
　toll barriers 125, 139
　travel permits 128–129, 134, 139, 141, 150, 260, 267
　weapons 127
rōnin 27

samurai 25–27, 30, 40, 42, 46, 48, 60, 75, 82, 89, 99, 107, 130, 139–140
Sea of Japan 5, 9, 17, 78, 100, 103, 105, 108–109, 113, 116–117, 169, 245, 259

Setō Inland Sea 5, 8, 69, 71, 77–79, 91, 113, 160
Shinkansen 10, 156, 166–168, 171–176, 178, 215, 230, 238, 245, 262
 early development 172–173, 177
 operations, 1964 Summer Olympic Games 156, 172, 174, 178, 205, 262
 Shinkansen Railway Holding Organization 174
 Tōkaidō Shinkansen 172, 174, 262
shinōkōshō 46
Shintōism 20, 22, 31, 43, 57, 72, 142
shipbuilders, government subsidies to 83
shipping coastal routes. *See* coastal shipping routes
shōen 24, 26, 28, 30, 74, 77, 79, 89, 103, 125–127, 257, 260
Shōgun 25–27, 29, 32–35, 37, 41–42, 44, 46–47, 56–58, 60–61, 77, 80–81, 90, 92–93, 106, 117, 122, 129–134, 136, 157, 243, 256, 260
 Enemy of the Court 47
 vassals 26, 28, 30–31, 34–36, 106, 129
Shōwa Nankai earthquake 84
shugo 26, 28–30, 103
shuin sen 32
Society 5.0 11, 249, 255, 265–267, 269–272
 ageing population 54, 178, 245, 247, 271, 275. *See also* ageing society
 agile governance 269–271
 autonomous driving vehicles 267, 271–273, 275
 aviation safety and security 278–279
 Blue Ocean Strategy 279
 challenges facing Japan 255, 267, 269–271, 274–276, 278–279
 characteristics 266
 natural disasters and resilience 276–277
 personal mobility 267–268, 272–273, 275
 rural shrinkage 193, 275–276
 Science and Technology Basic Law 249, 265–266
 Smart City Public-Private Partnership Platform 266
 vision 255, 265–266, 271
socio-technical transition 7
sonnō jōi 43, 46
Summer Olympic Games
 Melbourne 3
 Sydney 3
 Tōkyō 57, 59, 172, 262, 272
Supreme Allied Commander of the Pacific 52

Taira Reforms 9
Temporary Funds Adjustments Law 51
tiers of government 4, 200
Tokugawa *bakuhan* 28, 34, 36, 38–39, 43, 57, 81, 92, 101, 105, 108, 116, 122, 127–129, 139, 258. *See also* military government: Tokugawa
 commerce regulatory framework 42, 59
 confiscation of *daimyō* lands 34, 47
 corruption 43
 fiscal-military state 34
 foreign trade 36–37, 40, 45, 128
 fudai daimyō 34–35, 129–130
 governance 29, 34–35, 39, 61
 integration of river administration measures 104
 monopolistic guilds 31, 40, 60
 Office of *Shōgun* 35
 paper money 42, 140
 provincial governments 34, 36, 137, 139
 road administration 121, 129, 135, 150
 sakoku edicts 37
 security 9, 35, 82, 122, 260
 taxation rice 41, 89, 93, 137, 141
 Tempō Reform 43, 60
 tozama daimyō 35
 village water management associations 104
Tōkyō Stock Exchange 61
ton'ya 40, 43, 60, 81–82

topography and rivers 9, 18–19, 21, 42, 70, 72–73, 76–77, 79–82, 84, 89, 92, 99–107, 109, 112–118, 121, 124–125, 129–131, 135, 141, 143, 158, 203–204, 225, 259, 277
transit-oriented development xii, 4, 10–11, 224, 234–239, 241, 249, 264. *See also* national land-use planning
transport fees 139
Treaty of Peace and Amity 44

uji 3, 20, 22, 57, 73, 92–93
  chiefs 20, 22, 57, 92–93
  clans 92–93

Wa 19–20, 72, 75, 89, 91
war. *See also* Korean War
  First World War 51, 83, 163
  Gempei War 78
  Imjin Wars 33
  Ōnin no Ran 30, 60, 77, 92

Pacific War 16, 51, 88, 113–114, 145, 151, 164, 185, 188, 198, 210, 216, 224, 260
Russo-Japanese War 50, 155, 162
Second World War 8–10, 57, 59, 69, 85, 93, 122, 171, 178, 183, 198, 209, 224, 257
Sino-Japanese War 50, 155, 162, 187
Southern Court and Northern Court 27–28
Woven City 243, 246, 249, 272

Yamatai 19–20, 58, 73, 89
Yamato Kingdom 15, 19–21, 56–57, 72–73, 76, 122, 125–126, 150, 260
Yayoi 8, 15, 17–19, 57, 71, 89, 102, 122, 259, 265

za 30–31, 60, 74, 127
zaibatsu 50, 52, 61, 187

About the Cover

"Transformation—From Steam Engines to Super-Conducting Maglev Railway Technology"

The composition of this oil painting by Jack Black (1948–) alluding to the maglev test track at Yamanashi, Japan, is based on the artwork of J. M. W. Turner, 1844, "Rain, Steam and Speed—The Great Western Railway at Maidenhead", and the sky is based on the artwork "The Fighting Temeraire, Tugged to Her Last Berth to be Brocken Up, 1838". Both original paintings are exhibited in the National Art Gallery, London.

The book cover is a composite painting in oil based on these two paintings. As a romantic artist, the topics tackled in these paintings are nostalgia for the past—as river boats were being replaced by steam engines—and the demise of the 98-gun sailing warship that once fought heroically at the Battle Trafalgar, and was now being towed by a steam-driven boat on the River Thames to be broken up as scrap.

The reproduction of this painting is allowed by permission from its owner, Yoshitsugu Hayashi, Senior Research Professor, Chūbu University, Nagoya, Japan, and was photographed by Mr Kiyoaki Suzuki.

The cover was designed by Anna Gatti.

About the Team

Alessandra Tosi was the managing editor for this book.

Sam Noble and Lucy Barnes performed the copy-editing and proofreading.

Melissa Purkiss typeset the book in InDesign and compiled the index.

Anna Gatti designed the cover. The cover was produced in InDesign using the Fontin font.

Luca Baffa produced the paperback and hardback editions. The text font is Tex Gyre Pagella; the heading font is Californian FB. Luca produced the EPUB, AZW3, PDF, HTML, and XML editions—the conversion is performed with open source software freely available on our GitHub page (https://github.com/OpenBookPublishers)

This book need not end here...

Share

All our books — including the one you have just read — are free to access online so that students, researchers and members of the public who can't afford a printed edition will have access to the same ideas. This title will be accessed online by hundreds of readers each month across the globe: why not share the link so that someone you know is one of them?

This book and additional content is available at:
https://doi.org/10.11647/OBP.0281

Customise

Personalise your copy of this book or design new books using OBP and third-party material. Take chapters or whole books from our published list and make a special edition, a new anthology or an illuminating coursepack. Each customised edition will be produced as a paperback and a downloadable PDF.

Find out more at:
https://www.openbookpublishers.com/section/59/1

Like Open Book Publishers

Follow @OpenBookPublish

Read more at the Open Book Publishers BLOG

www.ingramcontent.com/pod-product-compliance
Lightning Source LLC
Chambersburg PA
CBHW040323300426
44112CB00021B/2862